KU-009-988

SAVE
£10,000
WITH A NAIL

SAVE £10,000 WITH A NAIL

MORE THAN 1,700 PRACTICAL TIPS FOR A PROBLEM-FREE HOME

Published by The Reader's Digest Association, Inc.
London • New York • Sydney • Montreal

Put away your credit cards

Welcome to *Save £10,000 with a Nail*, your complete guide to preventative home care. Here are simple, inexpensive ways to make sure every part of your home and garden stays in tip-top condition for decades to come.

Save £400 with a sponge

Ten minutes of cleaning kitchen walls this way, and paint lasts forever.

Save £750 with a vacuum cleaner

Forget about floors – sweep your walls! Wallpaper will stay like new for years.

Save £800 with a bar of soap

Keep sash windows sliding smoothly with a regular soap rub.

Save £250 with a newspaper

A ball of newspaper is the perfect tool for replicating a textured finish on a plaster repair.

Save £1,000 with a chisel

Doing this common brick-wall repair yourself is both fun and easy.

Save £150 with a tissue

This simple check will show when your tumble dryer's door seal needs replacing.

Ready to start saving?

Then grab a few tools – along with some handy household items – and never again be surprised by an expensive home repair or crisis.

The power of a single nail

Let's just say that a fixing comes loose, making your gutter sag. You notice it dripping one rainy day as you come back to the house, but it's too wet to get up a ladder to fix it there and then, so you make a mental note that you really should nail it back into place at the weekend.

But, of course, you don't. It's still raining, then something more important comes up the following weekend, the weather dries up and you forget about it. And then winter comes.

The visible drip, as it turns out, was just one part of the problem and only happened when the heavy rain that day overspilled from the gutter that was also blocked with fallen leaves. In lighter rain, the water had been seeping through the now-rotten fascia board and into the loft for quite some time.

At this point in the tale, one or more things could happen: the continuing leak in the loft might trickle down into a wall or upstairs ceiling, causing mould to grow there. Or the water could seep into a ceiling light fixture and cause an electrical short – or even a fire. Still more seriously, perhaps, if the leak has already been dripping for more than a year, the structural roof timbers could be rotting.

This may be a worst-case scenario, but builders and handymen see things like this all the time – they call it benign neglect. Think about the homes you've lived in. If it wasn't the roof, it was the central heating. Or a blocked drain. Or damp. Or a cracked and uneven patio. What homeowner hasn't had to pay at least one really large bill for a repairman to fix a small problem that's turned into something big?

Some homeowners believe that major home repairs and refurbishments, because common, are inevitable – irritating and expensive, but all part of owning a property. But they're *not* inevitable, and this book can put an end to them happening in your house.

A health book for the home

Save £10,000 with a Nail has one main goal: to make sure your credit cards stay safely in your pocket. No more big, unexpected payments for home repairs. Here are hundreds of smart, easy and practical ways to prevent major home problems from occurring – with an emphasis on easy.

Don't take the book's title literally. Preventative nails here or there may not always lead to windfall-sized savings, but we hope the title's message is clear: even the most minor, everyday maintenance tasks can have significant and lasting repercussions on your home's appearance and condition. Think back to the disastrous gutter story for a moment: if that hypothetical homeowner had taken just a few minutes to get up on a ladder to nail or screw that gutter support back into place, the leaves in the gutter would have been discovered and the damage that we described could have been stopped or avoided. Taking half an hour or so to fix the sagging gutter and then clear the leaves, in other words, is like getting paid thousands of pounds for 30 minutes' worth of effort.

That story illustrates another of this book's main goals: to show you that preventative home care is often about stopping small problems from becoming big. Little problems do happen around a home all the time – even for professional carpenters and plumbers – but in the pages ahead you'll find easy fixes and touch-ups for most common house problems, plus maintenance tips to help you to recognise the early warning signs of potential problems and deal with them confidently, efficiently, promptly and economically.

We've organised *Save £10,000 with a Nail* very simply. After an introductory chapter, where you'll learn about the basic tools you'll need for the small fixes and preventative measures that fill this book, we gradually work our way through every room, part and system in and around your home. Here are preventive-care and maintenance tips and quick fixes for everything from walls to roofs, toilets to radiators, carpets to doorbells. Finally, we show you how to keep your home safe and secure against bad weather, intruders and pests.

This book is all about giving you the knowledge and confidence you need to maintain and enjoy the biggest investment that most of us will ever make – and you'll probably even increase your home's value and saleability in the process. Never was the phrase 'prevention is better than cure' more apt than in describing *Save £10,000 with a Nail*.

Here's to a happy, healthy home – and bank balance!

Contents

1 HOME CARE: ARE YOU READY?

The fact that you're consulting this book at all suggests that you understand how important home maintenance is. Maybe your house is in perfect condition, and you want to keep it that way. Or maybe you already recognise a few things here and there that need to be done and you want a little advice on how to do them. Whatever your situation, adopting a positive, can-do mindset is your first step in achieving a problem-free, well-maintained home without spending thousands of pounds on repairs.

Even if you're a DIY novice, relax. Making small repairs really is no more difficult than following a recipe, and many of the essential maintenance tasks that will keep your home in tip-top condition amount to little more than regular cleaning and vigilance. Do this and you'll catch small problems before they lead to big bills.

The first section of *Save £10,000 with a Nail* contains basic advice on how to get into the habit of doing your own simple home repairs and maintenance. We'll show you how to plan regular maintenance checks and where and when to ask for professional help. You'll also find a description of the basic tools you're likely to need and advice on how to take care of them. You'll be ready to maintain and repair in no time at all!

Home maintenance basics

We all know that minor problems can mushroom into major headaches in the blink of an eye; not fixing these problems while they're small will only cost you more money and aggravation in the end. It's worth remembering the old adage: 'An ounce of prevention is worth a pound of cure.' You can save a lot of pounds in repairs and restoration – and a great deal of anguish, too – if you put an ounce's worth of effort into maintaining your property.

The expense factor

Owning your own home doesn't come cheaply. In 2009, the average price of a home in the UK was £160,000, and that's not the end of your expenditures. Factor in council tax, mortgage interest and building insurance, then consider what the average homeowner spends in a year to maintain (or even improve) their property, and this can add several thousand pounds to your already hefty housing bill. This is why it's so important to prevent problems now, rather than wait until they blossom into full-blown catastrophes later and then get around to fixing them.

Can you remember the last time you wrote a repair man or builder a big cheque for something that you later discovered you could have fixed yourself? It probably felt like you were being robbed. But how were you to know that you could replace the washer on your tap yourself in 10 minutes? Many DIY beginners are spurred into action by the realisation that they can save a significant amount of money by doing small jobs themselves, and this book will help you to know what you can do and when it needs doing. Taking charge of your home's health and putting benign neglect behind you is tremendously satisfying. You'll have a healthier bank balance, a more fortified home and, perhaps most importantly, you'll remember that you and not the plumber or the builder are in control and in charge of your own life and home.

Paying attention pays off

When your home has many rooms and even more nooks and crannies, how can you stay on top of potential problems? And what does a 'potential problem' even look like? You probably know your home well enough to be able to find your way around in the dark, but how often do you really look at your surroundings?

The truth is, the best weapons your home has against deterioration are your own senses. It's your eagle eyes, sharp ears and even your keen sense of smell that will help you to spot problems early so that you can fix them

SMART HOMEOWNER
£125
The average daily rate for a general handyman to fix problems around the house that you could do yourself.

quickly. Maybe you'll notice a small hole or chip in your kitchen's plaster wall or detect a musty odour coming from your bathroom. Don't ignore what your senses are telling you: once you learn how to interpret these clues you'll be well on the way to expert home maintenance.

One of the best things you can do for your house is to 'visit' it regularly and get to know it inside out. Try walking around the perimeter of each room in your house. Feel the walls. Stand in the far corner of the room and look at the ceilings and floors from points of view that you don't usually have. Stand inside cupboards, if you can, and look out into your rooms. Close your eyes, take a deep breath and smell your living area. You'll get a good feel for what your house's 'normal' state is and this will help you to notice if something isn't right at a later date.

When you do this you're bound to start noticing things, good and bad, that you hadn't noticed before. You'll develop a new and refreshing appreciation for your living space and find yourself cleaning, lubricating, painting and making other such minor adjustments, just to keep it looking good and working smoothly.

Dedicate the same kind of thoughtfulness that you had when 'seeing' your home to repairing it. Plan work thoroughly, gather all the tools and materials you need before you start, proceed slowly and follow instructions carefully and you can be sure of having a home that makes you proud.

ONE OF THE BEST THINGS YOU CAN DO FOR YOUR HOUSE IS TO GET TO KNOW IT INSIDE OUT.

15 must-have items for home care and maintenance

They may not count as tools, but these household items are key to keeping your home clean and well maintained. Gather them together or buy them now and keep them somewhere convenient – many of the tips throughout this book assume that you'll have these indispensable items easily to hand.

- **VACUUM CLEANER**
- **BROOMS** (indoor and outdoor)
- **MOP**
- **SPONGES**
- **PLASTIC SPRAY BOTTLE**
- **SCISSORS**
- **PENCILS**
- **WIRE COAT HANGERS**
- **BUCKET**
- **ROPE**
- **DUSTPAN AND BRUSH**
- **CLEAN RAGS AND OLD TOWELS**
- **STEAM IRON** (for tasks such as softening vinyl flooring or reviving a carpet)
- **SCRAP WOOD** (assorted remnants and shims)
- **POWERFUL TORCH** (and spare batteries)

How a positive attitude can save you time and money

When embarking on home maintenance projects, a positive, can-do attitude will save you money, time and frustration. Bear these points in mind before you begin:

- **Be upbeat** Don't let unexpected problems and hiccups in the plan upset you and put you off. Keep a sense of humour and stay positive.

- **Be calm** Having too much nervous energy and rushing through a job usually lead to mistakes or even injuries.

- **Be prepared** Before you start, read all instructions carefully (in this book, and also on manufacturer's packages where applicable) and then follow them to the letter. Collect all the tools and equipment that you'll need before you embark on your project.

- **Be aware of the details** If you're replacing a roof tile, take a photo or draw a diagram of the old one to note how it fits into place. If you're replacing or repairing a tap, for example, notice the order in which the washers, screws and other small parts (left) are assembled and disassembled.

- **Be creative** If you don't have the tools or materials called for, you can often find substitutes that will work just as well. If you're replacing a brick and don't have a brick jointer to shape the fresh mortar, for example, use a lolly stick or a spoon. Sometimes this book suggests such alternatives, but if it doesn't, you can come up with substitutes of your own.

- **Be flexible** Sometimes one problem masks another and you have to stop in the middle of a job to fix the underlying fault. If you're patching a hole in a wall and discover a leaky pipe, fix the leak first, then return to the original job. You'll save yourself a lot of headaches later.

- **Be safe** Most accidents occur when people are tired or in a hurry. Take your time, wear the proper safety equipment, and know when to stop and when to call for professional help.

- **Be realistic** Many jobs require more time, money and skill than homeowners plan for. Think hard before you start a job – sometimes it really is cheaper and quicker to leave it to the professionals.

- **Finish what you start** As long as the tools and materials are out, finish the jobs you start, otherwise you could still be looking at that unpainted architrave a year from now.

COLLECT ALL THE TOOLS AND EQUIPMENT YOU NEED BEFORE YOU EMBARK ON ANY PROJECT.

Making time for home maintenance

If you're serious about protecting your home against deterioration and damage, you need to be observant at all times and do regular maintenance checks. Failing to look systematically for potential problems is only inviting disaster – or at the very least, huge repair bills. As unbelievable as it seems, a small fix here and a thorough cleaning there can keep your house and everything in it running smoothly. Neglect a small problem, though, and it will inevitably grow into a major one.

In the chapters that follow, we'll tell you how to nip all kinds of home maintenance problems in the bud. Some of what you read may be gentle reminders of what you already know but don't necessarily do. Much of it is simple common sense. But because we all tend to brush aside things that don't demand our immediate attention, it's a good idea to come up with a scheduling system to make sure that these checks and chores get done. It doesn't have to be a daunting programme of works but does need to make sense to you and be presented in a way that fits in with the way you live your life. Maybe you could take an hour out of each weekend to examine one area of the house – and then treat yourself to a nice lunch? Or if you regularly use your home computer you could program in a series of pop-up reminders. If you prefer paper and pen, make notes on an ordinary home calendar to do certain jobs on certain days.

SMART HOMEOWNER

5,000

The number of litres of water one dripping tap can waste in a year.

MAKE A DATE WITH YOUR HOUSE.

Getting the timing right

Generally, the best time to examine your home's exterior is in warm (but not scorching) weather; the best time to examine indoor systems is when they're not in use. Another good rule of thumb is to do your checks when the seasons prompt you. Autumn is the perfect time to give your home's heating system a once-over: cold weather is just around the corner and you may be already thinking about your heating bill. Late autumn is also when you should inspect your gutters and downpipes, once you've cleared out the last of the falling leaves.

Even though some chores can be done at any time and others are best done seasonally, there are certain tasks to which you should assign a particular season or month – even a specific date – so that there's no chance that you'll forget to do them. Checking your smoke alarm batteries is a good example. The chart on the next page lists the checks that should be part of your regular home maintenance programme. Add these and other jobs to your calendar or create your own chart. If you don't want to make extensive notes on your calendar, just write 'Check maintenance schedule' and then you can refer to a separate document.

Seasonal maintenance checklist

	spring	summer	autumn	winter
HOUSE EXTERIOR				
Check wood surfaces for deterioration	●		●	
Check that airbricks are clear	●		●	
Check that plants or soil aren't up against the house wall, breaching the damp-proof course	●		●	
Wash fascia boards and check for cracks or signs of rot	●			
Putty loose windows and replace cracked glass	●		●	
Replace worn or damaged draughtproofing	●		●	
Seal around windows and doors if needed	●		●	
Check for ants' and wasps' nests	●		●	
Lubricate door and window locks and hinges		●		
ROOF				
Replace damaged roof tiles or slates		●		●
Inspect flashing around chimneys, dormers, valleys and vent pipes	●			
Repoint chimneys	●			
Clean gutters, downpipes and leaf guards and check for damage or leaking joints	●		●	
GARDEN				
Check wooden fence panels and posts for rot	●	●		
Repair damage or wear in paths, patios and drives		●		
Clear debris from drains and gulleys	●	●	●	
Trim trees or large shrubs that may damage house or clog gutters	●		●	
Trim and tie back climbing plants on house walls	●		●	
HOUSE INTERIOR				
Check for and repair cracks in walls		●	●	
Replace cracked floor or wall tiles	●		●	
Check for and repair leaks in plumbing fixtures		●		
Renew damaged sealant around baths, showers, basins and tiled floors		●		
Clean discoloured tile grouting	●	●		
Inspect electric flex, plugs, switches, sockets and lamp holders for wear or damage		●		●
Inspect refrigerator door gaskets and replace if needed		●		
Check tumble dryer vent pipe and outlet		●		
Have heating system, boiler and any other gas-burning fires or appliances checked and serviced professionally			●	
Have chimney flue checked and cleaned			●	
Check smoke detectors and carbon monoxide detectors	●	●	●	●
Conduct a family fire drill		●		
Check basement for dampness, leaks, new cracks or movement in old cracks		●		

Building the perfect toolbox

Other than your positive attitude, the most important asset you have in your home maintenance arsenal is your collection of tools and household supplies. If you're just starting out, you don't need to have a fully equipped stock of tools and hardware, but every homeowner should have certain essentials on hand – as you take on more complex tasks, you can always add to your toolbox. Start by arming yourself with the beginner's basics described in the following pages.

What every homeowner needs

SMART HOMEOWNER

£80

The amount you'd spend to buy the 15 essential tools that every homeowner needs.

Hammers Probably the most basic of all tools is the hammer, which is used to drive nails into surfaces to join them together. Hammers come in various sizes and weights. Get one that fits your hand comfortably and is the right weight for your strength. Although there are dozens of specialised hammers, the most versatile is probably a good claw hammer (left) with a metal head and a hardwood (or sturdy glass fibre) handle. The claw part is used to extract nails.

Screwdrivers They come in many widths and lengths, with different tips to fit different screws. The two most essential screwdrivers are the slotted head screwdriver and the Phillips, which has a cross-shaped tip. A Phillips will also fit the star-shaped Pozidriv screws (see page 20), but not vice versa – so choose a Phillips if you only buy one cross-headed driver. When choosing a screwdriver, match the tip to the screw head's type and size – otherwise you may strip the screw or blunt the driver. The tip should fill both length and width of the slot in the screw head. A long screwdriver has more driving power, a short one gives more control and lets you work in tighter spaces.

Tape measures and rulers Measuring a job properly is vital if you want to get it right. The best multipurpose measuring tool is a retractable tape measure (below) – the flexible, spring-loaded metal rule that's contained in a small squarish case that you can clip to your belt or keep in your pocket. If you need to measure odd shapes, such as the circumference of a pipe, it's also a good idea to keep a cloth tape measure (a dressmaker's tape) on hand. A steel ruler makes a useful straight edge for cutting or marking, as well as for measuring: buy the longest you can. Finally, you may want to buy a folding carpenter's rule, a rigid rule made in hinged sections that folds easily and can be extended to give you the length you need.

Nails, screws and bolts Every homeowner's toolbox should contain a few basic fasteners. The most widely used are nails, which come in a variety of metals, styles and sizes for driving into a range of materials. Wire nails are round, with flat heads. Oval nails are better for not splitting wood. If you want to drive the nail below the surface, use a lost head nail, which has a very small head. Nails come in lengths ranging from 25mm to 150mm – the traditional 1 inch to 6 inch sizes.

Different types of screws are used for joining wood, sheet metal, plasterboard and masonry. Screws also come in various lengths and thicknesses and with different head types. The most common ones sold are slotted head screws, which just have one straight slot that runs across the entire head, and Pozidriv screws, which have a cross in the top of the head and smaller slots at 45 degrees to the main cross, making a star shape. These have, in many cases, replaced the traditional cross-headed Phillips screw, which is unsuitable for use with power screwdrivers (see right) – but you're likely to find both in your home. A Pozidriv screw can be driven in and unscrewed with a Phillips screwdriver, but not vice versa.

A bolt (below) is a flat-ended screw that, together with a nut, forms a mini-clamp that holds pieces together firmly, yet can be disassembled easily. A flat washer is usually placed between the bolt head or nut and the pieces being fastened to spread the pressure and protect the surface.

Drills and drill bits Many home maintenance jobs involve some drilling. You'll need a drill to do even simple tasks around the house, like hanging heavy picture frames. Using a hand drill over a period of time is tiring and you're likely to get less accurate, so a good electric drill makes a worthwhile investment. Better still, choose a good cordless drill (above) – one that operates at several speeds and in reverse and has a hammer action for masonry – and you'll be able to drill and screw everywhere, even if you're far from an electrical outlet. Bits for power drills come in many shapes and sizes – they are designed to be drilled into every kind of material, including wood, metal, plastic and masonry. Slotted and Pozidriv screwdriver bits are also widely available, so that you can use your drill to drive or remove screws. Don't use a power screwdriver with a Phillips screw as the bit is likely to slip out of the cross-hatched slots, potentially causing damage to surfaces and wear in the tool's motor. Pozidriv screws were developed to prevent this problem by giving a more secure fit.

Utility knife Probably the handiest cutting tool is the small utility knife, which comes with a variety of blades to cut wood, vinyl and other materials. A good straight-handled model will have a button that adjusts the length of the blade or retracts it into the handle for safety (right). Some models also have storage space in the handle for extra blades.

Level A spirit level will show you when a surface is perfectly horizontal or vertical – it's good for easy tasks like hanging pictures (as well as more difficult carpentry jobs). Simply place it on top of or against a surface and check its small, liquid-filled vials. When the bubble is at the centre of the vial, the surface is level.

KEEP YOUR TOOLS
TOGETHER – SAFE AND TIDY.

Basic wood saw Although a professional would use different saws to make rip cuts (with the grain) and cross cuts in wood, for most DIY jobs you can make do with a single general-purpose saw with a blade that is around 250mm long. A tenon saw (below) has a strip of brass or steel along the top edge of the blade to stiffen it. This makes it sturdy and easy to use but limits the thickness of wood that can be sawn through.

Hacksaw For cutting metal, such as a rusty nail or bolt, you'll need a hacksaw, which consists of a sturdy metal frame with a removable, narrow blade. The blades can snap, especially when you're cutting something tough, but they are replaceable. A junior hacksaw, which can be as small as 150mm long, is useful for jobs in awkward places. Hacksaws are also used for cutting plastic, such as curtain rails, and small wood mouldings.

Gap-filling tools If you find splits in woodwork, crumbling mortar in the chimney or gaps around a window frame, you'll need to fill the spaces with filler, sealant or mastic. To do so you'll need an assortment of putty knives and trowels and a mastic gun, a device that holds a tube of mastic or sealant and dispenses it with the squeeze of a trigger.

Choosing and buying tools

Price shouldn't always be the primary factor when choosing and buying new tools, but value for money is crucial. Cheap tools can be uncomfortable to use and may not last as long as more costly brands, but with the most expensive models, particularly with power tools, you'll be paying a premium for the brand name and maybe for extra features that you don't really need and are unlikely ever to use.

● **See how they feel** With hand tools, it's important that they should feel comfortable to hold and use – this is a very personal decision. Pick up the tool and hold it; move it a little as you would in use; feel the weight of the tool and the shape of the handle. Do this with a range of different tools and you'll start to get a feel for which suits you best.

● **Choosing handles** Wood-handled tools wear with years of use, growing smooth and even taking on the shape of your hand, but plastic or rubber handles may be lighter and more durable. They may also have a cushioned grip that makes them more comfortable to use, particularly for hammering jobs.

● **How much power do you need?** Power tools range from low-end budget models for £30 or less to professional models that can cost several hundred pounds. For most DIY jobs, a mid-range tool will be fine and your money will be better spent hiring a heavy-duty model on the rare occasions you really need one.

● **Stick to the tool for the job** Unless you're particularly restricted for storage space, choose individual power tools over multi-tools with interchangeable heads.

Indoor and outdoor ladders

You'll need a stepladder to reach high places inside the house. Ladders are graded for loading capacity: be sure yours will more than hold your weight, plus the tools and materials you'll be using. Stepladders come in various heights: a 1.8m ladder should be sufficient for indoor projects. Many stepladders can also be used in different configurations, for use in stairwells, for example, or as a platform. Look out for accessories, such as a clip-on tray for tools or paint, and make sure that the feet have non-slip covers.

For working outside the house, get an extension ladder – a nest of two or three ladders that can be extended or compressed to the right length. Many models have pulley mechanisms that make it easier to extend the sections. Ladders are made of wood, aluminum or glass fibre. The latter is a good choice: it's lightweight and won't conduct electricity, as aluminum or wet wood will do.

Sanding tools At the end of a woodworking job (or after filling small holes or cracks in your plasterboard or plastered walls), you'll have to sand the surface smooth before painting or varnishing it. You'll need an assortment of sandpaper grades, ranging from coarse to fine. It's also a good idea to use a sanding block (below) – a hand-held block that holds the sandpaper to give you a better grip and maintain a consistently flat sanding surface.

Wall fixings If you're driving a screw into either a solid wall or a plasterboarded stud partition wall, you'll need some kind of plug or fixing to give the screw's thread something to bite into. For fixing into brick or block walls, the simplest solution is a plastic wallplug (left). You drill a hole of the correct size using a masonry bit, tap the plug into the wall then drive the screw into it. For fixing things to plasterboard partitions, use a nylon or metal plasterboard fixing. These have a self-drilling outer thread that screws into the plasterboard and a smaller inner thread that takes the screw. For really heavy items, it's best to locate the timber stud and fix directly into that. If that's not possible, there are special plasterboard anchors or spring toggles that spread out within the cavity and pull tight against the back face of the plasterboard to obtain a secure fixing.

Pliers and clamps Pliers are good for hands-on holding. Clamps hold things for you and leave your hands free. It's a good idea to keep a supply of spring clamps and 'C' or 'G'-clamps (named for their shape – right) to hold items together while you're working on them or to hold a freshly glued joint while the adhesive dries. Slip-joint pliers – with serrated teeth on the forward parts of the jaws and corrugated teeth farther back (below) – are also useful. You can easily shift the jaws to hold objects of varying sizes using the set of teeth that fits best. Also get a pair of long-nose pliers for grasping small items or reaching into narrow spaces. For simple wiring jobs, such as replacing a plug, invest in a multipurpose tool: electrician's pliers that measure, strip and clamp wires and crimp wire connectors.

Spanners To hold, twist or turn nuts, bolts or plumbing pipes, you'll need some spanners. Your biggest must-have is an adjustable spanner (right), which has an adjustable head to fit various sizes of nuts and bolts. Look for one with jaws that will open to about 30mm – wide enough for a plumbing fitting. For plumbing work, you'll also need a pair of pipe wrenches or adjustable spanners (one for each hand). In time you may want to invest in a set of open-end spanners. The end of each tool in a set has an opening of a different size to fit varying sizes of nuts or bolts.

Maintaining tools

Money spent on good tools will be money wasted if you don't take good care of them. Follow these simple tips and good practice to keep the contents of your toolbox in good condition.

● **Tidy up after yourself** This sounds obvious, but the most important step in taking care of your tools is to make sure you put them away neatly when you finish a job. Store sharp tools with blade covers in place or the blade retracted to prevent it from getting nicked or blunted. Put spanners, drill bits, sockets, screwdriver heads and other tools that come as sets back in their box or pouch and make sure that none are missing. And never leave tools lying around, where they could get damaged, particularly outdoors.

● **Be battery-wise with cordless power tools** When you buy a cordless power tool it will come with one battery and a charger. Every five charges or so, make sure you let the battery discharge fully before you recharge it, rather than keeping it 'topped up', as this will help to prolong the battery's life. To avoid being left without power in the middle of a job, consider buying a spare battery so that you can keep one in use and one fully charged. If you buy several tools of the same make, the batteries may be interchangeable.

● **Keep a sharp blade** Chisels and planes (below) must be sharp to cut well and work safely. Many hardware shops will sharpen tools, or you can do it yourself with an oilstone. Allow a teaspoon of light

machine oil to soak into a new oilstone, then apply a little more, clamp the blade in a honing guide and rub it over the stone to sharpen the edge.

'Would-be-nice' extras for the DIY enthusiast

Squares Used in framing, roofing and stairway work, a carpenter's square is a rigid steel, L-shaped tool that helps you to keep corners squared at exact 90 degree angles. It also doubles as a measuring rule and a straightedge.

A combination square (right) is a steel rule with a sliding head, which lets you mark off 90 and 45 degree angles, and a sliding bevel that allows you to set any angle you like.

Electrician's screwdrivers When carrying out electrical work, you should use only a screwdriver encased in plastic. On an electrician's screwdriver only the tip of the metal blade isn't covered with plastic. This plastic coating helps you to avoid electric shocks. If you're in an emergency situation and you have to use an ordinary screwdriver to make electrical repairs, wrap overlapping layers of electrician's insulation tape around the entire shaft up to the tip and over any metal parts of the handle. Always be sure to turn off the power before you start any electrical work.

Nail bars If you need to remove a nail from a surface and the claw of your hammer won't do the job, use a nail bar, a curved metal tool with two angled blades. One blade is used for pulling nails and the other for prying apart pieces that are nailed together or for pulling off old mouldings, such as architrave.

Riveters and staplers To fasten metal to metal or metal to plastic you may need a pop riveter, a small tool that applies rivets easily with a squeeze of its handle. To fasten softer materials, get a heavy-duty stapler – either a hand-powered model (below) or a power stapler. You'll also need a supply of pop rivets and staples to fit.

Hammering aids Sometimes it's easier to drive a nail if you make a starter hole with an awl (below). Push this small, pointed metal tool into the wood where you want the nail to go. If you want to sink the head of the nail beneath the surface, use a nail set. This is a small punch with a narrow end that you position over the nail head for the last few blows of the hammer while you drive it below the surface of the wood. A stud finder is another useful aid, which will help you to locate the studs behind your plasterboard in stud partition walls. Inexpensive models work magnetically to find the screws or nails that secure the plasterboard. Electronic models measure changes in a wall's density.

Files and rasps
To shape or smooth metal or wood, you may need files or rasps (left), which are flat, round or triangular lengths of metal with rows of ridge-like teeth that cut into the material to be smoothed. Files are used on metal and rasps on wood. Because files get clogged up with the material they remove, a file card – a small, two-sided tool with a fine brush on one side and a coarser one on the other – is a useful accessory to brush away the debris and keep the file cutting properly. A half-round rasp, with one flat and one curved surface, can be used for shaping convex and concave curves.

Surforms
The Surform range of shaping tools all have perforated blades that work like a miniature cheese grater, removing wood in a series of fine shavings. The range includes planes and files in several styles, all with replaceable blades for when they become blunt. The Planerfile with its reversible handle is the most versatile.

Wood plane
When working with wood, a plane is a versatile and useful stand-by, such as for trimming a bit from the top of a sticking door. A good first purchase is a small block plane that smooths and trims wood and makes fine finishing cuts. An adjusting wheel under the palm-rest controls the position of the blade and how much wood is removed with each pass. Because of its small size, a block plane can be used in one hand, whereas larger planes require two hands.

Chisels
A chisel is a sharp, usually bevelled blade used for cutting or shaving wood or metal. Wood chisels are generally fitted with wooden handles and are either driven by hand or struck with a mallet. They are ideal for cutting mortises, or recesses, for hinges or locks. Cold chisels are struck by hammers and are used to cut sheet metal or chop off bolts or rivets. A stonemason's chisel (also called a straight chisel) is used for cutting concrete block and stone.

Brick bolster
The spade-shaped bolster chisel has a 100mm wide blade and is used with a 1.2kg lump hammer for cutting bricks. Choose one with a hand guard.

Cable and pipe detector
This small battery-powered device detects the presence of electricity cable and plumbing pipes buried in the house walls. Some will also locate ceiling joists and the timber frame inside a partition wall by detecting the line of fixing nails that holds the plasterboard cladding in place. Use it as a precaution to check for hidden pipes or cables before driving nails or drilling holes for wall fixings.

Household supplies

Many maintenance tricks can be accomplished with household supplies that you use every day. Here's a brief overview of which items under your kitchen sink (and stashed in your drawers and cupboards) can help you to keep your home shipshape.

SMART HOMEOWNER
NO COST
For many jobs, you don't need to buy anything special – just use what you have already in your cupboards.

Cleaners and lubricants

Dirt clogs moving parts, blocks the free flow of air or water and corrodes delicate materials. So one of the easiest ways to keep your home in good repair is to clean every nook and cranny clean.

Household cleaners Most cleaning jobs are easily done using common cleaning substances, including washing-up liquid, vinegar, bleach, talcum powder and household ammonia. Although ammonia is found in many commercial cleaning products, always take great care when mixing your own solutions – never mix ammonia with bleach and always use it in a well-ventilated area. A couple of squirts of washing-up liquid in a bucket of warm water makes a good window-cleaning solution or, for a much more powerful clean, caustic soda will shift most stubborn grime and can be used to unblock drains, too. You may not think of either as a household cleaner, but you can make use of the mildly abrasive properties of toothpaste to remove water marks in a sink or make a paste or solution of bicarbonate of soda for cleaning glass, tiles, porcelain and stainless steel.

Compressed air Sometimes all you need to get something clean is to get dust out of a confined space – for example, from inside your smoke alarm, power drill, computer keyboard or other electronic equipment. But don't blow it out with your mouth – that will add moisture to the mix, which may make the dirt stick even harder. Instead, use compressed air, which comes in an aerosol can with a nozzle extension. With the press of a button you can blow away dust or other loose, light debris.

Lubricants A little oil goes a long way in keeping your household running smoothly. For most jobs, a lightweight lubricant, such as 3-IN-ONE oil, is sufficient, but you may need other products. Two of the most popular are silicone spray, available under many brand names, and an anticorrosive penetrating oil in a spray can, such as WD-40. Silicone spray is a water-resistant oil with a silicone base that can lubricate almost anything. It works especially well on porous items, such as plastic parts, and is a good lubricant for locks, hinges and sliding doors. Because it's water-resistant, it can also be used as a rust retardant. Spray-on penetrating oil is also ideal for lubricating and resisting rust and can double as a cleaning agent. In fact, it's good for any number of home uses, including removing stubborn sticky labels and polishing fingerprints off brushed stainless steel kitchen appliances.

The best tape for the job

While tape doesn't usually have as much holding power as liquid or paste adhesives, it can do many things other adhesives can't, such as sealing ductwork or insulating electrical connections. Use this chart to help you to understand which type to choose for a job.

Tape	Description	What it's used for
Duct tape	Heat and moisture-resistant tape made of strong, plastic-coated cloth.	For temporary repairs and seals; despite its name, don't use it on ducts.
Metal foil tape	The true duct tape, made from heavy aluminium foil with strong adhesive.	Used to seal seams and joints in heating ducts.
Masking tape	Lightweight tape made of paper. Various grades or ratings are used for different tasks – longer-rated tapes are less adhesive and will peel off from walls more easily. Painter's tape is often blue or purple.	Holds glued items together while they dry; also used by painters to cover areas that aren't to be painted.
Electrical tape	Flame-retardant, stretchable vinyl tape that comes in a variety of colours.	Insulates cable cores in electrical switches, sockets and connections.
Carpet tape	Plastic or cloth tape with adhesive on both sides. Waterproof carpet tape is available for outdoor use.	Used to secure carpets and rugs to the floor.
Joint tape	Paper or mesh tape – paper is cheaper and easier to use, but messier.	For covering and strengthening the joints between sheets of plasterboard.

DUCT TAPE IS IDEAL FOR TEMPORARY REPAIRS.

The best glue for the job

When properly used, a good adhesive makes a bond that may even be stronger than the material itself. Various adhesives are available: the chart below will help you to decide which you need for the job at hand.

Adhesive	Description	What it's used for
Wood glue	Thick white liquid, also called PVA (polyvinyl adhesive), applied from a squeezy bottle.	Repairing woodwork or furniture.
Superglue or instant glue (cyanoacrylate)	Liquid adhesive in a tube; also available in gel form. **Caution:** Don't get any on your skin.	Liquid version bonds nonporous materials, including metals, vinyl, rubber and ceramics. Use the gel for porous materials like wood.
PVC cement	Paste that's applied with the applicator attached to the container cover. Some types require priming with a PVC cleaner. **Caution:** Gives off harmful fumes, so use only in a well-ventilated space.	Joining plastic plumbing pipes and fittings – acts as a solvent that melts plastic and welds the parts together.
Asphalt roof cement (plastic roofing cement)	Mixture of solvent-based bitumen, mineral stabilisers and other fibres. It's applied with a trowel.	Fastening asphalt roof coverings and flashing.
Epoxy	Waterproof adhesive that comes in two tubes of either liquid or putty – mix in equal parts and apply quickly.	Bonding wood, china, glass and most other materials; especially good for bonding dissimilar materials.
Grab adhesive	Builders' general-purpose adhesive mastic, applied from a cardboard tube fitted into a mastic gun.	Can be used to stick almost anything to anything, even skirting boards to walls.

TO REPAIR BROKEN CHINA
USE AN EPOXY ADHESIVE.

Tool safety

Working with tools can be dangerous, especially if the equipment is not properly maintained. If your saw is dull or your drill bit is blunted, you have to exert more energy to do the job. When you do this, your tools may wander off course and cause you nasty cuts or other injuries. Do your home maintenance safely by keeping your tools in pristine condition and by keeping a few common-sense safety rules in mind. Ban children and pets from work areas, avoid distractions, don't over-exert yourself and work at a steady pace.

SMART HOMEOWNER

90%

The percentage of eye injuries that could be prevented if DIY-ers all used the proper protective eyewear.

Use a chisel blade cover for safety

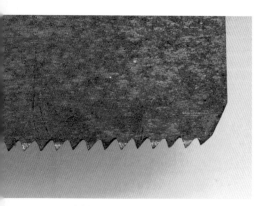
A blunt saw is a dangerous tool

Storage and maintenance of hand tools

● **Give every tool its own home** When you're not using your tools, keep them in assigned places where they won't be damaged by other tools. Store cutting tools where their sharp edges won't be blunted, and where they won't damage other tools – or your fingers. To prevent rust, store tools in a dry place and spray a rust-inhibiting coating on steel tools or put a few packets of clay or silicone desiccant in the toolbox or cabinet. Packets of dessicant come with most new tools and with many other household purchases, including new shoes and furniture – or you can buy them at DIY stores. If there are children in your household, always put tools away at the end of a job and keep them under lock and key.

● **Store saws and chisels in protective blade covers** This keeps the tools from being damaged or causing damage when you're rummaging in your toolbox looking for something else. If the tools don't come with blade protectors, make your own: get a couple of plastic report-cover spines from a stationery shop and slide them over the teeth of your saws or cut slits into tennis balls and slip chisel blades inside.

● **Keep tools dry** Water can rust a blade or warp a wooden handle. If a tool gets wet, wipe it with a soft, dry cloth before you store it. If it's sweaty or greasy, clean the tool with a damp cloth and then wipe it dry with a clean, dry cloth. Avoid oiling hand tools. If oil gets on the handle, your grip might slip and you could be injured.

● **Keep saws sharp** There's a saying that it's easier to cut yourself with a dull knife than a sharp one, and it's true of saws as well. Stay safe by cleaning and sharpening the blades on your cutting tools before they get damaged or dull. If they're past repair, replace them. To tell whether your saw needs attention, examine its blades under a magnifying glass. If the teeth are rounded (not sharp and pointy), take the saw to a hardware shop for resharpening. If a handsaw gets clogged with resin from cutting soft wood, clean it with oven cleaner, then spray the blade with silicone.

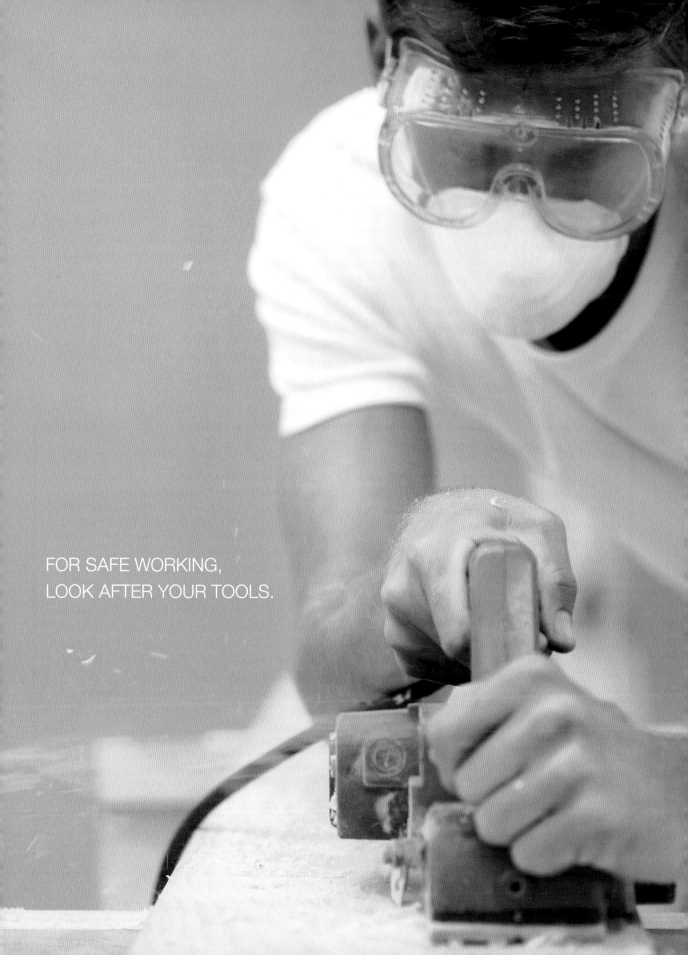

FOR SAFE WORKING,
LOOK AFTER YOUR TOOLS.

take care!

Before working with flammable or toxic substances such as paint or PVC cement, extinguish any gas pilot lights in the room, open windows and turn on a fan to ensure proper ventilation. Above all, don't smoke. Only buy as much flammable or toxic material as you need for the job in hand, no matter how great the saving might be for buying in bulk. Dispose of leftovers as recommended by the manufacturer, or contact your local council recycling department for instructions.

Power tools

Always follow the manufacturer's instructions for maintaining and operating your power tools. If you've lost the owner's manual, check the manufacturer's website – they usually post up old manuals for all of their products. Follow this general advice for working safely with power tools:

● Keep power tools unplugged whenever they aren't in use and disconnect the batteries of cordless tools. Many accidents happen by brushing against the on/off switch of a tool and turning it on.

● If the tool's air vents become clogged, clean them with compressed air or a vacuum cleaner. A blocked vent can cause the tool to overheat.

● If your project is dusty or will make a lot of sawdust, attach a vacuum cleaner to the tool's vent pipe if possible to suck up the waste. This will not only help with the clean-up but also reduce the chances of a fire.

● If you have cordless tools, use only the battery and charger that came with the unit.

● Never charge batteries for tools in temperatures below 4°C or over 40°C. Batteries rely on chemical reactions that slow down in cold weather and cease altogether when it's very hot. High temperatures release vapours from the battery and will diminish its capacity.

Safety smarts for DIY-ers

When you're using tools or machinery, always wear sturdy shoes with slip-proof soles. Roll up your sleeves and tie back your hair. Keep your hands free by carrying your hand tools in a tool belt or a bucket and, above all, use the appropriate safety equipment.

● Wear heavy work gloves for jobs that could hurt your hands and rubber gloves when handling toxic materials. Don't wear gloves when cutting or drilling – the tool could slip out of your hands and injure you.

● For grinding, filing, chiselling or any other work that involves dust or flying chips, wear safety goggles.

● Wear a dust mask when sanding or doing other work that might create particles that could irritate your respiratory system. The most effective masks are marked 'BSI-approved' and carry the BSI Kitemark® (see page 177). They are generally thicker than cheaper masks and have straps for a tighter seal.

● If you're going to be subjected to harmful vapours or fibres (such as from insulation), wear a respirator. The best models come with interchangeable cartridges to filter out the harmful effects of toxic dust and fumes from specific materials, such as paints and adhesives.

● If you'll be kneeling a lot, wear protective kneepads or kneel on a folded blanket or thick layers of newspaper.

● When you use a loud power tool, protect your ears with foam earplugs or earmuff-style ear defenders.

● Always keep a fire extinguisher to hand.

Getting professional help

Whatever your level of experience, there will always be certain projects that are best left to the professionals. Almost no one is qualified to work in all fields of home repair and improvement and some jobs must, by law, only be carried out by approved tradespeople. Follow this advice to make sure you get the best value from your contractors and don't pay more than you absolutely need to.

Hiring tradespeople

● **Work within your comfort zone** Steer clear of work that feels dangerous or requires skills that you don't have. For example, if you know heights make you dizzy, don't attempt any jobs on the roof or at the top of a ladder. Be realistic and call in someone else when it makes sense.

● **Use only registered, approved contractors** Don't undertake any job that the Building Regulations state must be done by a licensed professional (see page 34). If you're caught, you may have to pay a fine and then have the work redone by a professional. Even worse, if your home sustains severe damage, as in a fire, your insurance company won't pay up if you haven't fully complied with the Building Regulations.

● **Ask around for top-quality tradespeople** For small jobs, you can hire a lone worker, such as an electrician or plumber. For larger jobs, you may need a contractor, who can co-ordinate all the various trades. The best recommendations are by word of mouth: ask neighbours, suppliers and other building tradespeople for workers they would trust.

● **Take your pick of the contractor crop** Interview at least three contractors and get an itemised estimate from each one. The best may not be the cheapest: opt for quality and durability over a lower-cost, potentially shoddy job, and you'll save money and hassle in the long run.

SMART HOMEOWNER
50%
Average percentage of the cost of a minor kitchen refurbishment that you'll recoup when you sell your home.

smart idea

Don't pay more than a quarter of the cost of the job as a down payment and always hold back as much of the payment as you can until the project is completed to your satisfaction. The more the contractor wants up front, the greater the likelihood that he has bad intentions.

● **Spell out your expectations in a contract** Once you've chosen a contractor, work out a written agreement that specifies the work to be done and the materials to be used. Get the following in writing:

● A description of what the job entails, including who will acquire and pay for any required planning consents or building control approvals (make sure you have copies of all the relevant paperwork).

● Materials to be used, including brand names, colours, stock numbers, weights and other details.

● How long the job will take. For a big job, consider including a monetary penalty if the job isn't finished by a certain date.

● The dates and times that workers will be on the premises, along with the names of any subcontractors who will have access to your property.

● An estimate of the cost (and a maximum price).

● Titles and terms of the individual's or contractor's insurance policies, including workers' compensation and liability policies.

● A statement of responsibility for any damage caused to your property.

● A guarantee of all materials and workmanship.

● A declaration that your warranties or guarantees are transferable when the house is sold.

● A guarantee of clean-up and removal of debris daily and after the job is completed.

When you need a professional

There are some instances where building work is controlled by the law and you must always seek professional help. You may invalidate your insurance or incur a fine if you attempt to do specialist work yourself, and when you come to sell your home you'll be required to present certificates to back up work that has been done on it.

Representing the best in electrical engineering and building services

● **GAS WORK** One of the main areas off-limits for DIY is any kind of gas work, which should only be carried out by an engineer on the Gas Safe Register. Look for the Gas Safe Register logo on a contractor's letterhead or business card or contact the Gas Safe Register (see page 37) if you want to check your plumber or gas fitter's credentials.

● **ELECTRICAL WORK** Much electrical wiring work is also now 'notifiable' to the local authority building control department (see page 169). Home owners can do some minor repairs, such as replacing existing light switches or sockets in some rooms, but if you do any new wiring work yourself you must pay to have it inspected by the Building Control Officer. Otherwise you must use an electrician who's qualified to part P of the Building Regulations. The Electrical Contractors Association (ECA) or the National Inspection Council for Electrical Installation Contracting (NICEIC) can verify whether an electrician is suitably licensed (see page 37 for contact details).

● **REPLACEMENT WINDOWS** All new replacement windows must have a window energy rating of 'C' (see rating card left) or above, or have a whole window 'U' value (rate of heat loss through a structure) of 1.6 W/m2K. If you're replacing windows or doors, you'll need to either go through the Local Authority Building Control process or have the work done by a company registered with the Fenestration Self Assessment Scheme (FENSA – www.fensa.org.uk), who will certify that the installation work complies with the current Building Regulations. Homeowners will receive a FENSA Energy Rated Compliance Certificate which will be required by your purchaser's solicitor if you sell your home in the future.

What to ask a **prospective contractor**

Question	Why it's important to ask
What's your address and phone number?	You should be wary of contractors who only give a mobile phone number or who are unwilling to divulge their address – it will be impossible to find them if you have a problem with their work.
How long have you been in business?	Many fly-by-night tradespeople do shoddy work in one town and then vanish after a year or two. Try to find a tradesperson who's been in business locally for at least three years.
Can you give me references for clients who have used you for similar projects?	If the references are few or aren't recent, ask why. Check with the Trading Standards Department to see if any complaints have been filed against the contractor.
Will you show me before-and-after photos of similar projects you've done?	This is a good way to see what kind of work the person does. Better still, ask some previous customers if you can come to their homes to see the contractor's work – you'll be able to talk to them about their experiences at the same time.
Will you explain what the job will involve and how long it will take?	Having the contractor explain the project shows that 1) they know what's involved, and 2) they are willing to communicate with clients.
Can you give me a guaranteed end date?	Though few jobs ever go exactly as planned, you should have some assurance that the project won't drag on for months.
Will you provide a written estimate and set a maximum price for the job?	Everyone has heard the horror stories about contractors who charge their clients thousands of pounds more than they thought the job would cost. Always assume that big projects will go 10 to 15 per cent over budget and factor in a contingency fund at the outset. It's a good sign if the contractor is willing to honour the estimate price even if the project takes longer than anticipated.
What is your payment schedule?	Steer clear if the contractor asks for a hefty down payment (they might say it's for materials) before any work begins. This might indicate that they are not established enough to have accounts with local suppliers and don't have the cash reserves to pay for them out of their own pocket. For big jobs, negotiate a fee structure in which you pay over three or four instalments (the last one being the largest).

ASK QUESTIONS TO SIZE UP POTENTIAL CONTRACTORS.

Understanding quotes and estimates

● **Get everything in writing** Before embarking on any major renovations or projects, it's a good idea to get all the details, such as price, deadlines and materials, on paper, just to make sure there's no confusion later in the job.

● **Remember that estimates are just that: estimates**
When you ask for an estimate, a contractor looks at the job, calculates what materials will be required and how many hours the job will take, then gives you an estimate of the total cost. The actual bill may be higher or lower, depending on unexpected problems that the contractor might encounter during the job. Working in a piecemeal way, paying by an hourly rate and for materials actually used, means that the contractor is compensated fairly for time spent on the job, but the downside is that expenses can snowball and, if you don't feel the contractor is working efficiently, create conflict. Because they aren't binding, estimates are best used for small jobs, and when you've hired people you know and trust.

● **Know that you can count on quotes** A quote differs from an estimate in that a quote is a binding document. The contractor still gives an estimate for the job but the work is done for a set price, regardless of how long the project takes. A quote for a project will often be higher than an estimate, since the contractor has to factor in surprises that they may encounter. Nonetheless, most homeowners and contractors feel more comfortable working from a quote, especially on large projects.

Smart places to put your money

As a homeowner, the smartest place to invest your money is in updating the rooms and spaces you enjoy most (assuming your house is structurally sound, safe and dry). Property developers will have a more business-like view, but if you aren't planning to move in the forseeable future it makes sense to create the home that you want, not what you think a potential purchaser might one day want.

Nonetheless, it pays to keep the resale potential in mind when you carry out major works. Be wary of schemes that might seem strange to other people, as they will narrow your pool of potential buyers. Avoid splashing out on a brightly coloured bathroom suite that won't be to many people's taste, for example, and think hard before knocking two bedrooms into one to create the 'wow' master bedroom suite as it might not outweigh the advantages of having an additional room. Done well, home improvements will usually recoup at least part of their investment when you come to sell.

Most estate agents will tell you that if you're about to put your house on the market the best place to invest your time and money is in inexpensive, cosmetic spruce-ups. It's hard to beat a coat of paint for freshening up a room. New handles on kitchen units and new carpets, though considerably more expensive than paint, can also help your home's appeal.

Increasing 'kerb appeal' is another smart tactic and will create a favourable first impression for prospective buyers. New house numbers, a freshly painted front door and a new coat of sealant on the drive will help to make your house more attractive at little cost.

If you know that your house really needs a new kitchen or bathroom, ask local estate agents whether they think it's worth doing before you sell. In general, these are the areas with the best payback in recouping your costs, but if you're doing the work just to sell, many buyers would rather do it themselves to their own taste, and are likely to rip out whatever you put in.

Trade organisations and specialists

If you need advice on a job or recommendations of accredited contractors in your area, contact the relevant specialist organisation or trade federation from this list.

Architects
Royal Institute of British Architects (RIBA)
66 Portland Place, London W1B 1AD
Tel: 020 7580 5533
Email: info@inst.riba.org
www.architecture.com

Building
Chartered Institute of Building
Englemere
Kings Ride, Ascot
Berkshire SL5 7TB
Tel: 01344 630700
Email: reception@ciob.org.uk
www.ciob.org.uk

Federation of Master Builders
Gordon Fisher House
14-15 Great James Street
London WC1N 3DP
Tel: 020 7242 7583
www.fmb.org.uk

Institution of Structural Engineers
11 Upper Belgrave Street
London SW1X 8BH
Tel: 020 7235 4535
www.istructe.org

National Federation of Builders
B&CE Building, Manor Royal
Crawley, West Sussex RH10 9QP
Tel: 08450 578160
www.builders.org.uk

RICS (Royal Institution of Chartered Surveyors)
12 Great George Street
Parliament Square
London SW1P 3AD
Tel: 0870 3331600
Email: contactrics@rics.org
www.rics.org

Damp, rot and infestation
British Pest Control Association
1 Gleneagles House, Vernongate
South Street, Derby DE1 1UP
Tel: 01332 294288
www.bpca.org.uk

Property Care Association (formerly BWPDA)
Lake View Court, Ermine Business Park, Huntingdon PE29 6XR
Tel: 08443 754301
Email: pca@property-care.org
www.property-care.org

Decorating
Painting and Decorating Association
32 Coton Road, Nuneaton
Warwickshire CV11 5TW
Tel: 024 7635 3776
Email: info@paintingdecorating association.co.uk
www.paintingdecoratingassociation.co.uk

Electricity
Electrical Contractors' Association
ESCA House, 34 Palace Court
London W2 4HY
Tel: 020 7313 4800
Email: info@eca.co.uk
www.eca.co.uk

NICEIC (National Inspection Council for Electrical Installation Contracting)
Warwick House, Houghton Hall Park
Houghton Regis, Dunstable
Bedfordshire LU5 5ZX
Tel: 0870 013 0382
www.niceic.com

Gas
Gas Safe Register
PO Box 6804, Basingstoke
RG24 4NB
Tel: 0800 408 5500
Email: enquiries@gassaferegister.co.uk
www.gassaferegister.co.uk

Glass and glazing
Glass and Glazing Federation (GGF)
54 Ayres Street, London SE1 1EU
Tel: 020 7939 9101
www.ggf.org.uk

FENSA Ltd (the Fenestration Self Assessment Scheme)
54 Ayres Street, London SE1 1EU
Tel: 020 7645 3700
Email: enquiries@fensa.org.uk
www.fensa.org.uk

Heating and ventilation
Heating and Ventilation Contractors' Association
ESCA House, 34 Palace Court
London W2 4JG
Tel: 020 7313 4900
Email: contact@hvca.org.uk
www.hvca.org.uk

Insulation
Energy Saving Trust (EST)
21 Dartmouth Street
London SW1H 9BP
Tel: 020 7222 0101
www.energysavingtrust.org.uk

Plumbing and heating
Association of Plumbing and Heating Contractors Ltd
12 The Pavilions, Cranmore Drive
Solihull B90 4SB
Tel: 0121 711 5030
www.aphc.co.uk

Chartered Institute of Plumbing and Heating Engineering
64 Station Lane, Hornchurch
Essex RM12 6NB
Tel: 01708 472791
Email: info@ciphe.org.uk
www.ciphe.org.uk

Security
Master Locksmiths Association
Unit 5D, Great Central Way
Woodford Halse, Daventry NN11 3PZ
Tel: 01327 262255
Email: enquiries@locksmiths.co.uk
www.locksmiths.co.uk

Walls and floors take a beating like no other part of the house. We think nothing of driving a picture hook into a wall or showering the tiles around the bath with a jet of water. Constant traffic – often from dirty or hard-soled shoes – pounds the floors and stairs; people with bags or children with toys bump and scrape walls as they pass. It's all in a day's work for the surfaces in your home.

Eventually this abuse takes its toll. Floors need refinishing and tiles replacing, and walls need painting or their holes and cracks filling. This chapter shows you how to slow or minimise wear and tear, with actions as simple and cheap as using a cleverly positioned rug to extend the life of your floor, or vacuuming the walls once a year to prolong the life of paint or wallpaper.

A little maintenance and a few small repairs can help to avoid the major repair or replacement jobs we all dread. Here you'll find out how to replace a single broken floor tile and rescue the rest of the floor, how four screws and a doorstop can save you from a wall repair that could cost hundreds, and how, by reacting quickly and appropriately to a spillage, you can save your carpet from disaster.

SAVE £200

The cost to reline a 6m x 2.4m wall after damage by a water leak, including new plasterboard and other materials and debris removal.

Plasterboard walls

The walls in most modern homes are made of plasterboard, either screwed to a wooden framework or fixed to the brick or block wall behind with 'dabs' of plaster. Plasterboard is maintenance-free but prone to nicks, dents and tears, and is easily damaged by careless fixings or ruined by a leak.

Care and maintenance

● **Look out for leaks** Water will destroy plasterboard, so stay vigilant for signs of dampness, such as brown spots appearing – even if no water is obvious. If you discover evidence of moisture, check for a leaky pipe in the vicinity – it may be running through the wall cavity or above or below the wall in a ceiling void. Damage can also be caused by water consistently splashing out of sinks, baths or showers, or seeping through poorly grouted or sealed joints in tiling, while a persistently damp atmosphere in a poorly ventilated bathroom will also eventually take its toll on the walls. Water can seep in from outside, too, through a leaking roof or eaves.

● **Take care with fixings** Lightweight fixings, such as picture hooks, can be hammered into plasterboard, but if you attempt to fix anything heavy using the wrong fixing you'll almost certainly end up with a hole to fill and perhaps an even bigger problem. Always use plasterboard fixings that screw into the board, or cavity fixings or anchors that open out within the cavity and grip the inside face of the board. If you are fixing something really heavy, like a bookshelf, try to locate a stud and fix to that or, with a dry-lined brick wall, use long fixings and drill into the brick behind.

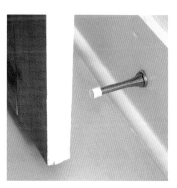

● **Install doorstops** Without a doorstop to act as a buffer, the repeated knocks from a doorknob or handle, or even just one carelessly banged door, will damage the wall and can even make a hole. Equip each interior door with a solid doorstop, screwed into the door, skirting board or floor, or if you want an inconspicuous doorstop, choose one that mounts on top of a door hinge.

Anatomy of a plasterboard wall

Plasterboard is used to clad internal partition walls, where it's screwed to a framework of timber or metal 'studs' (below), or to 'dry line' the inner face of external brick or block walls, where it's usually held in place with dabs of plaster. The structure determines how best to fix to the wall. For a sturdy hold, use plasterboard fixings, which splay out within the cavity behind the board or, for heavy items, try to locate and screw into a stud or drill and fix into the brickwork behind.

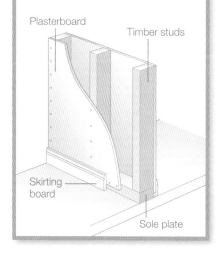

Plasterboard

Timber studs

Skirting board

Sole plate

● **Prevent wall damage with chair rail moulding** Another common cause of dents and scrapes on plasterboard are chairs or tables that bump against the wall in a dining room or eating alcove. The answer: chair or dado rail moulding fixed to the wall. Put it at the correct level for your chair backs, using instant-grip adhesive, pins or screws, and you'll protect the wall and add style to the room.

Easy fixes

● **Quick fixes for scratches and dents** If a plasterboard wall has not been coated with a thin 'skim' coat of finishing plaster, it can be easily damaged by knocks and bumps. Fortunately, it's just as easy to repair. Just apply fine surface filler, a little at a time, using a putty or filler knife. If the damage is more than 5mm deep, do the job in stages. Fill the hole about halfway, let the filler dry, and then fill it to the surface – if you apply too much filler at once, it will crack as it dries. Once the filler is dry, smooth and level the patch by sanding with some fine abrasive paper wrapped around a sanding block, or by wiping with a damp sponge (left) to feather the edges of the repair.

A damp sponge gives a smooth finish

Which filler should you use?

DIY stores stock a bewildering array of similar-looking packs, tubs and tubes of filler, but for everyday DIY you just need one for plaster, one for woodwork and another for filling gaps. Use this guide to help you to choose which you need for the job in hand.

For internal decoration

● **CRACKS AND HOLES IN PLASTER** Dry-powder interior filler, a mixture of chalk and plaster of paris, is the cheapest option for making small repairs in plaster. Mix as much as you need with water and it will set within a couple of hours. As the filler dries, it will shrink slightly, so it's always best to overfill the hole and then smooth off the excess with sandpaper when it's dry. You can buy a 500g pack for around £2 or a 25kg sack – 50 times as much – of Universal One-Coat Plaster for around £5.

● **FILLING GAPS** Flexible fillers are sold in tubes to fit into mastic guns or smaller squeezy tubes. They are based on the same acrylic compound used in frame sealants and are useful for filling gaps between windows and walls. Sometimes called decorator's sealant, flexible fillers can be painted over within a few hours. They remain flexible for a few years, but will dry and crack after that, especially if the joint filled is more than a few millimetres wide or deep.

● **REPAIRING WALLS OR WOODWORK** Ready-mixed fine-surface filler comes in tubs or tubes. The filler is based on high-magnesium (dolomitic) lime and stays soft as long as it's covered, but sets hard when exposed to the air. These are quick and convenient, useful for repairing both walls and woodwork, but are much more expensive than dry-powder fillers.

For exterior repairs

● **EXTERIOR MASONRY** Exterior-grade filler is usually cement-based and may take days to harden. Use it on exterior render or masonry, although old brickwork is better repaired with a traditional lime-and-sand mortar mix.

● **DOORS AND WINDOWS** Exterior woodwork is best repaired with a two-pack epoxy wood filler, which is more flexible than cement-based fillers.

● **Filling cracks** Cracks in plasterboard are often too fine for the filler to bond securely in place. What's the solution? Enlarge the crack by cutting along both sides with a craft knife to create a V-shaped groove about 5mm wide at the surface. The groove eliminates irregularities and provides enough surface for the filler to adhere to. If the crack is along a seam, remove any loose joint tape and scrape out crumbling joint filler. Fill the groove with a suitable filler, and smooth it with a filler knife. Let the repaired area dry, sand or sponge it to a smooth finish and then touch up the paint.

● **Replacing popped nails** These days plasterboard is usually screwed into place, but older walls may have been fixed with nails and, from time to time, one of these nails will start working its way out of the wall, squeezed by the framing as it dries. If you see a nail popping out, take a small, flat nail bar and prise the nail out. Slip a scrap of wood

smart idea

The last stage of any wall repair is to sand the repaired area and then smooth and paint it. But sanding even a small repair creates a lot of fine white dust that's guaranteed to be walked all over the house. To keep the mess to a minimum, wipe the filler instead with a damp sponge. It will smooth the surface as well as sandpaper and leave you with far less mess to clean up.

How to patch damaged plasterboard

The easiest way to patch a small hole up to 125mm across is to glue a plasterboard offcut or piece of MDF behind the damage and then gradually build up the repair with filler. First, use a padsaw to enlarge the damage into a neat, straight-sided hole. Thread string through a backing piece that is slightly larger than the hole, apply coving adhesive or filler to the edges then guide it through the hole and pull it tight against the back of the wall until it has stuck firmly. Cut off the string before you apply the filler. Larger holes should be repaired with a plasterboard patch as shown below. Caution: always check that there are no cables or pipes behind where you'll be working.

1 First square off the hole. Use a knife or padsaw to enlarge the damage until you reach the studs on either side, then score and remove strips of board to expose half of each stud.

2 Fit timber crosspieces, the same size as the existing studs, cut to fit tightly across the gap. Hold these in position with G-cramps and nail diagonally through them into the studs.

3 Cut a plasterboard patch to fit the hole, making sure the board is the same thickness as the original. Nail the patch to the frame you have created, with the ivory side facing outwards.

4 Lightly sand the edges of the patch to remove any burrs, then use joint compound or finishing plaster to fill the gaps. Sand the filler once it is dry, then patch up the decoration.

between the bar and the wall to avoid damaging the surface. Then drive a drywall screw in just above or below the pop, dimpling but not breaking the surface paper with the head of the screw. Fill the repair area with fine surface filler, and smooth it with a filler knife. Let it dry, smooth with sandpaper or, better still, a damp sponge, then touch up the paint once the wall is dry.

● **Stopping recurring cracks** Perhaps you filled a crack and now, two months later, it's back. That's usually because of settlement, a common problem in new houses, especially around the corners of windows and doorways. The house will eventually stop shifting, but until it does, the trick is to fill any small reappearing cracks with a flexible acrylic filler (sometimes called decorator's filler or mastic), which can be painted over. Flexible fillers cannot be sanded, but a clever trick for getting a perfect finish is to put on a latex glove and wipe the filler smooth with your finger.

Filler knives

Equipment spotlight

A filler knife has a flexible steel blade that makes it easy to press filler into gaps and holes and to scrape the surface smooth. Do not confuse a filler knife with a stripping knife, which looks almost the same, but has a much stiffer blade and will be difficult to use effectively. Plastic spreaders are also available, and most tubs of ready-made filler come with a small plastic spreader for the job. It's a good idea to buy at least two filler knives, with different blade widths – a 25mm and 50mm. This makes it easy to build up several coats of filler, each a little wider than the last, to give the best results when filling a deep hole.

Repairing battered corners

Outward-projecting plasterboard corners are vulnerable to damage but, fortunately, easy to repair. Outside corners should be protected by a metal piece, called a corner bead; it wraps around the corner, is nailed to the plasterboard (left) and then covered with joint compound. If a corner bead is bent, tap it gently back into shape with a hammer and file any sharp edges smooth. Since the existing corner bead will provide backing for any repair you make, you can fill gaps with quick-setting joint compound.

You can also reinforce corners with joint tape bedded in joint compound (left). Use corner tape, which incorporates metal reinforcing strips; crease the tape down the centre and make sure to position it with the metal strips facing inwards, against the surface of the wall.

Plaster walls

A wall made of plaster is more durable than one made from plasterboard. But although scratches and dents are easy to fix, replastering – or having a major repair done – is expensive, difficult to do well yourself, and one of the messiest jobs you can imagine. Anything that breaks the bond between the plaster and the inner wall means major work, so follow these tips and take care of your walls.

SAVE £400

The cost to remove crumbling plaster from a 6m x 2.4m wall, clear the debris and replaster the wall.

Anatomy of a **plaster wall**

A plaster wall is built in stages. In older houses, the plaster is probably applied to a solid wall of bricks (near right) or blocks, or over a framework of timber laths (far right). Behind the smooth topcoat may be one or two coats of coarse render: a 'scratch coat' that bonds the plaster to the wall behind and which is scratched to help the second 'floating coat', a sandy mix, to stick. You may even find traces of horsehair in old plaster walls. Minor repairs can be done to just the topcoat, but if damage is more extensive you'll need to chip away and build up all the layers, or even strip away the plaster entirely.

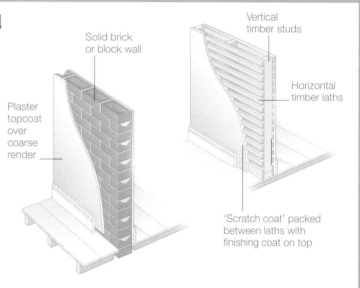

Solid brick or block wall

Plaster topcoat over coarse render

Vertical timber studs

Horizontal timber laths

'Scratch coat' packed between laths with finishing coat on top

Care and maintenance

● **Investigate the source of your cracks** The way plaster cracks can often tell you what's causing the problem and how serious it is.

● Small diagonal cracks above a window or door are rarely sinister and can simply be patched. In a new house, straight cracks in skimmed plasterboard walls that follow the joints between the boards are common and not usually a sign of anything serious. Diagonal cracks, often running in opposite directions, are the result of settling. Patch them and forget about them; they'll stop once the house stops settling.

● If the cracks are large, uneven in width, or recessed, the problem may be structural. Cracks zig-zagging up brick or block walls following the mortar joints may also be due to settlement, or construction shrinkage. But vertical cracks that go through bricks or blocks can indicate foundation failure. Talk to a chartered building surveyor or structural engineer and have the underlying problem remedied before you repair the plaster.

● **Patch small holes as they occur** The weight of loose plaster creates stress on the surrounding plaster. Once the process starts, it continues pulling even more plaster loose. Small holes are easy to fix – don't neglect them or they might become large holes.

● **Install doorstops** A doorknob that bangs into a wall can damage not only the area it hits but a lot of the surrounding plaster too. Make sure that all doors are equipped with sturdy doorstops.

● **Keep your tools clean** It may sound fussy, but make a point of washing and rinsing your tools and pans thoroughly before you mix a second batch of patching plaster to finish a job. Otherwise, the leftover plaster activates drying compounds in the new plaster and it can harden before you get it from the sink to the wall.

● **Plaster's biggest enemy: water** Leaking pipes, water that spills out of showers and roof leaks will stain and eventually ruin plaster. Brown spots on your wall can indicate leaks. Fix the leaks first; then repair or repaint the plaster. Before painting over a stain, coat it with a stain block to prevent show-through.

Easy fixes

● **Patching with the right materials** Making surface repairs to plaster is easy if you select the best patching compound for the job:
 ● Repair small cracks in plaster with fine surface filler. Widen a hairline crack with a craft knife or your filler knife until it's about 2mm wide so the filler has more plaster to stick to.

Rake out loose plaster before patching

Fixing a **damaged corner**

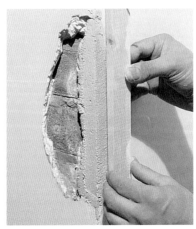

The easiest way to patch a damaged external corner is to use a planed timber batten as a plastering guide. Pin the batten flush to one edge of the corner with masonry nails, leaving their heads projecting so you can remove them again easily. Then plaster up to the batten (far left). When the plaster has dried, remove the batten carefully and repeat the process from the other side of the corner (near left). Finish by rounding off the new corner with some fine abrasive paper.

- There's no point putting filler over loose plaster – the repair will soon fail. Use your knife to rake out crumbly plaster and loose debris from a crack (left) before you start to apply the filler.
- Patch holes with patching plaster – a special mix that's stronger than plaster and seldom requires more than one coat.

- **Duplicating your wall's texture** If you want a repair to be invisible you need to make its surface match the surface of the older surrounding plaster as closely as possible.
- If the wall is textured, duplicate the texture. Depending on the effect you need, try dragging a comb, brush, crumpled newspaper or sponge across the wet plaster.
- If the wall has a sandy surface, let the patch dry and prime it ready for painting. Then apply a topcoat of latex paint mixed with sand.
- If the wall is smooth, just smooth the new plaster or filler with a putty or filler knife (right). Scrape the knife frequently on a clean piece of wood as you work to clean off any specks of dried plaster and keep them from scratching the surface of the repair.

Make the filler as smooth as the wall

How to repair a hole in a plaster wall

1 Tap around the hole. A hollow sound indicates plaster has separated from the wall behind. Chip away loose plaster with a cold chisel and hollow out around the edge of the hole a little so that the patching plaster will sit slightly behind the sound plaster that remains. Brush away any dust and debris.

2 Dampen any exposed bricks with a light spray of water. Start applying ready-mixed plaster to the wall with a plasterer's trowel (below) or a wide filling knife. Don't attempt to fill more than 50mm deep in one layer.

3 Build up deep areas in layers, allowing each to stiffen before applying the next. If the wall is to be papered, fill the patching plaster flush with the surrounding wall, then smooth it with fine abrasive paper or a sander (below) when it's completely dry.

4 If the patch is deep and the wall is to be painted, only fill the ready-mixed plaster to about 3mm below the level of the surrounding wall. Once this is dry, complete the job with a coat of skim plaster to give a smooth, paintable finish.

Apply the plaster with a trowel for best results

A power sander gives a professional finish

Painted walls

If you need an incentive to take care of painted surfaces, just think about all the furniture-moving, scraping, sanding, splatters and brush-cleaning that go into painting a room. Most of us don't think about the paint on our walls until it starts to look drab or dated, but all it takes is periodic dusting, prompt spot and stain removal, and the occasional patching of scrapes and chips and you can get years of extra life out of your paintwork.

SAVE £400

What you would pay to have an average-sized room (4m x 6m) with neglected walls prepared for decoration and repainted.

Care and maintenance

● **Dust your way to clean walls** The easiest way to stay on top of the dust, dirt and cobwebs that shorten the life of your paint is to run a duster over your walls every couple of months – it shouldn't take more than 10 or 15 minutes to do an entire room. There's no need to take down pictures or move furniture: areas that are covered don't get very dirty. Don't forget the ceiling; despite gravity, dust collects there, too. Vacuuming with a soft brush attachment works just as well and so does the old-fashioned approach: a clean, white cloth wrapped around the head of a broom.

● **Wash kitchen and bathroom walls** Remove residues from cooking and steamy showers by washing the painted areas of kitchen and bathroom walls and the woodwork at least once a year. Do other rooms, too, if they are regularly used by children or a smoker, or have a fireplace or wood-burning stove. Start from the bottom. Rub gently with a natural sponge and a soap-and-water solution (see below). Wash and rinse a small area, then move up and do an area that partially overlaps the one you've just cleaned. Dry the wall with an old towel when you've finished.

● **Make your own wall-washing soap** DIY stores sell sugar soap for cleaning painted walls before you redecorate, but it's too harsh for a light spring clean. Instead, a homemade soap mixture will do a great job of cleaning painted walls. Just mix 200ml of ammonia and 1 teaspoon of washing-up liquid in 4 litres of water. This simple solution is inexpensive, simple to make and at least as good as any commercially available cleaners.

● **Test painted walls before cleaning them** It's safe to wash glossy and vinyl silk finish paints, which are commonly used in kitchens and bathrooms and on woodwork. Most modern matt and satin paints are also washable, but always test them in an inconspicuous spot before you start. If the paint leaves a chalky residue on your sponge, don't go any further.

● **Wash high-traffic areas** Even if you don't need to wash an entire room, the areas around switches in particular may need an occasional clean. And so does that area behind the sofa or the bed, where somebody's

WASH HIGH-TRAFFIC AREAS.

hair leaves a greasy spot. Dust and dirt also tend to accumulate on walls behind TVs or other electronics and above radiators. If dusting doesn't get them clean, wash the area with a mild soap-and-water solution (see above).

● **Seal in lead paint** Until 1992 many paints contained harmful lead, to which you can be exposed if you're sanding or stripping the surface and which can be dangerous for small children. If you have walls that haven't been decorated for many years, the most reliable way to test suspect paint is with a laboratory test – you can find places to test paint by looking on the internet – or you can buy easy home-testing kits. If you do have lead

smart idea

Apply a light coating of spray starch to walls in high-traffic areas. The starch makes it easier to clean off dirt and grime. Next time you decorate, choose a washable paint finish for walls that get grubby.

Clever wall stain removers

If your walls have ...	You should ...
Crayon marks	Spray the area with WD-40, then wipe with a soft cloth.
Small spots and smudges	Rub gently with a pencil eraser.
Large spots	Make a paste from bicarbonate of soda and water. Apply it with a soft cloth and wipe clean with a damp sponge.
Ink and marker stains	Wipe with a rag dampened with methylated spirits.
Grease marks	Wipe with a rag dampened with white spirit.

Saving leftover paint

When you paint a room, save the leftover paint for touch-ups. Water-based paint will keep for 10 years and oil-based paint for up to 15: long enough to outlive the decoration of the room.

● On the lid, write the paint's colour and reference number, purchase date and the room where it was used. On the outside of the tin, mark the level of the paint so you can tell how much is left without opening the lid.

● Store a part-used tin upside down so that any skin that forms will be on the bottom when you turn the can upright. Or cut a disc of kitchen foil, using the lid as a template (right), and press it down gently on the surface of the paint. If you have more than half a can, just put a piece of cling film over the top for an extra-tight seal and replace the lid securely.

● A small amount of paint will keep better in a small container. Decant the paint into a screw-top jar (left), rubbing petroleum jelly around the rim first, so that the paint doesn't make the lid stick. Alternatively, pour the paint into a plastic food bag, squeeze out the extra air as you seal the bag, then put the bag in the original can and seal the can.

● When you reopen stored paint, stir it vigorously; if it blends well, it should be fine to use. If it's lumpy, strain the paint into a paint kettle through a piece of material cut from a pair of tights.

5 tips for a great paint finish

The secret to a professional paint finish is choosing your materials carefully. Here are some guidelines:

1 CHOOSE THE RIGHT COLOUR Take paint colour charts home and pick the colour during daylight in the room you'll be painting. Buy a tester pot of the colour you choose, paint a good square of it on at least two of the walls in the room to see it in different lights, and live with it for a while before you make a final decision.

2 CHEAP PAINT IS EXPENSIVE You're more likely to save money with a top-of-the-range paint. Cheap paint usually requires at least two coats to cover what's on the wall, instantly doubling your cost. Low-quality water-based paint also gets chalky as it ages and needs to be repainted sooner.

3 GET THE RIGHT FINISH Paint comes in gloss, silk, eggshell, satin and matt finishes. Use gloss or satin on woodwork for a hard-wearing finish. In areas likely to get dirty – kitchens and bathrooms – use washable paint. The glossier the paint, the more durable and easier it is to clean. Flat matt finishes, on the other hand, hide wall defects and touched-up areas better.

4 MATCH, DON'T MIX Consider using the same colour paint on woodwork and walls even if they're not the same sheen. You'll have to do far less masking before you start work, and touching-up later on is simpler, since paint splashed from the walls onto the woodwork (or vice versa) will be virtually invisible.

5 PICK THE RIGHT APPLICATORS The brushes and rollers you choose are crucial in achieving a professional finish.
● Select a short-nap roller for smooth walls and a longer nap for render, concrete and textured surfaces. Make sure the roller has slightly bevelled ends that won't drag paint onto adjoining surfaces. Choose a nylon-wool blend roller for oil-based paint but an all-nylon roller for water-based paints, as the water will swell natural fibres.
● Similarly, choose a natural bristle brush for oil-based paints and synthetic bristles for water-based ones. Look sideways at a brush before you buy it. A good brush comes to a dull point; a cheap one is cut square. Inspect the bristle ends, too. Split ends (properly called flagged ends) help to spread paint for a smoother finish.

paint, seal it in with two coats of high-quality new paint. As long as the new paint remains sound, the lead will be contained and present no danger.

Easy fixes

● **Touching up damage** To keep paint looking fresh, try to touch up damage as soon as it happens, using paint left over from the original job. Fill and sand holes first, as described for plasterboard walls (see pages 42-43) or plaster (see pages 46-47), then repaint the repair, feathering the new paint over the surrounding area with light brush strokes. Coat a stubborn stain with stain sealer before touching it up or the stain will bleed through again. If a leak has caused paint to peel and bubble, fix the leak source, then scrape and sand the area and repaint it.

How to prepare a wall before painting it

A paint finish will only be as good as the work you do to get the walls ready for it. Here are four steps to take before you put on the finishing coat.

1 Put on rubber gloves and wash the walls with sugar soap. This strong cleanser, widely available at DIY and hardware stores, dulls the finish so that paint will adhere better. Rinse the wall with a sponge and water after washing until the water runs clear. Let the wall dry. Wash off any mildew with a 50/50 mixture of water and bleach, and rinse it well.

2 Repair holes and cracks in the plasterboard (see pages 42-43) or plaster (see pages 46-47). Scrape off loose paint and blend in areas with chipped-off paint by sanding the edges of the surrounding paint or by skim-coating the area with filler. Fill scratches and dents in woodwork with wood filler, then sand. Fill gaps between the wall and door or window frames with decorator's mastic (which can be painted over) and smooth the seams with your finger – wet it first or wear a latex glove to stop the mastic sticking.

3 Apply masking tape over skirtings, architraves and other mouldings where they meet the wall; the newer blue tapes are easier to use than traditional masking tape. Protect the floor with a dust sheet.

4 To keep stains from bleeding through the new paint, seal them with stain sealer, available at DIY and paint stores. Oil-based and shellac-based sealers block stains better than water-based ones. Then coat the entire wall with a water-based primer, which is easier to clean up but just as durable as the oil-based equivalent. If you're painting over a dark colour or a patterned wallpaper, it's worth giving the room a coat of primer to cut down on the number of coats of the more expensive top colour you'll need.

Fill damage to skirtings and walls

Seal gaps around frames

● **Computer-match your paint colour** What can you do if you need to touch up a repair but you have none of the original paint left over? You don't have to repaint the entire room: just slice through the paint on the wall with a sharp trimming knife in an out-of-the-way area and lift off a good-sized chip. Take the chip to a DIY or specialist paint store that has computerised paint-matching equipment, and they will be able to match the colour with a custom-mixed paint. The service is usually free; the paint may be a little more expensive than the original off-the-shelf tin, but it may save you from having to repaint the entire room.

● **Avoid contaminating paint as you work** If you're using leftover paint to touch up a repair, there may be dried paint, dirt and possibly even some rust around the rim of the old tin. To avoid picking up specks of this dirt on your brush and transferring them onto the wall, decant a little of the paint into a paint kettle (right) – line the kettle with aluminium foil first, to make cleaning it quick and easy.

Decant a little paint for a small job

Wallpaper

Few modern wallpapers are actually paper. They are just as likely to be made out of vinyl or some other similar material; but this makes them easy to care for, and an occasional cleaning is all that's needed to keep them looking good. You may have to fix the odd tear, curling seam or bubble, but this is a lot less time-consuming and expensive than repapering the room.

SAVE £750

What you would pay to have wallpaper in an average-sized room (4m by 6m with a 2.4m high ceiling) stripped and replaced.

smart idea

If you don't have a seam roller, try using an ordinary rolling pin or a perfectly cylindrical, straight-sided pot or jar from the cupboard to press down a seam you have fixed.

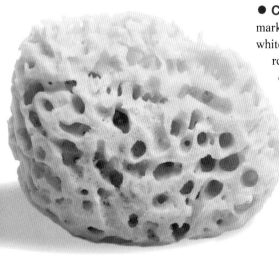

Care and maintenance

● **Vacuum your wallpaper** The best thing you can do to keep the wall covering in most rooms looking pristine is the simplest: vacuum it. A soft-brush attachment on a vacuum cleaner works best and is essential if the paper is flocked or has any kind of texture. Start at the top of the wall and work your way down, doing a couple of panels at a time. Be careful of cobwebs. Lift them off with the vacuum; if you try brushing them away, they may streak the wall. Depending on how dusty your house gets, dust the walls every few months. A duster or clean white cloth wrapped around the head of a broom will work well on flat, non-textured wall coverings.

● **Give your kitchen wallpaper an occasional wipe** In rooms where wall coverings are exposed to grease, steam or active youngsters, dusting is not enough: a light washing every few months is in order. Luckily, the wall coverings used in such areas are usually waterproof sheet vinyl. Give them a quick swipe with a natural sponge dampened in water with a squirt of washing-up liquid. Make sure that the sponge isn't too wet so that water doesn't seep under the seams and loosen the covering, and don't leave water on for more than a minute. Clean from the bottom up so that dirty water squeezed out of the sponge doesn't flow down over the dirty areas and leave streaks. Even if the covering is labelled 'scrubbable', it's best not to scrub hard or use abrasive or strong household cleaners. Rinse with a sponge dampened in clean water, then pat the wall dry with a towel. If the paper needs a second washing, let it dry thoroughly first.

● **Clean delicate coverings with dough** If you need to clean dirty marks off a small area of a wall covering that isn't washable, try using white bread. Scrunch up a slice in your hand until it feels doughy, then roll it onto the dirty area of the wall. The dough should pick up the dirt off the wall covering, but don't let a dirty piece of dough rub back onto the wall – keep taking fresh slices of bread until the mark has disappeared.

USE A NATURAL SPONGE ON YOUR KITCHEN WALLPAPER.

Which wall covering is best where?

Do you want to choose the best new covering for a particular room? Or work out what kind of wall covering you have already? Here's a selective guide to wall coverings and where they are best suited. Always consider the practicalities of how a room is used as well as the decorative effect you want to achieve if the covering is to stand the test of time.

FOR LIVING ROOMS AND BEDROOMS

● **Vinyl-coated paper** is paper that has been coated to make it resistant to dirt, grease and moisture. You can wash it with a damp sponge. It's the most common and best all-round wall covering.

● **Duplex paper** has a top surface, often with a relief pattern, bonded to a backing paper and is strong and easier to hang than other relief wallpapers.

● **Relief wall coverings** such as Anaglypta, are embossed with a pattern and are good at hiding imperfect walls. These wall coverings can be easily painted over.

● **Flock wallpaper** has a fabric pile bonded to a backing paper.

● **Natural fibre wall coverings** are made of grass, jute, cork, hemp, sisal and other natural materials laminated onto a paper backing. They can be very decorative and are good at hiding a wall's imperfections, but they are tricky to hang and to clean.

● **Foil coverings** are made by laminating a thin sheet of foil onto a paper base. They add drama and reflected light to a room, but are unforgiving of flaws in a wall. If a wall is less than perfect, apply lining paper first.

FOR HALLWAYS

● **Paper-backed vinyl** consists of a solid vinyl surface laminated onto a paper backing. It's washable and, since the paper backing gives extra strength to the vinyl, durable – qualities that make it good for high-traffic areas like hallways.

● **High-relief papers**, particularly woodchip or Lincrusta, aren't a good choice in narrow passages or halls, as they are rough to the touch.

FOR KITCHENS AND BATHROOMS

● **Sheet vinyl** has no paper backing. It's by far the best choice for kitchens and bathrooms because it's resistant to moisture, stains and grease, and is easy to clean. The absence of a paper backing makes sheet vinyl fragile and it will not withstand a lot of wear and tear. Use a paste that incorporates a fungicide when hanging wall coverings in bathrooms and kitchens to help to combat the effects of moisture.

● **Test textured or special wallpapers before washing** Natural coverings – grass, reed, hemp, cork, leather or fabric – and uncoated wallpaper are easily damaged by water and cannot be washed. To find out if a wall covering is washable, squirt a little washing-up liquid in water and dab some on the wall in an out-of-the-way spot. If the material darkens or absorbs water, or if the colours run, the covering isn't washable.

Easy fixes

● **Fixing curled seams** If your wallpaper has started to curl up at the seams, it's easy to fix. First, moisten the area with warm water to make the material pliable. Lift the edge carefully and slip seam adhesive under the edge using a strip of card or a toothpick. If the paper is solid vinyl, use vinyl-to-vinyl adhesive. Flatten the seam gently with a wallpaper seam roller and wipe away any excess glue.

● **Regluing peeling borders** Wallpaper borders, which are often used across the top of walls or at chair rail height, are notorious for peeling at the edges. They are often self-adhesive, as normal wallpaper paste will not stick to washable or vinyl wall coverings, but you don't need wallpaper paste to make the repair. Just dab a little white PVA glue onto the wall and on the underside of the border with an artist's brush and roll the edge gently with a wallpaper seam roller to fix the border back into place.

● **Popping wallpaper bubbles** An air bubble underneath the surface is a common wall covering problem, usually caused by leaving a dry spot on the back of the paper when hanging it. The solution is simple. Use a sharp trimming knife or razor blade to make two cuts at right angles across the bubble (below left). Peel back the flaps and apply a little paste with a small paintbrush (below right). Press the flaps back into place with a paperhanging brush and wipe off any excess adhesive with a damp sponge. Roll gently with a wallpaper seam roller to flatten the joints, if necessary.

Seam adhesive is strong wallpaper glue designed to keep the paper around seams from peeling, and it's also used to repair a seam if it starts to come away from the wall.
A seam roller is a nylon, wood or steel roller about 25mm wide, on a short handle. Roll it along seams to press both sides into the adhesive. Don't push too hard or you'll leave a permanent indentation once the glue dries. Never use a seam roller if the paper is textured or flocked: it will leave indentations no matter how gentle you are. Use a natural-bristle **smoothing brush** instead.

Cut through the bubble

Paste the repair

● **Painting or repapering over existing wallpaper** If a wall covering is untextured, firmly attached to the wall and only one layer thick, you can paint or repaper directly over it. To make sure the paper is firmly attached, run your fingers over the wall. If you hear a crackling sound, it means that the paper is loose. Putting paint or wallpaper paste over it will only make it more likely to come off. Check the seams and corners by trying to prise them up. If the paper adheres tightly to the wall, you're in luck.

● To paper again over wallpaper, just apply the new covering straight over the old. Try to stagger the seams by starting in a different place.

● If you paint over wallpaper, be careful not to overload your brush and apply paint too heavily. Even with care, the moisture from the paint may soak into the paper and make bubbles appear – but don't panic. As the paint dries, the paper should shrink back to a smooth finish.

smart idea

Painting over a wall covering isn't always a perfect solution – the covering's seams can show through. One way to disguise them is with a decorative painting technique, such as sponging or rag rolling.

Secret weapons against **wallpaper stains**

If your problem is ...	You should ...
Fingerprints	Rub off gently with a pencil eraser.
Candle wax	Hold a double layer of paper towels over the spot and press the towels gently with a warm iron.
Grease or other oily stains	Apply a paste made of cornflour and water. Let it dry, then vacuum it off. If you're worried about using water on the covering, use talcum powder or cornflour alone.

Align patterns to cut a patch

How to patch a wall covering

It's always a good idea to save a little paper from each room in case you need to make a patch to repair a damaged section. The technique below makes a neat repair on paper with a strong geometric pattern; if you need to patch plain or irregularly patterned paper, tear rather than cut the patch so that the feathered edges will blend in with the surrounding paper when you paste it in place.

1 Cut a piece of the leftover paper so that it's larger than the area you need to patch, but small enough to handle easily. Put it over the damaged area, and align the patterns. Tape the new paper in place with masking tape, and use a sharp trimming knife to cut through both layers of paper.

2 Remove the tape and set aside the top layer, which will become the patch. Peel off the damaged paper, apply paste and stick the patch in place.

Skirtings and architraves

Woodwork isn't just for decoration – it serves a practical function, too. Skirting boards and chair, or dado, rails protect a wall from damage. Architraves around doors and windows, skirtings and ceiling coving seal and camouflage the gaps where walls meet floors, ceilings and door or window frames. Over time, they get dirty, chipped and even loose. Letting problems go can mean having to refinish or replace the moulding, so it pays to keep them in good condition.

SAVE £55

What it would cost to replace shaped skirting boards with a decorative moulded edge yourself around an average 6m x 4m room.

smart idea

When you're reinstalling moulding and need to remove the old nails, it might seem natural to drive the nails out from the back. But if you do, the nail heads will splinter the front of the trim as they come out. Instead, use an old carpenter's trick: clamp locking pliers on each nail and pull it out through the back. Put the new nails in different places, through predrilled holes.

Care and maintenance

● **Wash your woodwork** The best way to keep skirtings and architraves looking their best – and free of the dirt and grime that can eventually ruin their finish – is to simply wipe the woodwork in a room every few months with a sponge dampened in a mixture of washing-up liquid and water. Rinse with a damp sponge and then dry with an old towel to prevent spotting. Most moulding has a gloss or semigloss varnish or paint finish, which can withstand a quick wipe down. Architraves around doors are especially prone to collecting dirt – don't forget to clean the top edge, but do it carefully, as this is often left unpainted.

● **Keep it dry** Most internal mouldings are made of softwood, although some decorative rails may be MDF. Both these materials are vulnerable to damp and will quickly swell or start to rot if they get wet. The key to preserving moulding is to keep its finish in good shape and to protect the woodwork against prolonged exposure to moisture. That means closing windows, wiping trim around sinks and showers, and placing pet food and water bowls far from your skirtings. The biggest threat of all to skirting boards is wet mops – take care to wring out as much water as possible so that excess water doesn't seep under the skirting and slowly start to rot it from within.

Easy fixes

● **Using screws to fix warped moulding** If your skirting is warped slightly or if you just fear a nail on a chair rail or architrave might pop through again, use a narrow-guage (3mm) woodscrew instead. This will hold better than a nail and won't bend while you're driving it in. The disadvantage is that the head is larger and more obvious than a nail, but you can minimise the visual impact. First drill a countersink (a depression the same diameter as the screw head and slightly deeper) and then continue drilling a pilot hole with a bit the same diameter as the screw shank. After you've driven in the screw, conceal the head with a little wood putty.

● If you need to screw back a loose or warped length of skirting board on a solid wall, drill through the skirting (including a countersink hole), then switch to a masonry bit to drill into the brickwork behind. Push a wall plug into the brick, and use a long screw to fix the skirting back. Then fill and refinish the skirting to hide the head of the screw.

● **Renailing loose trim without damaging it** If you've ever tried driving a loose nail back into trim to fix it in place, you probably discovered that it doesn't hold very well. When renailing loose moulding, bear these following tricks in mind.

● Use a new nail, driven in to one side of the existing nail's position. Nail into concave sections of the moulding (right), where the nails will be most unobtrusive and you're less likely to damage the surface as you hammer. Use a small ball-pein hammer and a nail punch. You can either pull out the old nail with pliers if you can grasp the head and remove it without damaging the wood around it, or sink it further in, below the surface, using a hammer and nail punch.

● To avoid splitting the moulding, predrill a hole for the new nail using a fine wood drill bit. Drive in the new nail; then use a nail punch to sink the head slightly below the surface. Fill the new hole and the old one with wood filler that matches the finish if it's bare or varnished wood, or fill then sand and touch up on painted woodwork.

● **Closing gaps in door-frame corners** The corner joints in architraves are prone to opening up, but it's an easy problem to fix. Drill a pilot hole for a panel pin through the top piece, put a bead of wood glue in the gap and then drive in a nail (right) to pin the joint together. If the gap is wide, use a mitre clamp to pull the corners back together before you fix them with the nail. To protect the wall from being damaged by your drill and hammer, insert a piece of thin cardboard behind the architrave.

Close a corner gap with a nail

● **Fixing unsightly skirting board gaps** Skirting board can often start to pull apart at external corners, leaving a gap that is not only unsightly but exposes the skirting to moisture when you are mopping the floor and won't protect the wall as well as it should. If your walls are plasterboard, as long as the pieces were originally cut to the right length, you should be able to bring them together by screwing into the wall. To test, try squeezing the ends together with your hand. If you can close the gap, drill a pilot hole close to the corner and use a narrow-gauge woodscrew to pull the skirting in to the studwork at the corner of the wall. Then do the same with the other side. If you can't close the gap or your wall is plaster, fill the gap with flexible sealant or wood filler.

Ceilings

It pays to look after your ceilings, particularly in older houses, where they are likely to be lime-sand-and-horsehair plaster. Pulling one of these down to replace it is a filthy job. Modern ceilings are made from sheets of plasterboard, covered with a thin skim of plaster, which are easier to fix into if you use the right plasterboard fixings. In both cases, you should look out for cracks and signs of damp and fix them promptly to prevent problems escalating.

SAVE £100

The cost of materials to replace an unsound 6m x 4m ceiling with new plasterboard, not including removal and disposal of the old ceiling.

DUST YOUR CEILING EVERY FEW MONTHS.

Care and maintenance

● **Dust your ceiling** It may seem to contradict the law of gravity, but dust can collect on ceilings, where it attracts more grime and may discolour the paint. Whisk away cobwebs when you dust and run a duster wrapped around a broom head over the ceiling every few months. As well as cleaning the surface, this gives you a proper look at your ceilings and helps you to spot the early signs of problems, such as cracks or leaks.

● **Be wary of textured finishes** Artex is just one, albeit the best known, brand of a thick textured paint used to make decorative patterns on ceilings. It was fashionable in the 1970s, and has also proved popular as a way of covering up cracks in the ceiling behind it. If you have an old textured ceiling, be especially careful about checking for cracks or movement that may be coming from bad cracks beneath the surface.
  ● All textured finishes may contain white asbestos (chrysotile) – Artex included this in its ingredients until 1984 – so never sand a textured ceiling. If you want a smooth finish, try stripping the coating with a steam stripper. Bag up the strippings while they are still damp (it is when they are dry that they release their harmful fibres) then seal the bags and contact your local council to find out how to dispose of them. An easier option if the ceiling seems sound is to apply a skim of smooth plaster over the top.

Easy fixes

● **Seal signs of water damage** Plumbing leaks from above can leave unsightly stains on a ceiling, but if you just paint over them they will soon show through the new paint. Seal them first with a proprietary stain block then paint or paper over the repair.

● **Foolproof tips for filling gaps** The best way to deal with fine cracks in a ceiling is to start by making them wider. Scrape out the crack a little to give the filler a bigger area to adhere to, dampen the area with a light spray of water then fill the crack with fine surface filler. When the area has dried, sand it, then touch up the paint or paper over the repair.

Ceramic tiles

Glazed ceramic tiles are exceptionally durable and almost entirely care-free; it's the cement-like grout in between the tiles that's more likely to cause problems by absorbing dirt or mildew or crumbling. Broken tiles are fairly easy to replace and joints can be cleared and regrouted or sealed, but you need to act promptly. Left too long in wet areas, damaged tiles or grout around showers or behind sinks will allow water to seep in and destroy the plaster or plasterboard behind.

Care and maintenance

● **Wipe down your tiles** Just wiping regularly with a damp sponge will keep glazed ceramic tiles clean. Do it every time you shower, while the walls are still steamy and before water marks form. If you wash the tiles, avoid soapy or oily cleaners. An alternative is to add a capful of methylated spirits to a bucket of water and wipe the tiles with that. In hard-water areas, a splash of vinegar in a bucket of water will help to wipe away limescale deposits.

SAVE £300
What you would pay to have old tiling, cracked grout and water-damaged plasterboard removed and replaced around a bath.

● **Keep the grout clean, too** Routinely wiping your tiles should help to keep the grout clean, too. But if the grout gets dirty, bring it back to its original colour with commercial grout cleaner. Some spray on; others brush on with a narrow applicator. After applying the cleaner, leave it on for a few minutes, or as directed, then scrub it off with an old toothbrush.

● **Bleach grimy grout** For grimy, mildewed grout that stubbornly resists standard cleaning methods, mix 200ml of household bleach in 2 litres of water. Scrub it on with an old toothbrush, and let it soak for 10 to 20 minutes before rinsing with clean water. Rinse a second time and wipe the tiles dry with a clean cloth. If that doesn't do the trick, rake out and replace the grout (see page 61).

Easy fixes

● **Sealing grout and porous tiles** Once you've got your grout clean, it's easy to keep it that way by sealing it. Make sure the grout is thoroughly dry, and then apply a silicone sealer (available at DIY stores). Put it just on the grout, using a fine artist's paintbrush – the sealer can stain glazed tiles if you are not careful as you work. Grout manufacturers generally

take care!

Never use abrasive scrubbers or scouring powders on ceramic tiles. They will dull the finish, which can make tiles more susceptible to dirt. Also avoid muriatic acid, a strong product that professional cleaners use: it's tough to work with and, when improperly used, can partially dissolve the grout. Never use steel wool to clean grout either: it's much too abrasive.

recommend resealing grout joints twice a year, particularly in areas that are prone to dirty or greasy splashes, such as a splashback behind a cooker or a kitchen worktop. If you have porous tiles, such as slate, stone or travertine, you can seal the tiles and the grout at the same time by applying a combination tile-and-grout sealer.

● **Matching your grout's colour** Unless your grout is bright white, the hardest part of regrouting a small area is matching the colour of the new grout with the rest of the wall. Even grout that originally came ready-mixed will probably have faded or darkened with dirt since the tiling was first done. The cheapest way to buy grout is as a white or coloured powder that you mix with water to the consistency of toothpaste – you must be precise with your measurements to get a consistent colour between batches, as a little more powder or water can make a difference to the shade of the mix. To match the colour of new grout with the old, you may need to mix two different shades together. Get a colour chart from your local tile shop and match it against the grout on your wall. Make up a few sample batches of grout, varying (and noting) the amount of each colour, then let the samples dry at least overnight and choose the closest match.

Use a mastic gun for a neat job

● **Sealing joints that flex** The joints where wall tiles meet the bath, or where two walls meet, are particularly vulnerable to water infiltration and damage. These joints also need to be allowed to flex since the bath moves as it empties and fills. The solution is to apply colour-matched silicone sealant (left) in the joints instead of grout. Fill the bath before sealing the joints so they don't stretch later.

● **Replacing cracked tiles** You can't repair a cracked tile; you have to replace it. You'll need a hammer, a cold chisel, a notched plastic trowel, a grout saw and ready-mixed tile adhesive. Wear work gloves and goggles, as shards of tile are sharp. Start by cutting out the grout around the tile with a grout saw. Then break up and remove the damaged tile and the

Grouting tools

If you're replacing a lot of grout, there are a couple of tools that can speed up the process. For a small job, you can probably make do with what you have to hand and use the applicator that comes with the new grout.

● To remove a lot of old grout, use a small, handheld grout saw or scrape it out with a trimming knife. Take care not to chip the edges of the tiles.

● To regrout a large area, use a rubber-bottom grout float or squeegee (right) then wipe off the excess and smooth the joints with a sponge, rinsing it often. For a smaller area, just press the grout into the seams with your rubber-gloved finger, smoothing the finish as you go.

How to grout tiles

Doing a professional job of grouting your tiles will protect the wall behind and increase the life of your tiling. Use a grout saw or trimming knife to remove cracked or crumbling grout, vacuum out any debris left in the joints then wash the area well before you start grouting.

1 If you're not using ready-mixed grout, start by making up a batch of the mix. Waterproof, epoxy-based grout sets quickly, so only mix a little at a time. Experiment with the mix if you need to match an existing colour (see page 60). Press the grout firmly into the gaps between the tiles, using a rubber squeegee or a sponge.

2 Use a clean, damp sponge to wipe away the excess grout straight away; once grout sets (particularly waterproof grout or combined, ready-mixed grout and adhesive) it's hard to remove.

3 To give the tiling a neat finish, smooth over all the joints with a thin piece of dowelling, a pen lid, lolly stick, toothbrush handle, a sponge or your finger (wearing rubber gloves). Use whatever you have to hand and experiment to get a good match with the existing grout if need be. Let the area dry until a cloudy haze appears on the tiles, then polish with a clean rag or screwed-up newspaper. Don't wait too long or the haze will harden and be difficult to remove.

old adhesive under it with a cold chisel and hammer. Apply adhesive to the back of the new tile with the trowel and press it into place. Let the adhesive dry for at least 72 hours, then apply grout.

● **Finding matching tiles** If you don't have any matching tiles left from the original job, wait until you've removed the broken tile, then take a large scrap to a tile shop and try to match it. A close, but not perfect, match may be good enough under the sink or low in a corner, but if the tile is in a conspicuous spot, choose a contrasting colour and replace a couple of other tiles to make it look like a deliberate design. Remember that floor tiles are thicker than wall tiles, so make sure you get a suitable match.

● **Touching up chipped tiles** You can touch up a chipped tile using appliance touch-up paint or the resin made for repairing baths, but it's tricky to find a perfect match. Instead, you can stain the chipped area with a marker pen or paint, then – after it dries – coat it with clear nail polish.

Wood flooring

For natural beauty and durability, you can't beat a wooden floor. With a little regular care, a floor can go decades without needing to be sanded and refinished or even requiring a new coat of varnish. The problems to look out for are those that affect the surface finish – scratches and scrapes, water damage and spills or stains.

SAVE £350

What you would pay a floor refinisher to sand and refinish a hardwood floor in a 4m x 6m room.

How is my floor finished?

Most wood floor finishes look fairly similar, but for proper maintenance you need to know whether the finish is shellac, varnish, polyurethane varnish or wax. Here's how to figure out what's underfoot:

WAX turns white a few minutes after you drip some water on it.

VARNISH flakes when scratched.

SHELLAC flakes when scratched and will dissolve in alcohol or methylated spirits.

POLYURETHANE won't flake, whiten or dissolve.

Care and maintenance

● **Vacuum your floor every week** Rubbed underfoot, the fine grit in dust acts just like sandpaper and will slowly wear through your wood floor's finish. Keep dirt at bay by vacuuming with an attachment that has a brush or a felt surface that runs along the floor – some vacuum cleaners come with a 'parquet' head. Rotating brushes or a beater bar can scratch the finish, so disengage the bar on an upright cleaner if you can. A dust mop or one of the newer microfibre sweepers will work just as well.

● **Use an extra-long 'walk-off' doormat** While vacuuming and spot-cleaning are fine, keeping the dirt out in the first place is even better. Get the longest mat you can for just inside the front door – the longer the mat, the more people will rub the dirt and moisture off their shoes as they walk in, even if they don't stop to actually wipe them.

● **Watch the hairspray** And the furniture polish. Both can cloud your floor's finish if 'overspray' is left to build up. Wipe sprayed-on areas immediately with a damp cloth and if there is one place where you always use the spray, give it a more thorough clean every few weeks with an ammonia-free window cleaner.

● **Keep out the rain** Water can not only ruin the finish on a wood floor but can penetrate deep into the wood and stain it. Close windows when you're expecting rain. Put trays under potted plants and, of course, immediately wipe up any water spills you see.

● **Protect high-traffic zones with rugs** A hard-wearing rug is the easiest way to reduce wear on a floor's finish in busy areas, but make sure it doesn't have a backing. Vinyl or rubber backing traps moisture, which can ruin your floor's finish and stain or damage the wood. You can stop a hessian-backed rug from slipping dangerously on a hard floor by attaching anti-slip tape around the edges or using a length of anti-slip underlay.

PROTECT HIGH-TRAFFIC ZONES
WITH RUGS.

WIPE UP SPILLS AND DIRT IMMEDIATELY.

Filling **large gaps**

As boards shrink over time, gaps open up between them, making a floor draughty and dusty. Narrow gaps can be filled with mastic from a sealant gun – choose a colour close to the colour of your boards or one that will absorb the colour of your stain when you refinish the floor. Gaps wider than 6mm can be filled with thin fillets of wood. Cut long slender wedges, coat the edges with wood glue and then hammer them into place with a mallet (below) as far as you can. Once the glue has set, use a power sander to remove any wood that is still proud of the surface.

● If a floor is full of gaps, you may have to re-lay it, although a better option may be to install a new tongued-and-grooved floor on top (see pages 67-68).

● **Remove residue with no-wax wood floor cleaner** Wipe up spills and dirt immediately, then use a floor cleaner to remove the residue. Dirt can damage the finish or become ground in and liquids can damage the finish or stain the floor, but as long as the floor's finish is sound and you act promptly, your wood floor will shrug them off.

● **Know the rules about using waxes and restorers** You can rejuvenate a wax finish with more wax, but never use wax on shellac, varnish or polyurethane. It not only makes the floor slippery, but also makes the job harder when the time comes to give the finish a fresh coat. If the floor is finished with polyurethane, use a polish made for polyurethane. If it has another type of finish, buy a general-purpose floor restorer and test it in an inconspicuous area first to make sure that it won't peel off.

Easy fixes

● **Colour in deep scratches** If a scratch is lighter in colour than the floor, it means the damage has gone right through to the raw wood. Use a furniture touch-up marker that matches the colour of the floor and dab it on to replace the stain. Let it dry, then apply a coat of the finish used on the floor. Apply additional coats if needed to build up the repair.

● **Touching up floor scratches** You can touch up a light scratch on a varnished floor with clear nail polish. Thin the polish by about half with lacquer thinner and brush it over the scratch with the nail polish brush. Let it dry thoroughly. Sand it gently flush with the surrounding finish using a medium-grade paper wrapped around a block of wood. Keep sanding with progressively finer grades until the sheen matches the surrounding floor. The finer the grit you sand with, the shinier your floor will be. Car spares shops usually stock finer grades of abrasive paper than DIY stores.

● **Making patched holes blend in** Patch small, deep holes with wood filler, using a shade darker than the floor colour. The patch will never be invisible, but if it's slightly darker than the surrounding wood, it will look like a tiny knot instead of a badly matched repair.

How to sand and revarnish a wood floor

Chipped, scratched or crazed varnish cannot protect the wood floor beneath. Although you may need to hire a sander, refinishing the floor is a far easier and cheaper job than replacing boards that have been damaged as a result of a neglected finish. Wax polish will clog up the sanding paper, so remove any wax with a wax stripper before you start.

1 Start by mopping to get rid of surface dirt and check for any nail heads that may have worked loose and will tear the sanding sheets. Hammer them in with a nail punch. Start at the edge of the room, with your back against the wall and slightly away from the skirting board. Move along the length of the boards at a slow, steady pace, lifting the drum as soon as you reach the skirting board and need to turn around.

2 When you've finished the room, go back over the metre or so of floor at the beginning of each strip, where you were standing before engaging the drum. Use a handheld sander to finish the edges, vacuum the finished floor, then dust it with a clean, dry, lint-free cloth

3 Apply varnish using a long-handled paint roller and paint tray. Plan your exit, so that you can paint your way out of the room. Work in criss-cross passes of the roller, then finish off by running it parallel with the boards. Use a paintbrush to finish the edges and cut in around obstacles like pipes.

● **Replacing a damaged board** If you have a board that is too damaged to touch up, you can lift and replace it. Floorboards are usually held in place by floor brads (cut nails) and can be prised up from the joists, but check first that they aren't screwed down
● If your boards are tongued-and-grooved, run a jigsaw along the edges to cut the damaged board free from the ones on either side.

● **Finding matching boards** It can be difficult to find an exact match in colour and grain pattern if you need to replace a damaged board. The best solution is to lift a good board from the edge of the room or from beneath a piece of furniture, use that to make the repair and replace the out-of-the-way board with a new one or with the damaged one.

● **Replacing loose wood blocks** Parquet or teak block floors are made from individual blocks of hardwood originally bedded in bitumen then sanded flat and sealed. These floors are difficult and expensive to replace, so it's worth looking after them. If blocks have worked loose, use a special solvent-based adhesive called Lecol to soften the bitumen and allow you to push the blocks back into place. If you need to replace a block, try local architectural salvage yards or ask a timber merchant whether they can cut you a block of matching wood.

10 quick strategies to tackle a wood floor's greatest enemies

Here are a few secret weapons that will help you to remove messes and stains from your wood floor quickly and simply:

1 CHEWING GUM
Any finish Cool the gum with a bag of ice until it's brittle enough to crumble; then remove with a plastic scraper.

2 CRAYON OR CANDLE WAX
Wax or penetrating stain finish Put a brown paper bag over the crayon or wax and heat with an iron until the bag absorbs the stain.

Shellac, varnish or polyurethane finish Use a cleaner designed for hardwood floor finishes.

3 DARK SPOTS AND INK STAINS
Wax or penetrating stain finish Treat like water stains. If they remain, soak with bleach or vinegar for an hour. Wipe with a damp cloth, then wipe dry. Sand lightly with fine sandpaper then stain to match the original colour. Reapply wax with a cloth.

Shellac, varnish or polyurethane finish Use a cleaner designed for hardwood floor finishes.

4 DRIED MILK OR FOOD STAINS
Wax or penetrating stain finish Rub gently with a damp cloth. Rub dry, then reapply wax.

Shellac, varnish or polyurethane finish Use a cleaner designed for hardwood floor finishes.

5 GREASE AND OIL STAINS
Wax or penetrating stain finish Saturate a cotton cloth with hydrogen peroxide and place it over the stain. Leave it for 30 minutes, then soak up any liquid with a paper towel. Rinse with a water-and-vinegar solution, then plain water. Let the area dry, then buff with a cloth.

Shellac, varnish or polyurethane finish Use a cleaner designed for hardwood floor finishes.

6 HEEL SCUFFS
Wax or penetrating stain finish Apply a small amount of wax with fine wire wool; rub in and buff with a cloth.

Shellac, varnish or polyurethane finish Use a cleaner designed for hardwood floor finishes.

7 MOULD OR MILDEW
Sand and refinish areas where the mould or mildew is beneath the surface.

Wax or penetrating stain finish Apply a cleaner designed for wood.

Shellac, varnish or polyurethane finish Use a cleaner designed for hardwood floor finishes.

8 SCRATCHES
Wax or penetrating stain finish Apply wax.

Polyurethane finish Fix with a touch-up kit made for urethane finishes and sold at flooring stores.

Shellac or varnish finish Fix with a hardwood floor finish restorer.

9 WATER STAINS OR WHITE SPOTS
Wax or penetrating stain finish Rub with fine wire wool dipped in wax. If the stain or spot remains, sand with fine sandpaper. Follow up with medium-grade wire wool dipped in mineral spirits. When mineral spirits evaporate, stain to match original colour. Apply wax and buff.

Shellac, varnish or polyurethane finish Use a cleaner designed for hardwood floor finishes.

10 WAX BUILD-UP
Wax or penetrating stain finish Remove the old wax with a stripper made for wax. (Don't use furniture stripper.) Remove residue with a cloth and fine wire wool. Let the floor dry, then wax and machine buff.

Shellac, varnish or polyurethane finish Don't wax these finishes. It can make the floor dangerously slippery and interfere with subsequent finishes. If you have used it, take it off with a commercial wax remover.

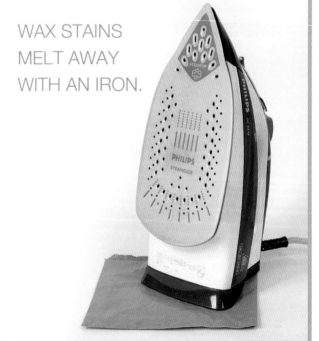

WAX STAINS MELT AWAY WITH AN IRON.

Laminate flooring

Even houses with solid concrete flooring can have wooden floors thanks to planks that glue or click together to give the impression of a solid wood floor. Laminate flooring is usually based on MDF or chipboard; the cheapest planks have a photographic image reproduced on a plastic coating to give the wood effect, but others have a veneer of real wood. At the top of the range, boards are solid wood, tongued and grooved for easy, click-together installation. There are a few essential tips to remember when fitting a floor like this and some simple golden rules for maintenance.

Care and maintenance

● **Buy the best for challenging situations** Fitting the cheapest laminate flooring is likely to be a false economy in high-traffic areas, such as hallways or family rooms. The boards are thin and the wood-effect coating is plastic, which could easily wear through in just a couple of years, exposing the chipboard beneath. The only solution then is to replace the floor. It's worth spending as much as you can afford on flooring in the busiest parts of your home, as the results will be much more hard-wearing. A compromise is to choose a laminate with a real wood veneer that can be up to 3mm thick. The base is still chipboard, but the wooden surface will stand up to more heavy wear.

● **Be mean with water when washing** You should avoid soaking any wooden floor with a sopping mop, and this advice is even more critical when you're cleaning boards with an MDF or chipboard base. If water is allowed to seep into the joints between boards, the base boards will start to swell and eventually the surface will start to lift and bubbles appear. Squeeze your mop as dry as you can or use a plant spray mister to dampen a sheepskin mophead and polish the floor with that.

● **Protect against scratches** The surface veneer is easily scratched, but if the scratch goes through to the backing board beneath it's harder to disguise than on a solid wood floor. Do what you can to avoid scratching your floor by sweeping and vacuuming regularly to pick up abrasive specks of dust. If you're moving furniture across a floor, always lift it up, don't drag it.

● **Look out for leaks** Water leaks are the enemy of laminate wood floors. Just like water carelessly splashed when cleaning (see above), water spills or leaks will quickly ruin your floor. Be vigilant for signs of leaks from pipework or radiators and places where condensation forms and may drip.

SAVE £750

What you would pay to replace damaged laminate planks in a 6m x 4m room, including installation.

- **Leave room for expansion** Gaps open up in wooden floors fixed to joists as the boards expand and contract over time and in changing atmospheres. In a tongued-and-grooved, 'floating' wooden floor, the boards expand and contract as one large sheet, so it's vital that you leave 15mm expansion gaps around the edges of the room when the floor is laid. These can be hidden by timber mouldings tacked to the skirting boards or by removing the skirtings themselves before you lay the floor and refitting them over the floor once it has been installed.

- **Choose a waterproof option** Most MDF-based laminate planks are unsuitable for use in wet areas, such as kitchens or bathrooms, but there are waterproof options now available. You can choose stone-effect finishes as well as wood. These make a quick and easy alternative to laying stone tiles over timber floors, which are prone to flexing and cracking the grout.

smart idea

Cushion the feet of your furniture to help to prevent chairs, table legs or other furniture that often gets moved from scratching the floor. Self-adhesive felt pads are cheap and easy to fit and over time could save you from a costly floor replacement.

Easy fixes

- **Label parts for easy reassembly** If you have a floor that clicks together, rather than one where the planks are glued to one another, it is possible to lift and replace a damaged board rather than replacing the whole floor. Be systematic and take care to avoid damaging any more boards as you lift them. You'll need to work backwards across the room from where you finished laying the floor, lifting each row in turn. Label each plank on the reverse as you go – row 1, plank A, B, C; row 2, plank A, B, C; and so on – to make it easy for you to put them back together. Use the damaged plank as a template if you need to cut the replacement to fit.

Know your options for **floating floors**

There are three main differences in the composition of boards for floating floors, although they are often all commonly referred to as 'laminate flooring'. Some planks need to be glued or nailed in place as you install them, others click together without any additional materials. But they should all be installed over an insulating underlay, and it's vital that the surface you are laying on is both flat and sound. The thickness of the top layer and the entire board varies according to cost and quality – it's worth remembering that the thickest boards will probably raise the surface of the floor higher than that of the adjacent rooms.

- **LAMINATE** boards range from the cheap and cheerful to some excellent wood-veneered options. The base board may be MDF or chipboard, coated with a plastic or thin real wood veneer. The thinnest boards are barely thicker than a vinyl floor covering, at around 7mm.

- **ENGINEERED WOOD** boards are made from layers of real wood glued together – in different directions for strength – and compressed to form a strong board that's stable enough to be used over underfloor heating. The top surface is usually a single piece of sawn timber, between 0.5mm and 6mm thick, with the finished thickness of the boards ranging from 10mm to 15mm.

- **SOLID WOOD** is the most expensive option, as each board is just one piece of wood, ranging from 15mm to 21mm thick. Boards may be tongued and grooved or shaped to click together and, once installed, they can be treated and maintained like a solid wood floor fixed to your joists, re-oiling or finishing them as needed.

Floor structure

We put a lot of strain on our floors. They carry the weight of all of our furniture and possessions and are subjected to constant trampling, so it's hardly surprising when they show signs of wear and tear. The two most common problems – squeakiness and bounciness – are easy to fix. When you lift a carpet to replace it, take the chance to give the floor beneath a service.

Easy fixes

● **Screw down loose boards** Sometimes a gap opens up between the boards and the joists below – closing up the gap to stop the boards moving should also stop the squeak or bounce. Locate the joists by following the line of nails or screws securing the boards (remember, boards always run at right angles to the joists) and drive in some 62mm (2½in) countersunk screws. Use a pipe and cable detector first to make sure you don't create an even bigger problem by screwing into a pipe or wire.

● **Working from below** If you can get underneath a squeaking floor, from the basement or cellar, it's easy to drive shims or wedges between the loose boards and their joists to stop them from moving. You can buy packs of plastic shims or cut some slender wooden wedges yourself. Put a little contact adhesive on both sides of the shim, then slide it into the gap and use a block of wood and a hammer to drive it in.

● **Quieting squeaks** Floors squeak when floorboards rub together or against nails. If the squeak is only a minor one, you can often fix it by brushing talcum powder between the boards as a lubricant. Alternatively, try tightening the grip of the nails by driving them a little further in with a nail punch (right).

● **Diagnosing the problem with bouncy floor joists** In an older property, if the floorboards are firmly fixed to the joists but the floor is still bouncy, it might be that the joists themselves are flexing. The herringbone strutting that braces them together may have worked loose or been removed by plumbers or electricians doing previous alterations. Lay a long spirit level over the floor to locate a sagging area, then lift a couple of boards to investigate. You can replace missing struts by cutting pieces of timber to fit between the joists or by using modern, galvanised steel replacements. Alternatively, the ends of the joists may have rotted due to damp in the walls. Lift the boards at the edge of the room to take a closer look, or hire a moisture meter to assess the joists' condition. Rotten sections can be cut out and replaced, but this is a job best left to the professionals. Make sure you also locate and fix the cause of the damp, such as a blocked airbrick (see page 155) so that the new joists don't rot too.

SAVE £250
What you would pay a carpenter for tracking down and fixing a large number of floor squeaks.

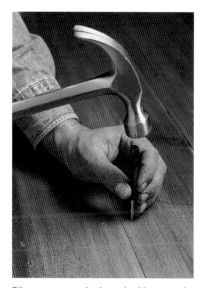

Silence a squeaky board with a punch

Vinyl flooring

Whether you choose tiles or sheet vinyl, the polyurethane finish of vinyl flooring gives it a long-lasting shine and makes caring for it a breeze. It's easier to replace a single tile than to repair damaged sheet vinyl, but follow these simple tips on careful cleaning and quick repairs to keep your floor looking its very best for as long as possible.

Care and maintenance

● **Keep out dirt and chemicals with a doormat** A doormat helps to keep your vinyl floor's two greatest enemies – dirt and chemicals – at bay. Grit in tracked-in dirt acts like sandpaper, removing the finish from your floor and even though you can't see them, chemicals from asphalt can stick first to your shoes and then to the floor, causing it to yellow.

● **Keep your floors clean** Get the dirt off before it gets ground in and your vinyl will last longer. Frequent sweeping is the best first defence. It's a good idea to get in the habit of quickly running a soft broom across the kitchen floor every evening after you have cleared away the cooking things and around entrance halls at the end of each day. Once a week is probably enough in rooms that generate fewer crumbs or mess from outside.

SWEEP FREQUENTLY TO STOP DIRT GETTING GROUND IN.

SAVE £700

What you would pay to have a new vinyl floor installed in a 4m x 6m room.

● **Learn low-impact cleaning techniques** Resist the temptation to blast away dirt with heavy-duty cleaners. Instead, clean vinyl using the mildest possible method. Sweep or vacuum it and wipe up spills immediately. To clean dirt that the broom or vacuum won't shift, use a mop dampened with warm – not hot – water. If all else fails, use soap, but make sure it's designed for your flooring.

● **Vinyl or lino?** If you have a very old or very new 'vinyl' floor, it may actually be linoleum, a jute-and-linseed-oil material with a wax coating. Lino was largely superseded by the crude-oil-based vinyl in the 1950s, but because it uses natural materials it's rising in popularity once more. Some manufacturers recommend stripping the wax and resealing lino every year with a water-based wax; follow the instructions on the packet.

● **Use the right cleanser** If vinyl needs cleaning, use a cleaner sold for vinyl floors. Clean lino with a mop or sponge dampened in warm water and detergent, rubbing just enough to loosen the dirt. Try not to rub off the wax; it's this that gives the floor its protective surface. Rinse with clean, cool water – no matter what the soap label says – otherwise you'll leave a residue on the floor. Try adding a teaspoon of baby oil to your cleaning water from time to time to restore the lino's natural oils.

● **Don't drench your vinyl** Water from an overly wet mop will work its way into cracks, seams and edges. Once there, it can destroy the glue bond that holds down the vinyl, causing it to come loose or corners to curl.

● **Rinse well to remove all soap** Soap may get your floor clean, but soap scum leaves a film that actually collects dirt. Until your floor needs a serious cleaning, stick to damp mopping with just water. When you do need to wash the floor, use two mops – one for washing and a second one, dipped in clear water, just for rinsing.

● **Preserve the sheen** Vinyl has a clear polyurethane coating that makes it shine. If your floor loses its shine, restore it with a polish or sealant made for no-wax vinyl flooring. Wax or mop-and-wax products won't adhere well to the coating and will leave behind a mess that you'll have to strip off. Make sure the floor is thoroughly clean and apply one or two thin layers of polish or sealant as directed. It should keep your floor shining for at least a year with only routine damp mopping. If you have a lino floor, a fresh coat of wax will restore a lost sheen, but use only the amount directed on the container label.

● **Fit furniture and large appliances with protective feet** The weight of heavy items (such as tables and refrigerators) that occupy permanent places in your kitchen can dent vinyl flooring. Prevent these dents by fitting your furniture with floor protectors (left), which you can find at most good hardware and DIY stores.

● **Put pads on your rolling casters** The surface of vinyl flooring can be damaged too by casters, as they roll to and fro over the years. Consider fitting chairs that have casters with felt pads instead. They will still allow the chairs to slide freely across the surface, but won't harm your vinyl.

● **For big moves, use a plywood path** More often than not, when we replace or move large appliances or heavy pieces of furniture, we drag or push them across the floor rather than lift them, but this can scratch and scuff a vinyl floor. To protect your vinyl, if something is too heavy or awkard to carry, lay a piece of plywood sheeting along the route that you are going to take out of the room and push or 'walk' the appliances out along the plywood path.

● **Shampoo away hairspray** If you have a build-up of hairspray on your vinyl floor, just shampoo it away. Mix a squirt of shampoo with a gallon of warm water, mop, then rinse.

SHAMPOO AWAY HAIRSPRAY.

Easy fixes

● **Fixing a blister** If a blister develops in a vinyl floor, it can start to wear unevenly, so fix the problem as soon as you spot it. Just slit the blister and about 1cm of the vinyl on either side of it with a trimming knife, then cover the spot with aluminum foil and warm it with an iron. Pull up each edge of the slit and slip vinyl adhesive under it with a putty knife. Press the blister flat and wipe up any adhesive that seeps out with a sponge dampened with water or the recommended solvent. Cover the area with a board, weighed down with a heavy object, for 24 hours.

● **Protecting exposed edges** Vinyl edges that end at a doorway or at the transition to another room need to be protected. If they're not, poorly glued edges might curl or a heel could catch and chip the vinyl or trip you. A screw-down metal threshold strip is simple to install, will protect the vinyl and prevent the floor from becoming a trip hazard.

● **Sticking down loose tiles** If you have a loose or curled vinyl tile, put adhesive under the edges with a trowel. Drive a small finishing nail into each corner and one along each seam, then fill the nail dimples with matching-coloured waterproof sealant.

● **Can't find a match for a tile you need to replace?** Steal one from under an appliance or cupboard, where the gap or mismatched replacement won't be noticed.

How to replace a damaged vinyl tile

Use aluminium foil and a warm iron

When replacing a tile, ask at your tile shop for the proper adhesive for your type of tile. Also get the right notched applicator; the adhesive manufacturer will recommend a specific notch size to control the amount of glue that goes onto the floor.

1 To make the old tile pliable and easy to remove, cover it with aluminium foil and warm it with an iron on moderate heat. Run the iron back and forth to heat the whole tile. When the tile is pliable, cut across the middle with a trimming knife and use a scraper to pry outwards to remove it. This will help you to avoid damaging surrounding tiles.

2 Scrape the old adhesive from the floor – warming the scraper blade with a hot-air gun can help. Make sure the new tile will fit the opening and cut it to size with a trimming knife and straightedge, if necessary.

3 Warm the replacement tile with your iron until it's flexible. Apply the adhesive to the floor with a notched applicator and set the tile in place. Clean up any excess with a sponge dampened with water or the recommended solvent. Cover the tile with a board and weigh it down with a heavy object overnight to ensure a strong bond.

How to patch damaged sheet vinyl

A gash in a vinyl floor doesn't have to mean a complete replacement. If you have a matching piece of vinyl or an offcut, you can make a repair that's nearly invisible.

1 Put a matching piece of vinyl that's larger than the damaged spot over the area. Align the patterns and tape it firmly in place. Cut through both pieces with a sharp trimming knife guided by a straightedge. Set the upper piece aside for use as a patch.

2 Heat the damaged area with a hairdryer or a warm iron placed over a sheet of aluminium foil (see 'How to replace a damaged vinyl tile', opposite) and prise it up with a putty knife, being careful not to damage or lift the surrounding area. Scrape up the old adhesive, warming it again with the hairdryer if it's difficult to lift. Test-fit the patch and sand or trim the edges if necessary.

3 Apply multipurpose tile adhesive to the floor, clean up any excess and let the floor dry. Put the patch in place, weigh it down with a board and let it sit overnight. Alternatively, fix the patch in place with some strong double-sided tape stuck around the edges.

4 To fuse the seams and make them unnoticeable, treat them with seam sealer, available at specialist flooring suppliers. Make sure you buy sealer with a gloss that matches the one on your floor.

Align the pattern before cutting a patch

● **Going vinyl 'shopping' in hidden places** If you can't find a matching piece of sheet vinyl to replace a damaged area in a visible location, borrow a piece from an inconspicuous place – such as under the fridge. You can cover the new hidden bare spot with a piece of inexpensive vinyl of any kind.

● **Out, black spot** If your vinyl floor has a small black spot that won't wash away, even after trying the baby oil trick (right), take a closer look. The most likely reason is that the colour in the vinyl has worn away, exposing the dark inner material. The cause of this wear is probably a chunk of dirt, a small stone or a nail head underneath the vinyl that has raised the spot just enough that foot traffic has worn through the top. With large damaged areas, the only cure is to replace the tile (see left) or patch the sheet vinyl (above).

● Repair kits are available from DIY and hardware stores and can be used to fix smaller areas of damage. The process involves mixing special paints (supplied in the kit) to match the floor colour, painting the damaged area and drying it with a hairdryer. Next, pour filler powder and bonding agent over the damaged area, level it, then let it harden for 15 minutes. Finish by brushing the clear acrylic finish over the repair.

● Genuine linoleum is much more resistant to marks and scratches. The colour goes all the way through the material, so damage is hardly noticeable and minor nicks and dents may even heal themselves.

smart idea

What can you do to remove black heel marks on your clean floor? Smear a drop of baby oil over the mark, wait a few minutes and then wipe it off with a rag.

A CERAMIC FLOOR IS
VIRTUALLY INDESTRUCTIBLE.

Ceramic-tile floors

In rooms that get the toughest treatment, such as kitchens and bathrooms, a ceramic-tiled floor is often the first choice. It's virtually indestructible – a weekly mop and your floor will more or less take care of itself. Although a chipped or cracked tile is almost inevitable in an active household, it's easily fixed, as is the day-to-day wear and tear that leads to stained grout and tiles dulled by water marks or soap.

Care and maintenance

● **Sweep or vacuum, then mop** Depending on how much you use the room and how much dust and grit the floor collects, the only regular cleaning a ceramic floor needs is an occasional sweeping or vacuuming. If you vacuum, avoid using a beater bar (the rotating brush). Once a week, after sweeping or vacuuming, mop the floor using a special floor-tile cleaner or a bucket of hot water with a splash of vinegar. Avoid oily or waxy cleaners as they will leave a film on the grout, which will attract dirt.

● **Bleach grimy grout** When dirt builds up on grout, it's time to bring out a scrubbing brush and a little elbow grease. Try a proprietary grout cleaner, available from DIY stores and tile suppliers, or mix 200ml of bleach with 2 litres of water. Make sure the area is well ventilated – open the doors and windows and turn on any extractor fans – and put on a pair of rubber gloves. Scrub the dirty areas with a nylon scrubbing brush and let the solution soak for 10 to 20 minutes. Don't scrub too vigorously or you could actually grind in the dirt. Rinse twice with clean water and wipe the area dry with a clean cloth.

● **Apply a sealer** Grout sealer keeps water and dirt from penetrating and staining grout, saving you a lot of work and possibly preventing damage to the underlying structure. If your tiles are glazed, take care not to get the sealer on the tile surface – use an artist's paintbrush to apply the sealer just to the grout joints. If the tiles aren't glazed, use a combination grout-tile sealer to seal the tiles at the same time as you seal the grout.

● **Only tile over a sound base** Never lay ceramic tiles directly over old floorboards. The natural flexing of the boards as you walk across the floor will cause the grout joints between the tiles to crack and this will ruin the waterproof quality and durability of the floor. Cover the boards first with a layer of 15mm exterior-grade plywood, screwing the sheets securely to the boards beneath, and seal the ply with a coat of wood primer before applying the tile adhesive. Remember that the floor level will be raised by up to 40mm by the thickness of the plywood, adhesive and the tiles themselves, and consider how this might affect the junction between the tiled floor and the flooring in adjacent rooms.

SAVE £300

What you would pay to have a mid-priced ceramic-tile floor replaced in a 3m x 2m bathroom.

take care!

Vinegar has developed a reputation as a miracle cleaning treatment, but sprucing up tiles is one job where you should leave it in the cupboard. Vinegar and other acids, like muriatic acid (brick acid), are often recommended for cleaning dirty grout and they do work – but that's because they dissolve the grout along with the dirt. Stick to proprietary grout cleaners or bleach.

Easy fixes

● **How can I tell if my tiles are sealed?** All stone tiles need sealing before they are laid, but with some matt-finish ceramic floor tiles, it's hard to tell if they are glazed or not. To find out, just sprinkle a few drops of water on a tile. If the surface darkens after a few minutes, the tile needs to be sealed to protect it. Ask a specialist tile shop for advice.

● **Perfect seams around the edges** What looks like a grout line between the floor and bath is actually a gap filled with sealant to keep water from seeping into the subfloor. Grout is prone to cracking as the bath moves fractionally in use, but sealant will flex and retain a waterproof joint. If the sealant starts to look ragged, rake it out with a screwdriver, getting the joint scrupulously clean, and reapply the bead of sealant, making sure you choose a waterproof sealant recommended for bathroom use. To get an ultra-neat finish, run strips of masking tape along either side of the seam and use an ice cube to smooth the sealant.

● **Touching up chipped corners** If there's a chip in the corner or along the edge of a tile, you can touch it up using matching touch-up paint if you can find the right colour. If the chipped area is deep, fill it with epoxy filler and let the filler dry before painting. If you can't match the shade of your tiles, colour in the damaged area with paint or a felt-tip pen and then cover it with clear nail polish.

How to replace a broken tile

It's relatively easy to replace a broken tile. If you don't have a tile left over from the original installation, take a chip of the damaged tile and the tile's dimensions to a tile store and get the closest replacement you can find. Wear safety goggles and work gloves to protect you from slivers of tile splintering from the surface as you work.

1 Remove the grout around the damaged tile with a grout saw.

2 Hit the tile with a hammer and cold chisel to break it, then chisel out the tile along the crack lines, working from the middle of the tile towards the edge. Then chisel the old adhesive out of the opening. Vacuum up any loose debris and clean any remaining grout off the adjacent tiles.

3 Apply tile adhesive to the back of a new tile using a notched trowel. Press the tile firmly into place and check that it's flush with the surrounding tiles; add or remove some adhesive if necessary. Let the adhesive dry overnight before grouting around the new tile (see page 61).

For neatness, spread adhesive on the tile, not in the hole

Carpet

VACUUM AT LEAST ONCE A WEEK.

It's warm, comfortable and attractive, but carpet also has valuable practical functions. It insulates against the cold, absorbs sound and cushions and protects the floor. On top of that, modern carpeting is highly durable, stain-resistant and easy to care for. Keeping it clean is the best way to prolong a carpet's life, but if accidents do happen there are ways to repair the damage so that you don't have to replace it prematurely.

Care and maintenance

● **Vacuum your carpet every week** Frequent vacuuming – weekly or more often, depending on traffic – is the best way to keep your carpet in good shape. Here's how to get the most out of your vacuuming efforts:

◉ **GO BACK AND FORTH** Set your vacuum cleaner for the pile level of the carpet unless your vacuum automatically adjusts. When you vacuum, use slow, even strokes and go back and forth several times, flipping the nap by going alternately against and with the grain. Finish with strokes that all go in the same direction.

◉ **USE YOUR HOSE AND ATTACHMENTS** Vacuum under furniture as well as you can, using the flexible hose and extension attachments that come with most vacuum cleaners. Twice a year, move the furniture and vacuum the area underneath really thoroughly.

◉ **GET RID OF FLUFF AND HAIR** New carpet sheds a lot of fluff. Don't worry, it's normal and will soon stop happening. If your vacuum cleaner won't suck up cat hairs, threads or other fine items, check that the bag isn't full (see below). If the suction is fine but the vacuum still won't pick up the fine stuff, use a lint roller or some doubled-over sticky tape to lift it.

◉ **CHANGE THE BAG** As the bag fills up, the suction power reduces. Changing your bag when it's about half full will keep the suction going strong.

SAVE £400

What you would pay for carpet and fitting in a 4m x 6m room, using a mid-range synthetic carpet and underlay.

take care!

Avoid carpet-cleaning methods that use shampoos, dry powders and powerful rotating brushes. They may cause harm from the force of the brushes or by leaving behind residual detergent or solvent. They most effective way to get your carpet clean is to use a professional steam cleaner.

● **Use protective runners or rugs** An easy way to prevent excess wear and dirt on your carpet is to put runners or throw rugs in high-traffic areas, especially hallways. The runners can be strips of offcut or contrasting carpet 'whipped' along the edges by a carpet supplier to finish them. It's much cheaper to replace a runner or rug than an entire carpet.

● **Lift, don't drag furniture** Never haul furniture across the room when you rearrange a carpeted room. Pulling furniture over carpet causes unnecessary wear, but, more importantly, can snag a loop of yarn, rip a carpet seam or bunch and wrinkle the carpet. If the carpet is nylon, the friction caused by dragging can actually melt the fibres. However heavy and awkward furniture is, always lift it to move it.

● **Block out UV rays** To prevent carpet from fading, try to protect it from prolonged exposure to direct sunlight. Draw curtains and blinds on the sunny sides of the house during peak daylight hours.

What kind of carpet should I buy?

There are two types of carpet pile: woven and tufted. Woven pile is formed by yarn stitched in loops. Tufted pile, which is plusher but not as durable or expensive as woven pile, is made by pushing tufts of yarn into backing fabric and sealing with another backing layer. It comes in varying lengths and styles, the longest being shag pile or Saxony. Some carpets have a combination of both piles; many have pile of both types that's curled or twisted and heat-set for greater durability and these are often easier to keep clean. A good underlay will improve the heat and sound insulation and the feel of the carpet, plus it can extend a carpet's life by up to 40 per cent. Another key to long life for a carpet is the material used to make it:

Tufted pile is soft

● **NYLON** is hard-wearing and a good choice for an area of heavy traffic, such as a hall. It's cheaper than wool. Nylon is stain-resistant and usually colour-fast, offering a range of brilliant colours that are dyed in the manufacture of the fibre, not after the carpet is woven.

● **POLYPROPYLENE** is stain-resistant and durable, but also flammable. Like nylon, the colour is added when the fibres are made, so it's colour-fast. The only shortcoming with polypropylene is that the fibres crush easily.

● **POLYESTER** has a luxurious, soft feel when used in thick, tufted-pile carpets. It's easily cleaned and resistant to water-soluble stains, but the pile is liable to flatten quickly.

Corded weaves are hard-wearing

● **WOOL** is very durable, luxuriously soft and thick and generally regarded as the best material for carpets. It's available in many colours and will stay looking good for years, but it's more expensive than synthetic carpeting.

● **BLENDS** of the materials above are also common. Wool-nylon, most often in a 80:20 ratio, combines the great look and comfort of wool with the extra durability of nylon. Other good combinations include acrylic-polypropylene and nylon-polypropylene.

● **Hire a pro to do the steam cleaning** Periodic steam cleaning – every 6 to 18 months, depending on room use – is the best way to keep your carpet looking as good as new. Even with regular vacuuming, dirt eventually works its way deep into the pile, beyond the reach of a vacuum. It's best to hire a professional carpet-cleaning company. It will use very hot water throughout the cleaning process as well as a powerful vacuum, which will suck up all the water that the cleaner puts down, leaving the carpets almost dry. The cost is generally less than £50 a room.

● **Or shampoo on your own** If you prefer to clean your carpets yourself, hire the most powerful cleaner you can – carpet cleaners are widely available to hire from DIY stores, supermarkets and dry cleaners. Follow the instructions closely and change the water frequently to keep it clean. Open windows and let the carpet dry thoroughly – preferably overnight – before walking on it or replacing furniture. Moisture left in the carpet can rot fibres and encourage the growth of mould and mildew, leaving you with a bigger problem than the grime you started with.

● **Change the room's traffic flow** To distribute the wear on your carpet and extend its life, move your furniture every few months in a way that changes the way people walk through the room. If you have a moveable rug, just rotate its position in the room.

TAKE YOUR SHOES OFF, BUT LEAVE YOUR SOCKS ON.

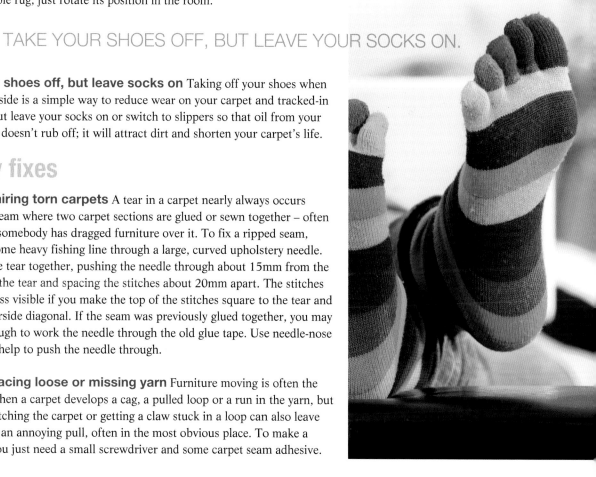

● **Take shoes off, but leave socks on** Taking off your shoes when you're inside is a simple way to reduce wear on your carpet and tracked-in grime. But leave your socks on or switch to slippers so that oil from your bare feet doesn't rub off; it will attract dirt and shorten your carpet's life.

Easy fixes

● **Repairing torn carpets** A tear in a carpet nearly always occurs along a seam where two carpet sections are glued or sewn together – often because somebody has dragged furniture over it. To fix a ripped seam, thread some heavy fishing line through a large, curved upholstery needle. Stitch the tear together, pushing the needle through about 15mm from the edges of the tear and spacing the stitches about 20mm apart. The stitches will be less visible if you make the top of the stitches square to the tear and the underside diagonal. If the seam was previously glued together, you may find it tough to work the needle through the old glue tape. Use needle-nose pliers to help to push the needle through.

● **Replacing loose or missing yarn** Furniture moving is often the culprit when a carpet develops a cag, a pulled loop or a run in the yarn, but pets scratching the carpet or getting a claw stuck in a loop can also leave you with an annoying pull, often in the most obvious place. To make a repair, you just need a small screwdriver and some carpet seam adhesive.

smart idea

Are you left with deep impressions in the carpet when you move the furniture? Bring the crushed fibres back to their original shape with a steam iron. Just set the iron on steam and hold it about 5mm above the carpet. Use a screwdriver to tease out and fluff up the pile.

If the yarn is still attached to the carpet, you can simply glue it back into place. First protect the area around the run with masking tape, then squeeze a heavy bead of adhesive into the run. Use the screwdriver to press each scab (where the original adhesive still clings to the yarn) down into the carpet backing until each new loop is at the right height.

If the yarn has become detached and is missing, count the number of carpet loops it will take to fill the run. Then pull a piece of yarn from the edge of a scrap (or hidden) piece of carpet, count the curls in the loose yarn then cut it to the right length to make your repair.

● **Replacing carpet tiles** Carpet tiles are usually fitted with self-adhesive or double-sided carpet tape, so it's easy to lift a damaged tile by slipping a filler knife under one edge. Replace it with a new one using the same type of tape. Rather than fitting a bright new tile that will stick out noticeably, take a tile from a hidden area and put the new one where it will be less obvious. To remove a stubborn stain on a carpet tile, try taking it up and washing it under cold water; let it dry completely before replacing it.

● **Repairing burns** A dropped match or cigarette will quickly burn a hole in a carpet. To fix a surface burn, snip off the charred tips of the tufts with sharp scissors. If the carpet is cut-pile, it helps to feather out the area by lightly tapering the nap in a circle a little wider than the damaged area.

How to patch damaged carpet

Patching a damaged area of carpet is easy. The only special materials you need are double-sided carpet tape, which is sticky on both sides, and carpet seam adhesive, both of which are available at DIY stores and carpet shops. Start by cutting out the damaged carpet with a sharp trimming knife and a straightedge. Use this piece as a guide to cut a patch from an offcut or a piece of carpet in an inconspicuous place, making sure that, if the carpet has a pattern, it matches.

1 Apply carpet seam adhesive around the edges of the hole and the patch. Try not to spread adhesive on the surface, but go around halfway up the depth of the pile. Leave it to dry.

2 Slide double-sided carpet tape partway under the edges of the hole in the carpet. Stick them to the floor or underlay and peel off the backing for the top layer as well.

3 Press the patch in place and tap lightly around the edges with a hammer to make a strong bond. Weigh the patch down with some heavy books until it has bonded.

Removing stains **from carpet**

Type of stain	How to get it out
Animal urine 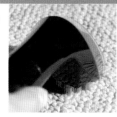	Immediately blot excess liquid with paper towels. Dab with a little fizzy water, then a spot cleaner made from 1 teaspoon of washing-up liquid and 100ml of warm water. Scrub with diluted carpet shampoo with an added splash of white vinegar, then rinse and blot dry. **A stiff-bristled carpet brush is a useful tool**
Blood	If fresh, blot with cold water (not hot). If dried, try a solution of 15ml of ammonia and 50ml of water. Leave to set for 30 minutes. Sponge off with cold water.
Chewing gum 	Freeze stuck-in chewing gum by covering it with a plastic bag full of ice cubes. Scrape off the gum with a butter knife once it's brittle enough to chip off the carpet. Vacuum up any remaining crumbs.
Coffee, beer and milk	Blot excess with paper towels then scrub with diluted carpet shampoo. When dry, use dry-cleaning solvent to remove grease from milk spills. Tackle stubborn stains by dabbing with a cotton bud dipped in 3 per cent hydrogen peroxide solution (sold in chemists).
Fruit juices and soft drinks	Blot excess with kitchen towel; sponge with a solution of 1 teaspoon of powdered laundry detergent and 1 teaspoon of white vinegar dissolved in 1 litre of warm water.
Grease, oil, lipstick and butter	Blot excess with paper towels. Sponge with dry-cleaning fluid, working from the edges to the centre of the stain. Try soaking up oily stains with a sprinkling of cornflour; vacuum it up once it's dry.
Paint 	Scrape up as much as possible with a wide-bladed knife. Sponge emulsion spills with cold water, working from the edges towards the centre, and remove gloss paint with white spirit or dry-cleaning solvent.
Shoe polish, ink and dried paint	Dab with dry-cleaning solvent or methylated spirits. Washable inks can be removed with warm water.
Wax	Scrape off as much as possible, then place a brown paper bag over the area and run the point of a warm – not hot – iron over it (don't let the iron touch a nylon carpet or it will melt the pile). The bag will act as a blotter and absorb the wax. Remove remaining traces with dry-cleaning solvent.
Wine 	Sponge red wine spills with white wine then blot with kitchen towel. Don't put salt on carpet stains; it may affect the colour and the dried salt can be difficult to remove. Treat white wine like a soft-drink spillage and blot with kitchen towel. Dried-in wine stains can be removed by soaking in a solution of equal parts of water and glycerine for an hour, then rinsing. Or try sponging with methylated spirits to make the stain fade.

SAVE £130

What you would pay for a handyman or carpenter to pinpoint and fix the squeaking steps on a staircase.

Stairs and banisters

The staircase is often the grand centrepiece of a home and it's certainly the most complicated piece of carpentry. Keeping stairs looking good requires little more than regular dusting, cleaning and vacuuming. Here are a few tricks that will make stair cleaning a breeze, along with easy carpentry secrets and balustrade repair tips that can save you the cost of an expensive replacement.

Care and maintenance

● **Vacuum from the bottom up** Carpet is always dirtiest just before you vacuum it, so you're just grinding in the dirt when you stand on an uncleaned step as you vacuum your way down the stairs. Instead, vacuum from the bottom of the stairs up, so you're always standing on a clean piece of carpet. Use a nozzle attachment to clean the edges of each step and the back of the step, where it meets the riser (the vertical section). Don't forget to vacuum the risers occasionally, too.

● **Buy extra extenders for your vacuum** If you have a cylinder, 'pull-along' vacuum cleaner or an upright with hose attachments, see how far up the stairs your hose will reach and consider buying a couple more extension tubes to fit onto the hose. These can extend your reach by a metre or more, enabling you to clean the entire flight of stairs while moving the cleaner just once or twice – speeding the job up and making it much lighter work.

● **Turbo-charge your vacuum** An air-powered beater brush, called a turbo tool, attaches to the end of the vacuum hose and brushes across carpeting on stairs in the same way as an upright vacuum brushes across a carpet on the floor. Use a turbo tool to loosen and suck up lint, hair and dirt that you would otherwise miss.

● **Keep your banisters clean** Dust painted banisters with a damp cloth. If the banister is especially dirty, add a couple of drops of washing-up liquid to warm water, but don't be tempted to scrub with an abrasive sponge or cleaner. When using soap, wring out the rag and wash small sections one at a time, rinsing them immediately with a second damp cloth. Dry thoroughly with a separate cloth. If your banister has a natural varnish finish, dust it with a soft cloth dampened with a little furniture polish.

TALCUM POWDER THOSE SQUEAKY STAIRS.

● **Powder a squeak** If you have a squeaky stair that needs silencing, sprinkle talcum powder into the seam at the back between the tread and the riser. You'll need to apply it again when the powder works its way out of the joint. Powdered graphite (just scrape a pencil lead) also works.

Anatomy of a **staircase**

The main parts of a staircase are the treads and risers. Treads are what you walk on; the rounded front edge is called the nosing. Risers are the vertical boards between treads. The treads and risers are supported by strings – boards with a zigzag edge for steps to rest on (called a cut or open string) or with slots that the treads slide into (a closed string). Some staircases have both types. The balustrade comprises a row of balusters topped by a handrail and is often the most elaborate and attractive part of a staircase. Balusters are the vertical pieces that support the banister or handrail. The newel post is the large post that the handrail is nailed to at the bottom and top of the stairs. Steps that fan to go round a corner are called winders; a half-landing is a platform where stairs turn by 90 degrees.

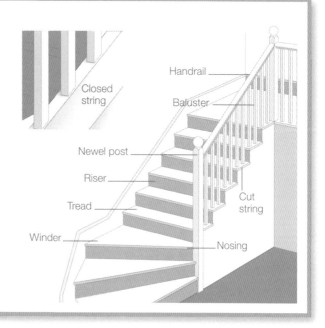

ISOLATE THE SQUEAK BY WALKING
UP AND DOWN THE STAIRS.

Easy fixes

● **Identifying the source of a squeak** Stairs squeak when you step on one piece of wood and it rubs against another. Isolate the problem by walking up and down the stairs to see which step is squeaking. Try to tell if the squeak is coming from the back, the front or the side of the step. Better still, if you can get underneath the stairway, ask someone else to walk on the steps so you can pinpoint the squeaky spots from below.

● **Sealing stubborn squeaks** One easy way to quiet a squeak is to apply a thin bead of sealant under the step nosing, to cushion the joint where the tread meets the riser. Do this from the upper side if the stairs aren't carpeted. After applying the sealant, run a plastic spoon or your

finger, wearing a latex glove, along it to remove the excess and push some of the sealant into the squeaky joint. Clean up any excess sealant as directed on the tube before it dries. If you can get to the steps from the underside – from an understairs cupboard, for example – seal the joints of the squeaky step from there, too, using sealant or polyurethane foam filler (left).

Brace steps to stop them creaking

● **Reinforcing steps** Stop steps from moving and you'll stop the creak. Screw one leg of an L-bracket to the riser of a creaky step (left), leaving a small gap between the other leg and the tread. Run a bead of glue between the tread and riser and then screw the bracket to the tread, closing the joint tightly in the process.

● **Reinforcing steps with wood blocks** Instead of brackets (above left), you can also secure wood blocks (left) beneath the stairs where tread meets riser. Drill pilot holes for the screws in each block. Apply glue to adjacent faces of the block. Put the glued surfaces against the tread and riser and then screw the block to each surface. Make sure that the screws are short enough not to protrude through the steps themselves.

● **Shimming squeaks** Some staircases are made with wooden wedges or shims under the stairs, which hold the treads and risers tight in the strings. If these shims work loose over time, the steps can start to flex and will creak as you walk up and down. If any are loose, squeeze a little wood glue onto the tips of the shims and tap them back into place (left).

● **Fixing a loose baluster** Most balusters are fixed to the handrail with nails, hammered in at an angle to go through the baluster and into the underside of the rail. If a nail works loose and the baluster starts to feel freer, pull out the nail, if you can, with pincers and replace it with a new nail, slightly longer and thicker (right). If you can't remove the nail, drive in a new one slightly to one side.

● Sometimes, fillets of wood are used between the balusters to hold them in place. The balusters sit in a groove in the underside of the handrail and the fillets fill the gaps between each baluster. If a fillet drops out, nail it (or a replacement, cut to fit) back into place (right). Don't use glue, in case you need to remove the balusters at a later date.

Nail a baluster to keep it in place

Wood fillets fill the gaps

● **Repairing a broken baluster** A broken or splintered baluster can often be glued back together without removing it. Brush the broken surfaces with glue. Draw rectangular pieces together with clamps, wipe off any excess glue and leave the clamps on overnight. Clamp round pieces by wrapping rope around the break and tying it. If the damage is minor, you can use masking tape instead of rope.

● **Removing a damaged baluster** If a baluster is so badly damaged that you cannot fix it, you will have to take it out and find a replacement. Some balusters are held in place by a moulding that runs along the side of the stairs. Prise off the moulding (left) with a chisel and carefully pull out the baluster. If the baluster is nailed in place, drive the nails all the way through the baluster and into the tread or railing with a hammer and nail punch and then slowly ease the banister out. If there's no visible way to remove a baluster, then there's no visible way you'll be able to put it back in either. That's the time to consult a carpenter.

smart idea

You can often order replacement balusters for a relatively new staircase at a timber yard. But if you can't locate a replacement, try this trick. Find a good baluster in a less visible part of the stairs and substitute it with the damaged one (or put in a new mismatched one). That way the odd one will be out of sight and the good one will be visible.

3 THE EXTERIOR

Maintaining the exterior of your house isn't just about keeping up appearances – and property values – it's also crucial to your comfort, security and safety when indoors. From chimney pots to foundations, your house is constructed from a wide variety of surfaces and materials that require year-round vigilance. Failing to spot problems in the early stages can result in headaches and hefty repair bills.

Structural elements in particular – like roofs – are costly to repair or replace, but it's possible to prevent or put off such expenses. In this section, we'll tell you when to schedule exterior check-ups, what equipment you need to get the job done and how to care for your home's doors, windows and roof to seal your home securely against the elements.

Exterior maintenance can require special equipment and some expert knowledge, especially when it places you up on the roof. Don't hesitate to call in the professionals when you need them, but remember: there's a lot you can do on your own to preserve the health of your home's outer shell and save your bank balance in the process.

Brick walls

Old brick houses, with solid walls 225mm or 330mm thick, are the ultimate in sturdy construction. Today, homes are often built with just 100mm of brick, used as a veneer or cladding over either a timber frame or lightweight blockwork, making a cavity wall. Whatever the build, bricks are sturdy and almost maintenance-free. Blows to the surface, moisture, crumbling mortar joints and plain old dirt may cause problems, but with a little care, you can avoid serious damage.

Care and maintenance

● **Inspect your exterior** Once or twice a year, walk around your house on a bright, sunny day and examine the bricks in the exterior walls. Make a note of any crumbling mortar joints, cracked bricks, mildew and other stains on the brickwork. You don't have to rush to fix the problems, but the sooner you do so, the better.

● **Keep your eyes peeled for moisture problems** After a heavy rainfall, check the house's downpipes and gutters to make sure no water is collecting on the ground near the outer walls or persistently splashing up onto the walls. Clear away any blockages and make any necessary repairs to gutters and downspouts. If standing water is a problem, build up the soil level slightly near the house so that it slopes away from the building.

SAVE £1,000
How much it would cost to have a 3m x 10m exterior brick wall pointed (the mortar replaced).

● **Mix your own mortar** You can buy pre-mixed mortar for repointing or replacing bricks, but you'll get a better match if you mix your own. Start by using a mix of one part cement, one part hydrated lime and six parts sand. Try a small area first, and if the colour or texture don't match the original, then try varying the proportions or using a different type of sand. Most pre-1939 houses, for example, were built with coarse 'sharp sand' and lime mortar (with no cement), giving an open-textured white finish. Post-1945 brickwork is more likely to have been put up with soft 'builders' sand, lime and cement, and has a smoother, yellow or orange finish. Whichever mix you use, remember that new pointing will look lighter and brighter than old mortar until it weathers in. New brickwork and pointing on Victorian houses can be blended-in by brushing on a dilute solution of soot in water.

● **Hose bricks before cleaning them** Before applying a cleaning compound to your bricks – for example, if you need to remove a difficult stain – wet the section of wall thoroughly with a spray from a garden hose. This will help the compound to

The anatomy of a **solid brick wall**

If your house was built before 1920, it's likely to have solid walls construted of brick or stone. Bricks are a standard size, so a solid brick wall is usually around 230mm thick; stone walls vary, depending on the type of stone used, but very old cottages sometimes have walls more than 500mm thick in places. Tall buildings, such as town houses and Georgian terraces, may have thicker walls on the lower storeys to support the weight of the bricks above.

Solid walls like these are strong. You can drill into them with a masonry drill and, provided you use appropriate fixings, hang heavy objects and shelves anywhere without fear of damage. They keep a house cool in hot weather, but can be cold in the winter. Damp seeping in from outside can also be a problem, as it can work its way through the bricks and any cracks in the pointing. If the masonry gets damp, it can be damaged in a heavy frost, when the water within the bricks freezes and expands. This can split the faces off bricks, which will then need to be replaced, or can cause a rendered covering to crack and fall off in chunks.

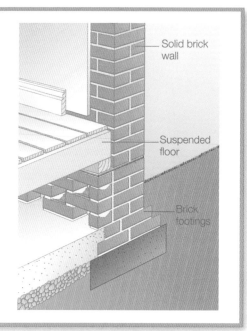

Solid brick wall

Suspended floor

Brick footings

take care!

When applying any strong cleaning agent to your bricks, wear protective goggles and gloves and cover nearby plants and grass with plastic. Don't use a metal brush, as it may scratch the bricks and leave behind metal particles that will rust. Avoid brick acid, too – it may stain or bleach bricks or corrode aluminium window frames if you have them. Before applying a cleaner to century-old bricks, or to bricks with a light or unusual colour or an unusual finish, test the cleaner in a hidden spot.

penetrate better and you'll get a much better result from cleaning. For most kinds of everyday dirt, all you need to clean your brickwork is a garden hose and stiff bristle brush. Work from the top down, wetting the wall and then scrubbing it clean.

● Don't dampen bricks that have a white, powdery deposit on them. This is called efflorescence and is common, particularly on new bricks. It's caused by salts in the bricks reacting with rainwater, but if you try to wash it off you'll make the problem worse. Brush away the powder with a stiff dry brush, repeating until all the salts have leached out and the efflorescence stops coming back.

● **Clean weep holes with pipe cleaners** Most cavity walls should have weep holes built in at regular intervals around the base of the wall, but also above and below window and door openings. They allow any moisture that penetrates the wall and trickles down inside the cavity to drain out of the building (channelled by metal flashing in the cavity), rather than seeping into the foundations, and also act as vents to allow a little air to circulate, minimising the risk of mould and condensation.

● A couple of times each year, inspect the weep holes in your brickwork to make sure that they're not blocked. Trapped moisture can rot windows, doors and timber joists inside, leading to thousands of pounds' worth of repairs. Clean them out with a pipe cleaner.

● **Painting brick walls** Although you can paint brick, it's not always a good idea. Painting brick changes it immediately from a relatively maintenance-free exterior into one that will need repainting every five to seven years. Also, if you or another owner later wants to remove the paint from the brick, the job will be expensive (and the results not guaranteed to be good enough to leave bare).

● If you have an already painted wall that needs redecorating, or if you need to paint new brickwork to match the rest of the property, make sure you use proper masonry primer and paint and wash the bricks thoroughly before you start. Apply the paint with a thick-napped roller or a masonry brush, with long, stiff bristles, working the paint into the rough surface in different directions before finishing with smooth, level strokes.

Easy fixes

● **Matching new mortar joints to old** The shaped mortar joints (the pointing) between bricks can get weathered away over time and might sometimes need to be patched up with fresh mortar. This is called repointing. It's often done badly, with messy, ragged joints, ill-matched to the surrounding pointing.

● To shape a new mortar joint to match the old ones, you don't need a bricklayer's jointer. To form the common concave shape, known as a bucket-handle joint, smooth the mortar with an ice-lolly stick, an old spoon or a piece of metal tube or hosepipe roughly the right diameter. For other shapes, carve a scrap of wood to the right shape.

● To trim away excess mortar (see page 92) from the base of a repointed weatherstruck joint – which slopes out away from the wall so that water drips clear of the bricks – you can make your own traditional tool, known

smart idea

If you're not sure whether your walls are solid or built with a cavity, the brick pattern can give you a clue. Solid brick walls include bricks turned to run through the depth of the wall, to give it strength. Their headers (the short sides) alternate with stretchers (the long sides) at the surface. Cavity walls are laid with only the stretchers visible, in a stretcher bond, overlapping half a brick at a time.

 ## The anatomy of a **cavity wall**

More modern houses usually have cavity walls, which are designed to improve the insulation of the house and to prevent damp penetrating from the outside. The outer layer may be brick or stone, partly or wholly finished with a coat of render (the wall is likely to be blockwork if it's rendered all over). Behind this is a gap 50-75mm wide and an inner layer, tied to the first with metal wall ties for stability. The inner thickness may be blockwork, which is cheaper than bricks and quicker to lay, but also a good insulator. The newest houses usually have a timber-framed inner layer clad with plasterboard, like an internal partition wall (see page 41).

Weep holes around the base of the outer leaf allow any moisture that penetrates the wall to seep out of the wall, rather than damaging the internal finish. They need to be kept clear to be effective.

The cavity helps to keep the house cool in summer and warm in winter by reducing heat transfer through the wall. The walls can be made even more efficient by including insulation in the cavity or within the timber panel of timber internal walls.

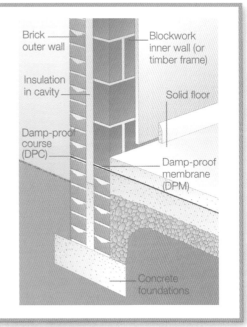

Brick outer wall

Insulation in cavity

Damp-proof course (DPC)

Blockwork inner wall (or timber frame)

Solid floor

Damp-proof membrane (DPM)

Concrete foundations

How to repoint crumbling brick joints

If the mortar in the joints between bricks is cracking and crumbling, you need to repoint it, replacing old, loose mortar with new. A bag of pre-mixed mortar (which comes with plasticiser) is convenient for a small repair, but it's much more economical to mix your own (see page 89).

1 Use a cold chisel to chip away loose mortar to a depth of around 15mm or until you reach solid mortar. Wear safety goggles and work gloves to protect you from flying chips of mortar. If you have a large area of wall to repoint, it may be worth hiring a hammer-action drill with a mortar-raking attachment to make the job quicker.

2 Brush out any loose debris left in the joints and rinse the bricks and joints with a hosepipe. Put some mortar onto a board, load a little onto the back of a pointing trowel and push it into the joints (above). Hold the board against the wall to catch any mortar that falls out as you work.

3 Let the mortar dry until you can press it gently with your thumb and leave a print. Finish the joints neatly to match the style of the existing pointing, using the trowel, a special pointing tool, such as a frenchman (above), or another tool that will re-create the shape of the joints on the rest of the wall (see 'Easy fixes', page 91). Using a timber batten to guide your tool can help to keep the joints straight and neat.

4 Before the mortar is completely dry, you can blend in the edges with the existing mortar using a sponge and 'age' it slightly for a better colour match (see below). Once the repair is dry, clean the bricks with a brush.

as a frenchman. Heat an old table knife or a strip of thin metal over a gas ring until it's pliable. Wear work gloves and goggles for protection in case the metal snaps, then clamp the knife in a vice and bend a 25mm section at the tip over to a 90 degree angle. Run the tool along the base of the joint, with its bend against the wall and the bent tip pointing down (see photograph, above right) and it will neatly slice away the unwanted mortar to leave a sharp finish.

● **'Ageing' new joints** New joints will stand out like a sore thumb if they don't match old ones in colour, but you can 'weather' new mortar to give it an aged look. Pat the mortar, while it's still a little damp, with a wet tea bag to stain it, or darken fresh mortar or repaired brickwork by brushing with a diluted solution of soot in water.

Get this stuff **off your bricks**

Type of stain	How to get it out
Dingy spots	Wearing gloves and goggles, apply spray-on oven cleaner. Leave it for 15 minutes, then scrub with a stiff brush. Repeat, then rinse with water.
Dirt	Hose off while scrubbing with a stiff brush. For a tough job, rent a power washer, but be careful not to damage the surface of bricks or dislodge any mortar with the jet.
Efflorescence (chalky build-up)	Brush off with a stiff brush. Repeat until the powder stops coming back, then wash and scrub the area (see page 90).
Graffiti	Wearing gloves and goggles, apply commercial spray-paint remover, following the manufacturer's directions.
Mould or mildew	Prepare a 50/50 mixture of bleach and water and pour into a plastic spray bottle. Spray on the mixture, wait an hour and then rinse the area well with water. Alternatively, scrub the area with full-strength white vinegar and a stiff nylon brush. To stop it coming back, locate the moisture problem that's causing the mould and fix it.
Paint	Blot wet paint with paper towels, then wipe with a rag soaked with paint thinner for oil-based paint or water and a little detergent for water-based paint. Scrape off dry paint then remove residue with paint remover.
Rust	Dissolve 500g of oxalic acid crystals (used in refinishing wood furniture) in 4 litres of water. Brush on, wait three hours, and then scrub and rinse.
Soot or smoke	Scrub with scouring powder then rinse well. For stubborn spots, make a paste of talcum powder and liquid chlorine bleach, apply to the stain and let it dry before brushing off.
Tar, oil or asphalt	Scrub with scouring powder. Make a paste of fuller's earth and paraffin (see page 94), apply and let dry. Brush off, then scrub again and rinse.
Water stains	Scrub with an acid-based commercial brick cleaner and a stiff brush.

STRIP THE BRICKS, NOT YOUR HANDS:
WEAR GLOVES TO PROTECT YOU.

Drilling out a damaged brick

● **Replacing a broken brick** Use a power drill on hammer action setting to drill all round the brick to its full depth, then chisel out the remaining mortar, being careful not to chip the surrounding bricks. Prise the brick out or break it out if necessary. Clean and dampen the hole, spread mortar along the bottom of the hole and the top and sides of the new brick. Support the brick on a trowel and slide it into place. Add more mortar to fill the joints, then shape them to match the other joints. If the brick is only damaged on the face, you can even turn it round and replace it good side outwards.

● **Disguising a mismatched replacement brick** If you replace a brick in a wall and the replacement doesn't match the surrounding bricks, try staining it the same colour as the existing ones using black tea, a solution of soot and water, or a little mud or garden soil mixed in water.

● **Seal out moisture** If water seeps into bricks, it makes the surface crack and flake when it freezes. If you spot frost damage, paint on a colourless, microporous, water-repellent sealant, which will keep out water while still allowing the bricks to breathe. Follow the safety advice on the packaging and paint the whole wall, as it can change the colour of the bricks slightly.

How to source matching replacement bricks

Bricks vary widely in colour and texture. The type used is often characteristic of the local area – and may be made from local materials. Stone walls may be built from chunks of local natural stone, such as Cotswold stone, or cheaper, manufactured blocks of reconstituted stone, which usually have a smoother or more uniform surface finish and colour.

● If you need to replace a brick or stone, it may be difficult to find a matching replacement off the shelf at your local DIY store. A builders' merchant is more likely to hold a stock of local varieties, but for older properties the bricks may be no longer available. Architectural salvage yards are a good place to go for materials like this. They will rescue, collect, sort and resell the intact bricks from demolished buildings in your area. Even if you cannot find a perfect match, an old and weathered close match will be less obvious when fitted than a bright new brick would be.

How to **draw stains out** of a brick

Remove stubborn stains, such as tar and oil, with a poultice made from fuller's earth or ground chalk mixed with paraffin or white spirit. Wipe the stain with a little of the paraffin or white spirit, hold a piece of plastic food bag or aluminium foil over the stain and pack the paste over the mark. Tape the poultice in place, sealing all the edges to stop it from drying out and leave it for a few days. The paste should draw out the stain, then you can wash the bricks clean.

Rendered walls

The hard external plaster known as render is a popular finish on new-build houses, but also a traditional feature of simple cottages, grand terraces, seafront promenades and homes all over Europe. It is a waterproof coating made from sand and lime or sand and cement, or sometimes a mixture of all three, and is usually applied to stone or blockwork walls. Apart from repainting, maintenance is rarely needed, but keep an eye out for cracks or other damage, which can allow water to get in, loosening the render's grip and possibly seeping through the wall to the inside surfaces.

Care and maintenance

● **Check for cracks** Once a year, examine rendered walls for cracks. You can ignore hairline cracks – they will disappear next time you paint – but seal larger ones (see opposite).

● **Use the duct tape test to spot a dangerous crack** If you find a long crack, attach a length of duct tape across it with epoxy. Watch the tape over the next two months. If it splits or twists, the wall behind the render is shifting and the foundation may be settling, which could cause significant damage to the entire house. Ask a structural engineer to assess the problem.

SAVE £600
What it would cost to have the exterior wall (6m x 5m) of a house stripped and re-rendered.

● **Beware of crustiness** Do you have a white crumbly or flaky crust forming on your wall? It's efflorescence. Salts inside the render are being leached out by moisture coming from inside. Get professional help from a mason or cement render specialist.

● **Bleach away ugly mildew** Grey or black stains on painted render are likely to be caused by mildew. To get rid of them, just clean the area using a solution of one part household bleach and three parts water. Wear rubber gloves and protect any nearby plants or grass with plastic sheeting.

● **The tap test for blown render** The bond between rendering and the wall behind can fail when moisture seeps between the two layers through cracks in the surface and then freezes. Check your render from time to time by tapping sections lightly with the handle of a screwdriver (right). If an area sounds hollow, it will need stripping off and replacing. Keep tapping to determine how far the render is loose and how big an area will need to be replaced.

● **Watch for pebbles falling like rain** Rendered walls on houses built in the 1930s are often finished with pebbledash, a render which has had pea shingle thrown at it while still wet. Over time, the pebbles start to fall off. It's normal to lose a few pebbles from time to time, but look out for signs of more serious failure, such as significant numbers of pebbles on the ground, and patch the wall if necessary (see page 97).

A hollow tap means loose render

Easy fixes

● **Using tape for neat crack repairs** If you find a crack that is no
more than 3mm wide, fill it with acrylic sealant. Clean out the crack with
a stiff brush, then, to keep the sealant from smearing, cover the crack with
a strip of wide masking tape. Slice the tape with a trimming knife to expose
the crack and fill it with sealant from a mastic gun. Smooth the surface with
a trowel or putty knife then remove the tape before the sealant hardens.

● **Freshen up with whitewash** A rendered and painted wall can
become dingy and stained with age. Give it a facelift the old-fashioned way
with whitewash. Make whitewash by mixing white Portland cement with
water to the consistency of pancake batter. Wet the wall with a hose and
apply the mixture with a masonry brush.

● **Time for a colour change** If you want to give your home a new
look, you can paint a rendered wall with masonry paint. Do the entire wall
in one session using the same batch of paint, to avoid colour variations or
visible joins. Be careful with your colour choice and pick something that
will be sympathetic towards the surrounding properties – bold colours will
not be to everyone's taste and may even reduce the value or saleability of
your home. In some places, particularly in conservation areas, there may
be restrictions on the colours that you can choose; check with your local
planning department if you are unsure. You'll probably need two coats
of paint. Apply it with a thick-napped roller for rough surfaces and use a
masonry brush to get into the crevices. Work the first coat into the render
by rolling or brushing in several directions.

● **Prepare before you paint** Fill cracks with a paintable exterior
sealant. If they are wide or deep, use pre-mixed repair compound. Clean
the surface thoroughly, but if you use a power washer, hold it a metre away
from the surface to avoid crumbling the render.

● **Flexible paint cuts down on maintenance** Elastomeric paint is
more pliable than standard masonry paint. It's a good choice for a rendered
wall as it will help to prevent hairline cracks appearing as the cement dries
out or flexes. It's sometimes sold as flexible masonry paint – look for it in
large DIY stores or specialist paint shops.

● **Painting pebbledash** An easy way to disguise patchy pebbledash
or cover up a repair is to paint it. Brush the wall gently with a soft brush
first to remove any loose material. Don't hose or pressure-wash the surface
as this is likely to dislodge more pebbles and could take weeks to dry out.
Apply two coats of masonry-stabilising solution, then two coats of masonry
paint, using a brush or long-haired roller to get between the pebbles.

How to patch damaged render

Use ready-mixed render or mix a small batch from six parts plastering sand, one part cement and one part hydrated lime, with just enough water to make the mixture workable – neither stiff nor sloppy. A batch will become too stiff to use after about 20 minutes.

1 Chip away loose render and any crumbling brick joints with a bolster chisel. Use a sponge to wet the area to be repaired to stop the render drying too quickly and crumbling. Apply a first coat of render to about 5mm below the surface, starting at the bottom and pressing the lower edge of your trowel into the wall as you sweep it upwards.

2 Let the render dry for around 20 minutes, by which time it should be starting to stiffen. Then use an old trowel to scratch a criss-cross of lines to make a key for the top coat. You could also do this with a square of wood with nails driven through it every 40mm or so. Leave the first coat to dry for at least 14 hours before applying the finishing coat.

3 Start at the top left and sweep the trowel lightly across the patch. Apply a little render at a time, until the patch is slightly proud of the wall. Before the render starts to set (after about 15 minutes), draw a straight-edged piece of wood upwards over the patch to level it with the wall. Smooth the surface gently with a damp sponge or wooden float.

● **Keeping out moisture** Preventing moisture from sneaking behind the finish is the most important step you can take to prolong the life of your render. Replace damaged or missing flashings around chimneys and vents as soon as you notice the problem and repair any surface cracks or damaged areas of wall immediately.

● **Pepper your wall with pebbles** If a patch of pebbledashed wall needs re-rendering, it's fairly easy to patch, though difficult to match. Repair the cement render just as for a smooth wall (see above) and reapply the stones while the render is still wet. Buy some matching pebbles from a builders' merchant (you'll need around 5kg for a square metre of wall), wash and drain them, then – with a coal shovel or a dustpan – fling a scoopful at a time at the wet render. Wash any pebbles that fall to the ground before you reuse them, then once enough pebbles are sticking to the wall, press them in gently with a wooden plasterer's float.

● **Try something new for a fresh coat** If the render needs replacing over an entire wall, consider using pre-coloured render. This is available ready-mixed or dry in pre-mixed bags that just need water added. Because the colour is mixed throughout the depth of the render, there's no coloured surface to peel or wear off and so you'll never need to paint it – just make sure you're happy with the colour first. Pre-mixed renders are also available with fibre reinforcement to help to prevent cracking.

take care!

You might think that coating render with a sealant is an effective way to prevent moisture problems, but this may just hold moisture in instead of keeping it out, which can cause serious underlying damage. Look for a microporous sealant that will let the wall breathe.

Timber cladding

A covering of wooden boards, or timber cladding, may not seem like the most durable outer finish for your home, and in Britain it's seldom used as more than a decorative feature on a small section of wall. But if the cladding is well cared for, it's just as waterproof as any other building material. Ignore signs of deterioration at your peril, though, as the boards will soon rot if water starts to get in, exposing the walls inside as well.

Care and maintenance

SAVE £200

Cost to replace a 2.5m x 5m area of deteriorated timber cladding on a house wall with new cedar boards, not including fitting.

● **Poke and prod the boards** Once a year, on a fine day, take time to examine the timber boards that make up any sections of exterior cladding. Using a screwdriver or an awl, prod any spots that are showing signs of rot to determine the depth of the damage. Scrape away the bad wood and replace it as you would if you were repairing a rotten wooden window frame or sill (see page 107).

● **Give cladding an annual bath** Every spring or summer, wash down your timber cladding. For a light cleaning, you don't need to use soap. Just wet the boards using a garden hose and scrub off surface dirt with a long-handled brush. Be sure to scrub under the edges of slats or shingles, where dirt tends to cling.

● **For tough dirt, use soap** If the wood is really dirty or beginning to show signs of mildew, scrub the cladding with a special cleaner designed for wooden decking; or mix together 1 litre of household bleach and 70ml of household detergent, such as a general-purpose, multi-surface cleaner, in 3 litres of warm water (don't use ammonia). This solution will remove heavy dirt and help to prevent mildew. Rinse the boards after washing with a garden hose. Every few years (or before painting the boards), clean your timber cladding with a power washer.

Easy fixes

Prise open a crack before gluing

● **Gluing splits back together** If you spot a split in one of the boards in your cladding, fix it promptly, before water starts to seep in. Gently lever the split open with a filler knife. If the split is large enough, slip a small wooden wedge under the bottom edge of the damaged board to keep the inside of the split exposed. Squeeze some exterior PVA wood glue along the exposed edge of the split, then remove the wedge, push the board back into place and wipe away excess glue with a damp cloth. Some strips of duct tape may be strong enough to hold the repair together while the glue dries, but if the board doesn't come together easily or if you find that the tape hasn't worked, drive several small finishing nails at an angle under the repaired section and bend them up to hold the bond tightly together. Remove the nails when the glue dries and fill the holes.

5 ways to fix boards

There are several ways to nail boards in place when installing timber cladding, but the framework behind is always the same: a frame of wooden studwork, covered by sheets of plywood or board and waterproof building paper.

- **SINGLE-FIXED BOARDS** are secured by nails driven through their faces, just above the top of the board below.

- **DOUBLE-FIXED BOARDS** are nailed closer to the edge, so that the nail passes through the board beneath as well.

- **HIDDEN NAILING** is neat – boards are nailed at the top edge, so that the nail is hidden by the board above.

- **SHIPLAP BOARDS** lie flat against the wall, with a notched lower edge that sits over the board below.

- **TONGUED-AND-GROOVED BOARDS** interlock to create a flat panel. Each board is 'secret nailed', by driving a nail down at an angle through the top edge of the board.

| Single-fixed boards | Double-fixed boards | Hidden nailing | Shiplap | Tongue and groove |

- **Using car-body filler on rotten boards** To repair rotted wood, dig away the rot with a knife or chisel, then fill the hole with car-body filler (available from DIY stores or car spares suppliers), smoothing or shaping the patch with a putty knife. Sand it to match the surrounding wood then prime and paint the area. It makes an exceptionally durable repair.

- **Banishing board bulges** All you need is a long wood screw to flatten a bulging board. Screw through the bulge into a stud behind: look for a pattern of nail heads to locate a nearby stud. To avoid splitting the board, drill a pilot hole first, then a countersink at the surface, too, so that you can fill over the head of the screw to hide it. Cover the screw head with exterior-grade wood filler, sand it smooth then prime and paint the area.

- **Making good use of roof cement** If you accidentally cut or screw through the building paper behind the cladding while making a repair, you will breach the moisture barrier that protects the walls behind. Seal the damage with asphalt roofing cement for a quick and effective fix.

How to replace damaged timber cladding

Timber cladding, also sometimes called clapboard or weatherboard, comes in a variety of widths and styles. The boards are nailed in overlapping rows to the sheathing behind (see page 99), often hiding the fixings behind the row above, but it's possible to replace a single damaged board or a small section of your cladding without stripping the whole area to get back to the repair. Follow the instructions below to cut out the damaged board, then take it to a timber yard to find the closest match.

1 Use a try square to mark cut lines on the section of board you need to replace. Locate the vertical lines of nails that indicate the position of timber support battens and make your cuts directly over the centre of a batten, so that you have a frame to fix into to secure the replacement section.

2 Gently lift the bottom edge of the damaged board using a nail bar resting on a wood scrap. Drive wooden wedges under the raised edge on either side of the cutting line to provide clearance for the saw as you cut through the board. Wedge a piece of scrap wood into the gap to protect the face of the board below and use a tenon saw to cut through the board (left).

3 Gently lift the bottom edge of the board overlapping the damaged one and wedge it as before. Use a padsaw to complete the cut through the hidden top edge of the damaged board.

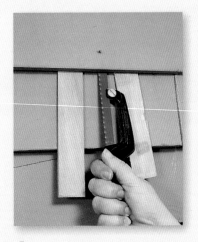

4 Free the board you are replacing by cutting through the nail holding it in place. Carefully drive in two wedges beneath the board above, one on either side of the fixing, then slide a mini hacksaw into the gap to cut through the nail (above).

5 If a nail head is exposed, use a nail bar to lever up the bottom edge of the board, resting it on a scrap of wood to protect the face of the board below. This will loosen the nail. Then hold the nail bar next to the nail head and tap it (left) to push the board back and pop out the nail head, so that you can pull out the nail.

6 Remove the damaged board and cut the replacement to size. Treat sawn edges with wood preservative then tap the board into place with a hammer and a piece of scrap wood. Pre-drill nail holes and secure the board with galvanised nails, nailing through the lower part of the replacement board about 5mm above the top of the board below. Use decorator's sealant to fill the joints and cover the nail holes, then sand, prime and paint the new board to match the existing cladding.

PVC-U cladding and fascias

It's sold as a maintenance-free option for replacing external woodwork, such as fascia boards behind gutters and wall cladding, as well as windows and doors, but PVC-U, or unplasticised PVC, can become discoloured, especially when exposed to traffic pollution. Also, extended exposure to sunlight can make it brittle.

SAVE £300

Cost to replace a 4m length of cracked PVC-U fascia board.

Care and maintenance

● **A spring clean keeps whites white** Over time, fascias, barge boards and cladding collect dirt and become chalky-looking, leaving a whitish residue that can break down into dark permanent spots if it's not removed. Use a mop or long-handled brush to scrub off the chalk, along with any dirt, grease or mildew with a bucket of warm soapy water.

● **Listen out for creaks** PVC-U expands and contracts constantly in changing temperatures, so roofline products – fascia boards, barge boards and soffits – and boards used as cladding should always be fixed loosely using slotted holes to allow them to move. If they are screwed down tight, they will creak as they try to move and may eventually crack. If you often hear your boards creaking, particularly in hot or cold weather, check the fixings and loosen them a little if necessary.

Easy fix

● **Repairing minor chips and cracks** To repair a shallow crack in a PVC-U board, use a toothpick to gently prise up one side of the crack, apply a little PVC epoxy cement from a vinyl repair kit, then press the crack closed.

SPRING-CLEAN WITH A BUCKET OF SOAPY WATER.

Can I paint PVC-U?

PVC-U boards won't chip or peel, as painted woodwork will, since the colour goes all the way through the material. But strong colours will fade over time, and white boards – especially if they face onto a busy road – will lose their bright white finish and begin to look grey. Fortunately there are paint products that can be used to revive shabby vinyl fascia boards, barge boards and cladding. Make sure you wash and rinse the boards thoroughly before you start, so that the paint will adhere well to the surface. You don't need to rub down before you paint for the first time, but make sure you choose a paint specially formulated for use on PVC-U. You can also buy PVC-U primers, which can then be coated with conventional exterior gloss paint. Once you have painted PVC-U boards, they will need repainting every few years, in the same way as exterior woodwork, and the old paint should be thoroughly cleaned and lightly sanded first.

ALWAYS PAINT THE OUTSIDE OF THE HOUSE IN SPRING OR AUTUMN, WHEN IT'S NEITHER TOO HOT NOR TOO COLD.

Painting your house

A sound coat of paint protects against the weather, so it's important to keep external paintwork in good condition. How often you have to repaint depends on climate, the quality of the paint and how well the surfaces were prepared last time, but once every five or six years is typical. If you clean and touch up your paint regularly, you can put off repainting for longer.

House painting tips

- **Only paint in spring or autumn** Paint when the weather is mild and the paint will stay wet longer, giving you more time to brush it out. Never paint on a rainy day or just before rain is expected, as the paint could be washed away before it adheres. Avoid windy days, too, as the wind will blow grit and dirt onto your fresh paint.

- **Choosing the right paint** Exterior-grade gloss paint is formulated to withstand the ravages of the British weather, so it's worth paying extra for – you'll almost certainly need to repaint much sooner if you choose a cheaper option. Always follow the manufacturer's instructions and use the undercoat and primer it specifies.
  - Use specialist PVC-U paint for painting plastic windows, gutters, soil and vent pipes and roofline products, such as PVC-U fascia boards, barge boards and soffits (see page 101).
  - Use special metal paint, such as Hammerite, to paint metal gutters, pipes and railings. As always, follow the instructions on the tin.
  - Use masonry paint for brick or rendered walls and apply it with a shaggy roller or masonry brush to push the paint well into the rough surface.
  - Use exterior woodstain or varnish on unpainted woodwork.

SAVE £750

Cost to have the wooden door and window frames of an average three-bedroom house with badly weathered paint prepared, primed and painted.

5 ways to **perfect preparation**

Here's how to get your woodwork ready for a great-looking, long-lasting paint job.

1 SCRAPE AND SAND-SMOOTH Scrape off all loose, cracked and peeling paint then sand down any scraped areas so that the difference between areas with and without old paint won't show through the new coat. Start with extra-coarse sandpaper, then switch to medium.

2 PRIME BARE WOOD Paint a coat of primer on areas of wood that have been scraped bare, applying a knotting solution to any visible knots first.

3 REPAIR DAMAGED AREAS Fill any holes, splits and damaged areas with wood filler.

4 SAND AGAIN Use abrasive paper wrapped around a sanding block to smooth the surface around any repairs and to give the old paint a 'key' so that the new paint will adhere well. Be careful if you choose to use a power sander as it removes wood quickly, even with the finest grades of abrasive paper.

5 PRIME AGAIN Use a damp cloth to wipe down the areas you have sanded, then apply primer to any bare wood or areas of new filler. Follow this with an undercoat or use a combined primer and undercoat.

● **Choosing the right brush** A 75mm brush is a good choice for painting flat woodwork – it will cover the surface quickly, making it easy to keep a wet edge of paint as you work, and give a smooth finish. For fiddly window frames and for cutting in around the glass, you'll need a smaller brush or, better still, an angled cutting-in brush (left).

● **Prevent paint blisters** The sun beating down on a fresh coat of paint can cause blistering, so don't paint areas that are about to be hit by bright sunlight. Instead, chase the sun through the day. In the early morning paint the north side of the house, move to the east side in the late morning and the south in the mid-afternoon. Paint the west side in the late afternoon (when the sun is weakening) or wait until the next morning.

For neat edges use a cutting-in brush

What's wrong with my paint job?

It looks like crocodile skin

POSSIBLE CAUSES Outer coat was applied over a poorly prepared surface – an undercoat that was not dry, too many undercoats or an incompatible paint, such as water-based paint used over oil.
SOLUTION Strip back to bare wood, prime and paint.

It's blistering and bubbling

POSSIBLE CAUSES Prick one of the blisters. If it shows paint inside, the temperature was too warm while painting.
SOLUTION Sand, clean and repaint.

POSSIBLE CAUSES If a pricked blister reveals bare wood, or if water comes out, moisture has seeped in from somewhere.
SOLUTION Fix any faulty sealant or leaky gutters. Strip paint and leave wood to dry before repainting.

It's flaking and peeling

POSSIBLE CAUSES When a surface is dirty or has too many layers of old paint, new paint cannot stick and will peel off. The surface may not have been 'keyed' to help the new paint to adhere. Or the wood beneath may be rotten.
SOLUTION Strip, prepare the surface well and repaint. Treat and repair any rotten wood.

It's mouldy and discoloured

POSSIBLE CAUSES Moisture and a warm, dirty surface, often caused by condensation settling.
SOLUTION Wash the area with a fungicide, let it dry, then repaint.

It's cracking and scaling

POSSIBLE CAUSES Moisture or pollution. Old paint often loses its elasticity, allowing moisture to seep in and lift off the paint.
SOLUTION Sort out the moisture problem, then strip and repaint.

It's shedding a chalky powder

POSSIBLE CAUSES Exterior paints are formulated to gradually release powdery chalk that washes off dirt when it rains.
SOLUTION This isn't a problem, but can indicate that it's time to repaint. New paint won't adhere to a chalky surface, so wash down the woodwork before repainting.

There are creases or runs

POSSIBLE CAUSES Paint will crease if it's applied over a coat that isn't yet dry. Runs occur when paint is applied too thickly.
SOLUTION Strip creased paint and redecorate. Brush out runs if the paint is still wet, or rub down and reapply the top coat.

Wooden windows

Sliding sashes or hinged casement: whatever the style of your windows, if the frames are made of wood, you'll need to take care of them if they are to last. Don't just look through them, but take a careful look at your windows from time to time. Follow these tips to keep them clean, watertight and easy to open and close and you'll save yourself a fortune on replacing neglected, rotten frames.

Care and maintenance

SAVE £800

Cost to replace a 1m x 1.5m wooden sash window, with a new frame and double-glazed unit, not including installation.

● **Keep sashes sliding smoothly** If a sash window has become stiff to move, clean the channels that the sashes ride in and rub them with a candle stub or a bar of soap. For longer-lasting results, lubricate them with silicone spray, which is available at DIY and hardware stores.

● **Clean windows regularly, frames and glass** Cleaning windows is essential to prolong the life of your frames. Clean every few months – more often if you're on a road with heavy traffic. Start by vacuuming or dusting the frames and sills, then clean their surfaces with a soft cloth and warm water and washing-up liquid. Finally, clean the panes, inside and out.

How to replace a broken window pane

Replacing a broken single-thickness pane is a straightforward repair. Measure the opening and ask the glass supplier to cut a new pane, of an appropriate thickness, to fit. If the broken pane is less than 800mm from the floor, you must use safety glass. For wooden frames, use linseed oil, universal or acrylic putty to fix the glass in place.

1 Wearing work gloves, carefully remove the broken glass. Use a glass cutter to score round the window then tap the glass with a hammer to break it out in pieces. Scrape out the remaining glass and putty with a hacking knife or chisel. If the putty proves stubborn, soften it with a heat gun. As you work, pull out the original metal glazing sprigs with pliers.

2 Dust the frame, apply wood primer and let it dry. Mould the putty in your hands until it's pliable then squeeze a 3mm bead all round the frame.

3 Gently press the glass into place – only push around the edges – so that it's well bedded onto the putty. Use a pin hammer or the edge of a chisel to knock new glazing sprigs into place against the glass, about 250mm apart and protruding about 5mm from the frame. Don't use the old holes.

4 Trim off any putty on the inside, apply more putty to fill the rebate and smooth it with a putty knife to give a neat, sloping finish with mitred corners. Leave the putty to harden for about two weeks before painting.

smart idea

Try erasing a shallow scratch in a windowpane with toothpaste. Use an 'extra-whitening' paste, as these contain the most abrasive; a gel will not work in the same way. Use a soft cloth to apply a pea-sized amount of toothpaste to the scratch, rub vigorously for a few minutes and wipe the glass clean.

● An old-fashioned technique is to wet the windows with a sponge or squeegee dipped in clear water, then rub them clean and dry using balls of scrunched-up newspaper, kitchen towel or a chamois cloth.

● Professional window cleaners use clean water and a squeegee, drawing it across the glass and wiping off dirty water between strokes.

● For very dirty glass, use 100ml of white vinegar in 2 litres of water, plus a squirt of washing-up liquid. Apply the solution to the glass with a spray bottle and polish off with a soft cloth.

● If reaching the outside of your windows is difficult, shut them tight and spray them with a garden hose. Do it gently, just misting the panes – too much pressure could force water into the house or crack a pane.

● **Overlap the glass with paint** When painting windows, it helps to seal out moisture if you allow paint to overlap onto the glass by 2mm.

● **Don't let paint cause a window to stick** Be careful not to close windows fully after they have been painted until you're sure that the paint is completely dry. Otherwise, when you come to prise or tug the windows open they can stick to the frames and damage your paint job. To prevent sash windows from sticking, open both sashes partway before you begin painting and start by giving the sash channels one thin, carefully applied coat of paint. Once the paint is dry to the touch, slide the sashes up and down a few times to make sure they are running freely.

Anatomy of a window

Two types of window are common in British houses: casements, which swing open on hinges at the top or side, and sashes that slide up and down. Horizontal transoms and vertical mullions may divide the frame into sections or slender glazing bars divide a window into many smaller panes. The most common problem with wooden windows is rot, mostly around joints, on the sill or where putty has failed. Moisture can cause the wood to swell, making windows difficult to open or close, or the wood may shrink, letting in draughts. Sashes may rattle if they are a poor fit in the frame or may fail if their cords break and they become difficult or impossible to use.

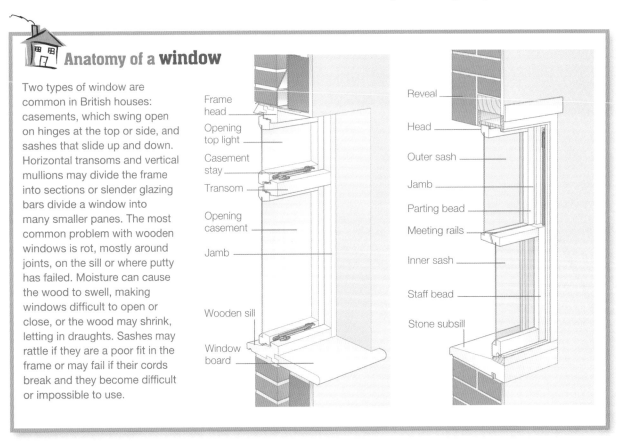

Frame head
Opening top light
Casement stay
Transom
Opening casement
Jamb
Wooden sill
Window board

Reveal
Head
Outer sash
Jamb
Parting bead
Meeting rails
Inner sash
Staff bead
Stone subsill

● **Look out for signs of rot** Rot will quickly ruin wooden frames and sills if it's allowed to take hold. Inspect your windows every spring, looking out for flaking or peeling paint that could indicate underlying rot or areas of obvious deterioration. Be especially vigilant in areas where water can collect, such as the undersides of windowsills and door frames.

Easy fixes

● **Replacing crumbly window putty** In addition to preventing draughts from coming in around pane edges, putty keeps water from soaking into the frames and rotting them. Replace cracked or brittle putty by carefully chipping it out with a chisel and spreading on a new coat. Knead the putty to soften it, then use your thumb to squeeze a bead into the frame (right) and a putty knife to smooth it out.

Putty keeps glass in and water out

How to repair rotten windowsills or frames

Rotted windowsills are easy to rebuild, using liquid hardener and a high-performance wood filler. Protect the rest of the wood with preservative before you repaint.

1 Strip away the paint and use a chisel to dig out the worst of the rot. Dry out wet timber with a hot-air gun.

2 Brush on generous amounts of wood hardener, until it stops soaking in. Leave it to dry and harden overnight.

3 Mix the wood filler a little at a time, to keep it workable – it will start to harden in about 5 minutes, or quicker in hot weather. Fill the damaged areas, building them up progressively if the damage is deep.

4 Sand the repair, filling small areas again if necessary. Drill 10mm holes, about 20mm deep and 50mm apart in the wood around the repair, push in wood preservative pellets and seal with the filler. Prime and paint the repair.

● **Giving the filler a grip** If you have to reconstruct a corner of a rotted sill with epoxy filler, put in a couple of screws first so that the filler will have something to hold on to.

● **Stop a rattling sash** A rattling sash window is a constant irritation, but one that's easy to fix. Sashes rattle when they are a loose fit in the frame. The simplest solution is to clamp them together when they are shut, using a fitch fastener (left). The cam-shaped clasp pulls the two sashes together as it closes – a Brighton catch is another option, which works by tightening a nut on a threaded bolt.

● If a fitch catch doesn't stop the rattle, you may need to adjust the staff beads that position the sashes. See opposite for how to remove them.

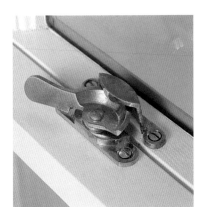
A fitch fastener gives a tight fit

● **Using carbon paper to figure out where a window sticks** Weather conditions and the natural settling of a house can lead to swelling and sticking in wooden casement windows, making them hard or even impossible to open or close. Pinpoint problem spots by slipping a piece of carbon paper between the window and the frame in different places around the perimeter, opening and closing the window as you go. Places where the window is binding will be revealed with carbon marks on the frame. Flatten the high spots on the window by sanding them down or by using a hand plane to remove a few shavings. Touch up the bare wood.

4 essential tips when shopping for replacement windows

Even well-cared-for wooden windows will probably one day need to be replaced, but your new windows should not only match the good looks of your originals, but help to pay for themselves by keeping your heating bills down. There are some important points to consider when buying new windows, as well as Building Regulations that must be followed.

1 MATCH THE ORIGINAL WINDOW, THEN GO ONE BETTER Changing the size of a window isn't an easy job, so replace existing windows with new units of the same configuration. Take the opportunity to upgrade single-glazed windows to double-glazed units and look into features that make them easier to clean (such as tilt-in sashes) and more secure.

2 GET TO GRIPS WITH THE BUILDING REGULATIONS All replacement windows must comply with Part L of the Building Regulations. This specifies minimum requirements for glazing (see point 3), stipulates that safety glass must be used in any windows that are within 800mm of the floor and that opening windows should not be made smaller (compromising fire safety) – and more. You'll be required to present

a certificate of approval when you sell your property to confirm that any windows fitted after April 2002 comply, so ensure that your installer is registered with FENSA (the Fenestration Self-Assessment Scheme) and can certify their own work, or apply to your local authority building control department before you start work, so that they can inspect and approve the work.

3 CHOOSE AN ENERGY-SAVING GLASS Double-glazed windows vary in efficiency according to their construction and the gas used in the gap, so choose the best you can afford, making sure that they comply with the Building Regulations and the minimum required energy rating or 'U' value (see page 34). The gap between the panes should be a minimum of 16mm and the glass should be 'low emissivity' to keep heat in when it's cold outside and out during hot weather.

4 WOOD OR PVC-U? Don't automatically go for the latest PVC-U double-glazing leaflet to drop through your door. PVC-U is often cheaper and lower maintenance than wood, but consider the age and style of your house and those around it: wooden windows that are sympathetic to your home can help to boost its value.

How to replace a broken sash cord

Sliding sash windows rely on counterweights for opening, closing and staying put. A cord attached to the sash runs over a pulley and down to a weight in a cavity inside the window frame. Over time the cords fray and break. You may need a helper to lift the sash in and out, but replacing the cord is a straightforward job. Always replace all four cords together – if one has broken, the others are probably wearing, too.

1 Use a chisel to prise off the staff beads on each side. Start in the middle to avoid damaging the mitre joints in the corners. Do the same to remove the parting bead between the two sashes once the lower sash is out of the way.

2 Ask a helper to lift out the lower sash as far as it can go. Tie a length of string to the upper part of any cord that is not broken, cut the cord and lower the weight to the bottom of the weight compartment. Do the same to remove the upper sash.

3 Prise off the pocket covers from the bottom of the weight compartment; they are usually just pushed in place. Lift out the weights, leaving their trails of string over the pulleys, ready for threading the new cords into place.

4 Where cords were broken, tie a small weight, such as a screw, to the end of a length of string and feed it over the pulley and down into the weight compartment. Untie the weights from the cords and remove the old cords from the channels in the sashes. Cut new cords to length: measure the height of the window from top to sill then add two-thirds again for fixing.

5 Tie one end of each new cord to a string coming over a pulley, working at the pulley end – start with the rear pulleys for the upper sash. Use the string to pull the cord through the weight compartment and out through the pocket. Tie the cord firmly to a weight and replace the weight in its pocket. Do this for each of the four weights, then push the pocket covers back into place.

6 Lift the upper sash onto the window sill and ask your helper to pull on one of its cords until the weight is just touching the pulley. Screw or nail the cord into the side of the sash, repeat for the other side then check that the window moves freely. Refit the parting beads, assemble and refit the lower, inner sash and replace the staff beads to finish the job.

PVC-U doors and windows

Windows fitted in the last 30 years are likely to have PVC-U frames – because they are cheap, secure and generally hailed as maintenance-free. The 'U' in the name stands for unplasticised and it's this that stops the PVC from being as flexible as raincoat material. But PVC-U is still more flexible than wood, so door and window frames need to be chunkier than their wooden counterparts to make them strong. The life-expectancy of your windows depends on the quality of the construction as much as the care you give them. Take note of the hinges and latches and look out for misting in the double-glazed units.

SAVE £400

How much it would cost to replace an entire window, rather than replacing a broken locking handle.

How to choose a supplier

Given that the quality of the product and its installation are crucial to the performance and longevity of your PVC-U windows, it's important to choose a supplier who is FENSA-registered (see page 108) and a member of the Glass and Glazing Federation (GGF). Members of the GGF who supply, fit or install replacement windows, double glazing, energy-efficient windows, doors and conservatories will have been trading for at least three years and vetted to ensure quality of service. You can search for a local contractor on these websites:
www.fensa.org.uk
www.ggf.org.uk

Care and maintenance

● **The question of cost and quality** The best-quality PVC-U window and door frames are stiffened internally with steel or aluminium alloy inserts. Cheaper ones may have reinforcement only up the sides where they are fixed to the brickwork and around latches and hinges. The cheapest may have no reinforcement at all, with hinges and catches simply screwed into the plastic and easily pulled out. The best doors will have a multi-locking system, where turning the key operates bolts at multiple points along the edge of the door.

● **Replacing window hardware** Cheap PVC-U windows are usually supplied with cheap hinges and latches – when they break, replacements can be hard to find in DIY stores and builders' merchants. Search online for specialist suppliers of window hardware or contact the original supplier of the windows. If you can get them, replacements are usually easy to fit, requiring no more than a few screws to fix them in place.

● **Internal misting** A big problem with all double glazing is misting between the two panes of glass. It's impossible to make the seal between the two panes completely watertight, so over time a small amount of water vapour will seep in. Most sealed double-glazed units incorporate a moisture-absorbing material within the spacer bars around the edges, and, in a properly made and installed window, this should keep the glass clear for at least 20 years. Poor fitting can damage the seals and, if this happens, you'll have no choice but to replace the unit. Make sure that the replacement is fitted according to British Standard BS 6262, which specifies a clear 5mm gap around all the edges of the glass, and drainage channels to prevent water being trapped in contact with the edge seals.

● **Spot the identity code** Look at the metal bead around the visible edge of a double-glazed unit and you should see a reference code. This will help you to identify the manufacturer of the window, and may prove to be a cheaper and easier source of replacement parts than starting afresh with a new window company, even if the window's guarantee has expired.

Window security

Windows are the main entry points for burglars, often because they are left unlocked or even open. Even if a burglar smashes the glass, it's impossible to open the window if it's securely locked, either by securing the window to the frame or preventing the handles being operated. These window locks are all easy to fit. Choose the appropriate option for your windows and you could save yourself not just money, but also the upset and inconvenience of a break-in.

Care and maintenance

● **Check locks regularly** It's no good having locks if they don't work – and it could even be dangerous if you cannot open a window to escape. Go round all your windows every six months and operate the keys to make sure that they all turn easily and lock securely. Lubricate stiff locks with a little spray lubricant, such as WD-40.

● **Keep keys to hand** Locking your windows will keep out intruders, but it will also keep you securely inside. Always keep keys close to the window they operate, but not where they can be reached through an open window. Make sure everyone in the house knows where they are and how to use them so that they can escape quickly and safely in the event of a fire.

SAVE 5%

Potential saving on your contents insurance if you fit key-operated, metal window locks to all accessible windows, as well as five-lever mortice deadlocks to external doors.

Easy fixes

● **Fit window restrictors for ventilation and safety** Locking your windows doesn't always have to mean locking them closed. Window restrictors fit into the hinged edge of a casement window and prevent it from being opened more than around 100mm – wide enough to let in air, but not wide enough for a child to fall out or an intruder to clamber in.
● Another option is a locking nightvent casement handle – available in many different styles to match your existing window hardware and replace the catch on a casement window. The handle engages and locks with a plate on the frame, just like a conventional locking handle (see page 112), but has a second notch in it to lock the window slightly ajar.

Locks need to turn freely

● **Fitting window locks** Most PVC-U windows are supplied with locking handles, but it's easy to fit locks to existing windows, whatever their style.
● For casement windows, surface-mounted locks fix the opening window securely to its frame. They are supplied with screws for fixing and only require careful measuring to make sure the two parts align. For large windows, fit two locks on each frame – one at the top and the other at the bottom – to reduce the risk of the window being forced.
● Sash window locks usually work by locking the sashes to one another and may be surface-mounted or drilled into the frame. With slim frames, take care not to crack the glass while you're drilling or screwing.

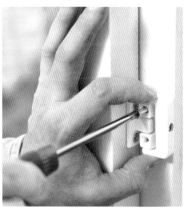
Check the fit before screwing home

Simple solutions for locking windows

Choose the right sort of lock to suit your existing window hardware and the type of windows you have. Most of the surface-mounted locks are suitable for wooden or metal windows: use wood screws for fixing to wooden windows and self-tapping screws for metal frames.

Casement windows

SWING BAR LOCK
A C-shaped bar fits to the opening window and swings over a plate mounted on the frame. A mechanical key screws down a locking bar to prevent the lock from opening.

CAM LOCK
When the two parts of the lock are aligned, a key turns a rotating shaft (or cam) that locks into the other half of the lock, fixing the two parts together.

MORTISE RACK BOLT
These common door locks are also suitable for window frames, as long as they are wide enough to accomodate the bolt – at least 35mm thick. The bolt is mortised into the opening window and a key turns the bolt into the frame.

LOCKING HANDLE
When locked, the handle cannot be moved without the key. Buy right or left-handed versions, depending on which way your window opens. Some models allow you to lock the window ajar for ventilation (see page 156).

STAY LOCK
Some stay locks come with handles and pegs, others just require you to replace your existing pegs with special threaded ones. A key-operated nut screws onto the thread to lock the stay in place. Depending on where you position the peg you may be able to lock the window open. Ventilation locks work in a similar way, with the nut and peg tightening on a short sliding bar that allows the window to be locked open.

Sash windows

SASH STOP
This simple solution stops the lower sash from sliding up. A locking nut screws into a threaded plate on the upper sash and creates a physical barrier to stop the window moving. Depending on where you position the plate, you can allow the window to open a little for ventilation. The window cannot be fully opened without completely removing the nut.

SASH WINDOW PRESS LOCK
A two-part lock that fits to the surface of the meeting rails and locks them together, and works only when the windows are fully closed. It can be locked by pushing the button, but not opened without the key.

DUAL SCREW LOCK
A long, key-operated screw fits through a barrel in the top rail of the inner sash and into a threaded sleeve in the bottom rail of the outer sash. The screw can only be inserted when the window is closed and must be fully removed to open it.

Doors

Constant use, banging and swinging: no matter what your doors are made of, what they look like or where they are, they probably see more use than any other moving part in the house. Hinges, handles, latches and locks are all prone to failure with frequent use, but most problems are easy to fix in order to make your doors swing freely and close effortlessly once more. Follow these tips to keep your doors weathertight, secure and squeak-free.

Care and maintenance

SAVE £400
What it would cost to replace an exterior, solid wood door that has deteriorated beyond repair.

● **Wash your exterior doors** Facing the elements and daily household traffic, the outside surfaces of entry doors can pick up dust and grime that not only dulls their appearance but also corrodes their hardware and finish. That's why you need to clean your door every few months.

● First, give the door a thorough dry wipe-down to remove any surface dust then follow with a cleaning solution. For stained wooden doors, use a wood oil soap; for painted finishes and PVC-U doors, use a good squirt of washing-up liquid in a bucket of warm water. Using a natural sponge, scrub the door in small circular motions, working from the bottom up. Rinse the sponge often as you work and make a new batch of cleanser if needed to avoid smearing the door with grubby cleaning water.

● **Polish the furniture** Once the door is clean and dry, give its door furniture some attention. Much modern brassware for doors – handles, knockers, letterboxes, keyholes and other items – is lacquered to help it to keep its shine. Abrasive metal cleaners will strip off this protective layer, so start by cleaning with a soft cloth and soapy water, drying and buffing the brass to a shine.

● If the brass is old or you know that it is not lacquered, you can use a metal polish. Protect surfaces around the pieces you are cleaning with cling film secured with masking tape, to avoid smearing the paste on the door.

● Clean glass or ceramic doorknobs with a soft cloth dampened with methylated spirits.

● **Tighten a loose doorknob** Do you have a doorknob that's wobbly? Simply loosen the grub screws holding the knobs in place on either side of the door and centre the spindle on which they turn so that it extends equally on both sides of the door. Then reposition the knobs and adjust the grub screws for a snug but not binding fit.

● **Lubricate locks with graphite** Never use an oil-based lubricant on locks; it can attract dust and grime. Instead, give locks an occasional blast of powdered graphite, a dry lubricant that comes in a squeeze bottle for easy application. It's sold at hardware and DIY stores and can also be applied to stiff latches and hinges.

smart idea
If you don't have any powdered graphite on hand (see left), just scrape off some pencil lead with a knife, collecting it on a sheet of paper. To get the resulting powder into the lock, rub it onto a key and insert it in the lock a couple of times.

A squirt of oil fixes a squeaky hinge

● **Silence hinges with a little oil** Keep hardworking hinges from squeaking with a touch of light machine oil such as 3-IN-ONE. An aerosol lubricant is a good choice for this job, as the straw attachment for the spray nozzle makes it easy to direct the lubricant to the right spot.

● To apply, prise up the hinge pin slightly by tapping a screwdriver with a hammer and aim a few drops or squirts of oil onto the shaft just above the hinge's upper barrel. Have a towel ready to catch any drips before they stain carpet or floors, then swing the door back and forth a few times to distribute the oil over the hinge mechanism.

● **Keep exterior doors weathertight** Sealing your exterior doors will help to keep the weather out and the heat in. Check all your external doors each year before the cold, damp weather arrives and inspect the condition of their weather strips and draughtproofing.

● Make sure draught excluders around the frame's top and sides are still making a good seal with the door. Just run your hand around the edges of the door when it's closed to feel for any draughts coming through gaps. Many different draught-proofing materials and kits are available for DIY installation. See pages 156-159 for more information.

● Install a brush seal along the door's bottom edge to stop moisture blowing in with the draught. A brush seal has a metal flange with a rubber strip that acts as a seal against the threshold when the door is closed.

● Threshold weather stripping is another easy-to-fit option and may be less obtrusive than a brush seal. A threshold strip closes a gap under a door with a rubber gasket installed in the threshold.

● A two-part excluder gives a snug seal, with a weather bar attached to the threshold and a deflector to the bottom of the door.

How to get a binding door moving smoothly

Changes in humidity and the natural shifting of your house may leave you with a swollen, sticking door, but you can often fix it using this trial-and-error approach. Once the door is closing smoothly, prime and repaint any bare wood.

1 Try tightening all hinge screws. Fix any screw holes that are stripped as described in 'Fixing loose hinges' on page 116.

2 If that doesn't solve the problem, hold a block of wood against the non-hinged side of the door frame and hit it with a hammer to see if that widens the opening enough to free the door.

3 If the door still binds, close it and examine it closely to find the sticking points along its edges – there should be a gap wide enough to slot in a 50 pence piece all round.

4 Sand down the problem areas, using first coarse, then fine sandpaper. If you need to remove more than 2mm of wood, you may find it easier to use a small block plane (right). Use two wedges to hold the door firmly while you work.

Easy fixes

● **Silencing rattling doors** If a door rattles, it's because it no longer fits snugly against the doorstop, the strip of wood on the frame that the door hits when it closes. An easy way to adjust the fit is to remove the strike plate – the catch on the frame that the latch goes into when it closes – and use pliers to slightly bend out its tongue-like flange, so that it will hold the door more tightly against the doorstop.

Anatomy of a **door**

In older homes, most doors are panelled (below) – they have a timber frame around the edges with four or six inset timber panels. Exterior doors are usually thicker (44mm) than internal doors (35mm) and may be made from hardwood rather than soft, but the construction is the same. On both interior and exterior doors, some or all of the panels may be glazed.

● Newer doors may look like solid timber panelled doors but are often hollow – internal ones may even be made from hardboard, making them light to hang and to use, but not very strong. Exterior 'composite' doors, such as PVC-U (see page 110) and GRP (glass-reinforced plastic), are often made in a traditional style.

● A typical external door is fitted to its surrounding frame with three hinges – two is usually enough for a lighter interior door. The position of the hinges can be adjusted to make a door swing or close better.

● Internal door frames have three sides and are screwed into the surrounding masonry or timber studs. Decorative architrave finishes the joints between frame and wall, and a stop bead all round provides an edge for the door to close against. Architrave can open up at the corners as a house moves (see page 57), and as the frame or door wood expands or contracts over time the stop bead may need repositioning to cure a rattle or a door that won't close.

● An external frame includes a threshold at the bottom, which projects from the frame and acts like a windowsill to deflect rainwater away from the building. A groove on the underside of the threshold (the drip groove) prevents water from collecting underneath, and a vertical 'check groove' in each jamb or side piece allows water that gets between the door and frame to drain away. A weather bar, running along the threshold, fits into a rebate cut in the bottom edge of the door and prevents rain from being blown inside.

Panel grooved into frame

Rail

Moulding

Muntin

Stile

Dowels

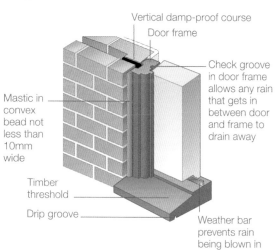

Vertical damp-proof course

Door frame

Check groove in door frame allows any rain that gets in between door and frame to drain away

Mastic in convex bead not less than 10mm wide

Timber threshold

Drip groove

Weather bar prevents rain being blown in

Use card to avoid a 'too tight' fit

Card strips will fine-tune hinges

● **More tricks for stopping rattles** If adjusting the strike plate doesn't stop a door rattling, try moving the stop bead so that it fits more tightly against the door. To do this, use a sharp trimming knife to free the stop from surrounding paint along both of its sides, then use a hammer with a wood block to tap the stop about 2mm so that it will be closer to the door. Close the door to test the fit, trapping a piece of card between the door and the stop (left) to create the necessary slight clearance: the door should hit the stop and the latch at the same time. If the positioning is right, hammer in some panel pins to secure the stop in its new position.

● **Curing a self-closing door** If a door swings shut and you don't want it to, it could be because its frame is out of plumb, either due to faulty installation or the natural settling of your house over time. An easy way to correct the problem is to increase resistance at the hinges so that the door moves less freely. Remove the hinge pins, which run down through the interlocking sections of the hinge, and hit them with a hammer to bend them slightly so that they fit more snugly into their hinge holes.

● **Fixing a hard-to-close door** Do you have to give one particular door an extra shove to get it to close all the way? It's likely that the door is either warped or has bound hinges – meaning that they are completely closed before the door hits the stop.
  ● If the door is warped, the best solution is to replace it. Close the door and check to make sure it's hitting all the stops along the top and sides. If it's warped, it will be obvious where it swings away from the frame.
  ● If the door isn't warped, try adjusting the hinges. Cut strips of thin cardboard the same length as the hinges and half their width. Put a wedge under the door to support it, then unscrew the hinges from the jamb, one at a time, and place a strip of cardboard in each hinge mortise against the barrel side of the hinge (left). Packing out this side of the hinge will give the door a little more movement – experiment with the thickness and numbers of strips needed to solve the closing problem.

● **Stop wood doors swelling and sticking** Wooden doors can be magnets for moisture, which causes them to swell and stick. If you plane a swollen door to fit in winter, you could be left with a draughty gap when the door shrinks again in better weather. A better solution is to keep moisture at bay by making sure that both the top and bottom edges of a door are painted or varnished to properly seal the end grain. Give paint strength and staying power with an undercoat of primer.

● **Fixing loose hinges** If some of a hinge's screw holes have become stripped, the screws just spin when you turn them. You have two choices:
  ● Replace the screws with ones that are the same size but about an inch longer, so that they will penetrate into solid wood in the framing.
  ● Remove the screws, and plug the holes with wooden toothpicks that have been dipped in wood glue. When the glue has dried, shave away the protruding toothpick ends with a trimming knife. Then drill new pilot holes, and drive the screws back into place through the hinge plate.

● **Filing door latches** If a door won't latch properly because the strike plate isn't aligned with the bolt, a little filing could do the trick. Watch closely how the latch bolt hits the strike plate on the frame when the door closes and look for wear marks left by the bolt to indicate where to file.
● If the alignment has shifted after adjusting the hinges, signs of wear won't help. Smear shoe polish on the end of the bolt or the latch instead, then close the door and operate the lock. The polish will leave a mark on the strike plate, showing you how far out of alignment the latch is.
● Carefully file the opening in the strike plate (right) to enlarge the hole a little at a time until the bolt fits in. You can also use your file to slightly round the edges of the bolt itself.

● **Replacing strike plates** If a door won't latch because the old plate and jamb are worn or damaged, buy a slightly larger strike plate and install it in place of the old one. You'll have to slightly chisel the mortise – the slot on the jamb that the plate fits into – to enlarge it.

● **Raising the strike plate** If a door won't latch because the bolt doesn't reach all the way to the strike plate, make the strike plate protrude further by putting one or more layers of thin cardboard between it and the door jamb. Remove the strike plate and use it as a template to mark cut lines on the cardboard where the holes need to be.

● **What to do when you need a new 'old' door** Sometimes a poorly fitting door cannot be adjusted to work and you simply need to replace it. In most cases, doors come in a small number of common sizes, making it quite easy to find a replacement to fit. Internal doors are normally 1,981mm or 2,032mm high, in standard widths of 686, 762, 813 and 838mm. External doors are usually 1,981mm high and 762mm or 838mm wide – all metric equivalents of the traditional imperial sizes.
● If you cannot match the style of an old door in the shops, architectural salvage yards are rich hunting grounds and usually have a wide selection of doors in the standard sizes.

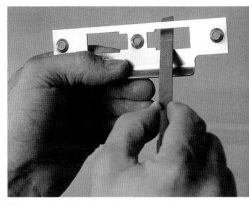

File a strike plate for a better match

smart idea

The bottom edge of an outside door should be painted to keep out moisture, but it's a tricky job to do. Use a scrap of carpet as your brush and suddenly it's easy. Apply paint to the pile side of the carpet, slide it under the open door and pull it back and forth for a smooth and easy coating.

Penetrating oil spray: **a lock's best friend**

GET A STUBBORN LOCK TURNING
If a lock is difficult to turn, first try a squirt of penetrating oil spray, such as WD-40, to clean and lubricate the mechanism. Have a cloth in hand to catch any drips. If this doesn't make the lock turn freely, the problem may be a poorly cut key. Have a new one made from a functional original – never have a key cut from a key that isn't original or small imperfections can be magnified.

REMOVE A TRAPPED KEY
It's not uncommon for older locks to trap keys as a result of dried-out, misaligned pins. Get your key out by giving the lock a dose of WD-40 or other penetrating oil spray and then rotating and jiggling the key. The key should come right out, but if it doesn't, pinch with one hand as your other fingertips touch the lock for leverage, and slowly wriggle it loose.

OPEN A FROZEN LOCK
If a lock freezes in wintry weather, you can loosen it by spraying a little of the lubricant into its mechanism – avoid oil-based lubricants as they will only make matters worse. Another way to thaw things out is by carefully preheating your key with a match before inserting it in the lock.

NO MATTER HOW SOLID THE DOOR, IT'S ONLY AS STRONG AS THE METAL THAT SECURES IT.

8 quick remedies to make your front door more secure

No matter how solid your door, it's ultimately only as strong as the metal that holds it in place. Here are a few simple hardware upgrades to consider if you want to increase your home's security.

1 HEAVY-DUTY MORTISE DEADLOCK A mortise deadlock is a low-cost, high-value addition to your security system. The lock's bolt closes into a plate recessed (or mortised) into the doorframe, making a secure fixing. A deadlock can only be opened with a key

and varieties include double-cylinder deadbolts, which are keyed on both sides, and single-cylinder deadbolts, which can only be opened from one side. Use only locks manufactured to British Standard BS 3621 and look for a mortise lock with a minimum of five levers for good security. If your front door only has a cylinder lock, make a mortise deadlock your first addition.

2 STRIKE BOX A strike box toughens up the entrance to your home and deters intruders by replacing existing strike plates with a structure that includes a metal pocket within the mortise in the frame, oversized plates and a solid connection into the wall stud behind the doorjamb with extra-long screws. To accommodate this addition, you'll need to enlarge both the hole chiselled into the jamb and the cover plate recess.

3 REINFORCEMENT PLATE A three-sided, wraparound metal reinforcement plate adds an extra layer of security by encasing a section of the door itself around its deadbolt. This will extend the door's edge by the thickness of the metal, so you may need to deepen the hinge mortises on the other side of the door to prevent catching and sticking.

4 LONDON BAR Chiselling away wood to fit a mortise lock into a door also weakens the basic structure of the door, making it susceptible to being kicked in from outside. A London bar is a steel strip that runs down the inside of the door frame, from top to bottom, spreading the impact of anyone trying to force entry and strengthening the door's hold.

5 RACK BOLTS An additional rack bolt at the top and bottom of an external door will also help to prevent forcing. The bolts are mortised into the opening edge of the door and open into holes recessed in the frame. They can be operated with a standard fluted-edged key or fitted with thumbturn knobs screwed permanently in place. These are an excellent option for locking the door at night when the house is occupied, as they are secure from the outside but easy to open without a key if you need to escape from a fire.

6 HINGE BOLTS To strengthen the hinged edge of the door, fit hinge bolts. These protrude from the edge of the door and close into steel keep plates recessed within the frame.

7 RE-KEY THE LOCK Changing the entry locks when you first move into a house is a good idea. Re-keying kits are available for most lock brands and allow you to change the key without replacing the entire lock for each door. The kits also allow up to six locks to be re-keyed for the same key, to minimise the number of keys you have for the house.

8 A WIDE-ANGLE PEEPHOLE This easy-to-install safety accessory is designed to fit any standard-thickness external door and avoids you having to open the door to unwanted callers.

Sliding doors

A slender frame, space-saving design and expansive glasswork are the secrets to the enduring popularity of sliding doors. They let in ample light and provide a picture view of the garden. State-of-the-art, concertina doors are like drawing back an entire wall, but less expensive, more traditional designs are also available, and include energy-conscious glass and well-insulated frames. If you make sure your doors are well secured against intruders, the most important task in keeping sliding doors moving smoothly is maintaining the mechanism.

SAVE £300

How much it would cost to buy a new 2m wide pair of sliding doors instead of a replacement door gear set.

Care and maintenance

● **Wipe metal frames with window cleaner** Many patio door frames are made of aluminium because it's affordable, rust-resistant and easy to maintain. They are also usually finished with a tough protective coating, so all that's needed to maintain their good looks is an occasional wipe-down. Whenever you have a bottle of window cleaner in your hand to clean the door's glass, use it on the frame as well. A squirt of all-purpose household cleaner in some warm water will also keep them clean.

● **Bottom rollers are best for strength** Sliding doors are fixed to brackets with rollers that move along the tracks. Lightweight internal sliding doors, such as for dividing rooms or for use in wardrobes, are usually hung from an upper track with top rollers and they work in a similar way to curtains. But this mechanism isn't usually strong enough for heavy, large, glazed patio doors, and they normally have their rollers at the bottom. If you're buying replacement sliding doors, look for high-quality, bottom-rolling options for low maintenance and long life.

● **Make the tracks run smoothly with wax** After you finish cleaning a patio door's bottom track, run the stub of a candle along the track in long, even strokes to help the doors to run smoothly.

● **Make sure the latch catches securely** From time to time, make a point of checking the latch on your doors. Sliding doors often move out of alignment with the mount on the frame, so that you need to lift or jiggle the door slightly to lock it. Slide the doors closed, while looking carefully at the latch. If it doesn't line up with the mount, loosen the screws slightly and realign the latch – there should be a little room for movement.

● **Choose a combination construction** Many homeowners prefer the natural look and feel of wood, but not the regular maintenance required to keep external woodwork up to scratch. Some of the latest sliding doors offer a combination of beauty and durability, with a wooden face on the internal side of the doors and a vinyl or aluminium cladding to shrug off the weather on the outside.

USE WAX FOR SMOOTH RUNNING.

● **Treat the track with alcohol** Dirt and grime are constantly settling in a patio door's bottom track, some brought in every time a person walks over the threshold, some just everyday house dust. When you vacuum the floor near the track, give it a once-over using a soft-brush attachment on the hose. Once a month, clean the track with a soft cloth dampened with methylated spirits to clean off any grease.

Easy fixes

● **Getting your door back on track** The heavy use that patio doors get in high-traffic areas can lead to occasional problems with sticking or juddery sliding. If this starts to happen with your doors, look carefully at the gaps along their top and bottom edges. If they are not uniform you need to adjust the rollers. Find the roller adjustment screws along the edge of the door's bottom rail, remove the button-size covers and turn the screws anticlockwise to lower the door in its track, or clockwise to raise it. Tweak the adjustment until the doors are level and running smoothly.

● **Don't ignore obvious obstacles** If your sliding doors stop sliding freely, don't panic and don't even reach straight for the screwdriver to make roller adjustments. Check the track first. The most likely cause is a pebble or other small object lodged in the roller track. Another common problem is a dent in the track, which can usually be straightened out carefully with a pair of pliers.

● **'Lock' your doors with a stick** Patio doors may be heavy, but burglars know how to exploit their weak points. Stop the doors from sliding open when you don't want them to by placing a cut-to-fit dowel in the lower track as an improvised lock. Sliding door latches are not difficult for an intruder to break, but this simple trick will prevent the door from being slid open and the intruder from gaining access.

● **A pin stops doors from sliding** A neater locking solution than the dowel described above, and a simple DIY installation, is to fit a sliding pin to fix the two doors together and prevent either one from being slid open. An unobtrusive bracket fits to the top corner of the inner sliding door, and when you want to lock it you simply slide a sturdy metal pin through the bracket and into a hole drilled in the outer door.

● **Get help to lift doors out** If you need to repair or replace the rollers or track in sliding doors, you'll have to start by removing the doors themselves. Even modestly sized glazed doors are really heavy, so make sure you have some help. How the doors come out depends on how they are hung, but to remove most bottom-roller doors you'll need to retract or wind the rollers fully into the door by turning their adjustment screws anticlockwise. This drops the door enough to lean into the room and clear the upper track. You may need to remove a retaining strip along the top edge of the door first – make sure your helper holds the door steady while you do this, then carefully lift the door out of the bottom track together.

CLEAN THE SLIDING TRACK WITH METHYLATED SPIRITS.

WASH AND WAX YOUR
GARAGE DOOR LIKE YOUR CAR
AND EXTEND ITS LIFE.

Garage doors

Your garage door is often one of the first things a visitor sees when approaching your house. Whatever the style and construction, it plays an important role in keeping your possessions secure, even more so if the garage has a connecting door with the main house, so it's vital to maintain it well and to keep it looking good, opening smoothly and locking securely.

Care and maintenance

● **Wash and wax your door** When you clean you car, give the garage door a once-over at the same time. By protecting its surfaces from dirt – and corrosion, if it's metal – you can extend a garage door's life. Dust the door both inside and outside, then wipe it down with a mild household detergent diluted in water. Spray lightly with a hose to rinse. If the door is metal with an enamel finish, apply car wax on the exterior after washing to seal out damaging grime and moisture.

● **Care for traditional wooden doors** Victorian terraces and most streets of 1930s semi-detached houses were built without garages, but with family cars came family houses with garages. Until the 1970s, most garage doors were made of wood, fitted in pairs and hinged down the sides like gates. If your garage still has wooden doors, protect the vulnerable bottom section from water that splashes up when it rains or moisture that can be sucked up from standing water by the wood itself. Keep the paintwork in good condition (see page 103 for tips on painting external wood), making sure that the door's bottom and side edges are painted, then run a bead of sealant along the joint where the bottom horizontal rail meets the panels, if there is one, to prevent water from seeping in when it runs down the door.

● **Test an automatic door's opener** If you have an automatic opening door, test its auto-reverse safety feature every month. Raise the door, place a piece of 50mm x 100mm timber flat on the ground in the door's path, and press the remote-control switch to close the door. The door should instantly reverse as it touches the wood. If it doesn't, it might not stop for a person or vehicle in the way, either. Adjust its sensitivity, following the guidelines in your owner's manual.

● **Lubricate all moving parts** You should oil all moving parts on a garage door every year. They are subjected to more wear from the weather than most other doors in the house and this light, but regular maintenance will help to keep them working smoothly. Apply lightweight oil such as 3-IN-ONE to roller and hinge pivots and a cleaner-lubricant, such as

SAVE £400

What you would have to pay to replace a single, up-and-over garage door with a new one.

take care!

An up-and-over garage door's weight is counterbalanced by either a torsion spring mounted on the header above the door or a pair of side-mounted extension springs above the roller tracks. These tightly coiled springs can cause injury if they snap or come loose. If they need adjustment or replacement, call a garage door installer. Always have both springs in a pair replaced if one fails. Also call a professional if the lift cables, attached to the bottom bracket, are frayed and need to be replaced.

Choosing garage doors

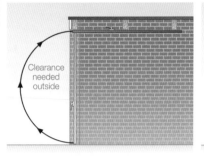

Retractable door

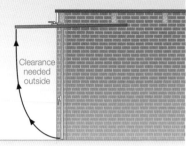

Canopy door

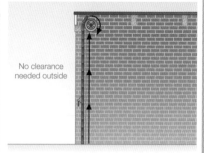

Roller door

Most new garage doors are an up-and-over design, sliding up into the roof of the garage with a system of tracks, springs, rollers or hinges when open, rather than swinging outwards on conventional hinges. The different designs need varying amounts of clearance in front of the garage and space inside for the open door.

RETRACTABLE DOOR A system of pivots and rails mounted in the roof of the garage enable this type of door to be tucked out of sight when open, but it requires the greatest clearance space outside.

CANOPY DOOR A section of the door overhangs the opening – like a canopy – when it is open. The required clearance in front of the garage is less than for a retractable door and the door and mechanism take up less space inside, too.

ROLLER DOOR Roller doors are the most compact option. They need no space at all for opening and their slim sections roll around a metal pole into a small boxed compartment just inside the roof – or even on the outside of the front of the garage if space inside is really limited. Sectional doors have wider panels, so do not roll up, but use the same mechanism and retract into the roof on tracks when open. Roller and sectional doors can be used with automatic opening systems to make the most secure garage door options. These doors fit behind rather than in the opening, so they make a good choice if the door space is an unusual shape or size.

smart idea

When working on an automatic garage door, always open it and disconnect it from its power source before you start. Then place G-cramps or self-locking wrenches on the track above and below one of the door's rollers to lock the door in place. This is much safer than propping the door open.

WD-40, to any springs. Don't overdo it, though – too much oil will collect dirt. Clean tracks that the opening mechanism runs on by wiping them with a cloth dampened with oil.

● **Be security savvy** Traditional, side-hung garage doors are often fitted using gate hinges, screwed to the outside of the doors. Even with a combination of bolts and locks securing the doors from the inside, these kinds of doors are vulnerable to intruders, as the hinges can simply be unscrewed to release the doors. Consider replacing the hinges with conventional butt hinges fitted within the frame. You'll need at least three heavy-duty hinges for each door to carry the weight, but these are much harder for an intruder to break through.

● Whatever style of garage door you have, if your garage has a connecting door with the main house, it makes an attractive entry point for a burglar. Make sure your garage is as secure as you can make it, by fitting high-quality locks and consider the options for additional locks on the frame, or a bar that locks to the ground in front of the door to prevent it from being opened.

● Next, take a look at the connecting, internal door. Do what you can to make this as secure as your front door. At the very least, fit deadbolts at the top and bottom that can only be opened from inside the house and that will protect the door against someone trying to force it.

● **Banish dirt and draughts** Leaves and dirt often blow in beneath up-and-over style garage doors, but it's easy to keep them out. Screw a length of proprietary, garage-door draught excluder (right) along the door's bottom edge. Make sure that the weatherstrip makes a good seal with the driveway beneath it, but is not so tight that it makes the door difficult to open. Drill evenly spaced holes through the metal edging and the door and screw it into place. Use self-tapping screws on metal doors.

● **Keep water away** Water splashing on the bottom of your garage door will eventually cause problems: rust on a metal door or peeling paint and rot on a wooden one. Make sure that your gutters keep water away from the door and that the surrounding landscape doesn't drain water onto the drive in front of the door. Clear away snow before it melts and refreezes, sticking the door to the driveway.

● **Send sports players to the park** To a child, a garage door makes a perfect makeshift goal or a bouncing board for some solitary tennis practice and it's easy to see why. But balls can easily dent a metal door, and repeated banging can cause any garage door's parts to loosen or become misaligned, so banish ball sports to the park or back garden.

Seal the garage against the weather

Easy fixes

● **Touch up peeling paint** Cracked and peeling paintwork not only looks shabby, it exposes the wood or metal beneath to the elements. Sand the affected areas until smooth, then apply a mildew-resistant primer and two finish coats of paint. On a rusty metal door, sand down to bare metal using emery cloth, treat the rust with a rust-repair product and then use a special metal primer before repainting the door.

● **Quieten the rattling** Loose components are usually the culprits behind noisy garage doors. Check and tighten the bolts on loose hinges and roller mounts and keep moving parts well lubricated to avoid a clanking door.

FRESH PAINT LOOKS GOOD AND PROTECTS.

● **When automatic openers stay shut** If your garage door's automatic opener fails, check the obvious possible causes first: a flat battery in the remote control, the plug disconnected or loss of power to the motor unit because the power supply has tripped off a circuit breaker. If none of these is the problem, operate the door manually, using the crank handle to turn the roller. Check the rollers and tracks for dents, blockages or other defects, then check the door itself for dents or damage that might be stopping it rolling freely. Finally, take the cover off the motor, operate the remote control and see whether or not the motor is trying to work, to try to locate the fault.

Ladder safety

Many repair and maintenance tasks are within the reach of a competent DIY-er working with care and a sturdy ladder. Clearing gutters, painting first-storey woodwork and repairing fascia boards or bargeboards at the eaves are all jobs that would otherwise require a scaffold tower or a professional. Make sure you have the right equipment and follow these simple pieces of advice and you can save yourself hundreds of pounds. If your roof is more than two storeys high, or steeper than average, always call in a professional, who will use a safety harness and other protective gear.

A safe ladder

SAVE £75

Average cost of a week's hire for a scaffold tower, rather than using your own ladder to get to a high-level repair.

● **Buy a strong model** Make sure your ladder can handle your weight and the weight of the tools and materials you'll be carrying – all ladders are rated for load capacity. Look out for integral safety stabiliser bars and extra-large feet, and even anti-slip rungs for added safety.

● **Does it wobble?** If you haven't used your ladder in a while, inspect it for loose rungs, cracks, dents, rot or rust. If a wood ladder feels shaky, tighten the nuts on the reinforcing rods. On an extension ladder, make sure that the safety feet pivot freely, that the sliding sections move easily and lock solidly into place, and that the pull rope, if there is one, is not frayed. Check a stepladder for loose hinges.

Ladder set-up

smart idea

If you plan to use a ladder to access your roof, make sure that the weather forecast for that day is good. Work on a dry, mild, windless day after the dew evaporates. Severe heat and cold, wet and icy surfaces, and gusty winds are all extremely hazardous when you're working at height.

● **Keep your ladder from sinking** If the ground is wet or muddy, set your ladder's feet on a base stabiliser (left). This also has a high-friction base to stop the ladder from slipping on hard surfaces. You can make your own stabiliser with a wide board or a piece of plywood staked into the ground. Nail battens to the board along three edges to stop the ladder from moving.

● **Check your ladder's angle** To make sure you've got your ladder at the correct angle, stand straight with your toes at the foot of the ladder. From that position, you should be able to stretch out your arms and rest your hands on the rungs at your shoulder height.

DON'T GO UP ON THE ROOF UNLESS THE WEATHER FORECAST IS GOOD.

● **Put socks on the ladder's tips** Before leaning a ladder against a fascia board, timber cladding or other surface that might be damaged, slip a couple of old thick socks over each top end to cushion it. Tie them in place with string. You can also use old rags or work gloves, or you can buy rubber covers that fit over the ends.

● **Get dressed for safety** Thick-soled shoes with a good grip are essential for working on ladders. Never wear slip-on shoes or sandals. If you're going to be standing on one rung for a long time, even thick-soled shoes will become uncomfortable: consider fitting a hook-on platform for the duration of the job. Don't forget a safety helmet to protect your head.

● **Take your ladder beyond the working point** Never stand on the top few rungs of a ladder to work, as you'll not have the sides to hold on to to steady yourself. Extend the ladder beyond the place where you'll be working and never stand on the top of a step ladder.

● **Is a window in the way?** If a job calls for you to rest the top of your ladder on a window, buy a U-shaped stabiliser bar that attaches to the top of the ladder to span windows, or improvise by lashing a length of timber at least 75mm x 50mm across the top of the ladder to span the window and hold the ladder safely away from the glass.

● **Be wary of opening doors** When putting a ladder in front of a door, lock and brace the door so that no one can unknowingly fling it open, toppling the ladder (and you). Warn other people in your household where and when you'll be working from such heights.

● **Avoid being shocked by power lines** When you are setting up or moving a ladder and when working on it, be careful to stay away from power lines. A metal or wet wood ladder is especially hazardous.

● **Do the bounce check** Before you start work, climb three rungs up, jump up and down and lean out from side to side to check that the ladder is solid and will not settle – reposition it if necessary.

On the ladder

● **Use a pull-up bucket** Don't carry your tools and materials in your hands while climbing a ladder. Instead put them in a bucket with a long rope (left) and haul them up once you're safely on the roof or at your working height on the ladder. Or carry them in a tool belt secured around your waist, with the tools evenly distributed.

● **Remember the 'three points of contact' rule** Use both hands to steady yourself as you climb, holding the rungs, not the sides of the ladder. When working, keep your weight centred between the side rails and always maintain three points of contact with the ladder – either two hands and a foot or two feet and a hand.

smart idea

Never store a ladder outside or in an unlocked garage. A burglar may use it to reach an unlocked window that would otherwise be out of reach. If you have to leave a ladder out, chain it securely to a tree or other immovable object.

A bucket makes a good carrier

Pitched roofs

A sloping tiled roof is the most common construction style, whether your house is four years old or four hundred. The covering may be slates or tiles and the shape may be a simple up and down slope or a more elaborate combination of pitches, valleys and hips, but the maintenance tasks and repairs have one common theme: to keep the covering watertight.

Working safely

● **Safety first** Never consider climbing up onto a pitched roof unless you have a scaffolding access tower installed. The one exception is if you have a Victorian house with a valley roof or 'butterfly' roof, which can be safely accessed via a loft hatch or roof window from within the building. Even with a scaffold tower, never attempt to work on your roof if it's more than two storeys high – leave that to the professionals.

● Always wear a hard hat when you're working on a roof and heavy-duty work gloves to protect your hands.

● Don't try to carry tools across a roof in your hands – you need your hands free to hold on to the ladder, and if you accidentally lose one of the tools it will slip down the roof slope and could seriously injure someone on the ground below if it falls off the edge of the roof. Use a tool pouch or tool belt, secured around your waist.

SAVE £30,000
A leaking roof that isn't fixed promptly could mean major repairs and replacement of the structural timbers.

● **Using an access tower** Scaffolding towers can be hired – usually for a minimum of a week – for as little as £50 to £75, depending on the size you need. Most hire companies will deliver for a small additional charge. Even with these costs and the additional work of erecting and dismantling the tower, you'll make substantial savings by avoiding the need to pay a professional to do the job.

● Choose a platform height of around 5m to reach the eaves of a two-storey building. The platform size varies and you can hire narrow towers for restricted spaces, such as in side passages between two properties.

● Make sure that the base of the tower is level and square. Use locking castors on hard ground to stop the tower moving when you are on it, and base boards to spread the load on soft ground.

● Fit a handrail and toe boards all round the platform and prevent the tower from toppling by using stabilisers or tying it securely to the building.

● **Spread the load across the roof** If you walk or crawl across the tiles themselves, you'll put a lot of pressure on the small areas where you are touching the roof covering as you move. A much safer alternative for you and your roof is to convert your ladder for roof work by adding a ridge hook (right). This has wheels for running the ladder across the roof, from the top of your access tower, to get it into position without dislodging any tiles. Slide it up beyond the ridge then flip the ladder over and slide it back down until the hooks are holding the ladder securely on the ridge.

Work safely with the right equipment

Anatomy of a **pitched roof**

A roof that's pitched means simply that it slopes. A single pitch rests on a wall at one end and slopes down to the eaves, but most pitched roofs are the duo-pitch type, with two slopes that meet in a ridge. The ends may be flat (a gable end) or sloping (a hipped end). Where two sections of roof change direction, a valley is formed.

PURLIN ROOF A horizontal beam called a purlin runs between the gable ends along each slope of the roof, midway between the ridge board and the eaves, to provide extra support for the rafters. This increases the unsupported span of the roof to about 7m.

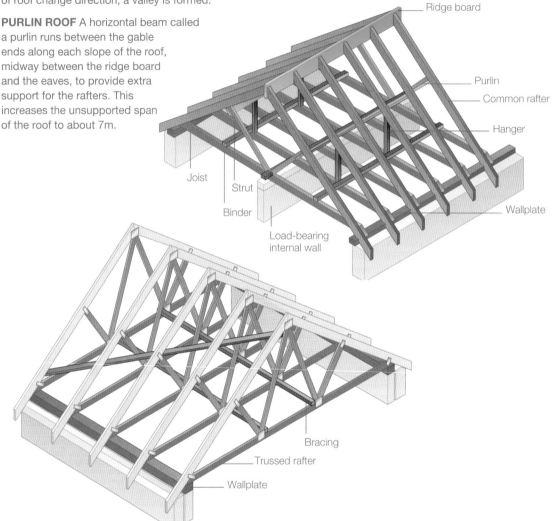

Ridge board

Purlin

Common rafter

Hanger

Joist

Strut

Binder

Load-bearing internal wall

Wallplate

Bracing

Trussed rafter

Wallplate

PREFABRICATED ROOFS Since the 1960s, almost all modern house roofs have been built using prefabricated roof trusses. Each truss combines rafters, joists and struts, constructed in a W-pattern to create an extremely strong frame that can span the external walls of the building with no need for internal load-bearing walls. The triangular structure is strong enough to support the roof covering, so the timbers used can be slimmer in cross-section than those in a traditional purlin roof, reducing cost and weight, and making them easier to fit.

The trusses are positioned 600mm apart and are nailed into place. There is no ridge board, but horizontal braces are fitted where the W-shaped internal supports meet the rafters and the ceiling joists, and diagonal braces are added across the underside of each section of the roof slope, running from the ridge to the eaves. These brace the structure to keep it from collapsing sideways. The roof structure is tied to the house walls with galvanised steel straps to prevent the roof from lifting or gable walls collapsing in high winds.

How to replace a broken tile

A broken tile can soon become a bigger problem, letting in water or allowing the wind to lift neighbouring tiles. Fix it promptly to save yourself from a much bigger and more expensive repair job. If your local builders' merchant cannot match your tiles, try looking in an architectural salvage yard.

1 Slide up the tiles that overlap the broken tile (right), tilt the broken tile sideways to separate it from the ones interlocked with it and lift it out.

2 Alternatively, use wedges to raise the tile to the left of the broken one and the one to its right in the course above (below right). This should release the broken tile so that you can lift it out without disturbing its neighbours.

3 If the tile is fixed in place, lever it upwards to release it from any clip that holds it to the batten. If the clip stays in place, the new tile may slip into it. If the clip is dislodged, there's no need to replace it – a few unclipped tiles won't matter. Sometimes alternate courses are nailed in place. If your repair is to a nailed tile, use a slate ripper to cut the nails before you remove the tile.

4 Lower the broken tile in a bucket on a rope to a helper on the ground then haul up the new tile in the bucket. To fit the replacement tile, slide it up into place. Fit it into the clip that was left behind, if there was one, but don't attempt to nail it down. Pull back into place any tiles that you pushed out of place and remove any wedges.

Care and maintenance

● **Catch problems early** Stand back from your property and inspect the roof regularly to spot problems early on. Use a pair of binoculars if you have some and check the ridges, tiles, verges and valleys.

● Look along the ridge and down any hipped edges. Ridge tiles should be set in a continuous bed of mortar. If the mortar cracks, tiles can be dislodged in high winds and water can seep in and rot the timbers beneath.

● Tiles and slates should be flat and uniform. Look out for any that seem to be slipping out of place.

● Check that valleys are clear of debris, such as leaves from nearby trees. If they are blocked, rain cannot drain freely away, and overflowing or standing water may seep into the roof space.

● Inspect the edges of the roof, along the verges, and make sure that the tiles are firmly bedded onto the masonry beneath and that the mortar is in good condition to prevent the tiles from being dislodged in high winds.

● **Spotting signs of a poor repair** Replacement roofs are expensive, and even paying a builder to make a substantial repair to a leaking roof is likely to cost at least a few thousand pounds, so homeowners are understandably often tempted to make cheap repairs or choose cheap materials for the job. While these will be fine as a temporary fix, they are not a permanent solution and will often end up costing more in the long

A slate ripper hooks round and cuts through the nails that secure slates and tiles to their battens, enabling you to remove a broken slate or tile without removing the whole run. Most tiles are not nailed in place but all slates are fixed with two nails – usually around half-way up, but sometimes at the top. Most hire shops will hire out slate rippers – it's probably not worth buying one for occasional use.

Rip through nails to remove a slate

term. Look out for these tell-tale signs of a bodged repair job on your roof and investigate and repair the source of the original problem.

● In many Victorian houses roofs have been re-covered using modern concrete interlocking roof tiles, rather than the original slates, as they are substantially cheaper. But they are also much heavier, and unless the timber structure of the roof was reinforced it will start to sag under the weight of the new tiles. If your roof is made of concrete tiles, inspect the rafters for signs of reinforcement and be prepared to install bracing yourself if there's none to keep the roof safe.

● Look out for anything sprayed or painted on top of the slates or tiles. This could be a black bituminous substance, with or without a mesh reinforcement, or red paint or sealant, used to stop a leak. In the long run, this is an expensive alternative to a proper repair job, as the covering cannot be stripped and the whole roof will need replacing.

● Look inside the roof space. Anything sprayed onto the underside of the tiles – such as insulating foam – may be a substitute for having a leak repaired and can lead to condensation and wood rot in the roof timbers.

Easy fixes

A sound slate will ring like a bell

● **Check the state of a new slate** Don't fit another flawed slate when you're making a repair. Test a secondhand slate to make sure it's in good condition by tapping it lightly with a hammer (left). A good slate will make a ringing sound and a cracked one will sound dull. Take a look at the underside, too, to make sure it's not powdery or crumbling.

● **Replacing ridge or hip tiles** Ridge tiles need to stick fast, so improve their grip by coating the tiles or slates beneath the replacement with PVA adhesive before you put on the mortar. If the old mortar won't chip off without damaging the tiles beneath, leave it and bed the new ridge tile in place with roof and gutter sealant instead, rather than a thin layer of mortar. Don't fill the gap at the apex of the roof with mortar, as this allows air to circulate and helps to prevent the timber from rotting.

● **A temporary fix for a broken slate** Cracks can be sealed until you can make a more permanent repair. Squeeze a bead of roof and gutter sealant into the crack (top right) or tape over it with self-adhesive flashing tape, pressed firmly home with a wallpaper seam roller (right).

● **Seal the verge** If mortar is loose or crumbling where the tiles meet the gable ends of the house, rake it out and replace it. Add a little PVA adhesive to the mortar to help it to adhere and paint PVA adhesive on the surrounding area as well. Push the mortar into the joint with a trowel, knocking it in with the side of the trowel to make sure that no air gaps are left within the mortar.

● Minor cracks in the mortar can be sealed with roof and gutter sealant. Choose a colour to match the mortar for an invisible repair.

Two quick fixes for a cracked slate

How to replace a broken slate

Slates may become cracked with age or by someone clambering carelessly on the roof. Use a bucket on a rope to lower the broken slate and haul up the replacement.

1 Cut through the nails holding the slate, using a slate ripper. Jiggle the slate from side to side to ease it out. Take care to collect all the broken pieces in a bucket – they could seriously injure someone on the ground if they were to fall off the roof.

3 Slip the new slate, with its bevelled edges upwards, under the course above. Wiggle it from left to right while easing it upwards until it lines up with the slates on each side. Its top edge should fit tightly over the batten to which the course above is nailed.

4 Fold the end of the metal strip up over the lower edge of the slate, then back on itself and press it down flat. This will stop the slate from slipping out of place, since you cannot nail in a replacement. The double fold helps to prevent snow and ice from forcing the clip open.

2 Take a flexible metal strip – called a tingle – 25mm wide and long enough to reach from the hole in the slate to its bottom, plus 100mm. Lead or zinc work well. Drill a nail hole 25mm from the end. Nail the tingle to the batten visible in the gap the slate had been covering.

Flashing

You probably don't notice it until it fails, but flashing lines the valleys between roof sections and fits around vent pipes, skylights and chimneys to prevent water from seeping in. If your flashing shows signs of corrosion, gets bent or isn't covered properly by the tiles around it, leaks are sure to follow, along with a substantial bill for water damage repair. Many flashing repairs need nothing more sophisticated than a roll of special flashing tape and could save you hundreds of pounds.

SAVE £250

How much you would pay to repair and redecorate a water-damaged ceiling, caused by poorly maintained flashing.

Care and maintenance

● **Get a good look at your flashing** When you check your roof (page 131), make sure to scrutinise all the flashing, too. Look out for corrosion, twigs and leaves clogging valleys, flashing coming loose from the chimney or pipes and lifted tiles that aren't covering flashing adequately. Check the joins where the house wall meets a bay window or porch roof, too, as these should be sealed tightly with flashing.

Easy fixes

● **Plugging small holes** First scrub the damaged spot with a wire brush to clean and roughen the metal surface. Then fill the hole with gutter sealant and smooth the patch with a putty knife. Wetting the knife with paint thinner will help to get a smooth finish.

How to patch using flashing tape

Rolls of flashing tape are available in different widths and colours to suit the repair you need to make. You can cut a small patch or use a longer length to cover a larger area.

1 Use a wire brush to clean any dirt and loose metal from the area to be repaired. Rub the area with abrasive paper to create a key for the adhesive strip to stick to. Wipe the area with a damp cloth and let it dry.

2 Brush on a coat of flashing strip primer (left) extending at least 50mm beyond the area of the repair in each direction. Leave it to dry for at least 30 minutes, or longer if recommended by the manufacturer.

3 Cut the flashing strip to extend at least 50mm beyond the crack or hole. Peel off the backing and press it firmly into place, using a wallpaper seam roller to smooth out any wrinkles and bed it down well.

● **Patching corroded areas** Scrub away the corrosion with a wire brush, then clean the surface thoroughly with soap and water and rinse. Cut a piece of glass-fibre mesh large enough to cover the rusted area and extend beyond it at least an inch on all sides. Apply a coat of plastic roof cement to the flashing area and press the glass fibre over it, then top with a second coat of the sealant.

● **Adhesive flashing** Metal flashing is usually laid within the joint between two courses of bricks when the house is built. It's mortared in place as the wall goes up (see diagram below), but it's a major job to use the same technique when replacing a section of flashing.

● Self-adhesive strip is a much easier 'retro-fit' option. Remove the damaged flashing, and clean and repoint the brickwork. Then paint flashing primer on the area to be covered and let it dry for half an hour. Cut two lengths of flashing strip each the full length of the repair. Peel off the backing and stick the first in place, with half its width overlapping the roof. Roll it with a wallpaper seam roller (above) for a smooth finish and a secure fixing. Apply the second strip so that it overlaps the top edge of the first and bed it down well with the roller.

How does flashing work?

Flashing is usually made of lead, but can also be zinc, aluminium alloy or modern stick-on lead substitute. It doesn't create a waterproof seal, but overlaps or is overlapped by the roofing, diverting rainfall so that it runs off the roof. Every joint is vulnerable, especially if it joins two materials that shrink or expand at different rates, such as metal vent pipes and clay tiles. Joints may also pull apart as the house settles. Chimney flashing is especially complex. To let the chimney move independently from the house, it has two-part flashing: soakers, interlaid with the tiles on the roof, overlapped by a stepped cover flashing attached to the chimney.

Easy fixes for common problems

Flashings fitted when a house is built are usually strips of lead, which can deteriorate with age. Depending on the extent of the deterioration, it may not be necessary to replace the flashing. Small repairs are quite easily achieved.

● **FINE CRACKS** If you notice a fine crack in a length of flashing, inject some bituminous sealant or other roof-and-gutter sealant into it using a mastic applicator gun and cartridge for an even application. Some sealants are available in different colours so you can choose one that will make the repair least noticeable.

● **SMALL HOLES OR SLIGHT CORROSION** If you catch them soon enough, a patch of self-adhesive flashing strip will make a sound repair over a small hole or where there are the first signs of corrosion. Use the method described for using self-adhesive flashing, above.

● **RENEWING FLASHING MORTAR** The top edge of a piece of original metal flashing is cemented into the mortar between two courses of bricks. As with all mortar, sometimes it starts to work loose and lets in water, even if the flashing itself is intact. You can repoint the joint (see page 92), but first push the edge of the flashing back into the gap between the courses of bricks. If the flashing springs out again, you can wedge it with blocks of wood (right) until the pointing has hardened. Remove the wedges and fill the holes with mortar to complete the repair.

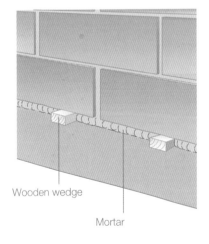

Wooden wedge

Mortar

Flat roofs

A flat roof provides less surface area to care for than a pitched roof but doesn't shed rain as quickly, so it's essential to keep it watertight. A flat roof has a lifespan of around 15 years, but with a little maintenance and some simple repairs, you can put off the need to re-roof the area for longer. The most common problems are holes, tears, blisters and loose seams.

SAVE £750

How much it would cost to replace the covering on a 4m x 8m flat roof.

smart idea

When the time comes to replace your roof, consider using one of the latest PVC or rubber-based coatings. They are more expensive than felts, but can last at least twice as long.

Care and maintenance

● **Check for surface damage** Every few months, inspect your flat roof. Depending on the architectural style of your home, you may be able to do this by looking out of a first-storey window. In other cases, you'll have to access your roof by climbing a ladder. Look for holes, tears, blisters and loose seams on a felt roof or for rust and pitting on a metal roof. Make repairs or add patches (see right) to prevent leaks. Also, check the edges of the flashing to make sure water can't seep under it.

● **What is your roof made of?** Traditionally, flat roofs were covered with alternating layers of builder's felt and hot tar, topped with a layer of gravel. Today, the more common covering is torch-on polymer roofing felt. This comes with its own bituminous backing, which is softened by a gas torch as the felt is rolled into place. It's easier to apply and doesn't require a coating of chippings.

● **Slather on the sunblock** To protect a felt roof against damage from the sun's ultraviolet rays, paint it with solar-reflective paint. This is a particularly good idea for roofs made of mastic asphalt or torch-on polymer felts that have a very sunny aspect, and will extend their life.

Easy fixes

● **Try a repair kit** You can give an old flat roof a new lease of life by trying a simple reinforcement fabric repair kit. Make sure the surface is as clean and dry as possible, then use a soft broom to apply a good coat of waterproofer. Note that you won't be able to clean the broom afterwards and will probably need to throw it and your shoes away.

How to patch a split using tape

Act fast when you spot signs of a leaking roof. Inspect the roof to find the split and fix it with self-adhesive roofing repair tape.

1 Scrape any chippings from the area around the split. Use a hot-air gun to soften the tar that the chippings are bedded in. Dry out any moisture within the split – the hot-air gun will be a help again – then fill the split with bituminous mastic. Prime the area round the split with a bitumen primer and allow it to dry.

2 Cover the split and a little of the surrounding area with a piece of self-adhesive roofing repair tape. Overlap the pieces if you need more than one, and use a wallpaper seam roller to make a firm seal. If you think the split may be over a joint between the decking panels under the surface, continue the repair to the roof's edge.

Unroll the reinforcement fabric and lay it in overlapping strips across the roof. Brush on a second coat of waterproofing and let it dry. Some kits recommend applying up to four coats.

● **Give your old roof a topcoat** After a while, many asphalt roofs become a patchwork of repairs. If this is true of yours, revive the surface by simply brushing on asphalt roof coating. If the roof has any slope at all, start at the highest part and work your way down.

● **Renew tar and gravel over a leak** If your old-fashioned felt-and-tar roof springs a leak, scrape the area clean of gravel and apply fresh roof tar. Be sure to replace the gravel before the tar hardens. If you can't pinpoint the source of a leak, cover the entire suspect area with tar.

● **Lancing blisters** If you find a blister on your asphalt roll roofing, the culprit is usually trapped moisture. Slit the blister down the middle with a trimming knife to release the moisture. Let the blister dry, then fill its cavity by squeezing in roof and gutter sealant from a sealant gun. Drive

A broom spreads waterproofer quickly

a row of roofing nails in on each side of the split, then apply more roof sealant to the slit and the nail heads. Cut a patch of similar roofing material a couple of inches longer and wider than the damaged area. Nail the patch over the repaired area and seal the patch's edges and the nail heads with the sealant.

IF LEAVES ARE LEFT OVER WINTER,
THEY WILL CLOG UP GUTTERS.

Gutters and downpipes

It's an unglamorous, messy job, and you can't stand back afterwards and take pride in how nice and clean they look, but clearing out your gutters is one of the most important household maintenance tasks you can do. Blocked gutters cause water to collect and overflow, seeping or dripping into surrounding areas or the foundations of the house and potentially causing damage with damp and rot. Clearing them is a simple task that could cost thousands if left neglected.

Care and maintenance

SAVE £750

Cost to replace 6m of deteriorated fascia board rotted by water from blocked gutters.

● **Clean gutters around Easter and Bonfire Night** Use these two memorable dates to remind you to clear your gutters. In spring, you'll remove winter debris, and by late autumn the last of the leaves should have fallen. If leaves are left over winter, they will clog up the gutters and downpipes, stopping heavy rain from draining away. The soggy mess will freeze in cold weather, so that rainfall just runs over the gutter's edges until a thaw melts the leaves.

● It can cost up to £30,000 or more to replace structural roof timbers damaged by a gutter leak.

MAKE EASTER AND BONFIRE NIGHT KEY DATES FOR CLEARING GUTTERS.

● **Be organised and systematic** Cleaning gutters is fairly easy but you need to work systematically. Here's how to go about it.

● Use a pull-up bucket. Attach one end of a long rope and an S-hook to the handle of an empty bucket (you can make the hook by bending a wire coat hanger), and put in a stiff hand-brush and a trowel or a scoop made by cutting the base off a plastic milk bottle. You can also make a scraper by nailing a piece of wood cut to the shape of the gutter to the end of a length of broom handle. Starting near the downpipe, climb a sturdy ladder up to the gutter, pull up the bucket with the rope and hook it over a rung of the ladder.

● Work from low end to high. Sweep all debris toward the higher end of the gutter (above right), then scoop it up (below right) and put it into the bucket. Clean only as far as you can reach comfortably, then move the ladder along to the next section.

● Once you've removed all the debris, use a garden hose to flush the gutter from the high end to the downpipe. This also lets you check for leaks and any other damage. If you see standing pools of water, that probably means the gutter is sagging and needs realignment. If the water won't flow out of the gutter at all, the downpipe is most likely clogged and needs clearing.

Improvised tools scrape and scoop up leaves with ease

Easy fixes

A blast of water clears a clog

● **Conquering leaking gutters** Most gutter leaks occur at the joints where two sections meet. To stop a leak, apply silicone sealant from a squeezable tube along the joint's inside seams. Smooth the sealant's edges so that they won't collect debris. If the leak recurs, disassemble the sections and put a bead of silicone between the parts at each seam.

● **Clear a blocked downpipe** The fast way to clear a clog in a downpipe is with a garden hose. Surprisingly, it's best to do it from the bottom up. Wrap rags around the nozzle of a hose and wedge it into the bottom of the pipe. You may have to remove a section to gain access if your downpipe sinks straight into the ground. Turn on the water full force. If that doesn't dislodge the debris, use a plumber's snake, working from the bottom up.

● **Diverting water from your house** Don't let water collect at or splash up onto the footings of your house. If your downpipe doesn't empty into an underground drain, attach a few feet of extra pipe to an elbow at the bottom to carry the run-off away from the foundation. Consider

How to **unblock a clogged soakaway**

The most efficient way to dispose of rainwater falling on your roof is to pipe it direct to the underground drainage system. But in many homes, of all ages, the rainwater downpipes flow into soakaways – holes in the ground filled with rubble. Ideally, soakaways should be sited at least a couple of metres away from the walls and in permeable soil, which will allow the water to drain gradually without waterlogging the garden.

● Unfortunately, some soakaways are little more than holes in the ground right next to the house wall. In houses with cellars or semi-basements, this can result in the cellar flooding every time it rains. Even properly constructed soakaways will eventually clog up with leaves and silt washed down with the rainwater.

● If you have a cellar that fills with water or a pond that forms on the lawn after a shower of rain, check to see whether your rainwater is flowing into a clogged soakaway. The easiest way to check is to lift the cover off the nearest inspection chamber and then use a hosepipe or bucket to run water through the gutters and downpipes. If you see a corresponding flow of water running through the inspection chamber, then you know that your drainpipes flow into the drains. If there's no obvious flow of water and you know that the downpipe

isn't blocked, then your water is probably going into a soakaway.

● Soakaways can be dug up and renewed, and this is a good opportunity to resite one that is too close to the house. Traditionally they were made by digging a large hole, around 1m square and 1-1.5m deep, filling it with rubble to around 300mm from the surface and covering with a sheet of corrugated steel, to prevent topsoil being washed down into it, before back-filling with new topsoil up to ground level.

● To renew a rubble soakaway, dig out the topsoil and save it to put back when you have finished, then dig out the clogged rubble and replace it with fresh, from a builders' merchant.

● The preferred modern equivalent still requires you to dig a large square hole, but the soakaway itself is a purpose-made plastic cage, available from builders' merchants. These are usually wrapped in geotextile before they are buried underground to prevent soil and silt from being washed in. Surround the tank with gravel then back-fill the top layer of the hole with topsoil once the drainpipe has been diverted into the hole.

digging a soakaway (see left) if there's no option of feeding into the drains, or at least fit a large water collection tank.

● **Tightening sagging gutters** Water cannot flow away freely if the gutter doesn't fall evenly towards the downpipe. The fall should be gradual, but not too shallow. If it's not even, puddles of water will collect in the sagging sections. The easiest way to straighten a sagging gutter is by adjusting the support that holds it to your house.

Add new brackets to cure a sag

● Traditional cast-iron gutters were nailed in place, straight into the end of a rafter, and to pull up a sagging section you just need to tighten the nail with a few blows from a hammer. If metal brackets have been used, use pliers to bend the strap that bridges the gutter to lift the outer edge.

● Most modern plastic guttering is fixed to fascia boards with u-shaped brackets. Add an extra support (right) if a gutter is sagging. Disconnect the gutter and lift out the sagging section. Tie a string line to the brackets to either side of the problem area, or lay a long straightedge on them to span the gap. Use this as a guide to position the new bracket: brackets should be between 600mm and 900mm apart. Reassemble the gutter and test the fall by pouring water into the gutter at its highest point. If puddles are still forming, adjust the position of brackets to increase the fall.

● **Patching metal gutters** If a gutter section is rusty and leaky, replace it. But if there's just one bad spot, the few minutes it takes to patch it is time well spent. Just scrape the area clean of rust with a stiff wire brush and wipe with paint thinner. Cut a glass-fibre patch large enough to overlap the damaged area by 50mm on all sides. Using a putty knife, cover the area with roof and gutter sealant. Smooth the patch into the sealant using a dry, wadded cloth. Cover the patch with another coat of sealant, feathering the edges to avoid creating ridges that could impede water flow.

Keep out leaves with a **gutter guard**

Wire or plastic mesh screens clip easily onto gutters to keep out falling leaves. They are supplied in short sections and match the standard gutter width. If you have a tree directly overhead or very close, though, these screens can sometimes get clogged themselves by heavy leaf falls clinging to them, diverting water over the gutters. In these situations, a more practical solution is to put a bulb-shaped leaf strainer in the top of each downspout. You'll still need to clear your gutters regularly, but the soggy leaves will be prevented from washing down into the downpipe and creating a much harder-to-clear blockage.

A strainer stops leaves at the top of the downpipe

Chimneys

Keeping it clean is the most important chimney maintenance task, as this reduces the chance of a chimney fire. But you should also look out for flashings around the chimney at roof level that have deteriorated, pots coming loose and mortar joints that need repointing. Ask your chimney sweep to check the chimney for you when he gives it its annual sweep.

SAVE £2,000

What you would pay a builder to replace chimney flaunching, reseat loose bricks and pot and reline a flue to make a neglected chimney safe to use.

Care and maintenance

● **Only burn well-seasoned firewood** Green, unseasoned wood contains up to 50 per cent water – it burns poorly and produces a lot of smoke, which leads to tarring on the chimney's walls. Only burn wood that has been seasoned for at least 12 months. Keep your firewood dry. If you store it outside, keep it off the ground and uncovered during good weather, then pull a tarpaulin over it when it rains or snows.

● **Look for obstructions** The best time to check a chimney is in the spring, right after you've finished using it for the winter. If it's safe to do so, work from the roof or a ladder and check the top of the chimney first – look for anything that might block it, such as a bird's nest. Then use a powerful torch to look down the flue for obstructions. If you find any you can't reach, call a chimney sweep.

● **Sweep away tar build-up** Over time, residual gases and resins from wood condense on the inside of the flue, mix with soot and form a dark coating of tars. If it's not removed regularly, this can block the flue or dissolve mortar joints, allowing smoke to leak through the sides of the flue. Worse still, the tar can catch fire and spread through cracks in the flue into your house. If you use an open fire, have the chimney swept once a year.

● **Cap your flue** If your flue doesn't have a cap, get one fitted. It will keep out foreign objects, birds' nests and water. If your chimney has more than one flue, put a cap on each.

Check chimney flashing

Faulty flashing lets in damp

● **Inspect the chimney flashing** Check your chimney each spring to make sure that the flashing where the chimney joins the roof (left) is securely in place and intact. Use binoculars to get a good look from ground level (see page 131) and combine this with an annual roof check-up.

● If the flashing is loose or corroded, it won't keep out water, and you'll soon start to see signs of water damage in the roof space and then within the house (below left).

● Chimney flashing is complicated to install – call in a professional to get it replaced.

● **Check for a damaged cap from inside** A missing or damaged chimney cap can result in moisture inside the chimney. An easy way to check a cap without climbing onto the roof is to place a single sheet of newspaper at the base of the flue the next time it rains. If the paper becomes fairly wet, the cap probably needs repair or replacement.

● **Trim back encroaching trees** Trees that overhang the chimney can be ignited by escaping sparks or create a canopy that can cause your fireplace to smoke. Trim back branches to at least 3m from the chimney.

● **Do a night-time inspection** At night, with most of the lights in your home turned off, ask someone to shine a bright light up the flue from the fireplace while you check all the exposed areas of the chimney throughout the house and in the roof space. If you see any light leaking through, it means that smoke and fumes can leak through, too. Repoint the brickwork and get the flue relined by a professional.

● **Blow up a balloon to keep out draughts** If you have an open fireplace that you don't use, it may be draughty, and you'll certainly be losing a lot of heat up it and out of the house. Even if you use the fire in the colder months, it's a good idea to block the flue when it's not in use.

● An easy fix is to stuff a black bin liner with newspaper, rolled to roughly the width of your fireback. Make a well-packed parcel just the right size to stuff up the chimney from the fireplace. Tuck it up behind the top edge of the fireplace, against the fireback, and it will help to prevent draughts.

● You can also buy a chimney balloon. Reach your forearm up into the flue and measure the dimensions of your chimney – front to back and side to side. It doesn't have to be an accurate measurement, but will guide you when choosing which size to buy, The balloon is inserted into the chimney and then inflated to fill the hole. You can deflate the balloon to remove it and use it again and again.

CHECK YOUR CHIMNEY USING TORCH LIGHT.

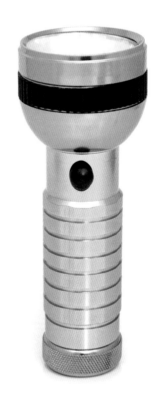

Anatomy of a chimney

Flues lined with clay blocks or, more recently, stainless steel pipes, allow smoke to draw smoothly up the chimney, without the tars seeping into the inside walls of the house. A chimney stack above the roofline prevents downdraughts blowing smoke back into the rooms below. Each flue is capped with a pot, set on a bed of mortar and secured by a mortar cap, called flaunching, around its base. Pots are often replaced by a cowl or concrete slab on disused chimneys.

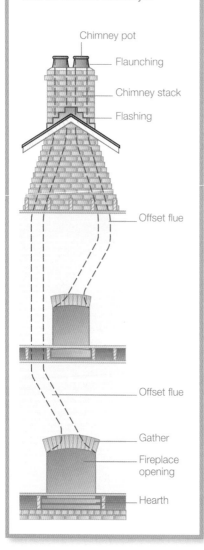

Chimney pot

Flaunching

Chimney stack

Flashing

Offset flue

Offset flue

Gather

Fireplace opening

Hearth

● **Steel flues for woodburners** If you plan to install a wood-burning or multi-fuel stove in an existing flue, factor in the cost of installing a stainless steel flue liner at the same time. Otherwise you may find that the tars from the wood condense inside the flue and these can migrate through to the decorative surfaces, causing stains on chimney breasts in upstairs bedrooms. This is because wood burns at a lower temperature than coal, so the tars condense more readily than they do with traditional coal fires.

● If you do install a stainless steel flue, it's not recommended that you burn too much coal in a multi-fuel stove, as the sulphur in the gases can corrode stainless steel. Make wood your main source of fuel.

Easy fixes

● **Check the chimney's crown** The crown, or flaunching, is the concrete bed on the top of the chimney stack that surrounds the flue and acts as a roof to protect the brickwork beneath. Include this in your chimney's health check. If it's seriously cracked, have it replaced by a professional – the chimney pot will need to be secured before removing the old flaunching and this is a dangerous and tricky job.

● If the flaunching is only slightly cracked, you can repair it with fresh concrete mortar or roof and gutter sealant. But take care to follow the appropriate safety procedures whenever you're undertaking any repairs at roof level: use a scaffold tower to access the roof and a roof ladder to cross the roof to the chimney. See pages 126-129 for more advice on safety when working at heights. If you're in any doubt, always leave this to a professional, who is properly equipped.

● **Filling joints in the chimney flaunching** If you find a gap in the joint between the flue and the flaunching, seal it with sealant rated for use on concrete. Apply a thick bead of sealant around the entire circumference of the flue where it meets the flaunching. Push the sealant down into the gap to fill it, then round it off and smooth it.

● **Blocking up unused fireplaces** If you have an unused fireplace and decide to close it off or brick it up, make sure that it's vented at the bottom and the top of the flue. At the bottom, the best way is to fit an airbrick in the chimney breast at or near ceiling height. At the top of the flue, either the chimney pot should have a perforated cowl mortared onto it, or – with the pot removed and capped off – an airbrick should be inserted into the side of the chimney stack. This will ensure a steady trickle of dry, warm air from the room below, up through the flue and the stack, to keep the whole thing dry and ventilated.

● Don't worry about losing heat from the room where the fireplace used to be – the tiny amount of heat lost through the airbricks will be more than compensated for by the fact that it keeps your downstairs room free of condensation and also helps to prevent dampness problems in the chimney stack. Together, this will save you hundreds of pounds in future maintenance and decorating costs.

Foundations and basements

When problems start with your foundations you need professional help. Damp is often the first problem, and is common in basements and cellars. Look out for signs of moisture and, more importantly, signals of cracking to make sure your home stays safe and dry.

Care and maintenance

● **Don't breach the damp-proof course** Foundations are separated from the house walls by a layer of damp-proofing. You can usually see this from the outside, as a wide line of concrete or a visible rubbery membrane. Keep an eye on the soil level outside and don't allow it to build up above this line, or moisture can seep directly into the house walls.

● **Preventing moisture in basements** Cellars and basements are prone to damp, and it's easy to understand why. But there are things you can do to minimise the problem.

● Improve ventilation by opening windows where possible in cool, dry weather and keeping airbricks and vents clear of obstructions (see page 155). If you have a tumble-dryer or bathroom in your basement, make sure that damp air is vented to the outside: run the dryer's vent pipe through a wall and make sure that a bathroom has an extractor fan. If condensation is still a problem, consider buying a dehumidifier for the space.

● Divert rainwater from the basement walls by making sure that the house gutters are draining efficiently and downpipes aren't discharging onto the ground near the wall of the house. Check soakaways to ensure that water is draining freely and not seeping into the house (see pages 140-141).

● Keep an eye on flowerbeds that surround the house and don't let the foliage become too thick close to the walls – this can prevent the house walls from drying out efficiently after a wet spell.

● Look out for leaks coming through cracks in the walls and fix them promptly. Gaps around external door and window frames will also let in water – seal them with frame sealant (see page 161).

● **What to do when cracks appear** If your house starts to develop cracks in internal or external walls or around the edges of solid concrete floor slabs, they could indicate foundation problems. The panel on page 146 explains common causes of cracks: some are serious, some can be patched up and forgotten. To get an accurate diagnosis, seek professional advice straight away. Inspectors from your local council's building control department will have a good knowledge of the local soil conditions; they should be able to spot the likely cause of your problems and recommend a contractor to help to fix it. Fixing foundations isn't a DIY job.

SAVE £150
The cost of repairing a patch of damp caused by soil piling up against an external wall and breaching the damp-proof course.

Common causes of **foundation problems**

Foundations rarely require any attention until they appear to stop doing their job. Small cracks in the walls begin to appear, then larger ones – often linking door and window openings, and zig-zagging up the walls through mortar joints. In extreme cases, cracks extend the full height of the building as if part of the house is going to fall away. Here are some of the most common causes of foundation problems.

● **DIFFERENTIAL SETTLEMENT** If an extension is built with different foundations from the rest of the house, the new part may settle and start to pull away. This was common in Victorian houses with bay windows and back additions, and is seen today with extensions built on inadequate foundations and not tied properly to the existing structure.

● **GROUND MOVEMENT** The ground beneath a house, especially clay, expands and contracts with the seasons. It can sink during a drought and heave when water within the soil freezes and expands upwards, causing the foundations to move with it. Trees close to the house can also cause this, sucking moisture from the ground as they grow, or no longer doing so if they are felled. Leaking underground drains may also saturate or erode the subsoil.

Ground sinks as tree drains ground in dry spells

● **OVERLOADING** Structural alterations, such as removing a load-bearing internal wall and installing a rolled steel joist (RSJ) to transfer the load to the walls at each end of the joist, can put pressure on foundations that were never designed to support that load. They can also fail beneath its weight, causing a wall to start to sink (see diagram below).

● **SUBSIDENCE** Many homeowners assume that this is the cause of their cracks, but fortunately it's rare and only occurs when underground chambers – natural or manmade, such as a mine – collapse.

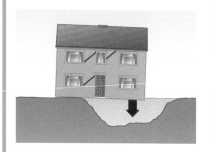

Ground swells if tree is felled

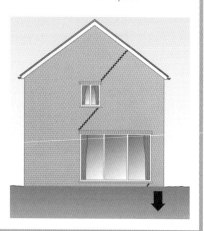

Easy fixes

● **Freshen up a smelly basement** Cellars and basements often have a musty smell, caused by mildew, a fungal growth. Increasing the ventilation in the space, using fans to increase air circulation and installing a dehumidifier can help to avoid the mildew forming. To get rid of existing mildew and the smell that goes with it, mix a solution of 25ml of household bleach and 1 litre of water in a spray bottle. Spray the walls and floors and scrub them with a nylon-bristled brush.

● **Give your floor a facelift** If a concrete floor gets dirty, use a stiff nylon brush to scrub it with a solution of washing-up liquid and warm water, with 4 tablespoons of ammonia added. Don't be tempted to scrub with a wire brush – bits of wire can be left in the floor and will cause rust spots. Once the floor is clean and dry, you can paint it with special floor paint.

Insulation

How comfortable you are inside your home largely depends on the effectiveness of your home's insulation. A properly insulated loft can also reduce your heating expenses dramatically. Give your home an insulation audit to make sure you're not wasting energy – and don't forget to seal the small gaps around pipes and wiring. Always wear protective gear when handling insulation materials.

Care and maintenance

● **Are your walls insulated?** Current building codes require homes to have insulated exterior walls, but this wasn't the case for houses that were built before 1965. If you're not sure whether your walls are insulated, use a hole saw to cut a small hole through a plasterboard wall inside a cupboard and inspect from there, or drill through the inner leaf of a brick cavity wall and inspect the drill bit for signs of insulation brought back out from the cavity. If the walls aren't insulated, consider having blown-in insulation installed – you may be able to get a grant to subsidise the cost.

● **Check the roof after a snowfall** To see how well insulated your roof space is, go outside after a snowfall and compare the amount of snow lingering on your roof with your neighbours' roofs. In a well-insulated home, the heat will be kept inside and the snow won't melt. If your neighbours' houses still have a good covering of snow and your roof is bare, it's a sign that your heat is escaping through the roof and you should increase your loft insulation.

● **Have you got enough loft insulation?** A poorly insulated loft can cost you plenty in terms of heat loss and high utility bills. Measure the depth of the insulation. If it's less than 270mm of glass fibre or mineral wool or 175mm of rigid PIR (polyisocyanurate) board insulation – the current minimum recommended depths for Building Regulations – add at least one more layer. These regulations only apply to new homes or conversions. You don't have to keep your home at these levels, but it makes sense to follow the guidelines to get the best from your heating.
 ● If your additional insulation will be deeper than the joists, you won't be able to replace any boards that were there before – don't squash the insulation down, as this will reduce its efficiency. If you want to reboard over the top of the new insulation, lay new battens at right angles to the existing joists, but the same distance apart, as most rolls of insulation are manufactured to this standard width. Screw the battens in place (nailing can cause cracks in the ceilings below), roll out the insulation between the new timbers and fix your boards on top once you've finished.

SAVE £115
Average annual saving on your energy bills when you install cavity wall insulation. Insulating solid walls can save up to £400 each year.

The barrier rule

Vapour barriers keep moisture out of your home. Whenever you install insulation, do it with the vapour barrier facing your living areas. The paper or foil facing on glass-fibre batts and blankets and on rigid board insulation serves as a vapour barrier, so install them the right way up. Loose-fill insulation requires a layer of plastic or polyethylene. Don't stack faced insulation – moisture can collect between the layers, reducing the effectiveness of the insulation, and may cause water damage inside your home.

● **Seal small gaps** It may be hard to believe, but those small spaces around the plumbing vent pipes and electrical cables in your roof can result in significant heat loss during the winter months. Pack wads of mineral wool insulation into the gaps as backing. Then fill in the spaces with expanding foam filler. Run a bead of silicone sealant around electrical junction boxes, allowing at least 24 hours for the sealant to set before you put any nearby insulation back into place.

● **Check for unwelcome wildlife** Loose-fill insulation material keeps your home warm, but can also make a comfortable winter residence for mice and squirrels. Check your loft insulation for any signs of unwanted guests in early winter. If you see droppings, disturbed areas of insulation or any signs of chewing, contact a pest-control specialist. Make sure that any pest-control service you use will remove the animals and eliminate their point of entry at the same time, to prevent them from coming back.

Easy fixes

● **Top tips for improving loft insulation** You can lay rolled blankets or precut lengths of mineral wool insulation on top of existing insulation. Working from the eaves towards the centre of the roof space, lay new batts over the tops of the joists at right angles to the existing insulation or unroll blanket insulation on top of the existing layer. Always wear work gloves and long sleeves when handling mineral wool insulation as it can irritate the skin. Wear a face mask to avoid inhaling any of the loose fibres.
● Take care as you work not to block ventilation gaps at the eaves.
● Be very careful where you kneel or crawl: you'll need to lift any boards you have in the loft to lay the new insulation, so take great care only to rest your weight on the joists.
● Leave water pipes below the insulation, to stop them from freezing, but electrical power cables (not lighting cables) must always run above the insulation to stop them from overheating.

smart idea

It's the air trapped in the minute spaces within insulating material that actually provides insulation. When adding insulation, don't pack it in or compress it too tightly as that will hinder its ability to stop heat loss.

● **Cutting insulation to fit** Glass-fibre and rigid insulation often need to be cut to fit properly into an allotted space. Cut rolled glass fibre or glass-fibre batts (precut lengths) by placing the insulation, faced side up, on a piece of plywood. Position a straightedge across the cut line, and press it down with your knee. Use a sharp trimming knife to cut through the material – use a knife shield attachment (above left) to compress the material as the blade cuts through and make the job easier. To slice through thick rigid foam insulation, place it on a solid, raised surface, such as a table or workbench, and use a jigsaw with a fine-toothed blade – or even an electric carving knife – to make the cut. Thin foam insulation can simply be scored with a trimming knife then snapped.

Options for insulating your walls

If your home has cavity walls (see page 91), you can have insulation blown or pumped in through holes drilled in the outer leaf. Solid walls can be insulated, too, by adding insulating material to the inside or out.

Cavity walls

Installing cavity wall insulation is a job best left to the professionals. Some experts claim that filling cavity walls can lead to dampness, especially in areas of the south and west of the UK that are exposed to regular wind-driven rain. The materials least likely to cause problems are foam and polystyrene bead insulation. Avoid blown mineral wool fibre if you live in an exposed location. In timber-framed cavity walls, the insulation can be incorporated into the inner frame during construction, leaving the cavity clear and avoiding problems with moisture.

Solid walls

External wall insulation is the most efficient option for solid walls as it keeps the whole structure of the house warm, and makes use of the heat-retaining properties of the walls themselves. But it does usually mean changing the external appearance of the property to a rendered finish. If your house is built with attractive facing bricks, or you live in a conservation area, external insulation is not usually a viable option.

Internal wall insulation can be added by building a 50mm x 50mm timber stud frame against the internal faces of all external walls and filling the spaces between the studs with rigid foam board (PIR) insulation. Staple a vapour barrier across the timbers and finish off with a layer of plasterboard, which can be decorated to match the rest of the room. You'll need to reposition all skirtings, architraves, light switches and sockets on each insulated wall, and you'll lose around 65mm of space from that end of the room

● **Don't forget the hatch** You can build up the insulation within your loft space, but if you leave out the loft hatch, you might as well leave it open. As part of the job when you're insulating the loft, cut an extra piece of mineral-wool insulation blanket or thick expanded polystyrene sheet slightly smaller than the area of the hatch. If you cut it to fit exactly, the extra thickness may stop the hatch from closing.

● To fix insulation blanket, hammer two or three nails along each edge of the hatch, then zig-zag string over the blanket and nails to lash it into place. Don't pull the string too tightly, as this will compress the blanket and reduce its efficiency. Alternatively, staple a sheet of polythene over the blanket to secure it.

● To fix a polystyrene panel to the hatch, stick it in place with polystyrene ceiling-tile adhesive.

● Fit a draught excluder around the loft hatch to finish the job.

● **Fire safety for lights** If you have recessed downlights that project into the loft space or other insulated roof space, it's crucial to leave a space around them to stop them from overheating or setting light to the insulation. The easiest and safest way to do this is to cover each downlight with a purpose-made galvanised steel cover or a fire-retardant fabric 'fire hood' before laying the insulation material over it.

● **Insulating floors** Once you've done all you can to insulate your loft and walls, you can still make a difference to your comfort and fuel bills by insulating the ground floors of your home.

● To insulate a suspended timber floor above an unheated basement or ventilated crawl space, fit the insulation beneath the floorboards, between the joists. If you can get under the floor, push glass-fibre batts – vapour

take care!

Be really careful if, in the exploration of your home's insulation, you find a light, flaky grey material. This could be vermiculite, a mineral used for loose-fill insulation that may contain asbestos. Don't move or handle vermiculite insulation unless you've had it tested by an approved laboratory and you're sure that it's safe. If you buy new vermiculite it should be safe to use.

Which type of loft insulation should I choose?

The structure of your roof may be the most important consideration – measure the distance between joists to assess whether it's regular and whether it matches the common sizes of batts or blanket insulation.

Type	Pros	Cons
LOOSE-FILL • Vermiculite granules, mineral fibre or polystyrene balls • Supplied in sacks large enough to cover 1m² • Natural or recycled options becoming more widely available, including sheep wool and recycled newspaper	• Can be poured or blown into awkward areas and irregular spaces • Low cost	• Can be messy to use • Joists need to be built up to achieve depth of insulation required by Building Regulations • Materials can shift or settle • Variable quality • May require mechanical blower
MINERAL FIBRE BATTS • Semi-rigid panels of mineral fibre insulation offer the same kind of material as blanket rolls, but in a less bulky format. Come in varying thicknesses from 25mm to 100mm • Also available in hemp and recycled cotton	• Easy to handle and transport • Can be trimmed to size • Come in standard joist widths to meet Building Regulations minimum depth requirements	• More expensive than the blanket roll equivalent • More than two layers required • Can irritate skin and lungs
SOLID BATTS • Expanded polystyrene sheets, or highly insulative boards, such as solid PIR	• Quick to lay • Convenient for insulating under suspended floors • Can be used on a roof slope	• Bulky to transport • Can be expensive
BLANKET ROLLS • The most easy-to-use option • Rolls of mineral wool or glass fibre fit in between joists • Thin high-performance options are also available	• Quick and easy to install • Comes in standard joist widths • Can be trimmed to size • Available with or without vapour barrier backing • Low cost	• Can irritate skin and lungs • Air gaps may form during installation

BLANKET ROLLS ARE THE MOST EASY-TO-USE OPTION.

Rest blanket on netting   Batts sit neatly on battens

barrier facing up – into the spaces between the floor joists. Secure the batts by stapling wire mesh (chicken wire) to the lower edges of the joists, or by pressing lengths of heavy wire – cut slightly longer than the width of the cavity – between the joists every 600mm or so. Bow the wires up slightly so that they hold the batts firmly in place, but aren't compressing them.

● If you can't get access below the floor, you'll have to lift the floorboards, a section at a time, and lay the insulation from above. Nail or staple 'hammocks' of garden netting between the joists to support the insulation (above left) or fix battens along the edges of the joists for solid insulation batts to sit on (above right).

● Insulating solid concrete floors is more complicated, as the only place to fit insulation is on top of the existing concrete slab. This means losing some height within the room and cutting the bottoms of all doors to clear the raised floor. Thin insulating fabric is sold to underlay wood board and laminate floors, but this is mainly a moisture barrier.

take care!

Always protect your skin, eyes and lungs when working with glass-fibre insulation. Wear a thick, long-sleeved shirt, work gloves, goggles and a face mask. You can protect yourself further by wearing overalls or a hooded sweatshirt and tucking your shirtsleeves into the cuffs of your gloves. Wash in a cold or tepid shower afterwards to remove any leftover fibres from your skin. If you're crawling around your loft, a hard hat is a good idea, too, for the inevitable collisions with the timber overhead.

'U', 'R' and 'K-values' What do they mean?

These mysterious ratings are often quoted in information about insulation, including the Building Regulations' aims for more energy-efficient homes thanks to increased insulation and reduced heat loss through glazing and gaps. But what do they mean and what should you be looking for? R-values and K-values rate how good a conductor of heat a particular material is. For insulation, you need a poor conductor to retain the heat within the building. Look for an insulation material with the lowest K-value you can find. The R-value designates a material's resistance to heat loss – in this case, the higher the R-value, the better. A U-value is a complex calculation that rates the overall ability of a wall, roof, floor or entire house to prevent heat loss. New extensions or house renovations may have to achieve a particular minimum U-value rating, and you may find U-values referred to when buying windows, but they are not usuallly used to rate insulation on its own.

Loose-fill is a flexible option

● **Loose-fill for awkward spaces** In many older homes, the spacing between ceiling joints visible in the loft is uneven. Joists are positioned at regular, conventional distances – generally 400mm or 600mm apart – and blanket roll and solid board insulation is all made with these dimensions in mind, so working with uneven gaps will leave you with a lot of cutting and wastage. In cases like this, loose-fill material is a better option. You can use vermiculite granules (left) or loose mineral wool, both of which are usually supplied in sacks containing enough to cover 1m².

● Don't just measure your loft space and order enough to cover it: deduct the area covered by joists or you'll have lots left over. Use plastic ventilator trays to avoid losing granules down cavity walls or through loft ventilation gaps and use a broom to push the insulation into hard-to-reach corners.

● To lay the recommended depth of insulation, you'll either need to build up the joists to 270mm thick to contain the loose-fill, or fill the gaps between the joists with loose-fill insulation and then lay additional blanket roll insulation on top.

How to insulate a roof slope

When you insulate the floor of your loft space, it makes the space within the loft very cold. If you want to store items that need to be kept warm and dry, a better option may be to insulate the roof slope, instead.

1 Use an open pair of scissors or a knife to cut batts of solid board insulation to fit the gaps between the rafters. Use any small offcuts in the eaves, to act as spacers that will help to maintain the air gap needed for ventilation.

2 Fit the batts between the rafters, then staple nylon garden netting to the rafters to hold the insulation in place (nailing could dislodge a tile or slate). You may need a helper to support the batts to stop them from falling out while you secure them.

3 Staple sheets of building paper over the netting, making sure these overlap by at least 100mm where they join. Tape along the seams with waterproof adhesive tape.

4 For an even better finish, screw foil-faced plasterboard to the rafters, positioning the foil side towards the roof. Use plasterboard drywall screws, which can be driven in with a power drill.

Double glazing

Replacing old single-glazed windows and doors with double glazing is one of the most cost-effective home improvements you can make. It may seem costly at the time, but do it well and you'll add value to your home, and the windows will start paying for themselves in lower heating bills from the minute they are installed. Any window can be double glazed, not just the ubiquitous PVC-U replacements, or you can fit secondary double glazing to create an insulating air gap without replacing your existing windows at all. Watch out for signs of deterioration that will reduce the efficiency of the double glazing.

Care and maintenance

● **Choose windows wisely** Replacement double-glazing window firms who put leaflets through your letterbox might inspire you to install new windows, but do your research first and choose your new windows and supplier with care. Cheap PVC-U windows can become discoloured and made brittle by ultraviolet light and grow grimy from traffic dirt, especially in homes on busy roads. Their catches and hinges are prone to breaking and, unless well designed, they can spoil the appearance of your home and reduce its value. Always buy the best you can afford – properly made and installed, sealed double-glazed units should last for 20 years or more, making them a worthwhile investment.

● **Make every day a clear day** The biggest potential problem with double glazing is internal misting between the two panes of glass. This is a natural deterioration when windows start to get old, but if it happens prematurely it's usually the result of poor-quality construction or installation. Cheap windows can sometimes mist up within a few years, or even months. To help prevent misting, make sure that your windows are certified as glazed in accordance with British Standard BS 6262, in addition to the required FENSA certification (see page 108). Not all FENSA member firms use this glazing method.

● **Keep windows and frames clean** Take care of PVC-U frames – they cannot easily be painted to freshen up their appearance like wooden frames can. Make sure you wash the frames whenever you clean the glass, wiping them with a soft cloth; open them and wipe around the edges, too. Don't use abrasive cleaners or scrubbers and never use washing-up liquid in the water, as this can attack and degrade the seals. Instead, mix a generous squirt of cream cleanser (car shampoo is ideal for this job) into a bucket of warm water.

● **Don't let hinges stick in their tracks** Most PVC-U casement windows open on hinges that run in sliding tracks at the top and bottom of the casement. These 'friction stay' hinges allow windows to stay open

SAVE £150

Cost to replace a sealed, double-glazed unit that has misted up because of failed seals.

WASH YOUR FRAMES WHEN YOU WASH THE GLASS.

Anatomy of a **double-glazed window**

It's the gap between the panes, not the glass itself, that gives double glazing its insulating properties. Even an air gap will help to reduce the amount of heat lost through a window, but most double-glazed units are filled with special 'inert' gases, such as argon, which are poor conductors of heat. The optimum gap between the two panes of glass in a sealed, double-glazed unit is 20mm. If the gap is too wide, convection currents can occur within it, transferring heat between the panes of glass, too narrow and the insulation will be poor. New windows should also be supplied with low-emissivity glass, which reduces heat transfer through the window, keeping rooms warm in winter and cool in summer.

Heat from the sun passes through the window

Inert gas fills the gap between two panes of glass to prevent heat loss

Low-emissivity glass reflects heat back into the room

SECONDARY DOUBLE GLAZING

If you don't want the upheaval of replacing the entire window, or if you live in a listed property where you cannot change the external appearance of your house, thoroughly draughtproof the windows (see pages 157-159) then fit secondary double glazing. The most common option is an aluminium-framed sliding window that allows access for opening the existing window, but fixed options are also available. Secondary double glazing offers greater sound insulation than sealed units and, in this instance, the insulation is most effective with as wide a gap as possible. The best soundproofing results are achieved by having different weights of glass in the secondary glazing and the existing windows, to avoid resonance. So if you have 4mm glass in the existing windows, use 6mm panes in the secondary glazing.

Dirty hinges will be stiff

in any position without swinging in a breeze. They are strong, to bear the weight of heavy double-glazed units, but also more complex than conventional hinges and with more moving parts. The tracks are prone to collecting dirt and will, in time, make the windows stick or stiff to open. Pick out any large obstructions, like leaves or small twigs that have blown in when the window is open, and use a vacuum cleaner to pick up loose dirt, then wipe the tracks with white spirit.

● Once a year, lubricate the hinges with a spray of silicone-based furniture polish – not oil, which can attract dirt and grime.

Easy fixes

● **Replacing broken hardware** If a handle or hinge fails on a window, or if you want to upgrade your window hardware by fitting locking handles, you can usually do it yourself with nothing more than a screwdriver. Be careful to buy an exact match in size so that you can use the same screw holes if your frames are PVC-U. Old holes in wooden frames can be filled and repainted if necessary. Some hinges are fixed in place with rivets, in which case it's wise to call for a professional repair.

● Even if only one hinge on a window is faulty, replace both hinges together to prevent uneven wear.

Ventilation

Draughtproofing and insulation are important, but it's important not to make your home completely airtight – all houses need to breathe. Most dampness problems in modern houses are caused by condensation and high humidity due to inadequate ventilation. This can lead to mildew on clothes and leather in wardrobes and black mould on the bathroom ceiling. Follow these tips for keeping your home warm, but fresh.

Care and maintenance

● **Check airbricks regularly**
Suspended timber floors need to be ventilated underneath by airbricks. These are set into the bricks in the external wall, usually one brick in size. They should never be blocked off or covered by raised paths or garden beds, as they are vital in venting away the moisture that rises up from the ground. Check airbricks every six months to make sure that soil or wind-blown debris isn't piling up against them, and clear them if necessary.

SAVE £250

Cost for a builder to install soffit vents into your roof space for ventilation.

● **Check window vents regularly** The Building Regulations require new windows to be fitted with 'trickle vents' that allow a small constant flow of air in and out. They fit in the top of the window frame, and some can be closed manually by sliding a tab on the inside. Check the vents once a year to make sure that they aren't broken and that they still open and close easily – and that they aren't all closed.

● **Vent the attic well** All homes have some form of loft ventilation, either screened vents in the gable ends, vents fitted within the tiles on the roof slope or soffit vents in the eaves (right).
● Cool air flowing into the loft through these vents prevents the warm, moist air rising from the house from condensing within the cold loft space, where it would settle as moisture on the roof timbers. Over time, this would cause the wood to rot, saturate the loft insulation and potentially spoil the plaster and decoration on the ceilings in the rooms below – all of them expensive but preventable repair jobs.
● Once a year, make sure all vents are open and free of obstructions and that insulation isn't blocking soffit vents or impeding the flow of air.
● When you install loft insulation (pages 147-152) make sure that you don't block any vents. Plastic ventilator trays (right) are designed to sit between the joists and create a backing for insulation to press against, while allowing air to circulate behind them.

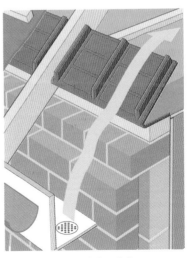

Air must flow freely in a loft

Choosing the right extractor fan

Before buying a fan, find out how much air it can move. Airflow capacity is given either in cubic metres per hour, or litres per second.

The fan extract rates required by the Building Regulations vary by room:

- **KITCHENS** 60 litres per second (215m³ per hour)
- **UTILITY ROOMS** 30 litres per second (110m³ per hour)
- **BATHROOMS** 15 litres per second (55m³ per hour)
- **SEPARATE TOILETS** 6 litres per second (22m³ per hour).

A typical 150mm diameter wall or window fan has an extract rate of about 280m³ per hour, which is more than enough to meet the Building Regulations requirements for ventilating any room, including a kitchen.

Night vents let in just enough air

● **Use fans in kitchens and bathrooms** Everyday activities like showering and cooking – even breathing and perspiring – introduce water vapour into the air and this should be vented to the outside of the building.
◦ All bathrooms should have electric extractor fans (although this doesn't stop you opening the window, too). Such a fan is a Building Regulations requirement for new bathrooms. Ones that are wired into the light switch and have a timer come on automatically when someone puts on the light and will continue to run for a set period after the light is switched off.
◦ Make sure your cooker has an extractor fan fitted above the hood to remove steam from cooking. The most effective ones vent to the outside, rather than recirculating moist air back into the room.

Easy fix

● **Fit locking night latches for window ventilation** If your windows don't have trickle vents, you can fit locking night vents for ventilation. These locking casement handles (left) can be closed tight or slightly ajar and locked for security – they are available in a range of styles and finishes.

How to install a soffit vent

Installing exterior soffit vents can reduce moisture in your loft in winter and keep it cool in summer. The vents are easy to install, although you'll probably need to put in more than one. Estimate one soffit vent for every 10m² of loft space. Note, too, that soffit vents draw air into the loft. To achieve proper ventilation, your roof should also have sufficient roof vents, which let air flow out of the loft. Follow these simple instructions for putting in a soffit vent.

1 Place the vent on the soffit and trace its area with a pencil. Measure 25mm in on all sides to make a cutting line. Erase the initial tracing to avoid mistakes. Drill holes on all four corners.

2 Using a jigsaw, cut along the outline to make the opening for the vent.

3 Install the vent over the opening, and screw it into place with stainless steel self-tapping screws. Be sure to angle the louvres so that air flows into the loft.

Draughtproofing

Without draught excluders on windows and doors, icy blasts blow in and precious heat leaks out. Checking the draught excluders every year is an important first step in keeping your heating bills as low as possible. Foam strips will perish over time, and other materials can stop working too if the door or window shrinks or shifts slightly. Fitting and replacing are both simple tasks – just make sure you choose appropriate products and buy the best you can.

Care and maintenance

● **Locating leaks** The best way to tell whether your draughtproofing is up to scratch is to light a stick of incense and, on a windy day, move it slowly alongside windows, doors, loft hatches and other fixtures where outside air might enter. When the incense smoke moves horizontally, you've found a leak that may require sealing (see page 160) or a draught excluder.
● You can also detect draughts by feel. Dampen the back of your hand and move it along the perimeter of exterior doors and windows – you'll feel coolness when air is coming through.

● **Inspect exterior doors annually** Draught excluders around exterior doors will shift as your house shifts and settles. Check once a year to see if weather stripping needs to be adjusted or replaced.

● **Prepare surfaces for draughtproofing** When applying self-adhesive draught excluder to windows, it's crucial to start with a clean, dry surface. Any residual moisture, dirt or oil will prevent the adhesive from adhering to the frame and forming a tight seal.
● If the area is dusty or grimy, use a small amount of methylated spirits on a cloth or paper towel to clean it off.
● Use a hair dryer on its highest setting to thoroughly dry the surface and remove trapped moisture.
● Before installing a draught excluder on a door, check that none of the hardware is loose and that the door latches tightly. Adjust it for a tight fit if necessary first (see pages 116-117).

Easy fixes

● **Stopping window draughts** An easy way to seal gaps around a draughty casement window is to install a self-adhesive foam strip all round the frame. Buy the best quality you can to get the longest life from your repair. Cheap foam strips can perish in just a couple of seasons – better-quality foam should last for five years or more. Use scissors or a trimming knife to cut lengths to fit, making sure to go right into the corners and butt lengths together neatly where they join. Peel away the backing a little at a time as you work so that long strips don't get tangled and stuck together.
● Seal draughty sash windows with brush strips (see page 159).

SAVE £25

Average annual saving on your energy bill when your house is fully draughtproofed. You could pay £200 for a professional to do the job or £100 for DIY materials.

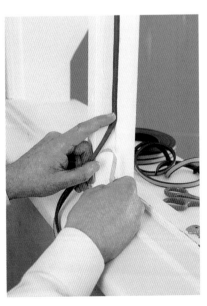

Foam strips seal out draughts

● **Replace threshold gaskets** External doors may have a threshold draught excluder: a rubber gasket that sits within a metal bar across the doorstep and seals the gap between the door and threshold. When it's time to replace a worn gasket, take the old one with you to ensure a good match. A gasket has two splines (narrow fins) that fit into grooves in the threshold. If the splines tear off as you remove the old gasket, use a narrow screwdriver to pry them out, and make sure no pieces stay in the grooves. To install a new gasket, press its splines into the grooves using your fingers, then push down with a wood block.

How to choose the right draughtproofing

When selecting draughtproofing, be sure to compare cost and durability. Felt is inexpensive, for example, but it's also one of the least durable and least effective types of draughtproofing material.

Type and description	Use	Pros	Cons
SELF-ADHESIVE RUBBER STRIP			
● Squashy rubber strips available in 'P' and 'E' profiles joint edges	● On casement windows and exterior doors ● Fix to the frame with the self-adhesive backing	● Tough and long-lasting	● Available in a limited colour range
BRUSH STRIP			
● Siliconised nylon pile is fixed into self-adhesive backing strips or a metal or plastic holder that's nailed in place to the frame ● Bristles make a seal with the door or window	● On exterior and patio doors, and sash and casement windows ● Designed to seal surfaces that move against one another	● Durable and effective in difficult situations, where friction of sliding doors can dislodge seals	● Self-adhesive options prone to coming unstuck on sliding doors and windows
SELF-ADHESIVE FOAM STRIP			
● Strips of foam around 6mm thick and 10mm wide, with adhesive backing for easy installation	● On doors and casement windows	● Effective and easy to install	● Variable quality: cheaper versions perish quickly ● Paint will harden foam and stop it working ● Usually only available in white
STRIP EXCLUDERS			
● A strip of nylon, rubber or plastic bristle, or a continuous strip of rubber in an aluminium mounting strip	● On exterior doors ● Screwed to the base of the door on the inside	● Height is adjustable to give a good seal with the floor	● Visible and unattractive, and tend to gather dust

● **Replace slipping draught excluders** Self-adhesive draught excluders can slip and shift over time, causing doors to stick or become difficult to close. If this happens, it's time to replace them – if you try to reposition the strips the self-adhesive backing won't stick back securely.

● **Stop draughts at the front door** You can fix draughtproofing around the edges and a threshold strip across the bottom, but don't forget the openings within your front door.

  ● A letterbox excluder fits over the inside of the letterbox opening – two rows of nylon bristles meet in the middle to keep out draughts, without blocking out the post. Horizontal internal flaps – in plastic or metal – also help to keep out draughts and can be fitted to the inside of the door with a strip of self-adhesive foam draught excluder to seal around the edges and soften the bang when it closes.

  ● Keyholes may be small, but if they aren't covered a breeze will still blow in. An escutcheon plate (right) stops that from happening. The plate hangs on a pivot in front of the keyhole of a mortise lock and is easily swung out of the way when you need to use the key. They can be fitted inside or out.

● **Keeping the weather out** A rain deflector is a useful addition to a front door and works in combination with a weather bar fitted across the sill to keep the door draughtproof and watertight. Some doors are supplied with a deflector already fitted in wood to match.

  ● The deflector is a simple device – its slanted edge diverts water that runs down the door so that it drips beyond the threshold and runs away from the house.

  ● The weatherbar on the sill fits neatly into a rebate cut into the bottom of the door and creates a seal to prevent rain from being blown in beneath the door on blustery days.

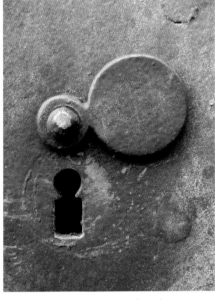

An escutcheon plate stops draughts

How to install draughtproofing on a sash window

Rigid brush strip is the most suitable material for sealing a draughty sash window, as the sashes slide over it easily.

1 Cut four lengths of brush strip, each the length of one of the sliding sashes. Don't use self-adhesive strip for sash windows, as the sliding of the sashes will pull it out of place.

2 Hammer pins through pre-drilled holes on the brush strip (above right) to fix the strip to the frame: on the inside of the inner sash and on the outside of the outer sash. Position them to make a snug seal with the windows. If you cannot access the outside of the window from a ladder, you'll need to remove the sashes for this job (see page 109).

3 Seal the top and bottom of the sashes with durable foam strips fixed to the frame or the sash.

4 Finally, fix a length of nylon brush pile strip to the meeting rail of the bottom sash (right) to seal the gap between the two sashes when they are closed.

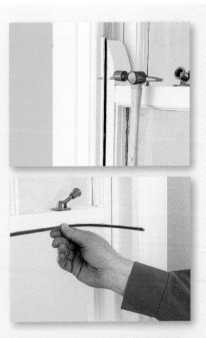

Sealing gaps

Sealant is one of the most versatile products around. It's relatively inexpensive, and the amount of money it saves you in energy costs and leak repairs more than makes up for what you pay for it. You can buy a sealant designed for use with virtually any building material found inside and outside the home—everything from plasterboard, glass, plastic, wood and tile to asphalt, concrete, metal, stone and brick. It may perform just one essential task – sealing gaps – but it does the job extremely well.

SAVE £800

Cost of replacing a wooden window frame rotted by water seeping through poorly sealed gaps around the edges.

USE A SCREWDRIVER FOR THE 'PROD' TEST.

Care and maintenance

● **A 'prod' test checks the seal** In early spring and autumn, examine all the points around the outside of your home where water could get in – around window and door frames, along the edges of timber cladding boards, around doorsteps and windowsills, or where pipes or cables run through the wall. Make certain that all joints are watertight and ready for the coming harsher weather in autumn, then check again in spring to make sure that frosts and heavy rain haven't weakened any joints over winter. The best way to test sealant is by poking it with a screwdriver. It should have some give. If it cracks or tears, replace it.

● **Prepare the area first** Clean the surfaces you are going to seal, otherwise the sealant won't adhere firmly and the seal will be useless. Wipe off any dust or dirt, and remove oils or deposits with white spirit or a manufacturer-recommended solvent. Most importantly, remove any existing sealant with a putty knife, razor blade or screwdriver. If you're sealing around a door or window frame, make sure that the paint is sound. Sand it, prime it and repaint it first, if necessary.

● **Stop up the tube** What can you do with a half-full tube of sealant? Either look for something else to seal, or reseal it and save it for next time. The trick to reusing sealant is to keep the remaining adhesive from hardening. Always clean the nozzle after use, then plug it with a rustproof, 50mm machine screw or nail. Wrapping the end of the tube with cling film can also help to keep the sealant from hardening. Some nozzles come with a cap to fit over the tip, or you can invert it to fit into the cut nozzle.
 ● You can buy packets of spare nozzles, which will fit most tubes as they are a universal size. These are a useful stand-by if you find that sealant has hardened within the nozzle when you come to use the tube again.

● **Warm up the mastic to make it flex** In cold weather, particularly if you store your tools and equipment in an unheated shed or garage, dunk a cartridge of sealant in a bucket of warm water for half an hour before you use it. Sealant gets stiff when it's cold, so the heat will help to make it more flexible and much easier to apply smoothly.

Easy fixes

● **Cut the nozzle carefully** The success of any sealing job depends on applying the right amount of sealant. One of the most common mistakes that DIY-ers make is cutting the nozzle too far down, creating a large opening that dispenses too much of the mastic. For best results, the hole should be about half as wide as the crack or seam you'll be filling. Cut the tube at a 45 degree angle to help you to make a neat job.

● Some professionals claim that a V-notch cut in the tip makes it easier to apply sealant round corners. Experiment and see what works best for you.

● Remember, you need to cut off the seal on the end of the cartridge itself, too, before you use a tube for the first time.

● **Tool the bead** To do its job, a bead of sealant needs to be tooled, or compressed, to fit into the seam. Ideally, it should be thick where it adheres to both sides of the joint but thinner in the middle. With practice, you can use the cut end of the nozzle itself to tool the sealant as it's applied. A wet finger also does the job, but be sure to wear latex gloves if you're using silicone, polyurethane, butyl rubber or any other sealant that may cause skin irritation. You can also use an ice cube (this is especially good because it will never stick), a lolly stick or plastic spoon.

● **Slow and steady** Squeeze the trigger of the mastic applicator gun to start the sealant flowing. Squeezing the trigger pushes a piston up inside the tube to force the sealant out of the nozzle. The trick for a neat job is to start at one end of the gap to be sealed and move the applicator slowly and steadily as the sealant is extruded, keeping a firm, steady squeeze on the trigger. You'll need to release the trigger and squeeze again from time to time. Stop the flow when you get to the end by releasing the locking bar on the piston, usually where your thumb is when you're holding the gun.

● **Keep in line with masking tape** If you're doing this for the first time, or need a straight, neat line of sealant in a conspicuous area, stick a strip of masking tape on each side of the seam before you start. Make sure the tape is straight and spaced evenly to the width of the tooled bead. Apply about 1m of sealant at a time, smooth the finish then slowly remove the tape.

● **Filling big gaps** Don't waste sealant on a gap that's wider than 5mm, or deeper than 10mm. It's unlikely to stick well, and you'll soon be doing the job again. To fill a deep crack, press a backer rod (available in different sizes at most DIY stores) into the gap before you apply the sealant.

● Fill wide or irregular gaps, such as where a pipe comes out through a wall, with expanding foam filler. This comes in an aerosol can and is applied through a nozzle directly into the gap, where it expands to fill the space. It's sticky and messy when first applied, but hardens to a heat, cold, water and rot-resistant finish after one or two hours. Once the foam has hardened, use a hacksaw or sharp knife to cut away the excess – wear a mask to protect yourself from inhaling the dust. The finished surface can be sanded, plastered or painted.

smart idea

Silicone sealant can degrade over time, so always test an old tube before using it. Squeeze a little onto a nonporous surface – if it doesn't cure (harden) within 24 hours, throw it away and buy a fresh tube.

Slow and steady makes a neat job

Foam expands into awkward gaps

Conservatories

When it's not warm enough to sit out, a conservatory can be a great place for you to enjoy the garden. But the glass means they can be too hot or cold for regular use. Follow these tips for keeping your conservatory clean and in good condition – and at a comfortable temperature. Loose or damaged seals, dirty and difficult-to-clean roofs and poor security are the most common problems.

Care and maintenance

SAVE £20

Cost for a window cleaner to clean the outside panes of your conservatory glass, including the roof.

● **Do a seasonal inspection** Prepare for rough winter weather with an autumn inspection of your conservatory's structural elements. Check for leaks, split or rotting wood, missing nails or screws, damaged steps and loose or damaged seals where the conservatory attaches to the house.

● **Think twice if you face south** The obvious place to site a conservatory is on the back of the house, off the kitchen or living space. But if this puts it in a bright, south-facing position, you may find that it is often far too hot to sit in on sunny days during the summer. The best location for a conservatory is on a north or west-facing wall, where it will be sheltered from direct sunlight for most of the day or for the hottest part. Consider other options, such as a sun room or other part-glazed structure rather than a fully glazed conservatory (see box, below).

● Air-conditioning units that also work as heaters in winter are worth considering, but are expensive to run and of limited use in a sunny space.

Planning for efficient **heating and cooling**

If you want to build a conservatory for year-round use, heating it and cooling it in summer will be expensive. Follow this advice for planning wisely to create an efficient space.

● The best option is always to have a conservatory that can be shut off from the rest of the house with doors. That way, excessive heat or cold in the conservatory won't affect the temperature in the rest of the adjacent rooms. Conservatories separated in this way don't need to conform to the latest Building Regulations requirements on insulated glazing, unlike those joined to the home by a permanent opening.

● Even the highest-specification glass will leak heat at a much higher rate than a brick wall. To minimise your heating and cooling costs, and improve the comfort of the new room, limit the glass area by creating a sun-room extension instead, with tiles or slates over

at least part of the roof. This is likely to require building control approval – check with your local planning control office first.

● When planning a conservatory or sun room, specify the best glazing you can afford. All double glazing should have a low-emissivity coating on the cavity side of the inner pane, but you can ask for this on both panes of glass. Choose double-glazed units filled with argon if you can, as these will insulate better than those with an air gap. And consider using solar-control glass for the outer pane – these have a subtle green, blue or brown tint to absorb heat from the sun, or a silver coating (like mirror sunglasses) to reflect it.

● **Watch out for leaks at the wall** A common problem with conservatories added after a house was built can be rainwater leaks at the junction between the conservatory roof and the wall of the house. This is most likely to occur in modern houses built with cavity walls (see page 91), where the outer leaf of brickwork above the conservatory roof line becomes an inner wall below it. When cavity walls are subjected to wind-driven rain, water can flow down the inside of the brick outer leaf until it reaches ground level or is intercepted by drainage channels and weep holes at lintels above doors and windows.

● Where a new conservatory roof is butted up against such a wall, a damp-proof tray should be fitted within the cavity above the roof line to make sure that rainwater cannot drip down inside. This involves removing bricks in the wall and is rarely done. If these kind of leaks are a problem in your conservatory, get professional help.

● **Prevent rot in wooden structures** Start your conservatory maintenance with the surrounding parts of the main house. Make sure that gutters passing over the conservatory are flowing freely and preventing rain from draining off the roof onto the conservatory below. Check that rainwater doesn't puddle or splash up onto or around wooden parts of a conservatory, where it could cause the wood to rot. Also make sure that soil or mulch in surrounding flowerbeds are kept clear of the wood.

● **Cleaning a glass roof** Keeping the glass clean is the biggest job in maintaining a conservatory. Cleaning the vertical panes is no harder than cleaning any normal window, but safely cleaning the roof can be more of a challenge. The best way is to use a squeegee on a long extension pole. Stand on a pair of steps if you need to to reach the roof comfortably, but never stand on or even lean on the glass itself.

● Self-cleaning glass is now available and is an attractive option. It's specially coated to prevent dirt from sticking, but relies on rain to wash the dirt away. In dry spells, the roof will need to be hosed down when it gets dirty.

Easy fixes

● **Increasing shade and ventilation** There's a large market in conservatory sun blinds to fit on vertical glass and the sloping roof. These may give shade from the direct rays of the sun, protecting furniture and shielding users from glare, but they don't stop the overall temperature from rising unless they are combined with suitable ventilation. Ceiling fans can help to move hot air away, but you need vents at low and high level to enable the air to carry away heat by convection.

● **Protect a glass roof** If you live in an area where heavy snowfall is common in winter, it may be worth fitting snow guards to the gutters above your conservatory. These netting structures stand up at the edge of the roof of your house and prevent large chunks of snow or ice sliding off and onto the roof of your conservatory.

take care!

It's important that the junction between the roof of a new conservatory and the abutting house walls is sealed with proper traditional lead flashing and not flimsy self-adhesive strips. When you're buying a conservatory, ask the supplier to specify what materials they are going to use and choose a supplier who will do the best job. Poor flashing will almost certainly leak, causing water damage, and can be an indication of other poor-quality materials and workmanship.

A LONG POLE MAKES ROOF CLEANING EASY.

Garages and carports

They provide protection against the elements for your vehicles, but increasingly garages and carports do double and triple duty as a workshop and covered storage area. Apart from the doors (see pages 123-125), garages and carports are relatively maintenance-free, but there are plenty of tips you can follow to make your garage a more functional storage and working space.

SAVE £350

Cost to have a double garage floor professionally painted with an epoxy coating.

take care!

A well-sealed garage can make a great work area or protected storage space, but it can also be a trap for carbon monoxide gas generated by cars and other petrol-driven machinery such as lawnmowers. Never run any such items in a detached garage unless the door is open for ventilation. Never run this kind of machinery in an attached garage even if the door is open, because carbon monoxide can seep through the garage walls into the house.

Care and maintenance

● **Give your garage floor a new look** The right finish will give your concrete garage floor an easy-to-clean surface and a polished look. Paints are available in a variety of colours, and the best contain a fine aggregate that gives a non-slip finish.

● Make sure the floor is clean before you paint. Wash it with a cleaner suitable for lifting oil stains and rinse with a hose, starting at the back of the garage and working your way forwards, towards and out of the door.

● If a previous coat of paint was peeling, roughen the surface with a commercial etching solution that will allow the new paint to adhere better.

● Allow the paint to dry for at least 24 hours before walking on it and as much as a week before parking a car on it.

● **Mark off your parking spot** Avoid damage to your car by marking off the parking zone within your garage. Use coloured tape or spray paint to mark the stopping point on the floor or suspend a tennis ball from the ceiling so that it hangs at the spot where you need to stop – either level with your bonnet or the windscreen.

Easy fixes

● **Keeping oil stains from setting** Oil drips are hard to avoid, but they don't have to hit the floor. Place a mat, offcut of carpet or a pan lined with cardboard under cars and leaking machinery to catch drips.

● If you miss a few, don't let them soak in. There are myriad products available for removing oil spills, but none works better than ordinary clay-based cat litter. If the stains are fresh, cover them with cat litter, wait about an hour and sweep it up. For old stains, pour paint thinner on the stain, cover with cat litter, wait 12 hours and then sweep clean.

● **Stripping out the elements** Seal the gaps around your garage door with weather stripping. Even if your garage floor or drive is uneven, you can create a good seal by tacking a length of brush draught excluder along the bottom edge of the door. Most garages are built just one brick thick and aren't insulated, but if you use yours to store things that need to be kept warm and dry, or if your garage is attached to your house, consider insulating the roof space and fit a solid door with draught excluders where it connects to the house.

7 tips for an **organised garage**

With just little time and planning, you can transform your garage from a cluttered mess into an organised, convenient oasis. Here are some easy ways for you to overhaul your untidy garage in just a weekend – or less.

1 Sort the contents of your garage into three piles: 'keep', 'sell/give away' and 'throw away'. If you're hesitating about a certain item, remember the two-year rule: if you haven't used or worn something in two years, it's time to let it go.

2 Group the 'keep' pile by season or by use, so that these items can be stored together when you put them back inside the garage.

3 Install cabinets or free-standing, open shelving units, if you don't have them already, for effective, off-the-ground storage. Bins and boxes in an array of sizes and shapes can be added for extra convenience, and transparent ones allow you to see what's inside without taking it down from the shelf.

4 Suspend overhead bins from ceiling joists. Up here is the best place to store a roofrack or roofbox, when it's not on the car, and if you've got a high roof in your garage you can use the space to store a lot of items that you don't need to access regularly.

5 Wall racks can be installed for easy access to sports equipment, garden tools, stepladders and more.

6 Stand recycling bins near the entrance to your home for easy sorting and disposal.

7 Create a workbench with pegboard panelling above it to make tools easy to find. Alongside it, fit cabinets or shelves for storing other tools and equipment.

4 HOME SYSTEMS

The plumbing and electrics in your home are a complex mass of components, all essential to keeping the whole place working. Think about them as systems, rather than a bewildering array of discrete parts and you'll start to understand how best to look after them.

There are limits to what a homeowner is legally allowed to do to fix or service parts of the plumbing and electrical systems. But key to keeping house systems running smoothly is regular maintenance, and this often involves little more than cleaning. Clean the coils on the back of your refrigerator and it will run more efficiently. Clean the striker on the doorbell and that faint chime will return to its original clear ring. It's as simple as that. In this section, we'll show you how to handle basic maintenance and repair jobs and warn you about jobs that you should leave to professionals.

Even when you do call in the experts, you can save time and money by doing some of the groundwork yourself by locating and diagnosing the problem. You will find advice on clues to look and listen for and simple diagnostic tests you can do yourself.

Of course, you can also save money by reducing the amount of electricity and water your houshold uses – follow these clever tips to cut your household bills.

ELECTRICS

You and the law

Faulty wiring really can be a matter of life and death. The risk of damaging appliances through electrical shorts plus the personal risks of electric shock or fire make it easy to understand why you should never attempt electrical repairs unless you're confident of your ability. Building Regulations stipulate that some jobs must be left to the professionals or checked and certified for safety after you've finished.

● **Building Regulations and electrical work** The rules governing electrical wiring work are set out in Part P of the Building Regulations. Householders can still carry out wiring work listed as 'notifiable' by the Building Regulations (see below), but it must be inspected by the local authority Building Control officer.

● Alternatively, the work must be carried out by a qualified electrician who is registered as being eligible to 'self-certify' his own work. When you come to sell your house, you'll be expected to provide certificates relating to any relevant electrical work done since 2006.

● UK rules do not apply in the Republic of Ireland. You must comply with Ireland's National Rules for Electrical Installations. Contact the local government office or the Electro-Technical Council of Ireland for details.

● **What you can do** Some minor electrical alterations and repairs are not covered by the legislation. You are still allowed to replace power sockets and light switches on a like-for-like basis, upgrade earth bonding, replace a faulty cable for a single circuit and add new power sockets, fused spurs and lighting points to an existing circuit. But you must not do any of this work in 'wet' rooms – kitchens and bathrooms – or outside.

● **What you cannot do** The jobs listed below qualify as 'notifiable jobs'. These must be carried out by a qualified, self-certifying electrician or scheduled with the local Building Control office and inspected and tested after completion of the job.

● You may not add sockets, fused spurs or lighting points in a kitchen, bathroom or outdoors.

● You may not wire and connect a new circuit back to the consumer unit.

● You may not extend a circuit in a kitchen or bathroom.

● You may not carry out electrical work outdoors.

● **Your supplier's rights** Your electrical supply company has the right to refuse to supply any property that it suspects may have faulty and unsafe wiring or wiring that doesn't comply with the Wiring Regulations. The company has the right to inspect and test any electrical work you've carried out yourself if it thinks it may be unsafe.

Ask the experts

If you're in any doubt about whether an electrical job is notifiable or whether you can do it yourself, contact your local building control office for advice.

● Even non-notifiable jobs must be carried out to a standard that meets Building Regulations, so call in a professional if you're unsure of your own abilities.

● Look for an electrician who is a member of the Electrical Contractors' Association (ECA) or on the roll of the National Inspection Council for Electrical Installation Contracting (NICEIC). Look for the logos below on the electrician's headed paper, card or advertisement.

Representing the best in electrical engineering and building services

Top tips for saving energy

There are lots of simple things you can do to cut down the amount of energy you use in your home. Following the advice in even one of these tips will help to reduce your household bills, but with a little effort you should be able to make substantial savings – and contribute towards lowering national greenhouse gas emissions, too.

SAVE £160

Average amount you can save on heating costs every year by installing cavity wall insulation – in an average home.

Care and maintenance

● **Insulate your home well** Adequate insulation in your loft and walls and insulating double-glazed windows throughout will help to cut down on your heating bills, by making your house retain heat better in cold weather and stay around 10°C warmer than an uninsulated home. But insulation can also help in hot weather, as you use less energy on fans and air-conditioning units. A well-insulated house can be up to 7°C cooler in summer than a non-insulated equivalent.

● For more tips on insulating your home, see pages 147-152; for tips on double glazing, see pages 153-154.

● **Pull the curtains at night** It's simple, but effective. When it's cold outside, even draughtproofed, double-glazed windows will lose some heat. In fact, windows can contribute as much as 20 per cent of the total heat lost from a home. This will make the rooms feel cold, and you'll probably be tempted to turn the heating up a couple of degrees to compensate. But you can reduce your heat loss by up to a third by hanging and using good-quality, heavy, lined curtains that fit snugly to the wall at the edges and have a closed pelmet at the top.

● **Think twice before using the hot tap** Every time you turn on a hot tap, you need to run off the cold water that has been standing in the pipe (the lag) before hot water starts running through. This can add up

Low-energy lightbulbs   Equipment spotlight

As part of a Europe-wide energy-saving directive, traditional incandescent lightbulbs are being phased out and replaced by low-energy compact fluorescent lamps (CFLs). These can last between 6 and 15 times longer than incandescent bulbs and use 80 per cent less electricity to run. Replacing all the bulbs in your home with CFLs will require a large initial outlay, since they are significantly more expensive to buy, but will immediately start to save you money on your electricity bill. Although they were initially only available in a limited range of shapes and sizes, you can now find a CFL to suit almost any lamp. If you don't want to splurge on a complete new set of bulbs, make sure you replace any traditional incandescent bulb that blows with a low-energy equivalent – you may already have found that you cannot buy the traditional bulbs any more as shops are no longer replenishing their stocks.

to a litre or more each time. If you use this simply to rinse your hands or swill a teacup, you're not actually waiting for the hot water at all but have still drawn it unnecessarily out of the tank where it will need to be replaced and reheated. Reach for the cold tap instead.

● Even if you don't have a water tank and use a combination boiler for instant hot water, this quick burst of the tap will have been enough to fire up the boiler for no reason. By the time you come back to the tap, the hot water you pulled off will probably have cooled.

● **Target big ticket areas** The two biggest categories of energy consumption in most homes are heating the house and heating the hot water. Between the two, they account for more than half the energy used each year. Concentrate on reducing your energy use in those areas first to make an impact on your overall consumption and the bills.

Certification Mark

Choosing new appliances

All new electrical appliances now bear an energy rating, making it easier than ever to compare them and their likely running costs. Always choose the best you can afford: A+ and A++ appliances are the most efficient. Check, too, that an appliance is 'Energy Saving Trust Recommended' by the Energy Saving Trust – look out for the logo (left) to be sure. Just as important is to buy appliances that are appropriate for your family's needs. If you're a small household, don't choose a large American fridge with far more room than you really need, or a large-capacity washing machine, or you'll still be using unneccessary energy.

● **Mind the gaps** If you add up all the gaps around the average home's draughty doors and windows, it can be as much as the equivalent of having a 300mm x 300mm hole in the wall. Spend £10 on self-adhesive draught-stripping and a few hours' work fitting it and within a few months you'll have earned back that £10 in energy savings. In fact, fitting draught excluders all round your home could cut your heat loss by as much as 25 per cent in winter.

● For tips on draughtproofing your home, see pages 157-161.

● **Turn down the heat** Turning down the thermostat by one degree can save you money, and you probably won't notice the slight difference in temperature. Fit a digital thermostat (see page 233) to give yourself precise control of your heating.

● **Wash on cool and line dry** You don't need a hot wash to get clothes clean with modern washing powders and liquids. Set your machine to a 30° wash cycle rather than 60° and you could use around 40 per cent less energy for each load of washing. And once the washing is done, head out to the line. Even the most efficient tumble dryer is a heavy user of electricity so, whenever the weather allows, try to dry your laundry outside on a washing line rather than in another machine.

EQUIPMENT LEFT ON STANDBY IS CONSUMING POWER
UNNECESSARILY: TURN IT OFF AT THE PLUG.

Easy fixes

● **Choose automatic ventilation** An extractor fan will pay dividends by preventing problems with mould and damp in bathrooms and kitchens. To do this properly, it must carry on running for a while after you've finished showering or bathing and left the steamy room. If it's left running for several hours or forgotten about entirely, though, it will be spinning electricity out through the vent along with the air.

● Replace any manual fans with automatic ones wired into the light switch to come on whenever someone enters the room and switches on the light.

● Choose a model that will switch itself off again automatically, either for a time after the light is switched off, or when a moisture sensor detects that the damp air has been cleared.

● **Go wireless for shed lighting** It's easy to forget to switch off a light, but if that light is in a shed or outbuilding without any windows it could easily be days before you go back and discover it's still burning brightly inside. Even if you have a power supply to your shed, it's worth considering installing a simple solar-powered light, connected to a small solar panel mounted on the shed roof.

● Because solar-powered lights aren't connected to the house wiring, this is one outdoor electrical installation that you can safely do yourself within the wiring regulations (see page 169).

Low-emissivity glass for new windows

All new double or triple-glazed panels, and any supplied in new or replacement windows, should be given a low-emissivity (low-E) coating. This reduces heat loss through the windows, and although the glass may cost 10-15 per cent more than uncoated equivalents the windows will reduce energy loss by as much as 30-50 per cent. Most double glazing just has a low-E coating on the cavity side of the inner pane, but you can improve its performance further by specifying it on both panes within each double-glazed unit (see page 154).

5 easy ways to cut your fuel bills

Some energy-saving measures, like installing loft insulation or double glazing, require time and money. But there are simple things, too, that anyone can do and which will save rather than cost you money.

1 Switch off lights Make it a habit and train your family too: turn off the light when you leave a room unless you know you'll be coming back quickly.

2 Think small in the kitchen Small cooking appliances are usually more energy-efficient than the equivalent functions on a conventional oven. Using the toaster will use less power than an electric grill, and the short cooking times of a microwave make it far more efficient than slow-cooking in the main oven.

3 Don't light up the whole street Outdoor security lights have many benefits: they make your home less attractive to intruders and help you to find your way along the garden path at night. But many of them are poorly adjusted, come on all through the night every time a nearby tree branch moves or car drives by, or stay on for far longer than necessary. Check security lights regularly to make sure they are working efficiently.

4 Switch off at the wall Leaving your television, DVD player or even microwave on stand-by is consuming power unnecessarily. Constantly switching often-used appliances on and off may be a difficult rule to abide by, but if you know you'll not be using something for at least a few hours, switch it off properly at the wall, and definitely overnight.

5 Don't heat empty rooms Turn off the radiators and shut the doors on rooms you don't use all the time, like spare bedrooms. They will soon warm up when guests are expected. Check from time to time to make sure items stored there aren't getting damp and give the room an occasional blast of heating if necesssary.

Electrical emergency

WARNING – the main on-off switch on your consumer unit, or fuse board, disconnects only the fuses or miniature circuit breakers (MCBs) and the cables leading out from it to the household circuits. It does NOT disconnect the cables entering via the meter from the service cable. Don't tamper with these cables. They are always live and at lethal mains voltage.

Before you start work

● **ELECTRICITY CAN KILL** – and doing your own electrical wiring work has obvious dangers.

● Always turn off at the main consumer unit and remove the fuse or switch from the MCB for the circuit you're working on (left).

● Make sure you know what you're doing – if in any doubt, employ an electrician. Remember that all wiring work must now comply with the Building Regulations (see page 169).

What to do if the power fails

1 If you have no power throughout your house, and neighbouring houses are also without power, there's a mains supply failure. Report it to the 24-hour emergency number under 'Electricity' in the phone book.

2 If your system is protected by a whole-house residual current device (RCD), check whether it has tripped off. Try to switch it on again if it has.

3 If it won't switch on, the fault that tripped it is still present on the system. Call an electrician to rectify it.

4 If you don't have an RCD, and your house is the only one without power, there may be a fault in your supply cable or your main supply fuse may have blown. Don't touch it. Report the failure as above.

Always switch off the power first

What to do **in the event of an electrical fire**

FIRE IN AN APPLIANCE If a plug-in appliance catches fire, switch it off at the socket and remove the plug. If the appliance is wired into a fixed, fused connection unit, turn off the switch or turn off the power to that circuit at the consumer unit. Smother the appliance with a blanket or rug, or use a dry-powder fire extinguisher. Never use water on an electrical fire.

A SMELL OF BURNING If an appliance is giving off a burning smell, turn it off and unplug it. Turn off the power at the consumer unit if you cannot disconnect the appliance. Get the appliance checked by an electrician. If the smell is coming from a socket, turn off the main power switch, allow the plug and socket to cool, then check the wiring in both (see pages 182-185).

Dealing with electric shock

WARNING If you get a minor shock from an electrical appliance, a plug, socket or other wiring accessory, stop using it immediately.

● Get a repair expert to check the appliance for earth safety, and replace damaged plugs and wiring accessories as soon as possible. Only use PVC insulating tape to make a temporary repair.

● If you get a shock from a socket outlet or other part of the household wiring, ask a qualified electrician to check your wiring and earth bonding as soon as possible.

● If someone receives a major shock, DO NOT touch bare flesh while the person is still in contact with the source of the current. If you do, the current will pass through you as well, giving you an electric shock too.

● Follow the steps below to deal safely, swiftly and confidently with an electric shock emergency.

1 Immediately turn off the source of the current if you can. Switch off and unplug any appliance involved in the accident if it's safe to do so, or turn off the power completely at the main switch on the house's consumer unit (see page 174).

2 If you cannot do this, grab the person's clothing and drag them away from the source of the current, or stand on some insulating material such as a book and use a broom or a similar wooden object to move the person or the source of the current.

3 Lay a conscious but visibly shocked person flat on their back with their legs raised slightly and cover them with a blanket. Call an ambulance. Don't give the injured person any food or drink. Cool visible burns with cold water, then cover them with a dry sterile dressing. Don't apply ointments.

● **IF SOMEONE IS UNCONSCIOUS BUT BREATHING** Place the injured person in the recovery position (above), lying on their side but slightly turned over towards their front. Tilt their head back and bring the jaw forward to help to keep their airway clear. Cover them with a blanket and call an ambulance.

● **CHECK BREATHING** Monitor the victim's breathing and heartbeat continuously until the ambulance arrives. Watch for signs of breathing, such as the chest rising, and listen closely for their breaths or feel for breaths as they inhale. Check for a pulse in the person's neck – it's usually stronger here than in the wrist. To get the right position, find a pulse in your own neck first and then look for a corresponding pulse in the injured person.

● **IF THE BREATHING OR HEARTBEAT STOPS** If either the victim's pulse or breathing stops at any point, give artificial ventilation or external chest compression as necessary, if you're trained to do so. Carry on until the ambulance arrives, swapping with another trained person if possible and necessary, but without a break.

Electrical safety

A few simple, regular checks and good habits to follow can help to keep you and your family safe from electrical problems and emergencies. Keep these tips in mind whenever you use an electrical appliance and take particular care whenever you do any DIY repairs or installations to follow the golden rules of electrical safety.

SAVE £200

Average cost for a day's work by a qualified electrician to trace and repair a fault caused by careless use of socket outlets or appliances.

Care and maintenance

● **Check flexes and plugs for signs of damage** Choose one room a month and examine all the electrical flexes attached to appliances and lamps within it, looking out for cracked or worn insulation, exposed bare wires and black spots – a particularly alarming sign, as these are generally caused by sparks from the plug or appliance.

● Inspect the plugs, too, and make sure that they are not cracked, that there are no bent or rusted prongs and that the flex and the internal wiring aren't loose – give the flex a gentle tug to make sure it's secure and open the plug if you can to check the connections inside.

● If you spot any of these problems, replace the flex, plug or both – or replace the appliance altogether.

Golden rules of electrical safety

Electricity is a powerful and potentially lethal force. As such, you should approach it cautiously. Professional electricians follow these guidelines – follow their example:

Always ...

● Wear safety glasses when working around electricity.

● Unplug a lamp or appliance before attempting to repair it.

● Turn off power to a circuit at the consumer unit before working on it.

● Use a voltage tester to make sure a wire isn't live. Do this before you touch the wire!

● Use plastic-handled tools for electrical work. Even better, do as electricians do and use plastic-handled tools with rubber jackets.

● Call in an qualified electrician if you're in doubt about the safety of any electrical repair or test (see page 169).

Never ...

● Stand on a wet or damp floor when working with electricity. Put as much insulation as possible between you and the source of a shock. Wear rubber-soled shoes and stand on a rubber mat.

● Touch metal plumbing or gas pipes or fixtures when working on electrical wiring or appliances. Touching these pipes and fixtures 'grounds' you and will allow any shocks that you might receive to course through your body.

● Use two hands to open a consumer unit, pull out a fuse or test a socket outlet or switch. If you use both hands and come in contact with electricity, a shock can run up one arm, through your heart and out down the other arm to the other hand in contact with the current. If a job can be done with one hand, just use one hand.

● Use aluminum or wet wooden ladders if you're working near overhead power lines or testing a live circuit.

3 electrical mistakes to avoid

Preventing trouble with your home's electrical system doesn't take much effort and has more to do with what you shouldn't do than things that you should.

1 Never splice damaged flexes, joining them together with electrical insulation tape. This may work as a very temporary measure, but isn't a safe repair and can easily cause a fire. Far better is to stop using the appliance immediately. Replace it or have it repaired by a professional. Damaged flexes can be cut and rejoined using a junction box, but these are bulky and inconvenient on most small appliances.

2 Don't overload your outlets. Using multiple extension sockets and 'octopus' plugs that turn a single outlet into multiple outlets can make the socket outlet overheat and cause a fire. Never plug one adaptor into another. Move appliances if necessary so that they can be plugged into other outlets, or consider asking an electrician to add more sockets where you need them.

3 Don't get too used to extension cords – they should be temporary, not a permanent solution to siting an appliance far from a socket. They can cause dangerous circuit overloads and can also be a trip hazard. Ask an electrician to move or add a socket instead.

TOASTERS CAN MELT FLEX – KEEP THEM AWAY FROM THE HEAT.

● **Pull the plug, not the flex, from the socket** If you repeatedly tug on the flex to unplug an appliance from its socket outlet you're bound to loosen some connections inside, which could cause a short in your system. Always grasp the plug firmly on both sides and pull it out straight from the socket. If a socket outlet is stiff to use, it could be that the internal workings are worn and it needs to be replaced.

● **Keep flexes away from heat** Electrical flexes often get tucked along skirting boards, under radiators or around the back of the toaster because they look untidy. But a toaster can melt through a flex and constant proximity to a radiator can cause the flex insulation to crack.

● **Keep socket outlets covered** If you have small children or pets in the home, it's a good idea to plug socket outlets you're not using with childproof covers. Some brands of electrical fittings have built-in safety features that prevent a child getting an electric shock by inserting something into one of the socket openings, but it's still wise to protect the sockets with covers to prevent their intenal workings being damaged.

● **Spot the signs of a hidden fault** If a plug or socket feels hot it could indicate a wiring fault. Other warning signs are flickering lamps, frequent fuses blowing or a circuit MCB tripping repeatedly in the consumer unit. Fix obvious faults or call an electrician to trace the problem.

smart idea

When buying electrical products, look for the Kitemark® (see symbol below). This certifies that the product has been thoroughly tested and designed for safety, and should withstand normal use over its lifetime, performing safely and reliably. Today, you'll mainly see a Kitemark on plugs, sockets and extension cables. Visit www.kitemark.com for more information.

Wiring, fuses and circuit breakers

The heart of your home's electrical system is the consumer unit. From here, electricity is distributed to all the circuits within the house via circuit breakers, which 'trip off' to protect each circuit if it draws too much power. Understanding how the consumer unit works can help you to know what to do if you lose power to some or all of the household circuits, but you should leave all repairs to a qualified electrician.

SAVE £200

The average cost of a day's work for an electrician to trace and fix a fault caused by an overloaded circuit.

Care and maintenance

● **Turn power off before doing any electrical work** Make the consumer unit your first stop when doing any electrical work. Trip the circuit breaker that controls the circuit that you're working on then use a voltage tester to make sure the switch or outlet you want to work on isn't still live. To turn off power to the entire house, trip the main breaker, which is usually larger than the others and coloured red. If you have a fuse box, remove the main pull-out block or turn the switch to 'off'.

● **Are you sure the power's off?** Always prove that there's no power in a circuit before you attempt to do any work on it.

● For as little as £10, you can buy a socket tester that plugs in like a

---

What's causing my circuit problem?

Circuit failure is usually due to one of two problems. Circuits can be overloaded, which is what happens when too many appliances are running on the same circuit, or they can be short circuited, which is when a worn live wire touches a worn neutral or another live wire, or the earth core, or any metal that's earthed, creating a short cut for a large current surge. Here's how to identify the problem.

● **YOUR CIRCUIT IS PROBABLY OVERLOADED** if you've just plugged a high-wattage appliance into a socket outlet and everything just stops working. Try moving smaller portable appliances to another circuit that's not being used as much. Switch off or unplug the high-watt load before resetting the circuit breaker, otherwise the breaker will probably trip again almost immediately.

● **A SHORT CIRCUIT** is the likely cause if you reset the breaker or replace the fuse and your circuit still isn't working. Do a little sleuthing to figure out what's causing the fault. First, unplug all lamps and appliances on the circuit. Then check the plugs and flexes for damage: if a fixture, switch or outlet is discoloured or has a faint burned smell, it's the likely source of the problem. Replace the damaged flex, switch or outlet if needed.

● **BEFORE YOU PLUG ANYTHING BACK IN,** reset the circuit breaker. If the circuit still doesn't work, the problem is probably in the internal wiring. Call an electrician to investigate further. Now, start plugging things in again one or a few things at a time. If the circuit fails only when you turn on a specific lamp or appliance, you have located the source of your short.

normal plug, but checks power to the socket and alerts you to a dozen or more different wiring faults. Use one to check that the power is off before you remove the faceplate from any socket and then again at the end of the job to check that the socket is functioning correctly and safely.

● For £5, you can buy a simple 3-in-1 circuit tester, which will test for power to a switch, such as a light switch. Leaving the switch turned on, turn off the power to the circuit you believe the light is on, remove the switch faceplate and ease it away from the wall a little. Without touching any wires or terminals with your fingers, carefully touch the probes to the wiring terminals within the switch to test for power.

● You can also use a circuit tester to test socket outlets, but you'll have to remove the faceplate first as you would for testing a switch.

● **Pay some attention to your consumer unit** Once a year, take a good look at your consumer unit for any signs of moisture or rust. If you see any, call an electrician as soon as possible to give the unit a thorough safety check. As part of your annual check, trip and reset all the individual circuit breakers to prevent corrosion from setting in. A corroded breaker may not trip when it needs to.

● **Upgrade your fusebox to a newer model** If your household wiring still comes from a fusebox, with cartridge or even wired fuses, make it a priority to have it replaced with an up-to-date consumer unit. Even older consumer units may be worth updating for greater safety and performance. It's never worth skimping on matters of safety. The circuit breakers that control each circuit in a modern consumer unit will trip to 'off' within milliseconds of a fault occurring on the circuit – fast enough to prevent an electric shock from being fatal.

● **Understanding circuit breakers** The MCBs that control and protect each circuit will trip off as soon as too much current is demanded on the circuit – usually a sign of a fault.

● Most modern socket outlet circuits should also be protected by an RCD. This monitors the balance of the live and neutral current flows around the circuit and switches off in a fraction of a second if it detects an imbalance, caused by faulty cable insulation or by someone receiving an electric shock. A consumer unit may have one RCD protecting all the circuits or just covering the socket outlet circuits.

● The latest wiring regulations require that most new circuits be protected by an RCD – new consumer units do this by controlling each individual circuit with a combined MCB and RCD, called an MCBO or RCBO.

● **Keep a torch near the consumer unit** If the lights go out and you need to access the consumer unit to reset a circuit breaker in the dark, you'll be glad to have a torch easily to hand. Attach a strip of heavy-duty Velcro to the wall and to the torch to hold it securely in place. Dedicate this torch to this job and this job only, so that you aren't tempted to use it for something else and forget to put it back.

USE VELCRO TO SECURE YOUR TORCH TO THE WALL NEAR THE CONSUMER UNIT.

Amps, volts and watts: **what do they all mean?**

● **AMPS** The amount of electric current that flows through a conductor such as copper wire is measured in amperes (amps, or A). The higher the amp rating of a cable or flex, the thicker its conductors must be.

● **VOLTS** The pressure that causes current to flow through a conductor is measured in volts (V). In the UK, current is delivered to homes and offices at 230V. Transformers within the home can reduce this for low-voltage lights and appliances.

● **WATTS** Electricity's power, or ability to do work, is measured in watts. The higher the wattage of an appliance, the more power it will use.

● **What to do when the lights go out** The most common cause of a blackout in a modern home is when a solitary light bulb blows and trips the whole lighting circuit. This often happens when you first switch on a light. First, check whether it's just the lighting circuit that has tripped: if your lamps, radio or other appliances still work then it's almost certainly the MCB protecting the lighting circuit that has tripped. Check at the consumer unit to see whether one MCB is flipped down when all the others are up and switch it back to 'on'. This should restore the lights.

● If a blown bulb is in a table lamp connected to the ring main, it can sometimes shut down the power to the whole house because the sensitive RCD that protects the socket circuit (see 'Understanding circuit breakers', page 179) detects the blown bulb as a fault. Reset both RCD and MCBs.

A SOLITARY LIGHT BULB CAN TRIP THE WHOLE LIGHTING CIRCUIT.

Understanding basic household circuits

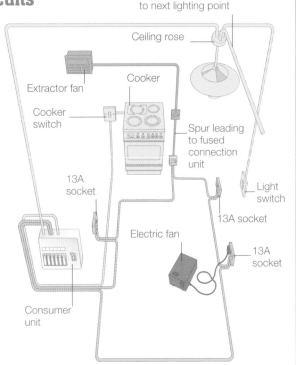

Lighting circuit cable continues to next lighting point

Ceiling rose

Extractor fan

Cooker

Cooker switch

Spur leading to fused connection unit

13A socket

Light switch

13A socket

Electric fan

13A socket

Consumer unit

▨ **LIGHTING CIRCUIT** The circuit runs out from the consumer unit, linking a chain of up to ten lighting points (or a maximum of 1,200W). Cables run from each light to its switch. The circuit is protected by a 5A or 6A circuit fuse or MCB, but it would be overloaded if each of the lighting points were fitted with a high-wattage bulb.

▨ **RING MAIN CIRCUIT** This is the house's main power circuit and is wired in a loop, or 'ring', that starts and ends at the consumer unit. Current flows to socket outlets around the ring, but in either direction, so the chain is not broken by one switched-off or faulty socket. The ring main can serve a floor area of up to 100m² and should be protected by a 30A or 32A circuit fuse or MCB. It can have any number of sockets or fused connection units on it, as long as its maximum total load doesn't exceed about 7,000W. Add extra ring mains to supply larger total loads and larger floor areas.

▨ **SOCKET OUTLET** The maximum load that can be supplied by a socket outlet taking a 13A plug is 3,000W. The plug is fitted with a 13A or a 3A fuse, according to the wattage rating of the appliance that's connected to it.

▨ **SPUR ON A RING MAIN** You can add extra sockets to a ring main by branching off the ring at a socket outlet or junction box and wiring a 'spur'. You can take a spur to a new single or double socket or fused connection unit (FCU) from any outlet on the ring as long as it's not itself a spur, isn't already supplying a spur or the new spur won't exceed the capacity of the ring main (see above).

▨ **SINGLE-APPLIANCE CIRCUIT** Appliances that use large amounts of electricity and are in constant or frequent use – a cooker, a fixed water heater or a shower heater unit, for example – should have their own circuit running from the consumer unit. They would take too large a proportion of the power available on a shared circuit and would be likely to cause an overload.

- **If you're not sure which circuit to turn off, listen to the radio** Plug a radio into the socket outlet you want to work on and turn it up loud enough that you can hear it from the consumer unit. Switch off circuit breakers one by one until you hear the radio go off. This way, you can be sure that the power to the circuit has been disconnected. It's a good idea to map out the electrical circuits in your house (see below) so that you know which sockets or lights are linked.

- **Replace blown plug fuses** If you have an old-fashioned fusebox, follow these simple but essential tips for working safely to change it. Make sure that you're standing on a dry surface. Using one hand only, open the fusebox, turn off the main power switch, grasp the blown fuse by its glass rim and remove it.
- Unlike a tripped circuit breaker, a blown fuse gives you a visual clue as to what caused the circuit to fail. Take a look at the fuse's glass window. If the metal strip inside is broken but the window is clear, the circuit is overloaded. If the window is discoloured, you probably have a short circuit.
- Replace the fuse with one of the same amperage rating, never with one of a higher rating. A fuse whose amp rating exceeds its circuit's capacity could overheat wires and cause a fire.

take care!

The positioning of sockets, lights and other electrical equipment in bathrooms, as well as your choice of appliances and wiring accessories, are strictly governed by the Wiring Regulations. Bathrooms are divided up into zones according to the position of the taps, bath, WC and shower, with different regulations for each zone. Never do your own wiring work in a bathroom and always seek professional advice from a qualified electrician.

How to map electrical circuits

When you're standing in front of a line of circuit breakers in the consumer unit and want to turn off the circuit that controls the living room sockets, how do you know which circuit that is? Map out your home's electrical system, then use the information to label the individual circuit breakers, or create a key and keep the map inside the consumer unit's cover.

1 Sketch a plan of each floor of your house, labelling all rooms and areas.

2 On the floor plan, mark the location of every switch, socket and light, using the symbols shown in the illustration key.

3 At the consumer unit, cut off power to the first circuit by tripping its breaker. Call this circuit 1.

4 Walk through the house, methodically turning on the lights one by one and plugging in and turning on a radio at each socket outlet or checking the operation of any appliance already plugged in. If a light or the radio doesn't go on, that switch or socket is part of circuit 1. Mark a '1' on your floor plan next to all the switches and sockets on the dead circuit.

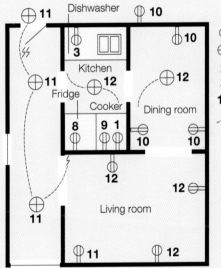

5 Repeat the process for all the other circuit breakers, using a different number for each circuit. You should find separate circuits for upstairs lights, downstairs lights, and upstairs and downstairs sockets. Often kitchen or utility room sockets are separated, and showers and electric ovens should also have dedicated circuits. A modern consumer unit has space for around 20 different circuits.

Switches and sockets

There may be miles of wiring behind your walls, but it's the switches and sockets (often called 'outlets') that give you access to the power. While usually long-lived and problem-free, sockets and switches can sometimes fail. Both can also be incorrectly wired, dangerous and yet fully functional, until something else goes wrong. Fortunately, switches and sockets are easy to check and replace, as long as you do it safely and carefully.

Care and maintenance

● **Power down before you start** This is a crucial first step to avoid injuring yourself. Before working on any socket or switch that controls a wired-in appliance or fused connection unit (FCU), always turn off the power to the appropriate circuit at the consumer unit (see pages 178-181), and then use a voltage tester to make sure that the power really is off.

● **Safety while you work** Always keep children and pets away from an open electrical wiring box and make sure that the main consumer unit is out of their reach. Never leave a switch or socket unattended with its faceplate not screwed home if you have children in the house.

An RCD (centre) is part of most mondern consumer units

● **Test RCDs every month** An RCD is installed in most consumer units (left), but you can also buy plug-in ones (see page 183). An RCD will instantly shut off power to everything on the associated wiring circuit or anything plugged into a plug-in unit as soon as it detects a fault (see 'Understanding circuit breakers', page 179).

● Test all RCDs every month to ensure that they are working. First, press the RCD's 'Reset' button to make sure the unit is on or check that the trip switch is in the 'on' position. Then plug in a radio at a nearby socket and turn it on so that you can hear it from the consumer unit. While the radio is playing, press the 'Test' button on the RCD – the radio should go off. Press 'Reset' again or flip the switch back to 'on' – the radio should come back on. If the RCD fails this test, have it checked by an electrician and replaced if necessary, as this is an indication that it would not trip and cut off the power if an electrical fault developed.

SAVE £400

Cost to replace a 32 inch television set damaged by an electrical short caused by an undetected fault in its plug or socket outlet.'

---

take care!

If an appliance makes a crackling noise, smells hot or sparks when you turn it on, don't risk a shock or a burn by unplugging it or touching the socket. First turn off power to the circuit at the consumer unit. Then, with dry hands, cover the plug with a dry towel and pull it out.

● **Stay safe outside** Even if your household socket circuits have built-in RCD protection, it's good practice to always plug in outdoor electrical power tools, such as electric mowers, hedge trimmers and shredders, plus any power tools like drills being used outside, into a dedicated RCD socket outlet or an RCD adaptor (left). Test it before each use and it will protect you from a potentially lethal electric shock if you should accidentally cut through a flex.

Exposed cores and poor connections

● **Ditch the heavy metal** Old metal switch and socket faceplates may look attractive but they are often inadequately earthed, and old connections and terminals make them potential hazards – a metal plate that comes in contact with a live wire can deliver a shock if you touch it. Plastic is the safer bet for most domestic situations, or switch to modern metal faceplates with up-to-date safety features and well-earthed connections and plastic mounting boxes.

● **Check plugs once a year** A few hours spent checking all the plugs on your appliances each year could save you hundreds of pounds and untold distress in fixing fire damage or replacing damaged appliances.
● Open up each plug and check that the connections are all secure, there are no loose wires, the flex is securely gripped by the plug, the pins aren't loose and that the plug itself isn't cracked. Lastly, check that the plug is fitted with a correctly rated fuse for the appliance it's attached to.

A neat plug is a safe plug

How to replace a socket outlet

Sockets can crack or be shorted out by a faulty appliance. It takes just a few minutes to fit a new equivalent faceplate – a job you can do yourself.

Use an electrician's screwdriver

1 Turn off the power at the consumer unit and switch off the MCB for the circuit the damaged socket is on. Use a voltage tester to make sure that the socket is dead. Unscrew the faceplate and ease it away from the wall.

2 Unscrew the three terminal screws behind the faceplate to disconnect the cable cores, or conductors. There may be one, two or three cores going into each wiring terminal, depending on whether the socket is on the ring main, on a spur or supplying a spur. Take note before you remove the wires and use an electrician's screwdriver for safety.

3 Check that the cores will reach the new terminals and carefully trim back the insulation to reveal longer cores if necessary. Fit green and yellow sheathing to any bare earth cores then reconnect the cores as before, screwing them firmly into the terminals. Carefully push the faceplate back to the wall and screw it home. Restore the power to the circuit and use a socket tester to check that the wiring is safe.

Replace broken boxes promptly

take care!

As part of a European harmonisation project, the colours of the insulation around the individual cores used in domestic wiring changed in April 2006 to match the colours used in flexes for plugging in electrical appliances since the 1960s. Since 2006, all new wiring has been done in the new colours, but when you remove existing socket faceplates you may find the old colours behind. In some cases you may find both colours together.
Live cores were red and are now brown.
Neutral cores were black and are now blue.
Earth cores that may have been bare should now all carry green and yellow striped sheathing.

● **Check flex for nicks or frays** When you check your plugs, check all the flexes too. The outer sheath must be intact, with no nicks, cuts or fraying. Any damage can expose the internal flex cores and you could get an electric shock from touching the flex. You can make a temporary repair by binding damaged flex with insulating tape, but always replace the whole flex as soon as possible.

Easy fixes

● **Keeping the plug plugged in** A socket that won't hold a plug snugly in its slots is defective or worn from heavy use. It's a potential fire hazard and must be replaced (see page 183).

● **Replacing like with like** The Wiring Regulations allow homeowners to replace damaged or faulty switches and sockets on a like-for-like basis, as long as they aren't in restricted rooms or outside (see page 169).

● **Getting a good grounding** All modern switches and sockets should be wired in to the main earth terminal block in the consumer unit. Earth cores used to be left bare, but it's now recommended that they should be protected with green and yellow plastic sheathing. Whenever you have a faceplate off a socket or switch, check the earth connection to make sure it's firm, and fit a short length of sheathing if there's none there. You can buy earth sheathing in rolls, which you cut to length and slide over the bare earth cores.

How to make safe connections

Whatever you're wiring – plug, socket, switch or junction box – the techniques of making a good and safe connection are the same.

● **STRIPPING WIRES** To connect wires you need to expose the metal cores inside. Start by removing around 40mm of the tough outer sheathing. The easiest way to do this without nicking the insulation around the cores inside is to bend the flex and cut it lightly with a trimming knife – the tension in the bent flex should split the sheath. Repeat on the other side and peel away the sheathing. Cut the individual cores to length so that they reach their terminals comfortably, then strip 15mm of insulation from the tip of each core. Adjustable wire strippers (left) do this job quickly and safely on all thicknesses of cable, removing just the insulation without damaging the metal cores themselves. Insert the wire in the correct size notch, then close and rotate the tool until the insulation is cut through and you can slide it off.

● **CONNECTING WIRES** Twist the strands of wire together to make it easy to insert the core into its terminal screw. With very thin flex, you may get a better connection if you strip away 30mm of insulation then twist and bend over the core. Push the core carefully but fully into the terminal, then tighten the screw. Tug each core gently to make sure that it's held firmly in place.

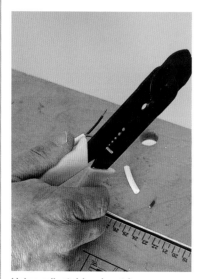
Using adjustable wire strippers

How to replace a switch

Some household appliances aren't plugged in, but are wired directly into a fixed switch, sometimes called a fused connection unit (FCU). You can install a switch to replace an existing single socket outlet – the faceplate fit is universal – using the existing wiring in the mounting box and connecting the new cores from the appliance flex.

1 Turn off the power at the consumer unit and take out the fuse or switch off the MCB protecting the circuit you'll be working on.

2 If the FCU is replacing an existing socket outlet, unscrew the faceplate and disconnect the cable cores from their terminals.

3 Prepare the ends of the cable and the flex for connection (see page 184), remembering to sleeve the bare earth conductor of the cable.

4 Feed the flex from the appliance into the back of the FCU. If there's a flex grip, release it sufficiently to let the flex through and then tighten it securely.

5 Make the connections within the switch for the cores of the appliance's flex. Connect the brown (live) core of the appliance flex into the terminal marked L and Load (or Out). Connect the blue (neutral) core to the terminal marked N and Load (or Out). Lastly, connect the green-and-yellow earth core to one of the terminals marked E or ⏚. If the FCU has only one earth terminal, don't connect the core yet. It will share the earth terminal with the power supply cable earth core and you should insert them both together when you're connecting the cable to the FCU.

Tighten the flex grip securely

Wire in the appliance flex

A metal box must be earthed

Don't overtighten screws

Connecting the switch to the power supply

1 If the existing switch or socket is on the ring main, there will be two sets of cores within the mounting box – a spur has one set and a socket that feeds a spur will have three. Remake the connections as you found them when you removed the original faceplate.

2 Connect the brown (live) cable core to the terminal marked L and Mains (or Feed, Supply or In). Connect the blue (neutral) spur cable core to the terminal marked N and Mains (or Feed or Supply or In). In wiring installed before April 2006, the cable core colours will be red for live and black for neutral (see page 184).

3 Finally, connect the green-and-yellow-sleeved earth core of the spur cable to the second terminal marked E or ⏚. If there's only one earth terminal, connect the earth cores from both flex and cable at the same time.

4 Add a 'flying earth' link to connect the earth terminal on a metal mounting box with the one on the switch faceplate.

5 Fit the correct cartridge fuse into the fuseholder in the FCU faceplate.

6 Fold the cable and flex neatly into the mounting box and press the faceplate against it. Screw the faceplate home, being careful not to over-tighten the screws and crack the plastic.

SWITCH OVER TO
LOW-ENERGY BULBS.

Light fittings

Broken or damaged ceiling fixtures are rare. They are generally replaced for decorative reasons, and this is a simple job to do yourself. Don't ignore them entirely, though: the plastic fittings can become brittle over time and crack, or pull-cord switches may break or fail. Whenever you replace a blown bulb, use a low-voltage replacement, and whenever you replace a light fitting, make sure the new one is suitable for use with low-voltage bulbs.

Care and maintenance

● **Don't exceed the recommended wattage** If a label on your light fixture or shade says not to use bulbs beyond a certain wattage, always heed the warning. Larger bulbs generate more heat in the socket than the fixture is designed to handle. Excess heat trapped in a fixture can shorten the life of a bulb, and over the long term it can cause the wire's insulation to break down and the socket to fail.

● **Sometimes it's best to leave the lights on** Turning off lights doesn't always conserve energy – turning a fluorescent light on and off frequently wastes power and shortens the bulb's life. If you're going to be out of a room for less than half an hour, leave fluorescent or compact fluorescent lamps on.

● **Switch over to low voltage** As traditional incandescent bulbs are gradually phased out, you'll have no choice but to replace blown ones with a low-voltage equivalent. Low-voltage compact fluorescent lamps (CFLs) are available in shapes, sizes and wattages to suit most light fittings, and are now also suitable for lights controlled by a dimmer switch. See the table on page 190 to help you to choose an appropriate wattage.

● **Replacing light tubes** How you remove a fluorescent tube depends on what type it is. Always take old tubes to a recycling centre. They contain trace amounts of toxic mercury and should never just be thrown away.
● Rapid-start tubes have two pins at each end. To remove a double-pin (rapid-start) tube, give it a quarter turn so that the pins line up with the slots in the sockets, then gently pull the tube out.
● Instant-start tubes have one pin at each end. One of the sockets that holds a single-pin tube is spring-loaded. Press the tube toward the spring-loaded socket and gently pull the opposite end out.
● Fluorescent tubes are now available in a range of colours, softening the traditional clinical white light associated with this sort of fitting. Their power output depends on their length and they are rated according to their diameter: 26mm is labelled T8, 16mm is T5 and the less-efficient 38mm, T12. The most efficient type is the triphosphor fluorescent tube. This gives out a natural tone of light and will last for up to 20,000 hours.

SAVE £12

Average annual electricity saving over the life of a bulb when you replace a 100W incandescent bulb with a 20W low-energy compact fluorescent lamp.

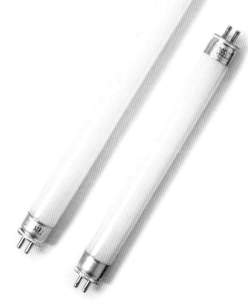

Count the pins to choose a tube

● **Give your crystal the white-glove treatment** When a crystal chandelier gets really dirty, your only option is to remove the crystals and wash them by hand. Regular maintenance, though, will help you to avoid such an arduous task. A couple of times a year, set up a stepladder and apply the two-glove cleaning method. Put on a pair of white cotton gloves, available at most DIY stores, and dampen one of them with glass cleaner. Rub each crystal with the damp glove then polish it immediately with the dry one. Wipe the chandelier frame with a dry cloth.

Easy fixes

● **Freeing a stuck rose** You should always unscrew a ceiling rose cover before you decorate – let it slide down the flex and protect the whole light fixture by wrapping it in a plastic bag. But if you or previous occupants haven't done this in the past, you may find that your ceiling rose is stuck fast with paint around the edges when you come to remove it.

● Turn off the power to the lighting circuit in that room by switching off the relevant MCB in the consumer unit (see page 174), then run the blade of a trimming knife around the edge of the rose to cut through the paint.

● If this doesn't free the rose, you'll have to break it instead. Wearing safety goggles and work gloves, crack the rose with a blow from a hammer. Remove the bits then replace the fitting with a new one (see page 189).

● **Fitting kitchen task lights** Wiring in a new lighting circuit in a kitchen is a notifiable job under the latest Wiring Regulations (see page 169), and should be left to a professional electrician. But you can install task lights yourself that plug into socket outlets and fix to the wall or the underside of your wall units to give you better working light on your worktops.

● You can fit a chain of lights around the kitchen, all plugged into one another, with just the first in the chain plugged into the power socket. These are sold in kit form, together with all the fixing clips, screws, cable clips and connecting flexes you'll need.

● Allow one fitting for every 500mm of worktop. Lay the fittings out before you start work, to make sure you're happy with the spacing. Make sure there's a socket within easy reach of the master light.

● Screw the fixing clips to the underside of the units, plug in the flexes that join the string of lights, then lift them into position and clip any excess flex under the cupboards. Plug in, switch on and test each light in turn,

● **Shield recessed lights with a fire hood** Spotlights recessed into the ceiling give a contemporary look and a crisp, bright light. But the lights themselves get very hot in use, and if they aren't properly protected they can cause a fire in the ceiling void above. When you next change a bulb in one of these lights, take out the surround, too, by releasing the clasps that hold it tight to the ceiling. Feel through the hole or shine a torch to see whether there is a solid or fire-retardent fabric enclosure above the light.

● If there's no sign of a fire hood, buy one for each light fitting in the room and push them through the holes to fit in place. To do this without disturbing the floor above you'll need to buy fabric hoods.

smart idea

If you have a dimmer switch in a room and nearly always use it on 'dim', replace the bulb with a lower-wattage one and go back to a conventional light switch. A low-wattage bulb will use less energy than a high-wattage bulb that's dimmed. Replacing a 100W bulb with a 40W one will save 60 per cent of its running cost.

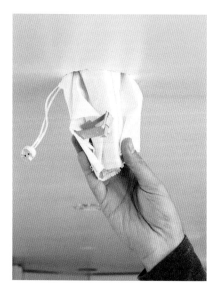

Shield recessed lights with a hood

How to replace a ceiling light fixture

If a light flex has discoloured or the lampholder has become brittle, it's easy to connect a new fitting without replacing the rose. If you want to replace the whole thing with a new rose or more decorative fitting, follow both sets of instructions given below. Remember that in houses wired before April 2006, the lighting circuit cores will be red and black, not blue and brown (see page 184).

Replacing a flex and lampholder

Unscrew the cover

Lugs support the flex cores

1 At the consumer unit, turn off the power and switch off the MCB protecting the circuit you'll be working on. It's not enough simply to turn off the light switch – the cables in the ceiling rose will still be live.

2 Remove the light bulb and shade, then unscrew the cover of the ceiling rose and slide it down the flex.

3 Using a small, electrician's screwdriver, loosen the terminal screws connecting the flex cores at each end of the row of terminals. Withdraw the cores from the terminals and unhook them from the lugs. If the flex has an earth core, unscrew the earth terminal enough to withdraw it. Don't dislodge the other cable earths.

4 Repeat the steps backwards to wire in the new pendant fitting, making sure to loop the pendant flex cores over the lugs in the rose.

Connecting a new rose

At each ceiling rose on a circuit, except for the last, there will be two circuit cables and a switch cable (the last light just has one circuit cable). You'll also need to connect the pendant flex cores. Remove the flex as above, and keep the power off.

1 Disconnect the existing ceiling rose, carefully unscrewing each terminal screw and gently prising out the cable cores. Take note of the connections to help you reconnect them to the new rose.

2 Undo the screws holding the ceiling rose in place and gently remove the rose. It may be stuck in place with paint – carefully run a trimming knife around the edge to free it.

3 Position the new rose or light fitting, feeding the cables through the holes or slots in the fitting. If you're replacing a rose like-for-like, you may be able to screw in the new rose using the existing holes in the ceiling.

4 In the central group of the three terminals, connect all the live cores (red or brown). Connect the neutral cores (blue or black) from the circuit cables to one of the outer groups of terminals, leaving the outermost terminal free for the blue core from the pendant flex.

5 At the other outer terminal, connect the neutral switch core flagged as live – you should see a blue core wrapped with a brown sleeve or a black one marked red.

6 Connect the flex cores to the terminals at either end of the row, looping them over the lugs for support. Finally, connect all the earth cores to the terminal marked E or ⏚ and fit the ceiling rose cover.

Connect all earth cores together

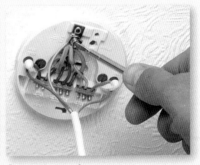

Connect cores in groups

Compact fluorescent lights

Choosing alternatives to traditional light bulbs isn't just about saving money any more. There's no doubt that compact fluorescent lights (CFLs) save electricity, last longer and pay for themselves within around 18 months – and at least twice again over the course of their life. But environmental issues have also come into play.

Installing compact fluorescent bulbs in your home is an investment in the future: just one CFL in every house would eliminate the amount of greenhouse gases that 800,000 cars emit over the course of a year. CFLs fit into all standard light sockets, use 75 per cent less energy than incandescent bulbs and last ten times as long. They now come in a variety of sizes and wattage equivalents, as well as in three-way and dimmable versions so that there's one for every sort of light fitting.

Conversion table for common wattages

Incandescent bulb	Compact fluorescent bulb
20W	5W
40W	10W
60W	15W
100W	26-29W
150W	38-42W

How much light do you need?

How bright (or how dim) you want your home to be is a matter of personal preference. But here are some rules of thumb to follow if you like a cheery, well-lit home.

Room	Wattage (compact fluorescent lamps)
Living rooms, family rooms and bedrooms	5W of compact fluorescent lights per square metre of floor
Kitchens, laundry rooms and workshops	10W per square metre of floor
Bathrooms	15W per square metre of floor and 30W per running metre of vanity top

If you have more than one light in a room or a lot of individual spotlights, divide the total wattage you need between them to avoid generating too much light when all the light fittings are switched on.

Before you go to the expense of installing (and running) additional lights, consider whether or not you're really making the best use of the natural light available. With good natural light, you can reduce the need for switching on lights. Always open blinds and curtains wide during daylight hours, and brighten dark rooms by decorating in light colours and using mirrors to reflect natural light. Try to avoid positioning desks and kitchen worktops in areas of poor natural light, where you'll always need to use an electric light.

Outdoor electrical fixtures

Having electricity outside can make a world of difference. It gives you power to run tools, security lights and even a pump for a decorative pond – all without having to deal with awkward and possibly dangerous extension leads. Outdoor sockets, switches and fixtures need to be protected from the elements and rated for use in wet conditions. Leave all outdoor wiring to a professional, but follow these tips for working safely and preventing risks from your outside electrics.

Care and maintenance

● **Clean the bulb sockets annually** Once a year, turn off power to all your outdoor light fixtures at the consumer unit, remove their light bulbs and use a ball of very fine steel wool (grade 0000) to clean corrosion from inside the sockets. This will help to keep the bulbs from jamming in the sockets and will make removing them easier when they need replacing.

● **Follow the rules and stay safe** The combination of moisture and electricity can be lethal, so always make sure your outdoor wiring complies with the recommendations set out in the Wiring Regulations (see page 169). Never install new outdoor wiring yourself: ask a professional electrician and get your outdoor wiring checked every few years.

● Never use power tools outdoors unless they are plugged in via an RCD, either into a dedicated RCD socket or using an RCD adaptor (see page 183). Always check that the RCD is working before you start work, so that you know that you're protected from potential electric shock in the event of the tool developing a fault or the cable being damaged.

● **Go solar** Using solar-powered rather than low-voltage outdoor lighting can save you money in two ways.

● There's no need to wire lighting into the household's ring main, so you don't need the services of an electrician to install your new outdoor system. It can take as little as 20 minutes to position and install six or eight solar-powered lights around the garden, either to illuminate a path or driveway or as a decorative feature.

● Some of the latest solar-powered landscape lights give off as much light as their low-voltage, mains-powered equivalents, but won't cost you a penny to run.

● **Weatherproof your electrical boxes** Sockets and switches that are exposed to the elements must be housed in weatherproof electrical boxes that stay weatherproof even when they are in use. The cover should seal even when something is plugged in. If your outdoor sockets don't come up to scratch, ask an electrician to replace them. Some covers can be retrofitted to existing boxes.

SAVE £350

How much you could save over five years by installing a 150W PIR (passive infrared) sensor exterior light rather than an overpowered and poorly adjusted 500W floodlight.

Solar lights are an easy outdoor option

Safety tips when working outside

The most important first step in working safely with power outdoors is to ensure that you always plug your tools into a socket with RCD protection. Most household circuits are now covered by an RCD within the consumer unit, but it's still safer to use a dedicated socket or adaptor (page 183) rather than running an extension lead out of a window from an indoor socket.

● Most electrical garden equipment is fitted with brightly coloured flex to make it easy to spot, so that you're less likely to accidentally cut through it with the mower or hedge trimmer as you work. If you need to use an extension cord to reach the furthest corners of your garden, invest in a similarly brightly coloured one for maximum safety.

● Plugging into a weatherproof external socket is a sure way to protect your electrical connections from moisture, but if you need to connect into an extension lead part-way down the garden use a waterproof enclosure (above) to keep the connection dry.

● Tripping on the trailing cable is a more common cause of accidents than cutting through the cable itself while working outdoors. Always unwind the cable fully before you start and lay it out smooth, without kinks or tangles. Drape the cable over your shoulder so that it trails behind you, or lift it up off the ground to a hook in your waistband, such as the Grass Snake Cable Grip.

● Always make sure you wear appropriate clothing and safety equipment to prevent slipping and injury.

Seal round outdoor electric fittings

● **Check seals and seams** Run a generous bead of exterior grade sealant around the joins between outdoor electrical boxes or lights and the house wall to seal out moisture. Most electrical fittings will have a waterproof rubber sleeve to encase the cable where it comes out of the wall. Check the sealant every autumn and rake it out and replace it if it's starting to crack or pull away from the wall.

● **Choose rugged fittings for outbuildings** In outbuildings, sheds and garages, electrical fittings can be more vulnerable to wear and tear and knocks, such as from moving heavy equipment, tools and bicycles than switches and sockets inside the house. Choose metal-clad fittings set on matching surface-mounted metal boxes: they'll withstand rough treatment better than their plastic equivalents. Run cables along the surface through conduit rather than chasing them into the wall.

Easy fixes

● **Removing a broken bulb with a potato** Outdoor light bulbs sometimes burst in their sockets because of exposure to moisture or sudden swings in temperature. Before you try to remove what remains of the light bulb, turn off power to the fixture at the consumer unit. Use a circuit or continuity tester to make certain that the power is off.

● You cannot grasp the broken bulb to twist it out without potentially cutting yourself, but a potato can help. Cut off one end to make a flat surface and press it firmly into the remains of the bulb. Turn the potato to unscrew the bulb. Once the bulb is out, clean the socket with very fine steel wool (grade 0000).

● If that doesn't work reach up into the bulb's metal base with needle-nose pliers, and open them until the tips are pushing against the inside of the base. Twist the pliers to remove the bulb.

A POTATO: SECRET WEAPON AGAINST BROKEN BULBS.

● **Keeping bugs away from outdoor lights** Porch and door lights left on at night attract a lot of insects, and they often find their way indoors. Here are a couple of ways to keep them at bay.

● Turn off outdoor lights when you don't need them. Consider installing motion sensors, which turn lights on when movement is detected and then turn them off again after a few minutes, before insects have a chance to start to congregate.

● Use yellow-coated, all-weather bulbs in outdoor fixtures. The yellow pigment makes light less visible – and therefore less alluring – to insects.

● **Light only when you need it** Security lights can be an effective deterrent to intruders as well as lighting a safe passage up your driveway or front path in the dark. But if they shine brightly into the night when there is no one there to need them, you'll be throwing away pounds in unnecessary electricity. There are several ways you can cut down on wasted outdoor lighting.

● Fit a PIR (passive infrared) sensor to your light or replace the light with one that incorporates its own sensor. These detect motion and switch on the light – generally a bright floodlight, but more decorative options are also available – when someone is approaching, switching it off again after a set period of time. They are combined with a photocell so that they only operate in dusk or darkness. You can get a security light with PIR for as little as £20.

● A PIR sensor is only worthwhile if it's carefully adjusted. If a moving bough on a nearby tree activates the sensor all night long, you may find that the bulbs and light actually wear out sooner than a simple light left switched on all night. Check your motion sensors every six months and adjust their angle or position if necessary.

● Dusk-to-dawn lights are controlled by a photocell that switches them on when light levels fall to a sufficiently low level and leave them on until dawn or for a set number of hours. Some incorporate a PIR that brightens the light when a visitor approaches.

Security lights can deter intruders

What to consider when planning garden lighting

There are several reasons to install lighting in your garden: for security, for safety and for decoration. Whatever lights you choose, take care not to fit them with bulbs that are more powerful than you need. Not only will you be wasting money on electricity, but the bright glare of floodlights and over-powered lamps looks unnatural and unappealing in a garden.

SECURITY Security lights are most effective if they are bright and targeted, but get this wrong and you can annoy your neighbours, cause a nuisance to passing traffic and lose any impact that might deter an intruder.
● High-wattage floodlights are available, but these are far too powerful for most domestic use. Choose a 150W light over a 500W one – it will still be bright enough without using your electricity to light up the whole street.
● Choose a security light with a built-in PIR sensor or buy a separate sensor and fit them together. This will switch the light on only when it detects someone approaching, but it's important to position and adjust it carefully to avoid it being triggered by pets or branches.
● Angle a floodlight towards the ground to illuminate the area close to the house and avoid shining a dazzling light into nearby properties or out onto the road.

SAFETY Lights can be extremely useful to illuminate a path, doorway, run of garden steps or a frequently used access, such as into the garage or shed. You don't need a bright floodlight for this: a bulkhead light will be more than adequate and ornamental lantern lights (above right) a far more attractive option within the garden. Fit lights at the entrance to a shed or garage with a PIR sensor so that they illuminate your approach and save you remembering to switch them off again. A dusk-to-dawn sensor is a good idea for lights at a front door and it can be combined with a PIR sensor.

DECORATION Low-level lighting can be run through borders to highlight garden ornaments or specimen plants. Fairy lights can be strung through trees. Pond lights can add a night-time dimension to water features, both in and around the water, and sympathetic but functional lighting can be used to make an outdoor space practical to use even late into the evening.

INSTALLING GARDEN LIGHTING All outdoor wiring is best left to a qualified electrician, but it's worth considering some practical installation tips when thinking about what sort of lighting to choose. All electrical cable must be protected from accidental damage in the garden. One way is to string it up above head height. This is seldom practial, as a length of overhead cable is vulnerable to damage or being caught when carrying ladders and the like. A better option is to bury it in a trench, and run it through protective conduit, so you should be prepared for your borders and maybe part of the lawn to be dug up as part of the installation.

Doorbells

It's easy to take for granted the bell or buzzer that announces visitors to your home – that is, until something goes wrong with it. The most common doorbells consist of one or more push buttons, a sounding device and a transformer that steps down household current to the lower voltage that most bells require. Except for keeping the sounding device clean, doorbell systems need little care. Follow these guidelines to diagnose any problems and find out what to do.

Care and maintenance

● **Use alcohol to keep your doorbell clean** If you can't hear your doorbell ding when visitors arrive, it may be because your bell or chimes are dirty. Dirt, oil or grime can slow down or stop the motion of a mechanical chime's plungers or a bell's clapper and gong. To restore the sound, remove the sounding device's cover and clean the plungers or clapper contacts with a cottonbud or toothbrush dipped in isopropyl alcohol. Electronic doorbells can't be cleaned – replacement is the only option if they stop sounding.

● **Bend the clapper back into shape** A doorbell's sound may be muted because the clapper isn't striking the gong quite right. This usually happens because the clapper arm is bent. Use pliers to gently bend the arm back into shape. If the sound from your mechanical door chimes is getting softer, check the rubber grommets (pads) attached to the unit's tone bars. If they are worn or hard and brittle, the tone bar won't ring out clearly. Buy replacements at a DIY or electrical supply shop.

Easy fixes

● **Check the power first** When your doorbell stops working the fault could be as simple as a lack of power. If your bell is wired in to the mains electricity, turn off the power at the consumer unit and check the wiring at

SAVE £200

What you would pay an electrician to install a new doorbell unit.

take care!

Doorbell and chime systems operate on low-voltage current, so it's generally safe to work on everything but the transformer without turning off power at the consumer unit. Even so, turning off the power before starting work is always a good idea and essential if you're planning to work on the bell's transformer, which is wired into the house's 240V mains circuit.

How to replace a doorbell

Replacing the sounding device, whether because it's faulty or you just want to upgrade it, is simple – just make sure that the new unit you buy matches the voltage rating of the transformer. With the power off, remove the existing unit's cover and disconnect the wires from their screw terminals, noting which wire went where. Detach the old unit from the wall. Run the wires through the back of the new unit and mount it on the wall. Connect the wires to the correct terminals on the new unit, then restore power.

both the chime end and at the buzzer outside. Many doorbells are battery-powered, so always check the batteries first when the bell fails and replace them if necessary.

● **Tightening and splicing wires** Loose connections and broken wires are common causes of doorbell system failure. Remove the push-button housing and check and tighten the wire connections behind the push button. Open the cover at the sounding device and check inside and at the transformer (with the power turned off at the mains). Check all the visible doorbell wiring for breaks, frayed insulation or other signs of damage. Wrap frayed wires with insulating tape and replace the wire as soon as possible. Splice breaks to restore the current by stripping both wire ends and joining them with a wire connector.

● **Getting the doorbell to ring** If your doorbell doesn't make any sound at all and the power hasn't been lost, or if the failure is an intermittent fault, it could be a problem with the push button. Constant use and exposure to weather and dirt can cause it to stop working by making the contacts dirty or by grit and dirt impeding the movement of the button. The button can also get stuck pushed in if the internal springs get bent or worn over time.
● To inspect the button, remove the screws securing its cover plate, if there are any. If the plate or button isn't fastened with screws, use a screwdriver or a flat knife to gently prise it up.
● Tighten the wire connections inside and check contacts and terminals for corrosion, removing any with fine abrasive paper. Gently prise up the metal contacts with a screwdriver blade if they seem pushed in (below).
● If there's still no sound, disconnect the button wires and touch their ends together. If the bell rings, the button is defective and needs to be replaced. Connect the existing wires to the new button's terminal screws and remount the button.

smart idea

Do you need to put in a new doorbell? Consider going wireless. Wireless door chimes can be installed in minutes without snaking wires inside walls and around door frames: unless you're building a new house or doing an extensive renovation, these wires will be messy and difficult to hide.

Unscrew the button plate

Gently prise up the metal contacts, bending them back into shape

Communications

Modern homes often have a spaghetti-like mass of cabling – for televisions, audio equipment, phones, computer hardware and more. Staying connected usually relies on good physical connections and taking care with the cabling. When something goes wrong, it's often caused by the simplest fault which you can easily fix yourself – a dislodged plug or wire. For more complex problems you'll need professional help.

SAVE £200

Cost for an engineer to replace and install a television aerial on the roof of your house after a loose one has fallen down.

Care and maintenance

● **Check the plugs and sockets** Every few months, check that the connections into your electrical equipment are all still firmly in place. A loose aerial connection will lead to a snowy picture; a loose SCART cable from DVD to TV can mean you have a picture, but no sound; a loose connection between two components of your home computer and it may not function at all.

● **Take a look up on the roof** Every autumn, make a point of checking your rooftop aerial to see whether it's still securely fixed. You don't need to climb up there to check – look up from the ground on a slightly windy day and make sure that it's not being blown about and doesn't look loose. If you have a pair of binoculars, use them to make a closer inspection.

● **Don't let cables get out of hand** Trailing cables aren't only a trip hazard – if someone does trip or accidentally pull a cable they are likely to weaken or break the electrical connections. Always try to avoid trailing cables around the room, but if this isn't possible, then keep them tidy.
● Tack phone extension leads to the skirting board with cable clips, using one clip every 300mm.
● Use a proprietary cable tidy to gather together all the cables behind a television unit, or stereo system with separate components. These simple plastic sleeves can cost as little as £10 but make a big difference.
● Tidy computer cabling under your desk with a wire cable rack or grid cable organiser to prevent dislodging connections with your feet.

Easy fixes

● **Boost a weak signal** If you use your television signal to feed more than one television set, you may find that it's not strong enough to give a good signal on each set. Every time you split a signal to go to another set, the signal to all the sets is weakened. An easy solution is to use a combined splitter and amplifier unit. Plug in the main 'in' cable from the aerial where it enters the house, then take out separate cable feeds for each of the television sets around the house. The splitter will need mains power, so position it near to a socket outlet.

● **Fixing a bad line** The wiring connections in phone sockets are particularly easy to dislodge and the cables themselves fragile. If a phone suddenly or intermittently stops working or doesn't ring properly but still has a dialling tone, it could be that the socket connections have worked loose.

● You must not tamper with the master socket that brings the phone signal into the house – only your phone supply company may open and do work on this. But you can fit new extensions from a modern master socket and rewire existing extensions if they are faulty.

● The phone signal is transmitted using low-voltage electricity and it will be weakened if it's split too many times or needs to travel too far. Don't put an extension more than the length of 100m of cable from the master socket. All phone equipment has a REN (ringer equivalence number) – it's usually 1, and a standard phone line will support a maximum of four in total. If you need to have more plug-in extensions (rather than wireless remote handsets) you can install a REN booster to increase the capacity.

● To rewire or replace an extension, disconnect the master socket then open the extension box. Strip around 30mm from the cable's outer sheath, then use a special phone cable insertion tool to push the thin inner cores into their appropriate connectors, following the original wiring.

Making a good connection

How to wire a coaxial plug

Aerial connectors for your television or FM aerial signal can work loose over time, leading to a loss of quality in the signal. Or you may need to extend the cable to reach from the wall socket to a new position or piece of equipment. Most aerials are connected via coaxial plugs, which are simple to wire yourself.

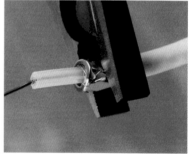

1 Strip away around 30mm of the cable's outer sheathing to reveal the wire mesh beneath, then fold back 20mm of the wire to expose the inner insulation. Use a pair of wire strippers to remove around 15mm of this inner insulation to leave a short length of the inner wire sticking out.

2 Slide the threaded cap onto the cable, followed by the cable grip. Use a pair of pliers to clamp the cable grip over the wire mesh. Feed the inner wire into the pin moulding then feed this into the body of the plug. Screw the cap and plug body together to enclose all the connections securely.

Top tips for saving water

As more and more homes are fitted with water meters, wasting water really is like washing money down the drain. Make a few small changes to your daily habits and follow some simple advice on fixing or maintaining your wasteful household fittings and you can cut your water consumption (and your water bill) considerably.

Care and maintenance

● **Water-wise washing** Most people would agree that a shower uses less water than a bath, but in fact a 5 minute power shower can use at least as much as a full bath – and many people shower for longer than that. Using a standard shower for 5 minutes a day will use around one-third as much water as a daily bath – a saving of 400 litres a week.

● The simplest way to minimise your water usage in the shower is to turn off the water while you shampoo or soap yourself. Follow the 'splash, lather, rinse' routine – get wet, switch the shower off, wash with the soap, then switch the water back on to rinse yourself off.

● Why leave the tap running while you brush your teeth? Doing this can waste as much as 5 litres of water a minute.

SAVE £160

Cost saving over one year when you swap your daily bath for a quick shower.

● **Choose mixer taps for a slower flow** Single-lever mixer taps can help to cut down on the water you run into the bath or basin. Because they mix the water as it flows, you can easily achieve the right temperature as you fill up. Putting in too much hot or cold water and then having to run more to correct it is a sure way to use more water than you really need.

● Some lever taps have a flow restrictor to reduce water usage. As you lift the lever to turn on the tap you'll feel a resistance and stop, but this isn't the maximum flow – lift a little further and the tap will run faster. But you should find that the lower level is usually adequate.

● **Make full use of a load** Only the latest, most sophisticated washing machines can adjust their water usage according to the size of the load – a feature known as 'fuzzy logic'. A washing machine can use around 14 per cent of the household's total water consumption, so use it wisely to avoid waste. Always wait until you have a full load before switching on.

● Machines with a 'fuzzy logic' feature analyse the water that drains from the first rinse in the cycle and will only rinse again if the clothes still have suds in.

Half-loads still use a full load of water

How to install a water butt

If you install a water butt on every downpipe around your property you may qualify for a small annual rebate on your water rates. You can fit water butts to collect water from sheds, greenhouses and garages, too – not just from the main house. Choose a water butt with a lid: it helps to prevent algae forming in the water and is safer for children and animals who use the garden.

1 Decide where you want your water butt to go and make sure you have a firm, level base to sit it on. You may need to lay a paving slab, properly levelled and bedded on sand, if the water butt won't be standing on a hard surface. Make sure that you have a stand to raise the level of the tap high enough to get a watering can comfortably beneath it.

2 The simplest and best way to install a water butt is to use a rainwater diverter kit, available in most DIY stores and garden centres. These allow rainwater to be diverted into the butt until it's full, when the flow reverts to draining away into the household drains. Position the water butt on its stand and work out where on the circumference the pipe from the downpipe will comfortably go into the water butt. Drill a hole just large enough for the pipe, around 100mm from the top of the water butt.

3 Use a spirit level to align the level of the hole entering the water butt with the downpipe. Measure up 5mm from this so that there will be a slight fall on the pipe leading to the water butt. This is your bottom cut line. Measure up another 30mm to mark your top cut line then use a saw to cut through the downpipe to remove the 30mm section.

4 Slot the diverter kit into place, making sure the arrow on the body of it is pointing down, then connect the flexible pipe to the water butt using the threaded tank connector. If the diverter has a lever-operated valve, switch it to the 'fill' position. Make sure the lid of the water butt is securely fitted and that the tap is turned off.

Recycle water in the garden

● **Choose models of efficiency** When you replace your washing machine or dishwasher, look for A-rated water-saving models. A standard washing machine will use 200 litres in one cycle; efficient machines will use half that, but the most efficient models use just 50 litres. A standard dishwasher requires around 36 litres for a cycle, but efficient machines can do the job with 16 litres – around the same as washing by hand.

● **Collect and recycle water** Gardens often need far less water than you think, and there's certainly no need to use a sprinkler on a lawn unless it's newly laid or seeded. But when you do water your garden, do it with rainwater collected in water butts or tanks. You can use a pump to deliver water to a hosepipe, but you'll use less if you target your watering to the plants that really need it with a watering can.
● Most garden plants actually respond better to watering with rainwater from a butt: it's warmer than tap water and not treated with chemicals.

● **Look out for signs of a leak** It's rare for a leaking pipe to go unnoticed for long inside the house, but if it runs beneath a suspended timber floor it could be a long time before any evidence is visible inside. Likewise, a leak underground within your garden may not be immediately obvious but could waste many gallons of water.
● Be alert for sudden, unexplained boggy patches appearing on the lawn or in a border. You can get your water supply company to come and

investigate by feeding a small camera through the pipes, looking for cracks, or you can use your water meter to help you to confirm your suspicions. Turn off all the taps and water-using appliances in the house and take a meter reading. Wait for half an hour then repeat the reading. If the reading has gone up, you probably have a leaking pipe. Contact a plumber or your water supply company for more advice.

Easy fixes

● **Stop drips and save £££s** A dripping tap can waste as much as 140 litres of water in a week. Always fix a drip promptly to minimise waste (see page 209). Remember, too, that if it's a hot tap that's dripping you're not only wasting the water, but also wasting energy heating water that is just dripping straight down the drain.

● **Keep track of waste with a smart meter** Some water supply companies will provide you with a free smart meter. This small, wireless, solar-powered device connects with your water meter (often buried underground in front of your property) and gives you information on water usage. You can see your meter reading, view your recent consumption and compare that with your average consumption, helping you to monitor your usage and act promptly if you see your usage starting to rise.

● **Time for a new loo?** One-third of the water usage in an average household goes on flushing the WC. How much water this takes each time depends on its age and style. Models fitted before 1993 usually have large cisterns and a single-flush operation, using around 9 litres each time you pull the chain. This is far more than necessary, but it's easy to cut it down without replacing the suite.
● Put a house brick or specially designed 'hippo' or water saver (available in DIY stores or from your water supply company) in the cistern and it will reduce the volume of water held inside, saving you up to 3 litres per flush.
● Modern slimline WCs use around half as much water as an old-fashioned model and many have a dual-flush option to reduce the water use even further. A half-flush for a slimline cistern takes just 3 litres.
● You can replace the flush mechanism in most WCs to retrofit a dual-flush function. Kits are available for push-button and lever flushes.

● **Roll up your hosepipe** Using a garden sprinkler can draw as much as 1,000 litres in a hour. And washing your car with a hose could use 17 litres a minute compared with around 30 litres in total washing with a bucket. Retire your garden hose and you'll be amazed what you could save.

RETIRE YOUR HOSE AND YOU'LL
BE AMAZED WHAT YOU COULD SAVE.

smart idea

Switch your showerhead for big savings: 'champagne' shower heads incorporate an aeration device, which has the effect of reducing water flow without any impact on the pressure. Replacing your showerhead with one of these can save 50,000 litres of water in a year.

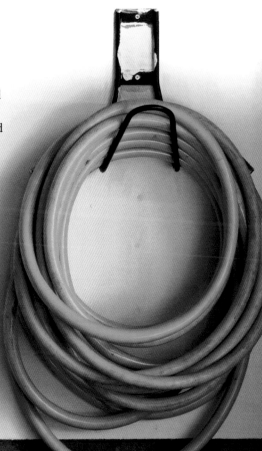

Plumbing emergencies

A pipe bursts, a toilet overflows, the washing machine floods your kitchen. The first step in dealing with most plumbing emergencies is to shut off the water supply to the whole house or to an individual fixture or appliance. The next steps are to stay calm and follow these emergency troubleshooting tips.

SAVE £90

What you might pay as a night-time call-out fee from a 24 hour emergency plumber.

Easy fixes

● **Damage control** If a broken pipe or overflowing appliance is flooding water into your home, take these steps immediately to minimise damage:
● Turn off the main water shut-off valve.
● Shut off electricity to the flooded area to prevent electrical shock, but only if you can get to the consumer unit without having to step through the water. Wading through water that's in contact with electrical outlets or appliances can give you a severe, possibly deadly, shock.
● Wear rubber boots and gloves if the leak was in a drain line or has been mixed with sewage. Disinfect the area thoroughly after it has been cleaned and allowed to dry.

How do I turn off the water?

When a pipe breaks or an appliance floods, your first job is to stop the water flow. Make sure you know where the main stop valve and all other valves are so that you can find them quickly in an emergency. To shut valves off, turn them clockwise. Or, if they are lever valves, turn the handle perpendicular to the pipe.

To shut off water here	Look for a stoptap or valve here
The entire house	On either side of your water meter – on an exterior wall, below a cover in the pavement or driveway outside your property – or in the house where the mains water comes in (often under the kitchen sink).
All the hot water in the house	On the pipe leading into your water heater or hot-water cylinder.
Kitchen sink	Underneath the sink – there are usually two valves, one for hot and one for cold water.
Bath	Either individual service valves on the tap pipes behind an access panel on the side of the bath or a stoptap within a bathroom cabinet.
Toilet	Under the toilet cistern.
Dishwasher	First look under the kitchen sink, where you'll probably find a valve on the line leading to the dishwasher. If not, pull out the dishwasher and look behind it.
Washing machine	Follow the short hoses that feed hot and cold water to the appliance. Where they connect to the plumbing, you should find two valves.

Emergency plumbing toolkit

When water is pouring out where it shouldn't, you need to act fast. Put together an emergency toolkit of the items listed below and keep it where you can easily fetch it in a hurry. If you 'borrow' a tool for another job, don't forget to put it back – if need be, buy duplicates that you can dedicate to this emergency kit.

- **SELECTION OF SPANNERS** for tightening and undoing compression fittings. Most jobs require either two spanners or a spanner and a wrench. A pair of large adjustable spanners are the most versatile option.
- **STILLSON WRENCH** for preventing pipes, taps or valves from twisting when undoing nuts.
- **PLUNGER** for clearing blockages in drains.
- **PLUMBER'S AUGER** for clearing more stubborn blockages the plunger cannot shift.
- **RADIATOR KEY** for bleeding air out of radiators.
- **STOPCOCK KEY** for turning off the water supply outside the house (usually under a cover in the pavement) if you cannot close the main stoptap within the house.
- **WASHERS AND 'O'-RING REPAIR KIT** for fixing dripping taps.
- **PIPE CUTTER** for removing sections of copper pipe.
- **JUNIOR HACKSAW** for cutting through awkward-to-reach pipes that the pipe cutter won't fit, such as ones close to joists or floorboards.
- **LENGTHS OF HEP$_2$O PLASTIC PIPE** (15mm and 22mm diameter) for replacing damaged copper pipe.

- **SELECTION OF PUSH-FIT PIPE FITTINGS** for emergency replacement of damaged lengths of pipe.
- **SOLVENT WELD CEMENT** for repairing leaking drainage pipes and rainwater downpipes.
- **BUTANE GAS TORCH, SOLDER AND FLUX** for repairing leaky soldered joints on copper pipes.
- **OLD TOWELS** for mopping up drips and leaks.

- Try to mop up the water as quickly as possible to prevent floor damage.
- In an emergency, patch a pipe however you can, although repairing or replacing a broken pipe is a job for a plumber. A good emergency repair is to clamp a short length of hosepipe over a leak, securing it tightly with jubilee clips or twisted wire.
- While your burst pipe is fresh on your mind, inspect the rest of your home's pipes and hosing. Broken or perished washing machine hoses are a common cause of household flooding. Standard rubber hoses weaken and crack with age and can eventually burst. To avoid what could be a costly problem, replace washer hoses every two years or so.

- **Help! My toilet is overflowing** When it looks like the water is about to spill over, stand back and trust the toilet's design. If the toilet overflows, turn off the toilet's shut-off valve or the main stoptap to the house if the toilet doesn't have a dedicated service valve. Bail out excess water, if possible, or just wait. Water will slowly leak through even the worst blockage, and the water level in the bowl will drop slowly to the point where you can begin plunging to clear the obstruction.

smart idea

If a washing machine or dishwasher floods, use beach towels and other large absorbent materials to build a dam around the spillage. Confining the water in this way makes it easier to mop up the flood.

● **No water comes from a tap** If no water flows from the kitchen sink cold tap, check that the main stoptap is open. If it is, call your water supply company to report the problem.

● If no water flows from other taps, check the cold water tank. It may have emptied because of a jammed or blocked ball valve. If it's empty, move the float arm sharply up and down to free the valve. If it continues to stick, ask a plumber to replace the valve.

● In frosty weather, there may be an ice plug blocking a supply pipe. If the kitchen cold tap is working, check the flow into the cold water tank by pressing down the ball valve. If there's no inflow, the rising main is frozen, probably between the ceiling and the cistern inlet. If the tank is filling, check the bathroom taps. If there's no flow from one tap, its supply pipe from the cistern is frozen. To thaw a pipe, see below.

● **The hot-water cylinder is leaking** Turn off the gate valve on the supply pipe from the cold-water cistern to the hot-water cylinder. If there's no gate valve, turn off the main stoptap and turn on all the taps in the house to empty the tank. This won't empty the hot-water cylinder, but it will stop water from flowing into it. Switch off the immersion heater, if there is one, and switch off the boiler or put out the boiler fire. Connect a hose to the cylinder drain valve, which is located near the base of the cylinder where the supply pipe from the cold water tank enters. Put the other end of the hose into an outside drain. Open up the drain valve with a drain-valve key or pair of pliers. You'll need to get the hot-water cylinder repaired or replaced by a plumber.

● **You cannot turn off the water** If the problem is on the tank-fed hot or cold supplies, you can tie up the float valve in the tank then run the taps and flush the WCs to empty the pipes. If the problem is on a mains-fed pipe, you need to turn off the rising main either at the stoptap inside your home or the outdoor stoptap in the ground.

● **Water is pouring from the loft** Turn off all the stop valves, open all the taps and position buckets to catch the water until it stops. If you can see a big bulge in the plasterboard or lining paper of a ceiling, position a bucket or large bin beneath it and use a sharp object to make a small hole, as gently as you can, to let the trapped water trickle out. Don't call an emergency plumber in a panic – all he'll do is turn off the water and present you with a large bill for the call-out. Wait until morning if the leak happens at night and try to locate the source of the problem before calling in the professionals.

● **Thawing a frozen pipe** Be very careful if you need to thaw a pipe. Water expands as it freezes and can push compression fittings apart, so that leaks occur when the water thaws. Be prepared to turn off the water supply and have buckets and old towels to hand. Strip off any lagging from the affected pipe and use a gentle heat, such as wrapping a hot-water bottle round the pipe or using a hair dryer. Never use a blowtorch, as it may melt the solder in nearby joints or cause a fire. Watch for leaks appearing and push joints back together and tighten them as necessary.

5 simple checks to prevent an emergency

1 Check the main stop valve. Turn it off and on again every few months and lubricate with WD40 if it's stiff.

2 Check the hot-water gate valve, either next to the hot-water cylinder or the cold-water tank in the loft. Close and open it every few months to make sure it turns freely.

3 Every few months, check all stop valves feeding tanks in the loft and all service valves to WCs, taps and appliances to make sure that they aren't stuck.

4 Make sure that all pipes in the loft or unheated spaces are lagged. Pipes in the loft should run beneath the loft insulation.

5 Check that your cold-water tank in the loft doesn't have insulation below it, as warmth from the ceilings below will help to prevent it freezing. An insulating jacket should cover the top and sides and be tucked into or joined with the surrounding loft insulation.

Sinks, basins and taps

Sinks and basins are the workhorses of your kitchen and bathrooms. They see a lot of action, so keeping them clean should be high on your list of home maintenance chores. They are also easy to take for granted – that is, until something (a blocked drain or leaking tap, for example) goes wrong. Follow these tips to keep your sinks, basins and taps in tip-top condition.

Care and maintenance

● **Scrub that dirty sink** You'd think that with all the soap and water that flow through sinks and basins they'd be perpetually clean. But soap deposits, food stains, rust and water spots all build up if you don't stay on top of them. How often you should scrub a sink depends on how much use it gets. Scrub a bathroom basin after about 30 uses and get into the habit of cleaning your kitchen sink last thing every night. A good recipe for a clean sink is a squirt of washing-up liquid added to a bowl of warm water. Dip a sponge in the mixture and scrub gently. To give the sink a more thorough going over, try an all-purpose cleaning spray or non-abrasive cleaner.

SAVE £100

Cost to call out a plumber to repair a dripping tap.

What kind of tap do you have?

The most common sink problem is a leaking tap. Repairs are simple but fiddly, as they often involve a lot of little parts that you need to keep track of and reassemble in the exact order in which you found them. Before attempting any repair, you need to know what type of tap you're dealing with.

● **COMPRESSION TAPS** A 'jumper' plate and rubber washer make a seal when the tap is closed to prevent water flowing out through the spout. In rising spindle models, the handle is directly attached to the jumper mechanism and rises up as you open the tap; non-rising spindle taps (above right) allow the jumper to move within the handle as it turns. Compression taps require several twists of the handle to turn the tap fully on or off. A worn washer is a common cause of leaks.

● **CERAMIC DISC TAPS** Instead of a washer and jumper, these taps use a cartridge containing two ceramic discs to regulate the flow. The discs have openings in them, and when rotated so that the openings line up water flows through. Each handle takes only a quarter-turn to operate the tap. Cartidges are made left or right-handed for mixer taps – make sure you replace a worn one with an equivalent, as they aren't interchangeable.

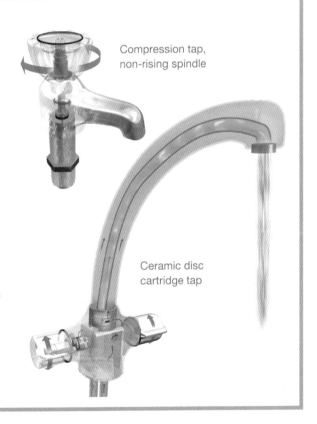

Compression tap, non-rising spindle

Ceramic disc cartridge tap

SINKS SEE A LOT OF ACTION,
SO YOU NEED TO KEEP
THEM CLEAN.

● **Make your porcelain sparkle** Here's a trick that will bring back the gleam to a white porcelain enamel washbasin or sink. Line the basin with paper towels and soak them with bleach. Let the towels sit for 30 minutes, then discard them and rinse with running water. Don't use bleach on coloured porcelain, though, as it may cause the colour to fade. Use a mild liquid detergent, vinegar or baking soda instead.

● **Protect sinks from scratches and stains** Replacing a kitchen sink makes no small impact on your wallet. Once you've got a shiny new one in place, follow these tips to keep it in 'like-new' condition:
● Install a perforated plastic mat in the bottom of your sink. This will protect the sink's surface from scratches and marks, and also protect your dishes and glassware from chips and breakages. Alternatively, use a plastic washing-up bowl inside your sink for washing dishes.
● Don't let fruit, vinegar, salad dressing or other acidic foods linger on the surface of a porcelain enamel sink. Long-term exposure to acids can cause staining and could permanently etch the surface.
● Don't use scouring powders to clean your sink. Instead, use the warm water and washing-up liquid formula described on page 205.

smart idea
Before breaking out the plunger to clear a blockage, use a funnel to pour 8 tablespoons (around 100ml) of bicarbonate of soda down the problem drain. Follow this with 500ml of boiling water, then flush through with hot water after 15 minutes.

A SURE REMEDY FOR STAINED SINKS – LEMON JUICE.

● **De-stain surfaces with lemon juice** When kitchen sinks get stained, you can often erase the spots with a paste made from 100ml of baking soda (bicarbonate of soda) and the juice of half a lemon. Dab a sponge in the mixture, rub the mark on the sink and rinse off with running water. This simple cleaning solution should work whether your sink is made of porcelain enamel, stainless steel or any other material – and won't damage the surface.

● **Use vinegar on your lime** The white spots and crusty sediments that are so difficult to clean off your taps are lime deposits from mineral-rich hard water. They are easy to remove with a secret ingredient that's probably already in your kitchen cupboard: vinegar. Soak a paper towel in vinegar and wrap it around the end of the spout or the area affected by the limescale build-up. Wait 10 minutes and then buff with a dry paper towel. This works well on all taps except brass or coloured fixtures – using vinegar on these surfaces may discolour them.

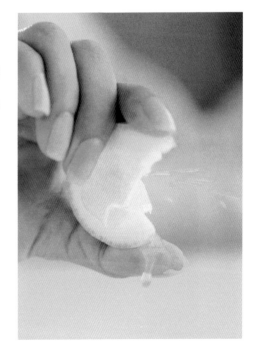

● **Use baking soda to make Corian gleam** Sinks made of nonporous, acrylic-based solid surfacing, such as Corian, are relatively stain-resistant and easy to clean. But they do need to be looked after to stop them getting water-marked and looking shabby. For routine cleaning, use soapy water or a cleaner specially formulated for solid surfacing. Rub out localised stains with a little baking soda (bicarbonate of soda) and water mixed to a toothpaste-like consistency. Apply the paste with a non-abrasive white scrubbing pad and rub gently in a circular motion until the stain has gone, then rinse thoroughly with clear water.

● **Avoiding hard-water damage to taps** If you live in a hard-water area, you'll be familiar with the limescale deposits that build up on taps, in sinks and on shower screens and tiles. You can clean the surface of taps, but the limescale can also build up inside, where it will damage the internal workings and eventually stop the tap from working.

● Once a year, give all your taps a check-up. Turn off the mains water supply or turn off isolation valves to each tap in turn. Remove the retaining

5 ways to clear a blocked drain

Any number of things can block a sink drain or cause it to drain slowly. Similarly, there are a number of ways to clear the problem – some easier than others. Start with the easiest solution, at the top of this list, and work your way down until water flows freely.

A plunger may shift a blockage

1 If the blockage is in a bathroom washbasin with a pop-up stopper, try pulling out the pop-up stopper manually, removing any accumulated debris and washing the stopper and plug hole with warm soapy water and a toothbrush. Replace the stopper and turn on the water.

2 If the drain is still blocked, try using a plunger. The overflow opening in the sink or basin will let air into the drain pipe as you're plunging, preventing the plunger from getting any suction. The solution is to stuff the opening with a wet cloth (left) before you start plunging. Position the plunger cup so that it completely covers the drain hole, then fill the sink with enough water to cover the cup. Make the first plunge a slow one to allow air to escape from the cup, then plunge vigorously up and down about 15 or 20 times and remove the plunger abruptly. Repeat several times as needed. Never use a plunger after you've poured chemicals, such as proprietary sink-unblockers, down the drain: plunging can cause harmful splashes containing harsh cleaning chemicals.

3 If you're this far down in the list and still haven't resolved the problem, it's time for direct action. Unscrew and remove the plughole cover, bend a hook in a coat-hanger wire and carefully feed it down the drain. Fish around for the plug that is blocking the pipe and try to pull it out slowly. Run some water down the drain, and then give it a good plunging to remove any build-up left in the pipes.

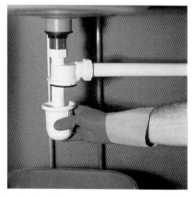

Unscrew the trap for access

4 You may also be able to approach the blockage from the trap under the sink or basin. Put a bucket under the trap and use a pipe wrench to unscrew the two couplings connecting the trap to the drainage pipes, or undo the base of a bottle trap (left) or the trap's drainage plug, if it has one, with an adjustable wrench. Let the water drain out of the trap, then probe inside for the blockage with the hooked coat-hanger wire.

5 If you still can't locate the blockage, it's probably lodged farther down the line – perhaps even in the main drainpipe. Try probing with a plumber's snake or auger if you have one, as these have a longer reach than a length of coat-hanger wire. If you don't have or cannot hire an augur – or if even this doesn't do the trick – it's time to call in a plumber. To save time – and money – tell the plumber what you have already tried.

screw from each tap to check that the headgear, the top of the mechanism, unscrews easily. If any parts are stiff, use penetrating oil to release the nuts and a wrench wrapped in cloth to brace the tap as you turn the spanner.

● If you can see limescale build-up inside, remove the small parts and soak them in vinegar or proprietary limescale remover. Smear the thread with lubricant before you reassemble the tap.

● **Wipe rust with WD-40** If you have rust spots on a sink or washbasin, you can get rid of them by wiping with a spray of WD-40 on a cloth and then rinsing thoroughly. For rust stains on porcelain enamel sinks, pour salt on half of a lemon and rub it on the stain.

● **Keep your drain draining freely** Mix 100ml of bicarbonate of soda (baking soda) with 100ml of salt and 25ml of cream of tartar. Keep the cleaning powder in an airtight, childproof container, then every few weeks pour 50ml of the mixture down each drain, followed by boiling water.

● The best way to keep your drains clear is to keep hair, soap, grease, food and other debris out of the drains in the first place. Never pour cooking fat down the drain – let it solidify then put it in the bin. Keep a drain strainer in your kitchen sink to catch debris before it's washed down with the water and do the same in your bath or shower to intercept hair before it can cause a blockage in the pipes.

Easy fixes

● **Replacing a washer in a compression tap** The first job is to remove the handle to get to the headgear, though how you do this depends on whether the tap is a rising or non-rising spindle design. You may need to lever off a cover to access the screw holding the handle in place. Wrap a wrench in a cloth before using it to undo the metal shroud covering the headgear in a rising spindle tap.

● With the handle removed, use an adjustable wrench to remove the headgear nut. Brace the tap with your other hand to stop it from spinning as you turn the nut, as this could weaken the tap's plumbing connection.

smart idea

Replacement rubber washers may only cost a few pence but you can often save yourself those pennies and a trip to the DIY store by simply turning over a worn washer and refitting it. There should be enough life left in the washer to stop the drip for a while longer.

A strainer helps to avoid blockages

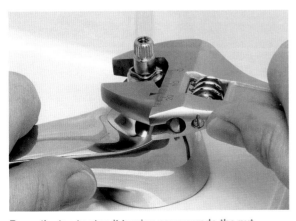

Brace the tap to stop it turning as you undo the nut

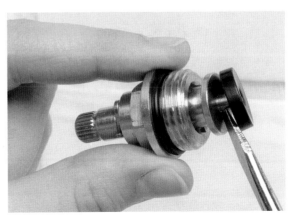

Lever off the old washer

take care!

Chemical drain cleaners won't only eat through a clog, they'll eat through anything, including your pipes (albeit slowly). Try to avoid these cleaners whenever possible. If you must use a chemical drain cleaner, wear rubber gloves, long sleeves and safety glasses. Never use a plunger on a drain into which you've just added a chemical cleaner. Water that splashes out of the drain as you work will be loaded with caustic chemicals.

• Lever off the old washer with a screwdriver (in some taps you need to unscrew it) and replace the washer with a duplicate. If the leak persists, the valve seat may have to be replaced. Call a plumber.

• **Unclogging an aerator spout** Some taps have a perforated plate over or just inside the spout to turn the flow of water into a spray. This is called an aerator. If water runs out of your tap slowly or without much pressure, the aerator may be clogged. Unscrew it and take it apart, if possible, keeping careful track of which part goes where. Soak the parts overnight in white vinegar, then scrub them clean with a toothbrush and rinse to remove any debris.

• **The sandwich bag and rubber band fix** If the aerator won't come off your tap spout, there's still a way to dissolve the mineral deposits that may be clogging it. Pour white vinegar into a plastic sandwich bag and use a rubber band or duct tape to secure the bag around the spout, making sure that the aerator is fully immersed in the vinegar. Let it soak overnight, then scrub the aerator with a toothbrush as above. Don't try this with brass or other coloured fixtures as it could ruin the finish.

How to repair a leaky cartridge tap

When a ceramic disc tap develops a drip, becomes stuck or difficult to operate or makes a thudding or banging noise when turned off, it's time to clean or replace the disc cartridges. You can tell whether you have a ceramic disc tap because the handle moves only one-quarter of a turn from off to fully open, whereas a conventional compression washer tap will turn several times from closed to open.

Remove the tap's handle to get inside

1 Turn off the water supply to the tap then undo the grub screw holding the tap's handle or handles in place. Use a spanner to undo the headgear, then carefully remove the ceramic cartridge. If the drip is from a mixer tap, you'll need to check both cartridges – make sure you keep them separate as right and left-handed cartridges aren't interchangeable.

2 Check the cartridge for any signs of wear and tear, such as scratches in the surface or specks of dirt lodged inside. If the cartridge appears worn, you should replace it, taking care to buy the appropriate left or right operating replacement. Always replace both hot and cold cartridges at the same time in a mixer tap.

3 Dismantle and clean a dirty cartridge using a damp cloth. Take careful note of how the cartridge is assembled so that you can put it back together again. A drip can be caused by a worn rubber seal at the base of the cartridge. If this looks damaged and if the rest of the cartridge looks otherwise intact, replace the seal.

Clean the parts then reassemble

4 Refit the cartridge and reassemble the tap, then turn the water supply back on. Check for any leaks and that the fault is fixed.

● **The first step in tap repairs** Before you set to work on any faulty tap, turn off the water that supplies it. Remember to turn off both hot and cold water supplies if the fault is with a mixer tap.

● If water-supply isolation valves (sometimes called service valves) aren't fitted in the pipework supplying the tap, you'll need to turn off the main water-supply valve for the house (see page 202) and open the tap until the water stops running.

● Take the opportunity to fit an isolation valve to the tap or taps you're working on while the water is switched off (see pages 222-223).

● **Plugging leaks in the trap** If water is leaking from a sink's drainage pipe, it's probably coming from the trap, or more specifically from the coupling nuts that hold it in place. Tighten a leaking coupling nut with two pipe wrenches, or with a pipe wrench and a pair of slip-joint pliers. Most drainage pipes are plastic, but if yours are chromed wrap the jaws of both tools with duct tape to keep them from damaging the surface.

● Grip the lower pipe with one tool and tighten the nut with the other. A quarter or half-turn is often enough to stop the drip, but if the leak persists, call a plumber.

smart idea

When doing work on a tap, it's vital to keep track of all the tiny parts. Put the plug in or place a saucer over the drain to keep parts from falling down it, and to make reassembly easier, line up parts in order as you remove them.

How to adjust a pop-up sink stopper

A pop-up stopper needs to be readjusted when it doesn't sit properly and either fails to hold water in the sink or doesn't lift high enough to let water drain out freely. The stopper is moved up and down by a three-part linkage consisting of a lift rod at the back of the tap, the clevis (a metal strip with holes in it) and the pivot rod, which supports the stopper or may actually be connected to it. If this linkage comes loose the stopper won't work properly.

To adjust the mechanism you'll need to work on the underside of the sink, which can be awkward. Make sure you clear out the area before you start, and keep all your tools (including a torch or, better still, a headtorch) within easy reach.

1 If a pop-up stopper won't seal tightly, first check for debris that might be preventing it from dropping far enough into the drain opening to keep water from escaping. Some pop-ups lift straight out, some are twisted out, while others require you to pull out the pivot rod to which they're attached. To take out the rod, use an adjustable wrench to loosen the retaining nut securing the rod to the drain body, then pull out the rod to free the stopper.

2 Wash the stopper (at a different sink) and check the rubber seal at the bottom of the stopper head. If it's dry or cracked, replace it.

3 Reverse the removal procedure in step 1 to reinstall the stopper. If the seal still isn't good, use pliers or your fingers to loosen the grub screw holding the lift rod and the clevis together. Pull the lift rod up, push the stopper down and retighten the screw (use a helper, if necessary).

4 If the problem persists or, conversely, if the stopper doesn't lift high enough to let water drain out freely, try moving the pivot rod to a different hole in the clevis. To do this, squeeze the spring clip on the clevis while sliding the rod out of it. Move the clip and the rod to the next hole up.

Baths and showers

Maintaining these bathroom stalwarts takes nothing more than a little regular diligence – but don't ignore those small leaks and drips that can lead to much bigger problems. If water from your shower seeps behind your tiles through cracked grout or faulty sealant and mould and mildew are allowed to flourish, you could eventually find yourself replacing the wall, not just the sealant or grout. Even worse, leaks from an upstairs bathroom can mean disaster (and big repair bills) for the room directly below. Follow these tips to head off headaches and hefty repairs.

SAVE £500

Cost to replace rotten floorboards caused by leaks from a poorly sealed bath, including removing the bath for access and reinstalling it.

Care and maintenance

● **Buy the right sealant** For durability and moisture-resistance, use a silicone-based bathroom sealant containing a mildewcide or fungicide. If you need to match a specific colour, get a high-quality acrylic latex bathroom sealant, which comes in a wide range of popular shades. Always make sure that surfaces are completely dry before applying sealant.

● **Use orange to banish rust** Orange oil-based wood cleaners don't just clean wood but also remove rust stains. Rub in the cleaner with a circular motion on the stain and rinse with water. Alternatively, try scrubbing the rust stain with a mixture of lemon juice and salt.

● **Wipe your bath and go** There's really no big secret to keeping your bath looking good: just wipe it down with water and a cloth or sponge after every use. This helps to prevent water spotting and soap scum build-up. When simple rinsing isn't enough, use a cleaner that's suitable for your bath's surface (either plastic or enamel), and rinse well after use.
  ● For porcelain enamel, make a paste of bicarbonate of soda (baking soda) and water, and scrub it on with a soft washing-up sponge.
  ● For glass fibre, spray on a general household or bathroom cleaner and wipe with a non-abrasive sponge.
  ● For stainless-steel fixtures, rub gently with a little bicarbonate of soda on a damp sponge.

WIPE YOUR BATH AND GO WITH A SPONGE AND WATER.

● **Make your bathtub shine** Blue-green stains on the sides of a bath are caused by water with high copper content. They are most common where a tap has been left dripping for a long time. To remove these stains, mix 1 tablespoon of cream of tartar with 1 tablespoon of bicarbonate of soda and add enough lemon juice to make a paste. Rub the paste into the stain with a soft cloth. Leave it on for 30 minutes, rinse and repeat if necessary.

● **Polish shower tiles to a gleam** Using dishwasher liquid or powder is a great way to keep tiled shower walls and floors sparkling. Mix 2 tablespoons of detergent with warm water in a small trigger spray bottle, and shake it to dissolve the detergent. Spray the solution liberally on shower walls and doors, let it sit for several hours and then scrub with a sponge. Use a sponge mop on the floor and to reach the top of the wall.

● **Keep shower doors crystal clear with vinegar** In hard-water areas, glass shower doors and screens can become opaque with mineral deposits and scum. To keep them clean, put white vinegar in a trigger spray bottle and spray it on the glass. Rinse well with water and dry with a soft cloth. If your doors have lots of mineral build-up, spray the door with vinegar and let it sit for a few minutes. Combine equal amounts of bicarbonate of soda and salt, rub the mixture over the door with a damp sponge and then rinse well.

● **Scale stops flow to a bathtub shower** To redirect the water to the showerhead in some baths, you pull up a plunger on top of the spout. If only some (or none) of the water is being diverted to the showerhead, the diverting valve is probably blocked with scale. You can often dismantle the valve by undoing a screw and either clean the scale off with a brush, soak the parts in vinegar or use a proprietary descaler. Most spouts simply screw on and off, but some require you to loosen a grub screw beneath the spout to release them.

Water-saving showerheads

Most showerheads, though not yet ones on electric showers, can be replaced with new efficient models that use far less water without compromising the power of your shower. Some manufacturers claim that the new showerhead will pay for itself in water and energy savings within as little as three months and that the new head will use only half as much water as a standard showerhead. Models sometimes known as 'champagne' showerheads incorporate an aerator into the showerhead, mixing air with the water to increase the volume of the flow while cutting the water usage.

How to replace a showerhead

Installing a new showerhead is not much harder than screwing in a light bulb, and it can do a lot to upgrade your bathroom. If you've got an old flow-reducing showerhead (or one that doesn't save water at all), you can replace it with a new water-saver that delivers a full stream of water while still reducing the flow rate.

1 To remove the old showerhead, use an adjustable wrench or pair of pliers to turn its collar anticlockwise. If the shower arm starts to twist as you turn the wrench, wrap the arm with a protective cloth or with duct tape and hold it in place with a pipe wrench while you unscrew the showerhead.

2 Wrap the shower arm threads with three to five clockwise turns of PTFE (polytetrafluoroethylene) pipe-thread tape to prevent leaks. If a washer is supplied with the new showerhead, install it following the manufacturer's directions. Screw on the new showerhead or handheld shower attachment and tighten with the adjustable wrench.

3 If you're installing a handheld shower attachment, screw the hose onto the attachment and the showerhead onto the hose using all required washers or gaskets.

smart idea

When applying sealant between the bath and the wall, fill the bath with water. The water's weight will open the gap between wall and bath as wide as possible, helping to prevent the sealant from cracking in the future.

Seal joints for a watertight bath

Easy fixes

● **Avoiding a blast of cold (or hot) water** A sudden change in temperature when you're showering is usually caused by a change in water pressure. This happens when an appliance (like your dishwasher or washing machine) is running and draws hot water at the same time as your shower, leaving you shivering. When you're showering and someone flushes the toilet, cold water is diverted from the shower to the toilet, leaving you with a potentially dangerous hot blast.

● The best way to avoid this is for all showers to be plumbed in with their own dedicated hot and cold water feeds, so that their flow cannot be interfered with by other appliances or plumbing fittings. But many showers aren't installed like this. An easy fix is to install a pressure-balancing, or anti-scald, valve, which maintains water temperature no matter what else is going on in the system. You can either have a pressure-balancing valve installed on the hot and cold-water pipes that feed the shower or replace the shower tap with a pressure-balancing model.

● **Filling in bathtub chips** A chip or nick in a porcelain enamel surface need not be permanent. Most DIY stores stock repair kits, ranging from simple touch-up paints to two-part epoxy compounds to build up the level of a deeper chip. The latter come in a variety of colours and are usually the best choice for a long-lasting and unobtrusive repair. Always follow the specific manufacturer's instructions, but this is what's usually involved:

● Scrub the chipped area with soapy water, let it dry then use a small piece of medium-grade sandpaper to remove any rust and give the epoxy a rougher surface to cling to. Mix the epoxy components together as directed and brush the compound onto the damaged area, but not beyond. Don't try to blend the new with the old. If the chip is deep, apply a second coat 8 hours later. Wait at least 24 hours before allowing the repair to get wet and a week before scrubbing it.

● **Sealing around the bathtub** The secret to stopping water from seeping through to the walls around the bath is a good sealing job. There are three key places that should be well sealed: between the bath and the wall, between the bath and the floor and between the wall and the plumbing fixtures. Inside wall corners on tiled walls should be sealed, too. Before applying new sealant, use a putty knife or a razor blade to remove old sealant and clean the gap well.

● **Unclogging a pop-up stopper** More often than not, when a bath drain gets blocked or is slow to drain, the culprit is a build-up of hair and soap scum in the plughole or on the bath's pop-up stopper, if it has one. Pull out the stopper and the rocker arm attached to it, remove the accumulated gunk and wash the stopper mechanism with soapy water and an old toothbrush. If cleaning doesn't do the trick, the stopper mechanism may need adjusting (see page 211).

How to plan a wet room

Wet rooms are increasingly popular in homes, where they offer a flexible use of space and a move away from the conventional kind of shower enclosure. In a wet room, the walls and floors are tiled and a drain sunk into the floor itself to allow shower water to escape. Putting up a glass or tiled screen is a good idea to separate the shower from the WC and washbasin area, but as long as your shower won't spray the toilet paper and the floor slopes gently towards the drain, a screen isn't essential. Installing a wet room is a job best left to a professional, but there are a few things to consider when planning your requirements to make sure that the room functions well and requires only minimal maintainence.

● Avoid using large, smooth tiles on the floor, as they will be dangerously slippery when wet. Mosaic tiles are a better choice within the shower area, as the grout lines and tile edges offer a better grip.

● Never lay ceramic floor tiles over wooden floorboards. As the boards flex naturally, the grout joints will crack and water will be able to seep into the timber below. You can minimise the risk of this by laying sheets of hardboard over the floor first.

● Always make sure your builder uses a professional waterproofing or 'tanking' product to seal the floor and walls before tiling. This will help to protect them from any moisture that seeps through.

● Consider the 'fall' of your drainage pipes when planning the layout of the room. Drain pipes need to drop 20mm for every 1m in length and this can restrict your options when you're working within the ceiling void of the room below.

● Specify a drainage trap that can be accessed from above for cleaning and to clear blockages.

The taps you find on your bath are available in the same types and with just the same operating parts as the taps on your sinks and basins, though they are sometimes larger. They can also drip and leak in the same way and repairing them follows the same procedures (see pages 205-211). The one problem with taps on baths is that accessing the tap's working parts can sometimes be tricky, as it may involve breaking into the surrounding tiles and wall. Further complicating matters are combination bath-shower taps in which a diverter valve directs water to either the showerhead or the bathtap spout. And faults with showers that have their plumbing sunk into the wall and tiled over can be costly and messy to repair if you go about it the wrong way. Unless you're confident in your skills, it's often wise in the long run to call a plumber to deal with bathtap and shower leaks.

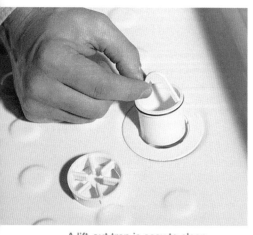

A lift-out trap is easy to clean

● **Plunging drains** If cleaning the pop-up stopper doesn't unclog your drain, try using a plunger. Position the plunger cup so that it completely covers the drain hole, then fill the bath with enough water to cover the cup. Hold a wet towel over the overflow vent to seal it and plunge vigorously to dislodge the blockage (see page 208). To create a tighter seal between the plunger and the drain, and to increase suction over the blockage, coat the rim of the plunger cap with a thick layer of petroleum jelly before you use it.

● **Going down under** If you can remove the bath panel to access the trap connected to the bathtub drain, you can attack a blockage from there. Loosen the two large nuts that hold the lower U-shaped section in place. Then, using a tray or shallow dish to catch any water or gunk, remove the section. Clear the trap and any other parts of the drain you can now reach (see page 208). If the blockage persists, call a plumber.

● **Unclogging strainer-style drains** Hair and soap scum lurking underneath a shower drain's strainer cover are the likely suspects when a shower gets clogged or drains too slowly. Usually, a quick cleaning or a bit of plunging is all it takes to get your bath or shower back in action.
● First, check the strainer cover itself. If gunk is visible in its openings, try cleaning them out manually. Run the water and see if that did the trick.
● If water still isn't draining properly, remove the strainer cover. Some types snap into place and can be lifted out with a screwdriver; others are held in place by screws. With the cover off, shine a torch into the drain and see if you can spot the blockage. If you can, try fishing it out with a hooked length of coat-hanger wire, taking care not to push the blockage even further down the drain.
● If the blockage still hasn't shifted, try clearing the drain with a plunger. If that doesn't work, call a plumber.

● **Unclogging your showerhead** A build-up of lime and mineral scale in a showerhead can reduce the shower stream to a trickle. To restore the flow to a fixed showerhead, pour white vinegar into a plastic sandwich bag and pull it up over the showerhead, making sure that the entire head is immersed in the vinegar. Secure the bag to the shower arm with duct tape and leave it on overnight. To clean a hand-held showerhead, unscrew it from its hose and rest the sprayhead in a shallow bowl of vinegar to soak overnight. Don't use vinegar on brass or other coloured finishes.

● **Easy access for clearing the drain** Waste pipes and traps from showertrays are almost impossible to access once they have been installed. Including a rodding eye on the waste pipe will help if you have a blockage to clear, but when you fit a new shower, consider specifying a top-access trap (left), which can be unblocked by simply removing the grid covering the drain and lifting out the trap for cleaning. These are often fitted in wet rooms (see page 215), where underfloor access isn't an option.

Toilets

Toilet maintenance is never high on anyone's list of favourite chores, but it must be done regularly to keep the fixture clean and in good working order. Blockages are the most common problem but can usually be cleared with a simple plunger. More draining on your wallet is the amount of water your WC uses each time you flush. Follow these tips to avoid unnecessary overflows, flushing failiure and wasted water.

Care and maintenance

● **Clean from top to bottom** When cleaning a toilet, start at the top and work your way down in this order: cistern, seat, inside of the bowl then the base. Use a spray-on bathroom cleaner, preferably one with ammonia. Spray the cleaner on the exterior surfaces and wipe it off with an absorbent dry cloth, and change rags as they become soaked. To clean inside the bowl, spray cleaner under the rim and on surfaces above the waterline. Use a rounded bowl brush to scrub first under the rim, then the bowl itself and finally the drain opening.

SAVE £30

The average amount you can save each year for each member of your household by replacing a standard toilet cistern with a dual-flush, water-saving system.

A PUMICE STONE IS A USEFUL TOOL FOR REMOVING 'TIDE MARKS'.

● **Use a pumice stone to get rid of toilet bowl rings** Its main purpose is to rub calluses off feet, but a pumice stone is also a useful tool for removing 'tide marks' caused by hard-water deposits. Keeping the pumice wet, rub it on the ring until it's gone. Pumice won't scratch white vitreous china, which is what most toilets are made of, but it will scratch enamel, glass fibre and other materials, so take care if you're uncertain what your toilet is made from. Pumice stones are widely available where cosmetics and medical supplies are sold, but you can also find pumice scouring sticks at hardware and DIY stores.

● **Flush away toilet paper only** Paper towels, facial tissue, bandages, nappies and personal sanitary products can block your drains, causing problems for you and maybe your neighbours, too. They will seriously clog up a septic tank if you have one. Toilet paper – and only toilet paper – is all that you should flush. Use the bin for everything else.

● **Peek inside the cistern** Every now and again, it's a good idea to take off the cistern lid and check up on what's going on inside (left). Here's what you should look for:
● The water level should be around 1-2cm below the rim of the overflow pipe. If it's too high, you may have a constant drip out through

the overflow pipe, wasting water. If it's too low, the toilet may flush sluggishly. See page 220 for tips on adjusting the water level.
● If the WC has a float valve with a ball, check the ball to make sure that it isn't cracked or waterlogged, as this will stop the flushing system from working efficiently.

Easy fixes

● **Stopping a leak** If you see water puddling on the floor under the toilet tank, try tightening the water supply pipe connections on the side of the cistern and the big plastic nut holding the flush pipe to the underside

How a toilet works

Most home toilets use a siphon flushing system, with an inverted 'U'-shaped pipe that prevents water leaking from the cistern into the pan in between flushes. The tank may be mounted at high level on the wall, with a pull-chain to flush, at low level with a short pipe connecting with the pan or 'close-coupled', where the cistern and pan are directly linked, but the operation remains the same.

Modern WCs are usually designed as dual-flush, with a two-part button or 'flush-and-hold' system to choose a reduced, 4 litre flush to save water or a standard full flush. A hole in the dome (see below) interrupts the flush by letting in air to break the siphonic action, but can be temporarily plugged to select a full flush.

Slimline cisterns may be too small to incorporate a ball float-operated system (below). Instead, they use a modified diaphragm valve (known as a Torbek valve) with a very short float arm and miniature float, or a vertical valve with a float cup that fits around the central column of the valve body. Both types are quiet in operation and fast to fill, although the float-cup valve system can be slow if the toilet is supplied with water from a storage tank rather than from the mains. In both cases, a plastic valve-operated flush mechanism replaces the siphonic system shown below and is activated by a push-button, usually in the cistern lid, not a conventional handle.

These systems have an integrated overflow and do not need an overflow pipe leading to the outside. Toilets with this kind of flush mechanism are not easy to maintain or repair yourself, and any problems usually require a replacement mechanism to be fitted.

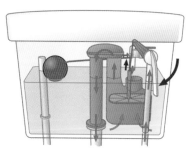
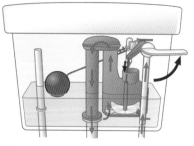
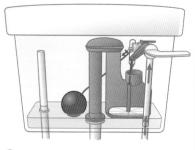

1 An inverted U-pipe in the cistern leads into the pan and at the other end opens out into a dome (siphon). When the flush is operated, a lift rod raises a plate in the dome and throws water into the crown of the U-bend. As the float sinks, the inlet valve opens to let in fresh water.

2 Openings in the plate are covered by a plastic flap valve held flat by the weight of the water. As water falls down the flush pipe, it creates a partial vacuum, causing water to be sucked up through the plate openings, raising the flap valve to let it through.

3 The base of the dome is about 10mm above the base of the cistern. When the water level falls below the dome base, air is drawn in and breaks the siphonic action, stopping the flush. The cistern refills until the rising ball float shuts off the inlet valve at the top of its travel.

How to clear a blocked toilet

When the water rises dangerously close to the top of the pan when you flush, you know you have a blockage either in the toilet's drain pipe or further along the soil pipe to the main drain. Start with the simplest solution first and proceed from there as needed. If clearing the toilet itself doesn't solve the problem you may need professional help to rod or jet-clear the outside drains.

1 Start with a plunger. Bail out excess water from the pan, leaving enough to cover the plunger cup. Put the plunger over the drain opening so it seals it completely. Plunge vigorously 10 or 12 times, then yank the plunger out with force. Repeat if needed. If you don't have a plunger, you can improvise by wrapping a plastic bag around a mop head. Secure the bag to the handle of the mop so that it cannot work free. Never use a plunger after a chemical drain treatment in case you splash yourself with dangerous chemicals.

2 Probe with a wire hanger. If you can see the clog, bend a hook in a coat-hanger wire and try to fish out the clog with it.

3 If neither the plunger nor the coat hanger have cleared the blockage, try a plumber's snake, or auger. This is a crank-handled tool (above) that winds a cable with a hooked spring tip through a toilet's 'U'-bend trap and into the drain. You can use the augur to grab the blockage and very carefully pull it back out through the trap or to push and break up the clog.

START WITH A PLUNGER.

of the cistern. On a close-coupled WC suite these connections might not be visible without dismantling the toilet and you may need a plumber's help to investigate. If tightening the connections doesn't work, it could be that the sealing washer between the cistern and pan or connecting pipe has perished. Replacing this is a job best left to a professional plumber.

● **Fixing flushing problems** If a toilet won't flush, first look inside the cistern to make sure it contains water. If it's empty then the problem is with the inlet valve or supply pipe. Adjust the water level if necessary (see page 220) and check that the isolation valve on the supply pipe is open. If water is still not flowing into the cistern, try dismantling and cleaning the inlet valve to remove any debris blocking it or replace the valve.
● If water in the cistern isn't the problem, check to see that the flushing arm (the lever connected to the pull-chain or handle) is connected to the hook at the top of the siphon and is lifting the plunger. Reconnect a broken or loose connection by hooking the 'S' or 'C'-shaped wire link back through the hole in the flush arm (right). You may need to reach under the

Reconnect a slipped link

smart idea

If you have an old-fashioned toilet with a large cistern you can still reduce the volume of water used each time you flush. Replace the flush mechanism with a dual-flush alternative if possible or simply put a house brick or a proprietary water-saving 'balloon' in the cistern to reduce the amount of water stored and used each time.

base of the dome and push up the plate inside a little to expose the top of the lift rod. If the flushing lever has broken, it can usually be replaced by a universal part, available from a plumbers' merchant or DIY store.

● Poor flushing can sometimes be caused by the flush pipe being pushed too tight into its housing in the back of the pan, restricting the flow. Try pulling the flush pipe slightly back (it's held in its rubber sleeve by friction only) and see if this improves the flush.

● A toilet's failure to flush can also be caused by a loose or disconnected handle. Remove the cistern lid, hold the handle with one hand and tighten the handle locknut with a wrench.

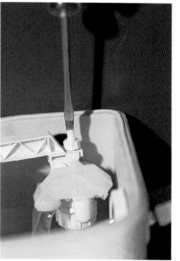

● **Adjusting the water level** To raise the water level in a toilet with an older float ball assembly, bend the metal float arm up slightly from the centre; to lower the water level, bend the arm down slightly. Newer models have a screw at the top of the float valve that allows you to adjust the float level by sliding it along the arm.

● With a plastic valve assembly (left) you can adjust the angle of the arm, and therefore the level of the water, by turning an adjustment screw at the valve end of the float arm.

A screw adjusts the water level

● **Remedy for a reluctant flush** If you find that you have to pump the handle repeatedly to make the toilet flush, first check that the cistern is filling fully and adjust the water level (see above) if necessary. If the water level is fine, you may need to replace the plastic flap valve inside the siphon unit. Replacement parts are cheap and easy to find and fitting is straightforward, though it might take a little time. You'll need to empty and disconnect the cistern – follow the instructions supplied with the new valve – so call a plumber if you don't feel confident enough to do the job.

TOILET MAINTENANCE IS CERTAINLY NOT HIGH ON ANYONE'S LIST OF FAVOURITE CHORES, BUT IT MUST BE DONE.

Septic systems

If your home isn't connected to the mains sewerage, you probably have a septic system to break down and dispose of household waste water. A well-maintained septic system will perform its job efficiently for decades while a replacement can cost as much as a new roof, so it's worth taking care of your tank and what you put into it.

Care and maintenance

● **Conserve water** This is one of the surest ways to maintain the health of your septic system. Large volumes of water, especially when delivered over a short time (as happens when too many showers are taken back to back or too many loads of laundry are washed in one day), can flush suspended, untreated waste particles into the drainage field, eventually clogging it.

● **Have your septic system inspected every two or three years** Also have the tank pumped as necessary to remove built-up sludge and scum. How often the tank will need to be cleaned out depends on its size and on the number of people in your home.

● **Take care what you send down the drain** Don't dispose of anything in sinks or toilets that the bacteria in the septic system can't break down. This includes grease, fat, oils, coffee grounds, any paper product other than toilet tissue, cat litter, disposable nappies, feminine hygiene products, condoms, bandages, aluminum foil and cigarette butts.

● **Don't flood the drainage field** Water constantly seeps from the septic tank into the drainage field, but if the drainage field is saturated with rainwater, the water from your septic tank has nowhere to go. Direct the run-off from gutters or drainage spouts away from the septic tank drainage field and into soakaways of its own.

● **Don't drive over the field** A drainage field needs oxygen to work; driving or parking over it compresses the soil and squeezes out the air.

● **Watch what you plant** Only grass should be planted over and near your septic tank and drainage field. Tree and shrub roots could damage the drainage system.

SAVE £7,000
What it would cost to buy and install a new septic tank and soakaway drainage system.

PLANT ONLY GRASS OVER YOUR SEPTIC SYSTEM.

Water supply and drains

The pipes that bring water into your home and take it away are prone to three common problems: leaks, blockages and noise. Fix minor leaks and sluggish drains before they become big headaches and be careful what you flush away and you can keep the plumber at bay. When a pipe problem occurs, how accessible the troubled pipe is often spells the difference between an easy DIY repair and one for the professionals.

SAVE £150

Cost for a plumber to locate the cause of noisy pipework and fix the problem.

Care and maintenance

● **Be kind to your drains** The most common cause of drain clogs is you – sending things down the plughole that should really go in the bin. Grease is a major culprit: it solidifies and collects along the sides of a pipe, attracting food debris and eventually blocking the pipe.
● Use a plughole strainer in your kitchen sink to catch scraps, and allow fat and grease to solidify, then scrape them into the bin rather than trying to flush them through the pipes with hot water.

● **Insulate your pipes** When the water in pipes freezes, it expands and can leave you with burst pipes or loosened connections that will leak when the water thaws. Insulation won't protect pipes during a very harsh and prolonged cold spell, but it will help during a short cold snap and should be sufficient to avoid freezing problems in most parts of the UK.
● Insulate any pipes that run outside the house or in unheated rooms, such as porches, and in the roof space above your loft insulation. See pages 226-227 for pipe insulation tips.

● **Fit isolators for easy maintenance** To do any repair or maintenance task on the plumbing in your home – even something as simple as replacing a tap washer – you need to turn off the water supply first and empty the pipes. All new pipework should now include service valves, or isolation valves, that allow you to isolate each individual tap, fitting

How your plumbing system works

Your home's water-supply system delivers water under pressure to fixtures and appliances. The soil and vent pipe (SVP) system relies on gravity to carry liquid and solid wastes to the main house drain, which slopes down to a sewer pipe or a septic tank. 'U'-shaped traps (sometimes called P-traps or bottle traps according to their shape) in the drain pipe of most fixtures hold water that acts as a seal to keep sewer gases from entering the house. Rodding eyes or clean-out plugs in the main and branch drains provide access for clearing blockages. Vent pipes connected to the drainage system allow sewer gases to escape and keep trap seals in place.

or appliance rather than cutting off the supply to the whole house while you work. With just a quarter-turn of a screw, the supply is stopped in an instant, minimising the mess and damage of a burst pipe or other fault.

● If you don't already have isolators fitted throughout your home, it's worth putting one in whenever you have the water turned off and a pipe disconnected as part of another job. Fit them in a convenient location in all supply pipes, such as to water tanks (right), taps, WCs and appliances.

Fit isolators on water supply pipes

● **Be sure to earth metal pipes** All metal pipework must be joined to the house's main earth bonding system to prevent electrocution from touching a pipe that has become live through an electrical fault. Check that you have an earth strap (below right) fitted to your pipework near where it enters the house, with a length of earth core leading back to the main earthing point. If a live wire touches a metal pipe anywhere in the house, the current will be conducted through the pipework and safely earthed.

● Plastic pipes and fittings don't conduct electricity, so a 'bridging' wire must be fitted between the metal sections on either side.

● In some older properties, the house earthing system may be connected to the rising main, but this should be changed to a common earthing point close to the meter. Contact a qualified electrician for advice and to check the earthing in your home.

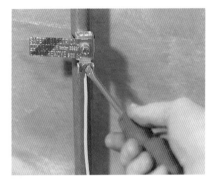
Metal pipework must be earthed

● **Water needs to drain downhill** Drainage pipes won't drain efficiently if they aren't fitted with the correct 'fall'. Whenever you plan to install a new fitting, particularly a bath or shower, where the waste outlet is already close to floor level, make sure that the waste pipe can slope down sufficiently to where it joins the main drain pipe or exits the wall.

● A pipe should fall by no less than 20mm for each 1m in length, but no more than 50mm for a pipe less than 1m long or 25mm for a longer pipe.

● To prevent self-siphoning, a standard 32mm drain pipe should be no longer than 1.75m. If your pipe needs to be longer than this, use a larger 38mm pipe, which can be up to 2.3m long. Take advice from your local Building Control Officer if you need to exceed this length.

● **Drain outside pipes before a freeze** Before winter, disconnect all hoses from outside taps. Inside the house, find the taps' shut-off valves and turn them off. Open each tap to let water drain out of the valve and pipes and leave the taps open until you restore the water supply in spring.

● An alternative to draining outside taps and their supply pipes is to fit them with an insulating jacket. Wrap a generous covering of insulation bandage around the tap and secure it with tape before covering the tap with a plastic bag to keeep it dry. Or buy a proprietary tap protector kit: these are cheap and easy to fit, and often allow you to continue using the tap while they are in place.

● **Prevent limescale with a water softener** If you live in a hard-water area (most of the UK south of a line between the Wash and the Bristol Channel), limescale deposits will build up on taps and in appliances, reducing the efficiency of heating elements in everything from kettles to the hot-water cylinder and washing machine. Fitting an ion-exchange water softener where the water main enters the house can greatly prolong the life of your appliances and pipes. Ion-exchange water softeners cost from £400 to £600; some require an electrical supply and all need to be replenished regularly with salt tablets or blocks. Always leave one tap, usually the cold tap at the kitchen sink, supplied by untreated hard water for drinking.

Easy fixes

● **Unsticking shut-off valves** When a water-supply shut-off valve isn't used for a while, it can get stuck or start leaking after you turn it. To fix a drippy valve, try gently tightening its packing nut with a wrench or opening and shutting the valve several times until the drip stops. To free a stuck valve, put a few drops of oil around the stem near the packing nut. Loosen the nut about one turn and retighten it by hand. Wait a few minutes for the oil to soak in and you should be able to turn the valve.

● **Draining the plumbing system** This is a possible, if temporary, fix for thumping or banging pipes and won't cost a penny. Begin by turning off the main water-supply shut-off valve. Find the lowest tap in your home and open it. Open a few of the highest taps as well. When the lowest tap stops dripping, close all the taps and turn the water supply back on. Expect some banging and spluttering when you turn on the taps again for the first time.

take care!

Clearing a blockage in a branch or main drain often requires a heavy-duty, power-driven auger or powerful water jet. This is definitely a job for a professional.

Water-hammer arrester

A water-hammer arrester is an air-filled cylinder or ball that's installed in the supply line near valves that are causing banging – water hammer – in the pipes. The air chamber acts as a shock absorber against the water-pressure spike and silences the banging. Many older homes have arresters that are simply capped lengths of vertical pipe. These become waterlogged over time as the air gets absorbed into the water supply. You can restore them by draining the plumbing system, but this is only a temporary solution. If water hammer persists, ask a plumber to install a proprietary water-hammer arrester, which comes equipped with a piston with rubber gaskets that isolates an air pocket from the water in the pipes. Screw-in water-hammer arresters (right) are also available for easy DIY installation.

● **Flushing air out of pipes** Once it gets into pipes, air will make a banging noise as it travels through them. If you suspect an air problem, turn on all the taps, hot and cold, and flush the toilets once or twice. If the noise persists, something else is causing the problem.

● **Locating a blockage** The first step to clearing a clog is finding it. If only one fixture is blocked, the problem is either in the fixture itself, in its trap or in the drain leading away from it. If several fixtures are clogged, the problem is in a branch line that all of them drain into, below the lowest stopped-up fixture and above the highest working one. If many or all fixtures are running sluggishly, the clog is probably in one of the main drain lines. A bad smell can signal a blockage in the roof vent on the system's main vent pipe and this may also make drains gurgle when you flush the toilet. For more on clearing a blockage, see page 208.

How to **silence noisy pipes**

Plumbing systems emit all sorts of noises: some are annoying but benign and others indicate trouble. To identify the troublesome pipes, follow the noise to its source if you can. Of course, locating and fixing a problem with pipes hidden within a stud wall is harder and may require you to break through the plasterboard for access.

● **RATTLING OR BANGING** when the water is turned on may be caused by a pipe that's loose within its strap, U-clamp, pipe hanger or support block. You can usually see exposed pipes vibrating, knocking against studs or moving within loosened supports. Resecure or tighten the supports or add more straps or hangers, as needed. If a rattling pipe runs through exposed joists, try installing pipe inserts – split plastic sleeves that fit around the pipe and slide into the hole in the joist. Quieting rattling pipes can be as simple as adding pipe clips (below right) or cushioning the pipe run with some insulation wadding (below left).

● **CLICKING, TICKING OR SQUEAKING** when the hot water is turned on may indicate that a now heat-expanded pipe is too tightly anchored. Loosen the clamp or strap or add a piece of rubber or felt between the pipe and its support that will compress as the pipe expands yet hold it firm when the pipe is cool.

● **THUMPING OR BANGING** when a tap or appliance is turned off is known as water hammer. It's caused by the spike in pressure that occurs when water moving under pressure is suddenly stopped by the closing of a valve. The problem is more common with certain appliance valves, which shut off almost instantly, than with hand-controlled taps. In addition to being annoying, water hammer causes pipes to shake, which can eventually damage pipes and valves and weaken connections. Install a water-hammer arrester (see box on page 224) to control the problem.

● **WHISTLING** may be caused by a shut-off valve that's not fully open or by high water pressure, which can worsen a water-hammer problem. Make sure all water-supply shut-off valves are completely open. In some cases, a pressure-reducing valve may have to be installed in the supply line near the water meter.

Hot water

Heating water for your taps is usually controlled by a separate system from your central heating, although both use the boiler and are generally controlled from the same timer system. Understanding which type of system you have is the first step in keeping it working efficiently and locating and fixing problems when they occur.

SAVE £20

Cost to replace an immersion heater element that has become caked in limescale.

Care and maintenance

● **Fit a timer for full control** If your house has an old gravity-fed central heating system (page 229) it's not economical to use the boiler to heat your water during summer, when the heating is switched off. Instead, use the electric immersion heater in the hot-water cylinder. Left switched on for long periods, an immersion heater will use a lot of electricity – fit a timer (left) to ensure that you have hot water ready when you need it and save you forgetting to turn off the heater.

● **Keep pipes warm** Hot-water pipes that run through uninsulated parts of the house, such as in the loft above the level of the insulation, will lose a great deal of heat, especially in cold weather. To minimise heat loss and save on energy, make sure that pipes are lagged with foam or blanket (left).

Wrap up pipes in cold lofts

● **Insulating pipes round a bend** Fabric wadding (left) or strips of self-adhesive foam wrap are versatile choices for lagging pipes. Simply cut strips to a workable length and wrap them round the pipe, overlapping each piece. At bends and valves, take care to cover the pipe thoroughly.

How to **prevent limescale problems**

Much of the UK has hard water – when it's heated, calcium and magnesium deposits (or limescale) solidify on the heating elements and reduce their efficiency or even stop them working altogether. This is a clearly visible problem in an electric kettle, but it's also happening out of sight in your washing machine, hot-water cylinder, dishwasher and shower. Even your pipes can become clogged up with limescale, reducing the water flow and eventually necessitating their replacement. Heavily scaled heating elements can raise your energy bills by as much as 25 per cent.

● An easy way to protect appliances is to use water softener tablets or granules with each wash. But it's harder to protect your hot-water system.

● The most effective solution is to fit an ion-exchange water softener (see page 224) where the mains water enters the house, to reduce the mineral content of the water flowing through your system. Always leave one tap that bypasses the softener to provide you with drinking water.

What sort of hot-water system do you have?

The most common hot-water system is a hot-water cylinder, usually sited in a cupboard, and heated either directly by an immersion heater element or indirectly by hot water circulating through pipes from the central-heating boiler. Even the systems that draw heat from the boiler usually also have an immersion heater as back-up in case the boiler breaks down or for when you need a burst of hot water quickly.

● **A COMBINATION BOILER SYSTEM** is often used in flats or small modern houses, where there's no room for a cold-water cylinder. In these systems, water drawn directly from the mains supply is heated on demand by the boiler whenever a hot tap is switched on. Working from the mains, you can be sure of a constant supply of hot water, but the flow rate is generally slower than stored water from a cylinder and it can take a long time to fill a bath. The flow of hot water can also be interrupted if someone switches on another hot tap in the house at the same time.

● **MAINS PRESSURE HOT WATER** can also be attained by using a sealed system with a hot-water cylinder fed directly from the mains rather than from a storage cistern in the loft. These systems give excellent pressure for showers and baths but need to incorporate safety features to allow for the greater pressure and the expansion of the hot water.

● Along with the boiler, give your hot-water system an annual check-up. The sealed-system water circulating from the boiler to the hot-water cylinder can corrode the pipes and elements or create a build-up of sludge. See page 228 for tips on keeping the system healthy.

● Plastic foam tubes (right) are quick and easy to fit, particularly on straight runs of pipework, as they slot straight over the pipe and simply clip into place. When you need to go round a bend, cut notches in one side of the insulation then bend the insulation round the pipe, with the notches inside the bend. Tape the piece in place with the next section.

Cut foam strips to fit round a bend

Easy fixes

● **When you have heating but no hot water** If you know the boiler and programmer are working because the radiators are hot, check the thermostat on the hot-water cylinder. It should be set to around 60°C; if it has been turned down it will have switched off the hot-water system.

● **Replacing an immersion heater** Elements can wear out over time or if they become coated with limescale, but an immersion heater element is easy to replace. If you notice that the water is taking longer to heat up, switch off the boiler and the power to the immersion heater. Turn off the gate valve to cut off water to the cylinder and open the bathroom hot taps and the drain valve on the cylinder to drain off enough water to work – around 4.5 litres if the immersion heater is at the top or the whole cylinder if it's lower down. Unscrew and remove the immersion heater cover, note the wiring connections then disconnect and remove the heater, using a large immersion heater spanner. Fit a new washer to the new element, if supplied, then reassemble the unit, refill the tank and restore the power.

● **Adjusting the temperature** The electric element of an immersion heater is controlled by a thermostat under a cover at the top of the cylinder. To adjust the water temperature, unscrew and remove the immersion heater cover and use a screwdriver to turn the pointer within the dial. Some twin-element heaters have two thermostats.

Setting the water temperature

Central heating

The modern alternative to independent heaters in each room, a central heating system distributes water heated centrally at a boiler to radiators around the home. This brilliantly simple solution has transformed home comfort, but there are many parts to the system with the potential for expensive repairs if a fault develops. Look out for problems with the electric pump, motorised valves, leaking pipe connections and air in the system.

SAVE £80

Cost for a plumber to solve minor heating problems that you can resolve yourself, such as an extinguished pilot light or turned-off radiator.

Care and maintenance

● **Check the system for corrosion** Every summer, before you switch the heating back on for winter, check the water in your radiators for signs of corrosion. Left unchecked, internal rusting can be very expensive to repair. Drain off a mugful of water from the drain valve at the boiler. Put it in a glass jar with two bright, non-galvanised nails, seal the jar and leave it for a week. If the water turns orange and the nails are rusty then there is some corrosion in the system. Treat the water in the central-heating feed-and-expansion cistern with a corrosion inhibitor (for sealed systems, see below) and ask a plumber to assess the damage for you.

Let trapped air escape

● **Let out the air** Check radiators from time to time to make sure that they are heating up evenly. If a radiator is hot at the bottom but cold at the top, it needs 'bleeding' to let out air that has seeped into the system.
● Use a radiator key (left) – brass ones are stronger than aluminium – and carefully turn it anticlockwise to loosen the bleed screw at the top of the radiator. Turn until you hear air hissing out and shut it tight as soon as water starts to appear. Hold a cloth under the valve as you work to catch any drips, as the water may be dirty.

● **Keep a sealed system healthy** If you have a sealed central heating system (see page 229), give it an annual dose of chemical corrosion and scale inhibitor. Special cartidges are available at most DIY stores – pump in the contents through a radiator air vent using a standard cartridge gun.

What sort of central heating system do you have?

The type of central heating system you have may depend on the age of your house. Most central heating systems work by passing hot water through radiators, with the water usually heated by a boiler, which switches on and off automatically at certain times of day.

A TYPICAL PUMPED SYSTEM

● A programmer switches on the boiler and the pump at preset times of the day. A room thermostat activates the pump (or opens a motorised valve) and the boiler if the air temperature is below the required level.

● The pump drives water around the system via the boiler, which heats the water. The water in the central heating system is separate from that supplied to the hot taps (see pages 226-227) and the two circuits may be controlled separately and switched on and off at different times. The motorised valve opens and closes the circuits to the radiators and hot-water cylinder as required by the thermostats.

● The same water is constantly circulated around the system. In an open system, in case of leakage or evaporation, the water is topped up from a feed-and-expansion cistern, usually in the loft. This cistern also takes up the expansion that occurs when the water heats up from cold.

● An open-ended pipe, called the open safety-vent pipe, provides an escape route for steam and excess pressure if the boiler overheats.

GRAVITY CIRCULATION

In some older central heating systems and in solid fuel systems, water is circulated by gravity.

● When water is heated it expands and weighs less than cold water. Hot water rises up a large pipe from the boiler to the hot water cylinder. Cooled water descends down the return pipe, pushing the lighter hot water up.

● Gravity circulation is reliable as it needs no mechanical assistance, but it requires larger 28mm pipes. The system is most efficient if the cylinder is directly above the boiler.

A SEALED SYSTEM

A sealed central heating system has an expansion vessel instead of an expansion cistern, and a pressure relief valve instead of a safety-vent pipe. The valve should be set permanently to 3 bar. Any water lost over time through minor leaks is topped up manually from the mains supply.

● A thermostat opens the motorised valve, which controls the circuits to the radiators.

● The valve turns on the pump to drive water around the system and starts up the boiler.

● The boiler has an overheat cut-out to prevent the system boiling should the standard thermostat fail. Most sealed systems use a combination boiler (see page 237). A boiler without overheat protection should never be fitted to a sealed system.

A pumped system

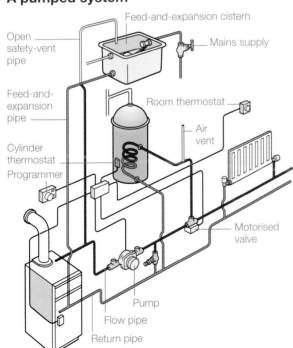

Open safety-vent pipe

Feed-and-expansion cistern

Mains supply

Feed-and-expansion pipe

Room thermostat

Air vent

Cylinder thermostat

Programmer

Motorised valve

Pump

Flow pipe

Return pipe

A gravity-fed system

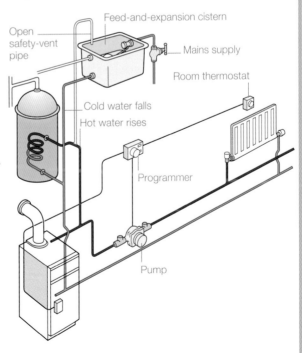

Open safety-vent pipe

Feed-and-expansion cistern

Mains supply

Room thermostat

Cold water falls

Hot water rises

Programmer

Pump

Getting the **right size radiators**

Radiators must be an appropriate size for the rooms they are in. A radiator that's too large will simply waste money and energy, calling on the boiler to heat up more water than necessary. A radiator that's too small will struggle to warm the room and you're likely to have the heating running for longer as a result.

● Start by calculating the size of the room in cubic feet. Measure the length and the width in feet, multiply them together then multiply this number by the height of the ceiling. Round the figures each time to the nearest foot.

● Multiply the volume by the factors below to give a figure in BTUs (British Thermal Units) for the room. All radiators have a BTU value, although some suppliers list the heat output in Watts – to convert BTUs to Watts, multiply by 0.293. When you're buying new, use your calculation as a sizing guide. If you want to check the sizes of your existing radiators, search for equivalent styles and sizes to find an approximate BTU rating.

● For living, dining and bathrooms, multiply by 5.
● For bedrooms, multiply by 4.
● For halls and kitchens, multiply by 3.
● For north-facing rooms, add 15 per cent.
● For rooms with french windows, add 20 per cent.
● For rooms with double glazing, subtract 10 per cent.

● **Let the heat radiate** A radiator with fins on the back can give off twice the heat of a flat-panel model, but if too much dust collects in the fins it will reduce the efficiency. Make a simple tool to clean the fins by attaching a piece of sponge or old rag to a length of coat-hanger wire, then push it down between the fins to keep them clean.

Easy fixes

● **Hushing noisy pipes** Humming is usually caused by the pump that moves the water around your heating system. Check that the pump speed isn't set too high – try turning down the speed control knob on the body of the pump (left) and see whether that makes a difference.

● Banging pipes could be caused by overheating. Turn off the boiler, but not the pump, and allow the system to cool. Turn the boiler back on and adjust the thermostat to maximum. You should hear a click as the boiler starts up – if you don't, then the thermostat could be faulty.

● If the banging is in just one section of pipe, consider swapping a couple of copper joints or even a length of pipe with plastic – this may help.

● **When nothing is getting warm** If neither heating nor hot water are working, check some simple things first, starting with the programmer to make sure it hasn't been switched off in error. Make sure that the power to the heating controller hasn't been tripped and that the relevant thermostats haven't been turned down by mistake.

A high-speed pump makes pipes hum

• Next, check the boiler to make sure that the pilot light hasn't gone out. If it has, follow the instructions in your user manual to relight it. For a combination boiler, check the water pressure gauge – the pilot light will not stay lit if it's too high or low (see page 236). A persistent drop in temperature probably indicates a leak somewhere in the system.
• If the heating is still not working, check the motorised valve that controls the flow of water, if there is one. Move the manual lever to open the valve – if it feels stiff, the motor could have failed. Call an engineer. If it moves and you hear a gurgling noise, you've cleared a blockage.

take care!

Never attempt repairs on a gas boiler. You must always engage a Gas Safe-registered engineer for any work involving gas (see page 238).

• **First check for a cold radiator** Before you call a plumber about a faulty radiator, make sure that the radiator is switched on and the valve is working. Turn both valves to close them and then open them again and see whether this solves the problem. Thermostatic radiator valves (TRVs) can sometimes jam closed – see page 234 for how to free them.

• **You can hear water rushing in the pipes** When air gets into the system, or if gas is produced as a result of internal corrosion, it can make it sound as though water is gushing through the pipes. Try bleeding the radiators to let out any air (page 228). If this doesn't work, there could be a more serious fault, such as a poorly located open safety-vent pipe in the loft – call a plumber to investigate further.

• **Radiators are cold downstairs but hot upstairs** This is usually a sign of a jammed pump, particularly if there's plenty of hot water in the taps. Try tapping the pump sharply with a mallet. If this doesn't work, turn off the heating, let the system cool then remove the screw in the centre of the pump and turn its manual starter (there may be a handle or you may need a screwdriver). A final trick is to turn the pump speed to maximum to try to clear any blockage – remember to turn it down again.
• Sludge in the system could also be the cause. Try adding system restorer to the feed-and-expansion cistern, leaving it for a couple of weeks and then draining and refilling the system.

• **Radiators are hot downstairs but cold upstairs** Start by bleeding the system (page 228) as air will rise and can fill the upstairs radiators.
• Next check the water level in the feed-and-expansion cistern. If it's empty, the ball valve has probably jammed and there's not enough water in the system to feed all the radiators. Call a plumber to replace the valve.

• **Tighten connections to fix a drip** A leaking radiator valve could need no more than a pair of spanners to fix it. Brace the pipe to stop it bending by gripping the nut below the valve with a Stillson wrench. Use an adjustable spanner to turn the nut between the valve and radiator. Tighten it no more than a quarter-turn, clockwise when looking from the radiator to the valve. If the leak persists, the valve may be faulty or need refitting.
• If the leak is from beneath the valve, call a plumber. If the leak is from a compression joint (a joint made with nuts), try tightening the nuts as above. If a soldered joint is leaking, you'll need a plumber's help.

Use a spanner and wrench to fix a drip

How to balance a radiator

Hot water is carried from the boiler to the radiators by a flow pipe, which branches off to supply each radiator. Cool water leaves each radiator at the opposite end and joins a return pipe carrying it back to the boiler.

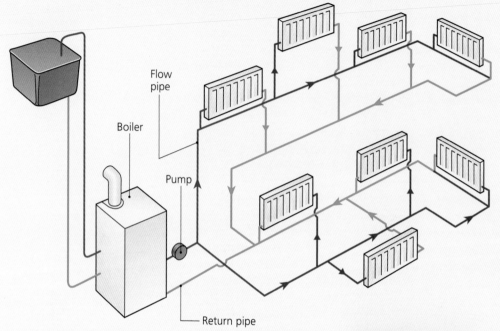

Flow pipe

Boiler

Pump

Return pipe

Water flows most readily round the radiators nearest to the pump, so the water flow through the circuit is balanced out by adjusting the lockshield valve on each radiator – this is the valve with a cover that doesn't turn. The valve at the other end turns by hand to switch the radiator on and off or may have a thermostatic valve fitted. The lockshield valves are set so as to make it harder for the water to travel through the radiators nearest the boiler. If the circuit isn't properly balanced, some radiators will get too hot and others will be cool.

1 Two or three hours before you intend to start work on the radiators, turn off the central heating system to allow the radiators to cool down.

2 Open all lockshield valves and handwheel or thermostatic valves fully. To open a lockshield valve, pull off the cover and grip the spindle with a pair of pliers to turn it.

3 Turn on the central heating system. Work out the order in which the radiators heat up, and label them accordingly. Start with the first radiator, and clip a radiator thermometer onto the flow pipe bringing water in and another onto the return pipe.

4 Turn down the lockshield valve until it's closed, then open it slightly. Adjust the flow until the temperature of the flow pipe is roughly 11°C higher than that of the return pipe.

5 Repeat for all radiators in the circuit, working in the order as labelled. The lockshield valve on the last radiator will probably need to be fully open.

Use pliers to turn a lockshield valve

Clip a thermometer to each pipe

Thermostats and heating controls

A modern thermostat and programmer are key to an efficient and effective heating and hot-water system. Older mechanical thermostats may need recalibrating to keep them accurate, but modern, digital models are more accurate and less likely to fail. Spending money to upgrade your system can pay dividends in energy savings.

Care and maintenance

● **Test your thermostat in autumn** Before you start using your heating for winter, perform this easy test. Tape a household thermometer (one that you know is accurate) to the wall next to the thermostat. Give the thermometer about 15 minutes to settle on its temperature reading then compare that reading to the thermostat's. If the difference between the two is more than 5°C, recalibrate your thermostat (see page 235).

● A simple check that your thermostat is working is to hold a switched-on table lamp underneath it for a few seconds. The thermostat should detect the rise in temperature and you'll hear a click as it switches off.

SAVE £55

Average annual saving on your heating bill by turning the main heating thermostat down by 1°C.

● **Go digital for clever control**
The latest digital programmers allow up to three control periods a day, and some have seven day settings, holiday modes and instant boost options for immediate heating. Most allow you to control your central heating and hot water separately.

Getting the temperature right

The average household room temperature is 20°C, though you may prefer it to be warmer or cooler. Most people like their bedrooms to be a little cooler and the bathroom warmer than the rest of the house – you can use the table below as a guide.

Room	Temperature
Living room	21°C
Dining room	21°C
Kitchen	16°C
Bedroom	16°C
Bathroom	23°C
Hall and stairs	18°C

● If you've just one thermostat controlling the heating for the whole house, it will turn the heat on or off depending on the temperature of the room in which it's situated. This isn't always the same as the temperature in the rest of the house and doesn't allow for any variation between rooms.

● For the most flexible temperature control and the most efficient use of energy, fit thermostatic radiator valves (TRVs) to all the radiators in your home. These are now compulsory on new systems and allow you to specify the temperature on a scale of 0-5 for each individual room, so that when the heating is switched on, only the radiators in rooms that actually require heating will warm up.

• With a digital, programmable thermostat you can have sophisticated control, allowing you to set different target temperatures depending on the time of day, raising the temperature in time for getting up in the morning and dropping it during the day when people are out at work or dressed and active in the house, for example. This minimises unnecessary use of the boiler and should save money on your gas bill.

• **Keep the thermostat away from draughts and sun** If the thermostat is in direct sunlight, in a room with a separate fire or close to a lamp, it may get warm enough to switch the heating off before the rest of the house is warm. Likewise, if it's in a draught, or near a poorly sealed external door or a window that you usually leave ajar, it may turn the heating on when it isn't needed in the majority of the rooms in the house.

• **Take care with TRVs** Thermostatic radiator valves allow you to control the temperature room by room (see page 233), but don't fit one on a radiator in the same room as the main thermostat. The TRV may turn off the radiator, allowing the room to cool slightly, and the main thermostat will activate the boiler to supply more heat when it isn't needed. If all the TRVs in the house are switched off, there will be nowhere for the hot water to go and the boiler can overheat.

• Always leave at least one radiator without a TRV to allow hot water to circulate through the system.

• **Don't heat more than you need** The hot water for the taps doesn't need to be as hot as the water for the radiators, so save energy by making sure that there's a thermostat fitted to your hot-water cylinder. This operates a valve to restrict the flow of water through the heating coil within the cylinder and will prevent water from being heated unnecessarily.

• The thermostat should be fitted around a third of the way up the side of the tank and must be in contact with the copper of the tank itself. If your tank has a loose lagging jacket, don't fit it over the top of the thermostat, but allow it to poke through a gap in the join.

Easy fixes

• **Adjusting the anticipator** A thermostat's heat anticipator tells it to switch off the boiler a little early, allowing residual heat to keep room temperature at the desired level. If your heating system cycles on and off too often or not often enough, the anticipator may need adjusting.

• Take the cover off the thermostat and nudge the anticipator pointer toward a higher setting on its scale if the system is cycling too often – adjust the other way if it isn't cycling often enough.

• **Free up a stuck pin** A thermostatic radiator valve can jam in the closed position, particularly if it isn't turned and closed regularly. Try tapping the body of the valve lightly – not the plastic valve head – with

take care!

If you remove a radiator to decorate, don't leave a TRV turned off, but keep it in place. Normal radiator valves can be turned off and should not leak, but in very cold weather a TRV may open itself and allow water to flow out of the disconnected valve. Always remove the valve and fit a decorating screw-cap while you are doing the work.

Use pliers to move a stuck valve pin

How to replace a central heating programmer

All new programmers have an industry standard backplate, making it easy to swap one for another with more settings such as 'weekend' and 'one hour boost'. If you have an old-style programmer, you'll need to rewire the backplate to suit the new programmer. Full instructions will be supplied with the new model.

1 Turn off the power supply to the programmer at the main consumer unit before you start work.

2 An old-style mechanical programmer with limited time settings and options can be removed from the backplate by turning off the power supply to the heating system and undoing the retaining screws.

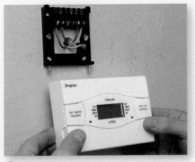

3 If your backplate looks like the example shown above, you can fit a new programmer directly to it. You may need to change the settings on the switch at the back to suit your heating system.

An older-style, gravity-fed hot-water system, which only allows the heating to operate if the hot water is switched on, is known as a ten-position programme. If you can turn the heating on without the hot water then you can leave the slide switch set to 16 positions.

4 The new programmer must be tightened onto the backplate so the pushfit terminals are secure. You can then switch on the power and set the on-off times.

5 If the new faceplate doesn't fit the old backplate, study the wiring carefully and label each wire clearly. Sketch the old connections, then disconnect the cable cores from their terminals.

6 Remove the old backplate and attach the new one, using the manufacturer's instructions and your sketch of the old programmer to wire it up correctly.

7 Push the new faceplate into position and restore the power to the programmer.

---

a mallet to jolt the pin out of positon. If this fails, remove the plastic head (it should pull straight off), grip the end of the pin with a pair of pliers and gently but firmly pull it upwards.

● If you manage to free the pin, move it up and down a few times to help to prevent it from sticking again straight away. Take care not to wiggle or bend it from side to side as you could break the pin.

● **Recalibrating the thermostat** Most manual thermostats are set to operate within a temperature range between 10°C and 30°C, but you can change this if you wish to. Pull off the control knob if you can, or you may need to remove the cover and unscrew the baseplate.

● The model shown on the right has two wire pointers in numbered notches on the back of the knob, one representing the 'on' temperature and the other 'off'. Simply reposition the wires to change the working temperature range of the thermostat.

● Not all thermostats are this easy to change – check the manufacturer's instructions for your model before you start.

You can reset a manual thermostat

Boilers

Gas burners efficiently burn a combination of gas (either natural or propane) and air to heat either air or water in your furnace or boiler. They are relatively straightforward devices. When trouble arises, it's generally just ignition problems and clogged burners. In addition to scheduling an annual professional inspection, you can enhance your burner's efficiency by staying on top of a few simple maintenance tasks.

SAVE £2,200

Cost to buy and install a new condensing boiler to replace one that has failed due to poor maintenance.

Care and maintenance

● **Give your boiler an annual health check** All boilers should be serviced annually by an expert heating engineer who's registered with Gas Safe or OFTEC (see page 238).
● A faulty boiler can emit lethal carbon monoxide fumes, but you'll also save yourself a potential four figure bill for buying and installing a replacement boiler if small faults, such as a worn seal or internal leak, aren't spotted and fixed at an early stage.

● **Checking the colour of your gas flame** To operate efficiently, a gas burner requires the correct gas-to-air balance. You can tell if the balance is correct by looking at the colour of the burner's flame:
● If the flame has a yellow tip and a 'lazy' flicker, your gas burner isn't getting enough air.
● If your burner is getting too much air, the flame will be blue with a sharp outline and a hard-edged inner flame.

How to relight the pilot

1 Turn off the gas knob and main electric switch to the boiler and turn the thermostat right down.

2 Wait for 5 minutes, then turn the gas knob to 'Pilot'. In older boilers, you may need to close both the main and pilot gas-supply valves. Wait 5 minutes, then open the pilot gas valve only.

3 While pressing the reset button or gas knob (depending on your model), light the pilot and wait for 1 minute before releasing the button or knob.

4 If the pilot goes out, wait 5 minutes and repeat step 3, this time depressing the reset button for a little longer than a minute. If the pilot still won't light, the thermocouple may be defective. Call a Gas Safe-registered heating engineer to service or replace it.

5 If you've a combination boiler and the pilot light won't stay lit, check the water-pressure gauge on the boiler display panel. If it reads below 1 bar, try repressurising the system by opening the valve at the end of the filler loop (the braided hose connecting the boiler to the mains). Turn off the water once the pressure has reached between 1 and 1.5 bar, then try lighting the pilot light again.

6 Once the pilot ignites and stays lit, restore the main gas supply and electricity to the unit and raise the thermostat to its original setting.

- If your burner has just the right gas-to-air balance, the flame should be mostly blue and soft-edged, with a blue-green inner flame.
- If you're concerned that your flame looks the wrong colour, call a service engineer and ask him to check the boiler.

● **Check the flame of an oil burner** The look of the flame in an oil-fired boiler will let you know if it's doing its job efficiently. If your boiler (or furnace) has an observation window, take a peek inside every so often. You should see a bright yellow flame with no trace of smoke. If the flame is dark orange or sooty, or if you spot smoke spewing from the chimney outside, it's time to call a service professional.

● **Keep the boiler house tidy** Between annual professional services, it's your job to keep the area around the boiler free from dust and grime, which can cause the boiler to fail. Never sweep dirt under the boiler unit: use your vacuum cleaner's hose attachments to clean around the edges of a boiler. Take a look outside, too, and make sure that plants aren't obstructing the flow of air from the flue.

● **Saving your life with a stick of incense** A gas boiler needs air circulation to vent fumes efficiently – a house that's too airtight prevents a boiler from getting the amount it requires. This leads to back draughting,

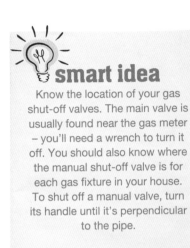

smart idea

Know the location of your gas shut-off valves. The main valve is usually found near the gas meter – you'll need a wrench to turn it off. You should also know where the manual shut-off valve is for each gas fixture in your house. To shut off a manual valve, turn its handle until it's perpendicular to the pipe.

How to choose a new boiler

The boiler you choose depends on the size of your house and household, whether you need it to supply heat and hot water, how many bathrooms you have to supply and whether or not you have room for a hot-water cylinder and a feed-and-expansion cistern. Floor-standing and wall-mounted models are available in a variety of sizes for all types of fuel: oil, gas, LPG (liquid petroleum gas), solid fuel and even electricity.

● **ALL NEW BOILERS** now have to be condensing models, apart from a few very rare exceptions where it isn't possible. Condensing boilers make more efficient use of fuel than conventional old-style boilers, as they extract heat from the flue gases as well as the heating system itself. A new condensing boiler can use as much as 30 per cent less fuel than your old boiler and will also reduce carbon emissions.

● **A CONDENSING BOILER** is easy to recognise by the plume of steam that escapes from its flue when it's in operation. For maximum efficiency, condensing boilers should be sited on an external wall to accommodate the balanced flue, which allows both combustion gases to escape and fresh air to enter. However, most

condensing boilers work with a fan-assisted flue, which makes it possible to mount the boiler on any wall and vent it through a flue to an outside wall or the roof.

● **COMBINATION BOILERS** heat water for the central heating in a closed circuit, but also heat water for the taps on demand from the mains water supply. When a hot tap is turned on, the water flows through the boiler, which switches itself on to heat the water. A combination boiler is a clever, space-saving option where there isn't room for a hot-water cylinder or feed-and-expansion cistern (page 229). They are expensive, but you only pay to heat the water that you actually use, so they are an energy-efficient choice. Most combination boilers can be used with gas or LPG, and some oil-fired models are available.

● **BUILDING REGULATIONS** now cover the installation of a new or replacement boiler. Any new boiler must meet minimum efficiency levels of 78 per cent for gas boilers, 80 per cent for LPG and 85 per cent for oil. The boiler must be installed by an accredited CORGI (for gas) or OFTEC (for oil) engineer and modern programmers and thermostats must be fitted at the same time.

Working safely with gas appliances

The Gas Safety (Installation and Use) Regulations make it illegal for anyone to carry out work relating to gas supply and fittings who's not 'competent'. In practice, this means leaving all work on your gas system, including the boiler, to an accredited professional. Always choose a qualified gas fitter who's registered with Gas Safe (see also page 34).

If your boiler is oil-fired, use a fitter who's registered with OFTEC (The Oil Firing Technical Association) or other Competent Person Scheme provider.

a dangerous condition in which flue gases are sucked down the furnace or chimney, allowing carbon monoxide to linger indoors. Carbon monoxide poisoning can be fatal. Here's an easy test you can do to make sure your home is getting enough fresh air.

● Close all windows and doors and your fireplace damper and turn on all household extractor fans (such as in your kitchen over the cooker hob and in all the bathrooms and toilets).

● Switch on the boiler to start heating water.

● Wait for 10 minutes to allow drafts to stabilise, then hold an incense stick below the air intake vents on the boiler's outer casing. If the resulting smoke is pulled up into the boiler, you've got enough fresh air for safe operation; if the smoke blows away it could be a sign of a back draught. Call a heating engineer to investigate further as soon as possible.

● **Adjusting the pilot flame** Older boilers have a permanently lit pilot light, which can deteriorate until the flame is so small that it keeps going out with just the slightest breeze.

● To adjust the pilot light, look for a pilot adjustment screw on the unit's combination control. Remove the screw cap, if there is one, and turn the screw anticlockwise to raise the flame or clockwise to lower it.

● Take care to follow the advice and instructions in your boiler's operating manual. If you're at all unsure, always stop work and call in a professional heating engineer, explaining what you've done so far.

7 golden rules of oil tank maintenance

Just like an oil-fired boiler, the steel or plastic oil tank that supplies it requires regular inspections and maintenance. If it's above ground, it can be at risk because of exposure to the elements. Underground tanks that fail can cause serious environmental damage that's expensive and time-consuming to remedy.

1 Have your tank professionally inspected every year before the start of the heating season, and between inspections keep an eye out for signs of trouble such as rust (on steel tanks), dents and leaks.

2 Make sure that the legs and foundations of an above-ground tank are stable and its surface is free of rust, oily stains that look like they're dripping down the sides of the tank (called 'weepage' by heating engineers) or significant dents. Rust and oily stains along the bottom of the tank are clear signs that it needs to be replaced.

3 Look for evidence of spillage near the tank's fill and vent pipes. Call your service engineer if you find any.

4 Whether the tank is indoors or out, keep the area around it free of debris so you can check underneath it for leaks. Make sure the tank and its fuel lines are

protected against possible damage by bicycles, heavy objects and debris falling from trees or the roof in high winds.

5 Keep the tank vent clear of snow, fallen leaves, birds' nests and other debris.

6 Underground tanks can corrode and leak without leaving telltale signs on the surface. If you've an underground oil tank, be alert to any sudden and unexplained increases in fuel usage, which can signal that the tank is leaking.

7 If you suspect a leak anywhere in the system, contact your service engineer or local environmental authority without delay.

Electric heaters

For quick and efficient heat, electric fan or radiant heaters are a useful and versatile addition to central heating – particularly in rooms without radiators, such as a conservatory. They require little more maintenance than keeping them free of dust, but always follow any safety guidelines for their use.

How to **use an electric heater safely**

Portable heaters are notorious fire hazards. Always plug heaters directly into a wall outlet never an extension cord, as most don't have sufficient capacity. Place your heater on a flat, dry, hard surface, positioning it at least 1m from combustible liquids and flammable items such as curtains and other soft furnishings. Make sure it's out of the path of children and pets and don't leave children nearby when the heat is on. Always let a portable heater cool completely before you move it to another location, whether it's a few inches or a few rooms away.

SAVE £20

Cost to replace a heater with a damaged or jammed blade.

Care and maintenance

● **Clean up before cold weather** Accumulated dust and debris can hinder an electrical unit's heating speed and output, so give electric heaters an annual spring clean before the weather gets chilly. With the heater off and cool, carefully vacuum the heating element, housing and any internal parts you can reach using a brush attachment. When they're not being used, store portable heaters in their original boxes or in bin liners that you've tied shut to prevent dust collecting.

KEEP DUST AT BAY FOR EFFICIENT HEATING.

smart idea

Kick-space heaters are a great way to add warmth to your kitchen. Set inconspicuously under your units, these heaters keep your feet toasty as they spread warmth at floor level. Some models are linked into the central heating, using hot-water pipes to heat the air; others have an electric heating element. But both types have an electric fan controlled by a thermostat to distribute the warm air into the room.

Easy fix

● **Fixing fan problems** If the fan in a fan heater stops spinning, turn off the heater, unplug it, allow it to cool and then investigate. If the blades seem to be jammed, remove the heater cover for access and clear away any debris. Give the fan a spin by hand to see if bent components are the problem, and try straightening them out, if possible, with pliers. If the fan seems to be loose, tighten the setscrew at the fan's hub. If none of this does the trick, the fan motor may be defective.

Refrigerators

It's the small things that cause the most damage to these appliances. Dust on your refrigerator's coils can lessen its efficiency and shorten its life, and algae and food particles can clog the drain. The good news is that with just a little care and attention your fridge should stay cool for many years.

SAVE £400

Approximate cost of a new, efficient, family-sized fridge-freezer to replace one that has failed due to poor care and maintenance.

Care and maintenance

● **Give your fridge room to breathe** Your fridge functions most efficiently when you give it a little space. Allow at least a 1cm gap on the left and right and 2cm behind it, and don't stack anything on top of the unit. If your fridge is in direct sunlight, consider moving it to a cooler spot or install a window blind to screen out the worst of the sun. If the fridge itself is hot, it will need to work harder to keep the food inside cool, so avoid positioning your fridge next to the cooker or a radiator if you can.

● **Clean from the top down** Every four to six months, clean the inside and outside of both fridge and freezer. Clean one shelf at a time, from top to bottom so that if you dribble crumbs, sauce, or even your detergent, you're not dirtying shelves you've already cleaned.
● Wipe the interior with a solution of mild detergent or baking soda.
● If the shelves are removable, clean them in the sink with warm water and mild detergent, but let glass shelves come up to room temperature before plunging them into hot water so that they don't crack. Dry them thoroughly before you put them back.
● Make sure that the drain hole at the base of the fridge is clear and finish by wiping the rubber door seals with the mild detergent solution, taking care to clear all dirt from within the grooves.

smart idea

A well-stocked freezer isn't just good news for mealtimes – it also keeps your freezer running at maximum efficiency as there's less circulating air that has to be cooled. Fill empty spaces in the freezer with jugs or food storage boxes of water. They will not only improve your freezer's performance but also help to keep the contents cold for longer in a power cut.

● **Defrost freezers to keep them cool** Unless your freezer is a frost-free model, with an automatic defrost system, defrost it every six months. A build-up of frost will reduce the freezer's efficiency and can cause the cooling system to fail.
● Wrap the frozen food in newspaper or blankets and put it somewhere cool while you work – a cold or, better still, snowy day is perfect for this job, as you can put the food outside to stay frozen.
● Turn the thermostat to 'Off' or 'Defrost', unplug the freezer and carefully scrape away ice with a plastic tool. Once the frost has all been removed, wipe the inside of the freezer with a baking soda solution, wash any removable doors or drawers and allow everything to dry before resetting the thermostat, switching the freezer back on and refilling it.

● **Vacuum dust from the coils** Your refrigerator's coils are notorious dust catchers, but they're simple to clean. Pull out the fridge to reach the back, unplug it for safety and use the hose and nozzle or soft brush attachment of your vacuum cleaner to clean dust and dirt from the grid of wire-like coolant pipes and around the motor.

● Clean the coils every three months, or more often if you have pets. Dirt and dust can inhibit the dissipation of heat, causing the unit to run poorly, cycle on and off too often, or not run at all.

● **Put your fridge on the level** A refrigerator is most efficient when it's level. Look for the unit's feet or castors (right) and raise or lower them with an adjustable wrench or by turning their leveling screws with a screwdriver. On some refrigerators, you may have to remove the toe plate to gain access. Use a spirit level to make sure the fridge is balanced.

A level fridge is an efficient fridge

● **Give door seals the paper test** If the door doesn't seal tightly, your food will spoil more quickly and your energy bill will rocket. Twice a year, put a sheet of paper between the door and the refrigerator unit and close the door. Try to pull the paper out – try this in several places around the door. If there's no resistance, the seal isn't working. If the seal appears stiff or cracked, replace it; if it looks good, lightly coat the flat surface with petroleum jelly to keep it from sticking.

Easy fixes

● **Fixing a saggy door** If your door seal is in good condition but still not sealing properly, the door may be warped or sagging. To fix it, take everything off the door shelves, loosen the screws behind the door seal or on the plate on top of the door, then grasp the door and flex it until it closes flush with the refrigerator. This is easier to do with a helper. Tighten the screws to hold the door in place.

When it's time **for a new model**

Refrigerators are switched on and running 24 hours a day, all year round. They account for around 20 per cent of the electricity used in an average home, so it pays to make sure that they run as efficiently as possible. When you need to replace your refrigerator, choose one with the highest energy rating you can (preferably A+ or A++) and look for the Energy Saving Trust logo on the appliance. The most efficient new models can save around two-thirds of the power used by a ten-year-old fridge, amounting to around £36 saved each year.

Cookers and hoods

Your cooker is the heart of your kitchen and, with that in mind, it's important to keep it in good working order. Regular cleaning is the key, but there are other simple checks you can do to make sure that your oven, grill, hob and cooker hood are always working as efficiently as possible.

SAVE £100

Cost saving by replacing a faulty cooker element yourself.

Care and maintenance

● **Anchor your oven** A freestanding oven should be fitted with an anti-tip bracket to keep it from toppling if weight is put on the door. Tipping ovens can start fires and cause burns. The anti-tip bracket is usually a U-shaped piece of metal screwed to the floor beneath the oven and hooked to one of the oven's rear feet, or a chain running from the back of the oven to a bracket on the wall. If your oven doesn't have one, the manufacturer might supply it for free.

● **Protect glass and ceramic hobs** Smooth cooking hobs are sleek and attractive but they're also easily damaged. To get the longest life out of them, avoid abrasive cleaners, never use the hob area for chopping and use only smooth-bottomed pans that won't scratch the surface.
● Never store heavy items like pans or canned food in cabinets above the hob. If they fall or you drop them while taking them out or putting them away, they will damage the cooktop and cause a very costly repair.

● **Look under the hood** Most of us only take notice (and action) when grease starts building up on the top of the cooker hood. But once a month you should clean the grease filter – many modern filters can be cleaned in the upper rack of a dishwasher, or fabric filters may be soaked in a

CLEAN UP COOKING SPILLS PROMPTLY.

degreasing agent then soapy water. Some recirculating cooker hoods have filters that cannot be cleaned; check your user manual if you're unsure.
● If your hood's fan is making more noise than usual, it could be a sign that the filter is clogged. While you have the filter off, wipe inside – and wipe the fan blades, if you can get to them, with all-purpose cleaner.
● Every six months, replace the filter. With a recirculating air cooker hood, you should replace both the grease filter and the activated charcoal filter that cleans the air.

● **Make it shine** Clean stoves transfer heat better and are more energy efficient than dirty ones. Here's how to keep yours in tip-top shape:
● Wipe up spilled food promptly – it's easier when spills are fresh.
● Avoid using abrasive cleansers and cleaning pads. Instead, spray a 50/50 mix of washing-up liquid and water and let it soak into burned-on food for a few minutes. Wipe with a clean cloth.
● If food cakes on one of your burners, clean off as much as you can, then turn the heat to high. The spillage should burn off.
● If you can dismantle gas burners, use a toothpick to clean the burner holes and wash the individual components. Dry them before reassembling, then turn the burners on for a few seconds to evaporate any excess water.

smart idea
Whenever a hob element or gas burner is removed for cleaning or repair, take the opportunity to clean the drip pan underneath it. Shiny clean surfaces reflect heat, making the cooker more energy efficient.

USE AN OVEN THERMOMETER ONCE A YEAR TO TEST YOUR OVEN'S THERMOSTAT.

● **Check the temperature** Once a year, use an oven thermometer to test the accuracy of an electric oven's thermostat. Set the temperature of the oven and allow it to warm up fully, then check the reading on the thermometer. If the temperature isn't accurate, you may need to recalibrate the oven (see page 244).

Easy fixes

● **Keep your cooker sides clean** Spills, stains and crumbs collect on the sides of a freestanding oven, but this is a mess (and potential fire hazard) that's easily avoided. Fit inexpensive T-shaped plastic gaskets, available in most DIY or hardware stores, slipping them between your cooker and the adjacent worktops. When the gaskets get soiled, simply remove them, wash them and reinstall them.

● **Keeping the flame burning properly** If the flame tips on your gas hob burners are orange rather than blue, it indicates that there is probably a problem with the burner.
● Wait until the hob is cool, then remove the burner, soak it in soapy water and give it a good scrub. Then clean the individual gas jets with a toothpick or darning needle. Use a fine wire to clean the tiny holes where the pipe from the pilot light connects to the burner.
● Orange flames aren't always bad news. They can be common in coastal areas where the colour of the flame might be affected by the salty air.

take care!

Never use commercial oven cleaners in a self-cleaning oven, as this can damage the appliance's interior surface. If you have a self-cleaning oven, set it to its cleaning cycle and give the oven racks a mild ammonia bath while you wait. Always let the self-cleaning cycle complete before opening the oven door.

● **Recalibrating your oven** If your oven's thermostat doesn't correspond with the temperature settings on its dial (see page 243), you can adjust the settings. Depending on the model, this can be an easy fix. On ovens with knobs, recalibrating may be a simple matter of turning screws on the back of the oven temperature knob. Ovens with digital (touch-pad) controls can sometimes be calibrated using a special keypad sequence. Consult your owner's manual for specific advice. An oven that cannot be recalibrated may have a faulty thermostat, which can be replaced by a qualified repair technician.

● **Replacing hob elements** If you have an electric hob, you heat your food on elements: coils of wire covered with nonconductive material. Modern hobs often have encased elements so that the elements themselves are protected from spills and damage, but they can still fail from time to time and exposed elements can reach the point where they no longer come clean. The good news is that most elements are easy and inexpensive to replace.
● Unplug the cooker then check how the element is connected – it may flip up, plug in or be soldered in place. If it's soldered, get it replaced by a professional. Other fittings, though, are easy to replace yourself. Plug-in elements can just be tugged out. With flip-up models, you'll need to remove a screw or two from an insulating block before you detach it.
● Take the element and the cooker's model number to an electrical supplier to source an exact replacement.

● **Adjusting warped doors** Staining or soot around the oven door can indicate that it's warped. To adjust the fault simply open the door and, on the inside panel near the corners, loosen the screws that hold the inner and outer panels together. Push down on the door while twisting it from side to side (be extra careful on doors with large glass panels), then carefully retighten the screws. Close the door and look for gaps – it may take a couple of tries to get it right. Another possible cause of warped doors is bent hinges, and these would have to be replaced by a professional.

● **Checking electric oven elements** If your electric oven isn't cooking properly, its element may be burning out. Disconnect the power to your oven by tripping the switch at the consumer unit, let it cool, then remove the screws that hold the element in place. You may need to remove the door to gain access – check your owner's manual for specific instructions. Pull out the element and test it with an electrical continuity tester. If the element is in working order, the tester's bulb will light; if it's faulty, replace it with a new one.

● **Replace a poor seal** Open your oven door and inspect the slender gasket, or oven seal, clipped to the front of the oven. Replace a damaged, burned or soiled oven seal with an identical part from a shop that sells appliance parts. The seal should just peel off, and you can then push the replacement into place. Don't attempt to replace seals on self-cleaning ovens; leave that job to a professional repair technician.

Peel away a perished seal

Waste disposal units

Below-the-sink waste disposals are powerful, but they're not invincible. You'll keep yours running smoothly for years to come if you follow simple guidelines, such as avoiding greasy foods and keeping the blades clean and free of obstruction.

Care and maintenance

● **A monthly freshen-up** Once a month, turn on your waste disposal unit and tip in a handful of ice cubes: this is a noisy but effective way of cleaning the blades. Next, run some cold water down the disposal chute, followed by a few lemon peels to get rid of bad odours.

● **Run cold, not hot, water** Hot water softens grease and that's a bad thing for your waste disposal unit. Fatty foods need to harden if they are to grind up, so flush waste through your machine with cold water. Better still, try to avoid sending grease down the drain.

● **Foods to avoid** The long fibres in celery and corn husks can get tangled in the disposal unit's blades. Shellfish shells are too hard and can damage the blades, as will any bones larger than small fish bones. Never throw coffee grounds down the disposal, either – they can clump together and clog the unit. Put them on the compost heap instead.

SAVE £75

How much it would cost for a service technician to dismantle and clean a waste disposal unit clogged with grease, fibres or non-food items.

Easy fix

● **Stop leaks with two screws** Your disposal unit is most likely to leak at either the drain pipe or the sink. Make sure that these fixing screws are always tightened and you can help to keep discarded food in your pipes, not inside your kitchen cabinets.

smart idea

To clean a smelly waste disposal unit, pour 100ml of bicarbonate of soda or washing soda crystals down the drain, let it sit for 30 minutes, then flush with cold water while the unit is on. Never use caustic soda or chemical drain-cleaner as the dangerous chemicals may splash out when the unit is switched on.

USE LEMON PEEL TO BANISH BAD ODOURS.

Dishwashers

The cleaner it washes your plates, the grimier your dishwasher gets. Left unchecked, dirt and dents can mean big repair bills, but giving this kitchen workhorse a once-over every now and again can keep your dishwasher problem-free for years to come. Check the moving parts that can weaken with age – like the doors, spray arms and hoses – and look out for early signs of rust and damage.

SAVE £500

How much you would pay to replace a modern, energy and water-efficient dishwasher.

Care and maintenance

● **Give the dishwasher a wash** Every six months, or sooner if the machine starts to look and smell grimy, give your dishwasher a thorough clean of its own. Either use a proprietary dishwasher cleaning product or pour a cup of white vinegar into the machine and set it to run a wash cycle (make sure that the machine is empty). Then clean the door edges and seals with a mild, non-abrasive detergent, such as washing-up liquid, checking that they are in good condition at the same time.

● **Clear blocked spray holes** Food and mineral deposits may clog the holes in your dishwasher's rotating spray arm, so when you clean the machine (see above) clear these too. Remove the dish racks, then unscrew the screws that hold the spray tower or hubcap arm in place. Lift off the arm (left), clean out the holes with a toothpick and scrub away hard-water mineral deposits with white vinegar and a nail or scrubbing brush.

● **Keep the filter clean** Every dishwasher has a filter or strainer in the base to catch food scraps before they are flushed into the drain and this will soon become clogged if you don't clean it regularly. How often you need to do this depends on how much you use your machine and how well you rinse cutlery and crockery before loading it. Start by doing this task weekly and increase the time interval if you find yours doesn't need cleaning that often.

● Remove the lower dish rack to access the base of the machine and lift out the filter. Some machines have retaining screws holding the filter in place and some have two-part filters that both need to be cleaned. Check your owner's manual if you're unsure.

● Wash the filter under running water, clean it with a washing-up liquid solution and rinse thoroughly again before refitting.

● To keep your filter clean for longer, get into the habit of scraping and rinsing plates and pans before putting them in the dishwasher.

5 common dishwasher problems

1 DISHES AREN'T GETTING CLEAN There are three possible causes, but they are all easy to fix. The simplest is careless loading of the machine. If dishes overlap or cutlery protrudes through the dish rack and stops the spray arm turning then the water and detergent cannot do their work. You may also be using insufficient detergent, or the sump filter may be blocked leaving dirty water in the machine during the rinse cycle.

2 CLEAN DISHES ARE STREAKED WITH WHITE These white streaks are mineral deposits from hard water and are an indication that either the salt levels in the machine are too low or that the softener unit is faulty. A simple test kit will allow you to gauge the hardness of your water and set the salt level on your machine accordingly. If topping up the salt doesn't eliminate the problem, call a qualified repairer to check the softener unit.

3 GLASSES ARE LEFT WITH RING MARKS This means you're using insufficient rinse aid. Check the rinse-aid level and the setting that determines how much the machine uses, and top up or adjust.

4 GLASSES ARE STICKY Too much rinse aid being used. Check the levels and setting, as above.

5 WATER IS STILL IN THE BOTTOM OF THE MACHINE A clogged filter, blocked drain hose or faulty drain pump could be the cause of water failing to drain away at the end of the wash cycle (see 'Keep the filter clean' on page 246).

● **Keep your washer well-stocked** For your dishwasher to work efficiently and clean well, you must keep the levels of rinse aid and salt topped up. If your dishwasher doesn't have a warning light to alert you when the levels are getting low, get into the habit of checking every week and refilling as necessary.

● Both too much or too little detergent can leave you with dishes that still don't look clean enough to put away. If you use powder detergent, experiment with quantities to find the right amount for you – areas with hard water will need more detergent than soft-water regions.

● **Replace hoses before they break** If your dishwasher has a standard reinforced rubber inlet hose, replace it every two years. These are prone to cracking and leaking, and a few pounds for a new hose could save you a big clean-up after a flood. Alternatively, you could upgrade to a braided stainless steel hose, which will last significantly longer.

● When you replace a hose, connect it with a worm-screw clamp, or jubilee clip, rather than the spring clamp often supplied with the dishwasher and replacement hose. These make a much more secure connection.

Easy fixes

● **When water won't drain away** If your dishwasher isn't emptying fully and there's still water in the base of the machine (the sump) at the end of the wash cycle, the strainer or filter may be blocked. Clean and replace them (see 'Keep the filter clean' on page 246).

● If this doesn't solve the problem, there may be a blockage in the drain hose. Pull out the machine, disconnect the hose and check that it's clear.

● If the water is still not draining away, it could be that the drain pump motor has a fault. This is a repair for a professional, but check the easy DIY fixes first to avoid an unnecessary call-out fee.

KEEP RINSE AID AND SALT TOPPED UP FOR CRYSTAL-CLEAR GLASSES.

Washing machines

When a washing machine fails, the biggest problem is often the flood that follows. This can be a costly disaster, potentially ruining flooring, kitchen units and plasterboard walls. Fortunately, most water-related faults are easy to prevent with routine care and sensible use.

SAVE £50

Cost saving from replacing a worn door seal yourself.

Care and maintenance

● **Don't overload the machine** Stuffing your washer with excessive loads of laundry is guaranteed to tax the machine's inner workings and leave you with clothes that haven't been cleaned. Follow the capacity parameters listed in the instruction manual and you'll get better results and a longer-lasting machine.

● If your household generates a lot of laundry, consider choosing a large-capacity model when you next buy a new washing machine. They are no larger on the outside than a standard model, but can accommodate up to 11kg loads – twice the capacity of many standard machines.

● **Balance is critical** In all washing machines – but in top-loading models in particular – off-kilter loads of laundry can put a great strain on the bearings and mechanism that rotate the tub. Save yourself the cost of replacing these parts by doing your best to load the machine evenly, putting large items in loosely and not bundled into a ball.

● When you have heavy or bulky items in the wash, listen out for the beginning of the spin cycle and interrupt the wash, if your machine allows it. Check that the load is spread evenly around the drum and redistribute the wet clothes, if need be.

● **More detergent doesn't mean cleaner clothes** Use only as much detergent as the package says – using too much won't get your clothes any cleaner and will cause an excess of suds that can even damage the machine. In soft-water areas – or if you have a water softener fitted in your home – you'll need less detergent than if your machine is fed with a hard water supply. Experiment with different quantities and use the minimum you can without compromising on cleanliness.

● **Replace your washer's hoses** The standard rubber hot and cold water hoses connected to your washing machine can harden, crack and burst over time, so it's worth replacing them as a precaution every two years. Consider a stainless-steel-reinforced hose, which lasts much longer and can withstand higher water pressure.

● Most hoses are easy to replace – just loosen the inlet connectors (left) to remove the old ones. Always make sure that hoses are as straight as possible, not bent, kinked or squashed as you push the machine back into place. When you change hoses, mark the date of replacement on the hose.

Tighten hose connectors by hand

Clean fluff and debris from filters

● Clean the lint filter Coins, buttons, fluff and fibres all get caught by the lint filter as the water drains out of the drum. Every six months, open the access hatch on the front of the machine, undo the filter cap and carefully pull out the filter (left). Remove the accumulated fluff and other debris and replace the filter. A blocked filter will prevent the machine from draining fully and may even cause a leak.

● Catchpots intercept debris Some washing machines don't have a lint filter but a catchpot instead, which traps items left in pockets or other objects from the wash before they are drawn into the pump with the dirty water. Every six months – or if you need to retrieve something lost in the wash – empty the catchpot. If you don't do this, items can still be drawn into the pump where they can cause expensive damage, while a blocked catchpot can stop water draining away and cause a leak.

● To empty the catchpot, pull out the machine, disconnect the power and the inlet hoses. Ask someone to help you and lay the machine on its front, resting it on a piece of wood or other support to stop the control panel being damaged by contact with the floor. (This support will also make it easier to get a hand-hold when you want to right the machine again.)

Empty the catchpot twice a year

● Pull off the clip that secures the sump hose to the catchpot – use your owner's manual to guide you if necessary. Remove the catchpot, empty it into a bucket or bowl (left), rinse and refit.

● Don't forget to clean your machine A monthly cleaning routine will help to keep your washing machine in good working order and prevent clothes getting dirty again as you empty a load of washing.

● If you use powder detergent, undissolved powder can build up in the detergent tray and beneath it. Pull out the tray completely and clean it thoroughly in the sink. Look inside the recess in the machine, too, and clean any dirt or detergent from there. Left-over detergent can be a sign that you're using too much or that your water pressure is low.

● If the door and its seal gets dirty, it can cause the seal to fail and water to leak out. Limescale often builds up on door glass and mildew can develop on rubber seals. Use an abrasive pad dipped in clear, warm water to scrub door glass clean and a sponge with a mild detergent to wipe the door seal. Leave the door ajar after a wash to allow the seals to dry to help to prevent mould and mildew appearing.

Easy fixes

● Clean the inlet screens Between the water inlet hoses and the washer you'll find small filters that clog easily, particularly if your water is hard. If the machine fills slowly with water or doesn't fill at all, blocked inlet filters could be the cause. Turn off the washer's water valves, then unscrew the hoses. You'll find the filters inside the valve bodies on the machine. Use a pair of pliers to pull them out, then rinse them under running water and gently scrub them clean with a toothbrush if necessary. If the screens are badly clogged, replace them. You can replace plastic screens with metal ones, but don't replace metal screens with plastic.

Blocked inlet screens are easy to clean

How to replace a door seal

1 Locate the outer clamp band securing the seal to the body of the machine and examine it carefully. You may be able to prise it off with a flat-bladed screwdriver, but some have a tensioning arrangement that has to be loosened first. Once you've removed the outer clamp band, locate the inner one, which secures the seal to the drum, and find out how this is fixed in place. You may need to loosen a clip to remove it, or you may be able to prise the band off with a flat-bladed screwdriver.

2 Once the clamp bands have been removed, use both hands to pull the seal away from the locating lips on the body shell and drum. Make sure that the drum and washing machine body are clean, then rub a smear of fabric conditioner into the groove that locates the seal on the drum – this makes fitting the new seal easier. If the clamp band has no tensioning adjustment, put it in place on the bottom of the seal first, then push the seal onto the machine with both hands, working in opposite directions towards the top.

● Before you refit the screens, check that the valves themselves are clear of debris, so that nothing gets pushed further into the machine.

● **Level your machine** A washing machine that's not level is likely to break down and wear out before its time. On most models, levelling is easy. Use a spirit level on top of the machine to check the level from side to side and front to back, and adjust the feet as necessary. Most washing machine feet are on threads that can be wound in or out of the machine with a wrench to raise or lower that corner slightly. Start by making both sides of the machine level from front to back, then check the back and front edges and make sure they are level from side to side. Once you're happy, tighten the lock nuts on the front legs to prevent the machine from jiggling out of place.

● **Got a leak? Look for clues in the water** You may not be able to fix a washing machine fault yourself, but doing some of the detective work to diagnose the problem can prevent wasting both time and money with the engineer. With a leak, you can learn a lot by inspecting the water before you clean it up.
● If the water is clear with no sign of detergent, the leak is probably occurring before the water reaches the detergent tray or drum and is likely to be from one of the inlet hoses or valves.
● If the water is soapy, it may be leaking out of the machine during the wash via a faulty door seal, sump hose or pump.
● Dirty water is likely to have leaked from a loose or perished drain hose.
● Before you call an engineer, check and tighten the hose connections that could be leaking and see whether this fixes the fault.

smart idea

Once a month, run your washing machine on the hottest wash you can, with no detergent and no clothes in it. This will help to clear out any undissolved detergent that can clog the workings and keep the inside of the machine sparkling clean.

Tumble dryers

Lint and airflow problems are the most likely causes of faults with a tumble dryer and they are simple to avoid. These simple machines, whether they vent damp air out of the dryer or condense the moisture into water, are a boon to a busy family, but don't take yours for granted – a build-up of lint doesn't just slow the drying process, it's also a fire hazard.

SAVE £300

How much it would cost to replace a poorly maintained venting tumble dryer.

smart idea

If your dryer is in a small, enclosed laundry room, leave the door open while the dryer is running. This will improve airflow to your dryer, which increases its efficiency. Alternatively, consider installing a louvred door on your laundry room.

Care and maintenance

● **Before every use, clean lint from the filter** This is the single easiest way to take care of your dryer. At least twice a year, augment your regular de-linting by washing the filter, if it's suitable for washing, and using a slim nozzle attachment on your vacuum cleaner to vacuum the area where the lint filter sits.

● **Take the lint screen test** If you regularly use fabric-softening dryer sheets, they can clog up the machine's lint filter with microscopic fibres and chemicals. Twice a year, remove your dryer's lint screen and hold it under running water. If the water beads up and rolls off, scrub the lint screen gently but thoroughly with mild soap and an old toothbrush. Let the filter air-dry completely before replacing it.

● **Vacuum underneath** Every six months or so, remove the dryer's kick plate or bottom panel at the front (some are held in place by screw clips, others can be prised off with a flat screwdriver, starting in the centre) and vacuum as much dust and lint as you can from under the machine. A build-up of lint here, where the temperature can get very high, could ignite.

● **Clean and inspect the dryer duct** At least once a year, use a long-handled dryer duct brush or a vacuum cleaner hose and nozzle attachment to clean out the dryer duct. Wait until the dryer is cool, then pull out and unplug the machine. From the back, disconnect the vent hose from the machine and where it vents out of the wall. Clean inside the hose, and inspect it along its entire length for snags or splits.
● The trick to using a dryer duct brush is to rotate it constantly as you insert it, and to pull it out frequently so you don't create a plug of lint in a hard-to-reach place.
● Vacuum around the vent pipe connections at both ends, too, and as far into the machine as you can reach.

- Make sure that the vent on the outside wall isn't obstructed or blocked by plants or accumulated rubbish.
- If your tumble dryer vents directly back into the room, clean the vent flap and duct and ensure that they aren't obstructed.

● **Help water to drain away** Instead of venting damp air, condensing dryers pass it over a cool surface to condense the moisture into water. This either collects in a tray that you must empty regularly, or drains via a hose into the household drains. Empty a drainage tray after every use or check the condition of the drainage hose once a year to avoid leaks.

● **Use a tissue to test the door seal** Once a year, while the dryer is in operation, run a piece of thin paper or face tissue around the edge of the door. If it's sucked in, the dryer door gasket isn't sealing. Note your dryer's make and model and order a replacement from an appliance parts store or online. Remove the old seal (it should come off with just a little prying), clean away the adhesive with white spirit and install the new seal using the adhesive supplied with it.

USE THE TISSUE TEST
ONCE A YEAR.

Easy fixes

● **Cleaning the moisture sensor** Most newer models have a moisture sensor to switch the machine off once the washing is dry. This is usually two shiny metal strips located near the lint screen. The sensor checks the clothes for dampness as they tumble past by using electrical resistance – the dryer the clothes, the greater the resistance. If the sensor gets coated with waxy, dryer-sheet residue, it becomes less effective. If you notice your dryer cutting out before the clothes are fully dry, clean the sensor with a squirt of gentle, all-purpose cleaner and a quick wipe.

● **Checking the length of your dryer duct** A general rule to follow is that a straight path from the dryer to the outdoor vent should be no more than 7m, with 1.5m subtracted for every right-angled bend. So if the path your duct takes requires two 90 degree bends, the total length should be no more than 4m. If the hose is too long, the dryer won't be able to vent the damp air efficiently and the dryer won't work properly. If a new dryer isn't working as well as you expected, check its position and move it if necessary.

Lawns
Trees and shrubs
Flowerbeds
Water in the garden
Drives
Steps
Patios and paths
Decking

5 THE GARDEN

Retaining walls
Fences
Sheds and greenhouses
Ponds

Working in the garden gives you the chance to enjoy fresh air and exercise, and save money at the same time. It doesn't matter how young or old you are, or how experienced or green-fingered: there are jobs anyone can do that will help to raise or maintain the value of your home.

The most important thing is good planning, especially when it comes to tending to your lawn and flowerbeds, which require specific jobs that change with the seasons. The rest is easy. In this section you'll find out how to keep your lawn lush and green without wasting gallons of water, how to fix a wobbly fence panel, get rid of the ants on your patio, keep your drive clean and safe and ensure your decking is a relaxing oasis, not a slippery, rotten eyesore.

Follow the tips on caring for trees, sheds, walls, ponds and more, and find out how to make the crucial small repairs (like patching a crumbling concrete step or adjusting the backfill in a retaining wall) that can spare you major work later on.

Lawns

A lush, green lawn is the Holy Grail of gardening and central to most people's idea of the perfect garden. You can spend a fortune on lawn treatments over a year, but there are some simple tips you can follow to keep your grass in good condition without resorting to expensive chemicals. But if your garden isn't suited to grass, don't try to fight nature – find an alternative, such as paving, and get on with enjoying your outdoor space.

Care and maintenance

● **Gauge when, and how much, to water** Grass should be watered deeply and on an infrequent (but evenly timed) schedule. Most types of grass need about 2cm of water every week, including rainfall. A light daily sprinkling will encourage roots to grow near to the surface, where they will be more dependent on you for their water; giving your grass a good soaking once a week will help the grass to set down deep roots, which will be able to draw water from the soil even in periods of drought.

● Most established lawns can survive a surprisingly long period of drought without being watered. The grass may turn brown and stop growing altogether, but hold your nerve and keep the sprinkler in the shed. As soon as the rains return your lawn should revive itself.

● Newly seeded lawns are an exception to the infrequent watering rule. They must be kept moist until germination and watered often while the grass establishes – daily, in hot weather.

● Do your watering in the early morning. Watering at night can invite fungus and disease, and watering during the heat of the day means more water will be lost to evaporation.

● **Don't let wildflowers take over** A patch of meadow, spotted with pretty wildflowers, will attract beneficial insects into your garden, where they will help to keep aphids and other pests at bay. But the success of wildflowers in the wild lies in their ability to spread and you can find yourself with what are essentially weeds all over your lawn. Designate a wildflower area and be vigilant for seedlings appearing outside this zone.

SAVE £700

Cost to lift, prepare and returf a poorly maintained, 6m x 10m lawn.

Dig out weeds with a knife

● **Uproot weeds** Weeding by hand is the best course of action, especially if you have only a few weeds. Grab them at their base when the soil is moist and use a trowel or weeding knife to dig up dandelions and other weeds with taproots. If you have a pervasive weed problem, herbicides may be your only option. These are potent chemicals, so always follow manufacturers' safety and usage guidelines. Spot-treat weeds with a spray or by using a paintbrush to apply the herbicide directly to the leaves.

● **Aerate your lawn** Make this a top priority every spring. To aerate, you can use a special tool – an aerator – to remove plug-like cores of soil, thatch and grass. This boosts growth by bringing water and fertiliser closer to the roots, eases soil compaction to help the lawn drain freely and removes thatch, which can stifle the growing grass. Don't sweep up the soil cores: they will provide a beneficial top-dressing as they break down.
● After you aerate, fertilise, water and, if needed, seed your lawn.
● Mechanical walk-behind aerators are expensive to buy but don't cost much to rent and will make light work of a large lawn. Inexpensive manual aerators are a good option for small lawns.

● **Don't cut grass too short** You may not have to mow the lawn as often, but cutting grass by more than one-third of its height will weaken the blades and make the lawn vulnerable to weeds and invasive grasses. Giving your lawn a trim rather than a close crop encourages deeper root growth and healthier grass overall.
● In shaded or high-traffic areas, or after a drought, lift your mower blades even higher.

● **Pick up the clippings or mulch?** Clippings are best collected and removed. Left on the lawn, they can encourage worms and disease and mat into a thick thatch that can even prevent water seeping into the ground.
● Some modern mowers can mulch the grass clippings as they go, chopping them very finely. In warm, wet climates this mulch will rot down and feed the roots, but in the UK this process is seldom fast enough and the mulch will simply build up. Leave the occasional layer of mulch as you mow, but don't do it every time.

smart idea
Apply fertiliser in spring or late autumn – never during the hot summer months, when it can cause turf burn or promote weed growth.

● **Choose the right type of grass** Before you buy any grass seed, find out which types of grass grow best in your area. Ask at a local garden centre, or ask neighbours with a good lawn what kind of seed they use.
● Next, read the small print. The make-up of seed blends can vary; check the contents for 'weed content' and 'other crop seed' and select a variety that lists '0 per cent' for each.
● Look out for the latest eco-friendly, 'smart' grass varieties. These have been bred to thrive on up to 30 per cent less water than standard grass.

● **What to do when grass won't grow** In shady, damp areas, and particularly in small gardens that are surrounded by fences on all sides, grass may never thrive, so consider the alternatives instead.
● Spreading, ground-cover plants need up to three years to establish but

Lawnmower

Take care of your mower and it will repay you with years of reliable service.

● Whether you have a cylinder mower or rotary, petrol or electric, the most important thing you can do for your lawn is to keep the blades clean and sharp so that they cut, rather than tear, the grass. Before each use, give the blades a light spray of cooking oil to prevent grass from sticking to them. When accessing the underside of a mower, always tip it so that the air-filter side of the engine is uppermost.

● Check the air filter once a year. If it's dirty, try shaking out some of the dust, but replace it anyway every two years.

● Keep the undercarriage clean. Caked-on grass and mud will encourage rust to develop and may stop the blade from spinning. Use a stiff brush to remove dry debris or a screwdriver wrapped in a piece of cloth for awkward areas.

● Change the oil in a petrol mower every spring, or after about 40 hours of use. While the engine is still warm, drain old oil into a container through the drain plug or, if necessary, through the filter hole. Refill with new oil.

● Stow it away for winter. Clean your mower thoroughly at the end of the season and empty any unused fuel from a petrol model.

can create a patchwork of colour and texture, interspersed with paths or gravel. Some can even be walked on – try *Lysimachia* (creeping Jenny) or a creeping thyme. Be wary of invasive species, such as ivy, ground ivy and periwinkle (*Vinca minor*), which could crowd out other plants.

● Small gardens can easily be paved. Make sure to lower the ground level slightly first to allow for the thickness of the paving, otherwise you can create damp problems in your house walls. The easiest option is to remove topsoil, lay a geotextile sheet to supress weeds and bed paving slabs on sharp sand. Fill the joints between the slabs by brushing in more sand. If you bed slabs on concrete or mortar and mortar the joints, you'll need to fit gullies into the drains to cope with rainwater run-off.

Easy fixes

● **Inspecting for thatch** Thatch is a layer of partially decomposed grass stems and roots that collects on the lawn's surface. Thatch develops more quickly if you don't collect the clippings when you mow. Annual raking or aeration will help to keep it in check, but if thatch gets too thick, it can prevent water and fertiliser from reaching the roots and can provide a breeding ground for insects or diseases. In turn, this can cause the turf to become spongy, making it more difficult to mow your lawn.

● To inspect your lawn for thatch, use a knife or trowel to cut a 10cm-wide and deep plug from your lawn. If the layer just above the soil is dark, spongy and more than 1cm thick, it's time to dethatch.

smart idea

Chemical treatments are both expensive and often harmful to the environment. But there are many organic fertiliser options for your lawn, including scattering your used coffee grounds over the grass. Spread them thinly – you'll probably only have enough for a small patch at a time – and allow them at least one month to break down before you put any more on top.

How to sow a new lawn from scratch

Sow grass seed in spring or autumn for the best results. The key to success is in the preparation; spend time and care digging and weeding the ground and you'll save yourself time and money in the long run, by encouraging a healthy, weed-free lawn.

1 Dig the ground thoroughly, removing any roots and weeds, and use a garden fork to break up any compacted soil to improve drainage. Level the soil, let it settle for two weeks then removce any weeds that have grown. Apply a top-dressing of fertiliser, then rake the surface level.

2 Tread the soil to firm it. Shuffle over the area with small steps, applying pressure with your heels; work systematically so that you don't miss any areas. Rake the surface again and pick out any stones. Use canes and string to divide the area in 1m squares to help you to sow evenly.

3 Measure out enough seed for 1m² and mark the level on a plastic cup that you can use each time. Using your hand, scatter the seed evenly, half in one direction then the other half at right angles. When you have covered the whole area, rake the surface lightly and water well.

Roll out new turf the day you get it

Dethatching your lawn First, mow your lawn to about half its normal mowing height, then make several passes with a spring-tine rake (a leaf rake), criss-crossing your strokes. If you have a large lawn, consider hiring a power rake for this job – it will be far quicker and do a more thorough job, too, though it's still worth finishing off with a hand rake.
● Dethatching will stress your lawn, so it's best done just before the active growing season. Reseed and fertilise the lawn after you dethatch.

● **Re-laying worn-out turf** Rolls of turf cost about 20 times more than buying grass seed for the equivalent area, but the results are instant and you can start to use the lawn straight away. If you need to replace a small area of worn turf, it is often worth the extra expense.
● Cut away the old turf and level the ground. Tread down the earth and rake it smooth, making sure that when the new turf is in place, it will be level with the existing lawn. Water the soil to encourage rooting.
● Lay new turf within 24 hours of delivery, otherwise it will dry out and begin to yellow. If you cannot lay it straight away, stack it in a shaded area or cover it and keep it wet.
● Lay strips in a staggered pattern (like bricks) to help to prevent visible joins. Roll over the new turf with a water-filled roller, which can be hired for just a few pounds. Keep the new grass moist for the first two weeks, then gradually reduce watering frequency. Fertilise after one month.

Trees and shrubs

Most people view trees and shrubs as long-term investments that add to the beauty of their homes and surroundings. Like all investments, they should be selected and maintained carefully and planted with enough room to grow. Keep older trees healthy with occasional pruning and you will help to avoid damage to your home from falling branches.

Care and maintenance

● **Take care around the roots** Most tree roots spread out only just below ground level. When surface roots appear above ground, cover them with around 5cm of topsoil or plant a ground-cover shrub to spread and conceal them. Never pile up soil over roots or around the base of a trunk, as this can encourage new shoots to sprout.
● If you want to plant under a tree, choose bulbs or perennials that can be planted once and then left: constant digging can damage roots.
● Avoid driving or parking your car over a tree's root zone.

● **Target water with a drip irrigator** Young trees and shrubs need about 8cm of water per week during their first growing season. Keep them hydrated by giving each its own watering system: use a thin nail to pierce holes in a 4 litre plastic jug or use a large plastic plant pot. Bury the jug or pot about a metre from the plant so that the spout sticks out just above soil level. Fill the jug with water, which will slowly seep out to the roots.

● **Keeping hedges in great shape** The best way to keep a hedge healthy and vigorous is to prune it regularly. Do this in spring and again in midsummer – and at the end of the summer for an evergreen hedge or in autumn for deciduous hedges, such as beech.
● Use hand shears to trim ragged growth, working from the bottom up. Aim for vertical or slightly tapering sides – step back from time to time to check your work – and use a string line to help you to get the top level.

● **Don't top trees** 'Tree topping' – drastically cutting back large branches on mature trees – is among the most damaging things you can do to a tree. Not only does it leave trees looking deformed and more prone to disease and decay, but the tree will ultimately grow back taller

SAVE £450

Cost for a tree surgeon to fell and remove a neglected tree that has become dangerous.

Prune roses to encourage blooms

and bushier. Always prune a tree with care, and never remove more than one-third of the crown in a single pruning.

● **Cut back for more flowers** It may seem illogical, but the best way to keep rose bushes full and healthy is by pruning them in early spring before new growth appears. For hybrid and floribunda roses, cut the strongest canes to about half their height; less vigorous canes should be cut back by a third. Make angled cuts about 5mm above and slanting away from outward-facing buds.
● Remove dead or damaged canes and suckers (shoots from the roots or the lower part of the plant's stem). Tear or pull out suckers at the base – cutting them will only result in more suckers.

● **Avoid trunk injuries** Take care when mowing up to a tree: bumps from a mower can damage the trunk and the sap system – which draws water and nutrients up from the roots – and this can kill the tree.

Easy fixes

● **Taming a neglected hedge** Overgrown hedges that have become woody at the base can be rejuvenated by cutting them right back to ground level. This drastic measure will leave you temporarily without a hedge, but the plants will send out new shoots from the stumps and roots. Keep your nerve and continue to cut back the new growth hard for the first two seasons and you'll be rewarded with a thick and healthy hedge.
● Mature deciduous hedges, such as beech, can be shocked by severe pruning and die, so tackle these in stages: the face of the hedge one year and the top the next, for example. If you cut back into wood that's no longer green, the plant won't produce new shoots, so prune cautiously.

Is that tree too close?

Any trees or shrubs planted right next to a building can be potentially harmful to the building itself. This doesn't mean that you shouldn't plant trees or shrubs close to the house or that you should tear down the pretty climber on your front wall, but check carefully every year for any signs of damage and fix problems before they get serious and turn into major repair jobs.

● Roots can work their way into footings, causing expansion damage to the brickwork as they grow, and the tendrils of climbing plants can get into mortar joints and push bricks apart.

● If your home is built on shrinkable clay soil (anywhere in the UK south of a line between the Humber and the Bristol Channel), you should be wary of trees growing within 10m of the walls, or within 20m for larger or fast-growing trees such as oak, ash, elm, poplar and willow. These trees can draw water out of the clay subsoil and contribute to subsidence problems in particularly dry summers.

● When in leaf, plants will shade walls. This can help to keep old houses with solid walls cool in hot weather, but can also block the drying effects of the sun and encourage damp problems.

● Fallen autumn leaves will collect around the base of a plant and can hold moisture against a wall unless you clear the leaves regularly.

● In hot weather, moisture can evaporate fast from bare soil in flowerbeds, contributing to subsoil shrinkage and even subsidence. So keep flowerbeds well planted with ground-cover shrubs, or lay paving next to the house.

How to prune a branch from a tree

Always take care when trimming a tree and never use a chainsaw above waist height. You may need a helper to do this job safely or, if the branch is more than 20cm in diameter, a professional tree surgeon. Try to maintain the shape of the crown and keep it symetrical.

1 To prevent the branch splitting and tearing the bark, use a sharp pruning saw or bow saw to make a preliminary upward cut, about a quarter of the way through the branch and 30-45cm away from the trunk.

2 Saw through the branch from above, cutting 2-3cm beyond the first cut, which will close and absorb the weight of the branch, making it easier for you to saw. Ask your helper to hold the branch to stop it falling.

3 Saw off the remaining stub by making a small cut on the underside, close to the trunk but not quite flush with it, and finish by sawing from above to meet this cut.

Keep hedges within the law

Homeowners in the UK have a legal obligation not to cause a nuisance to neighbours by having unreasonably high hedges – a ruling sometimes known as the *Leylandii* law, because of the popularity of these tall, fast-growing conifers as screens in gardens. There is no definitive ruling on how high a hedge may be, but the local authority may be called upon to adjudicate on whether a hedge is adversely affecting neighbours' enjoyment of their property and they can issue a formal notice instructing the hedge owner to cut back the growth.

● Where hedges grow alongside a road or pavement, the law is more clearly defined. Homeowners (or occupiers of rented properties) are resposible for trees and bushes that overhang the carriageway. Hedges should be kept cut back to the pavement edge or to the line of the property boundary and should be no higher than 2.2m. Tree branches should not overhang the road unless they are at least 5.2m high on minor roads or 6.6m on major roads.

● If overhanging branches obscure the road or pavement, the local authority can write to you, asking you to carry out any necessary pruning. If you fail to comply, they can carry out the work themselves and bill you for the full cost.

Flowerbeds

Garden centres and nurseries stock a wide variety of ornamental plants, but even if you look out for bargains, a well-stocked flowerbed doesn't come cheap. You can create blooming borders without it costing a fortune, though: start plants from seed or cuttings, make your own compost to feed the soil, mulch and water regularly, and shop wisely when you need to.

SAVE £20

Cost to buy the equivalent volume of compost as can be created from garden and kitchen waste in a 330 litre plastic compost bin.

Care and maintenance

● **Give plants a good start in a new bed** Early autumn is the best time to prepare a new flowerbed. Use a spade to remove the turf or top layer of soil, then place a tarpaulin alongside the bed. Dig up the topsoil and place it on the tarpaulin then add a generous amount (up to 25 per cent) of compost or well-rotted leafmould, and mix it thoroughly.

● Use a fork to loosen the soil in the bed to a depth of 15-25cm, removing any large stones, weeds or roots. Add another generous layer of compost, turn it over completely, and then shovel in the improved topsoil.

● Level the surface with a rake and you're ready to start planting.

● **Recycle old news into new blooms** An easy, labour-saving way to turn an overgrown patch of garden into a flowerbed is to cover the ground with a layer of 8 to 12 sheets of newspaper (black and white pages only) or a few pieces of cardboard. Lay about 10cm of compost or topsoil on top. The paper will kill everything growing beneath it and eventually break down into the soil, but it does require patience. Put down the paper in autumn and you should be able to plant in spring.

● **Maximise your harvest** Most plants grow fuller and have more flowers if they're pinched out occasionally. Use your thumbnail and finger to break the stem between two sets of leaves, snipping off the top growth.

---

4 tips for smart plant shopping

1 Only buy plants that that suit your planting site – don't hope that a sun-loving species might still thrive in a shady spot.

2 Look for healthy foliage, abundant new growth and unopened buds.

3 If possible, slip the plant from its pot and examine the roots, which should be firm and surrounded by a good amount of soil. 'Pot-bound' plants, whose roots completely fill the pot or even protrude out of it, have been poorly looked after and have probably been on the shelf for a long time.

4 Avoid plants with yellowed or wilting leaves, stunted or dead growth, weeds in the pot or moss on the soil surface – even if they are cheap.

How to make your own compost

Homemade compost is free food for your plants. Digging compost into your soil provides essential nutrients, helps to maintain a healthy soil pH, combat disease, retain moisture and boost the activity of beneficial soil organisms. Composting also helps the environment by reducing household waste.

While you can keep a compost heap in your garden, most people prefer the convenience of bins, which can be made from wooden slats or recycled plastic. The black plastic bins are usually fastest for rotting down, as they retain heat best.

The key to making compost is to mix 'green' waste (grass clippings, coffee grounds, kitchen scraps) with more fibrous 'browns' (fallen leaves, sawdust, shredded newspaper). You can also add eggshells, paper towels, shredded cardboard, paper bags and tea bags.

A balance of these ingredients will help to create a warm heap that will compost quickly. Cover an open heap to retain moisture and water it in very dry spells.

Don't add human and pet wastes (such as the contents of litter trays), meat or dairy scraps, plastics and other petroleum products, barbecue ash, diseased plant parts, perennial weeds, seeds or plants treated with herbicides and pesticides.

Garden waste needs around six months to rot down fully over the summer; longer over winter, when the temperature drops. 'Turn' the heap once or twice to mix it, which speeds up the process. When it's ready, your compost should have a sweet, earthy smell (if it smells foul, mix in more fibrous material and leave it a while longer). Spread it liberally around your garden and lawn and dig it in or let the worms pull it down into the soil.

A wooden cube is easy to build

Waste rots quickest in a plastic bin

An open heap can be large

- Another way to get more blooms from established plants is to prevent them from setting seed by deadheading them. If new buds are forming, simply cut off the spent blooms just above the bud. Otherwise, cut back to the base of the stem. Deadheading isn't effective for flowering bulbs and most perennials, but will keep annuals in flower for longer.
- Sacrifice some flowers to get fewer but larger blooms in peonies and chrysanthemums. Do this by removing buds or snipping off the small side-growths to concentrate the plant's energy just where you want it.

- **To fertilise or not?** Most established flowers don't require additional fertiliser if there's enough organic matter in the soil. Fertiliser is most beneficial when growing seedlings and when you plant them out. Some perennials, such as astilbes and clematis, thrive on a feed in early

DEADHEAD OLD BLOOMS AND MORE WILL GROW.

Rain gauge

Like lawn grasses, most flowers need about 25mm of water each week to thrive. But be careful not to overdo it with the hosepipe or watering can; too much water can cause root rot and encourage the growth of moulds and fungi. Place a rain gauge in your garden to keep track of how much rain has fallen and, therefore, how much extra water your plants really need. You can hide the gauge in a border or close to the house, or look for a decorative model that you're proud to have on display.

smart idea

You don't need costly slug pellets or other slug and snail-control products. Catch these voracious pests by burying a container half-filled with beer so that its opening is flush with the ground. Leave it overnight and empty out your catch in the morning.

spring. But too much nitrogen could mean spindly growth and too many leaves. Use farmyard manure with caution – most annuals can't tolerate it. Any manure should be well composted before it's put on your flowerbed.

● **Control pests the nontoxic way** One of the most common alternatives to pesticides is companion planting: grouping certain plants to ward off scavenging animals, insects and disease. For instance, planting a ring of garlic around rose bushes can protect them from aphids. Another effective way to control pests without chemicals is to attract wildlife into your garden to catch the aphids, slugs and other destructive culprits. Plant a variety of species, including plenty of native flowers, that will provide shelter, seeds, pollen and food and make your garden the most attractive on the street to butterflies, ladybirds, hedgehogs and birds.

Easy fixes

● **Mulching new flowerbeds** Mulch is not only good for your garden, it also saves you time and trouble. A layer of organic matter that blankets the soil, mulch keeps weeds at bay, retains moisture and improves soil fertility. Mulching materials include chipped wood or bark, pine needles, tree leaves, coffee grounds, grass clippings and even shredded newspaper. Mulch new flowerbeds to a depth of 5-8cm after planting. Mulch breaks down over time, so replenish it at least once a year, preferably in early spring, when most perennials are dormant. Take care not to lay the mulch too thickly: overdoing it may result in rot or soil imbalances, and provide a cosy home for insects or rodents.

● **Protect bulbs with chicken wire** Mice, squirrels, rabbits and other animals see your flower bulbs as tasty meals, not would-be blooms. When you plant bulbs to flower the following year, or in early spring, when the bulbs are dormant, place a layer of chicken wire on the ground (under the mulch). Anchor it by pushing the edges deep into the soil and this should prevent the pests from digging down. You can also mix rose bush prunings into the soil – animals will be deterred by the thorns.

MULCH FLOWERBEDS TO KEEP WATER IN AND WEEDS OUT.

Water in the garden

If your water supply is metered, you'll be all too aware how sprinklers and hosepipes can increase your bill in a dry summer. Even if you don't have a water meter, it's worth collecting as much rainwater as you can for watering the garden – far purer and kinder to your plants than tap water.

Care and maintenance

● **Collect rain in tanks and butts** Install as many water butts or larger tanks as you can to collect rain run-off from roofs and gutters. Put one – or several linked together, if you have room – at each downpipe, so there's water to hand wherever you are in the garden. In all but the driest summers you'll probably collect enough to satisfy your plants' needs.

● The easiest way to install a water butt is with a diverter kit (see page 200). This stops the butt overflowing and will help to prevent damp problems caused by overflowing water dripping down your house walls.

● Always fit a leaf strainer at the top of the downpipe (see page 140) to prevent the diverter becoming clogged with leaves, and check and clear the diverter if you see signs that it's not working properly.

● **To sprinkle or not?** A garden sprinkler attached to a hosepipe is an easy way to keep your lawn lush and borders well watered, but it can use as much as 1,000 litres an hour, and it's easy to water more heavily than you need to. Watering by hand is less wasteful and gives you a chance to really look at your flowerbeds as you go, so that you'll spot signs of pests or disease, plants that aren't thriving, sections of bed that are crowded and other potential problems before they get serious.

● **Recycling 'grey' water** Your household waste water can also be put to use in your garden. In new 'green' houses, the water from baths, showers, sinks and washing machines may be plumbed into a separate drainage system to a large, underground 'grey water' tank. Installing such a system in an existing house is a major task, but if you're serious about saving water, you can buy a pump or siphon to drain you bathwater to an outside tank via a hose through the bathroom window.

Easy fixes

● **Connect your hose to the water butt** If you have a lot of watering to do, the hosepipe is a tempting option, rather than repeatedly refilling a watering can from the water butt. For as little as £30, a simple water-butt pump allows you to use your hose for the water you have collected. Take care to plug the pump into an outside electrical socket that is protected by an RCD (residual current device – see page 191).

SAVE £150

The average cost of watering your garden for an hour a day over the summer months using a garden sprinkler.

smart idea

Water butts can collect algae and water-borne pests, so every autumn drain off the water and scrub the inside with soapy water. Disconnect the drainpipe or switch the diverter to 'off' and leave the butt empty over winter, when your plants won't need watering.

Drives

Concrete and asphalt are among the most durable of building materials, but they still require some maintenance to keep your drive in good condition. Asphalt needs periodic sealing and patching, while concrete can chip or flake and weaken around the joints between sections. Make small repairs to stop a small job turning into a major drive replacement.

SAVE £700

What you would pay to have an existing 3m x 16m asphalt driveway professionally cleaned and resealed.

smart idea

Kill weeds or grass growing in the crevices of paved driveways by pouring a pot of boiling water over them – you can even drain pasta or vegetable pans directly onto the weedy area. It's simple and doesn't cost a penny.

Care and maintenance

● **Clean concrete once a year** An annual scrub leaves concrete looking fresh and clears debris or stains that might make you slip. Wet the concrete, then scrub it with a stiff brush or broom and a mild degreaser or commercial concrete cleaner. Let the cleanser sit on the surface for 15 to 20 minutes, then rinse well with a hosepipe or pressure washer.

● **Don't seal in dirt** Asphalt or tarmac drives will last longer if you reseal them every two to three years. Sealant helps to prevent water seeping into cracks and damaging the base, and stops weeds taking root.
● Prepare your driveway for sealing by washing it with soapy water and a stiff bristle brush, followed by a thorough rinsing. Dig out any weeds or grass, and patch small cracks with crack-filler compound. Mix the sealer for the time specified – poor mixing is the main cause of subsequent problems. Work on areas around 3-5m² at a time, rather than in narrow strips. Use a sealing brush, squeegee or long-handled roller and apply two thin coats rather than a single thick one – it will dry faster and bond better. Keep off the surface for at least 24 hours.

● **Seal concrete joints with epoxy** Expansion joints let sections of concrete expand and contract in response to temperature changes. Over time, these joints can also become the primary points at which water seeps in under the cement and causes cracks and erosion. Seal any leaky joints in driveways with an epoxy joint sealant. Before applying the sealant with a mastic gun, sweep out the joint and scrub it clean.

● **Keep weeds out of block paving** Small blocks laid in staggered rows or a herringbone pattern make an attractive surface for a drive, but the joints between the blocks are usually filled with loose sand and so prone to growth of weeds. Keep weeds under control by regular brushing with a stiff-bristled, ridged brush designed for getting between paving blocks, or scrape them out with a weeding knife.

● **Keeping gravel neat** Gravel is a traditionally luxurious finish for a drive, but can easily start to look shabby and become home to weeds. Gravel should always be laid over a weed-suppressing membrane: if yours

Anatomy of a **drive**

Laying a new drive is a job for a professional, but is notorious for attracting shoddy workmen, who leave a neat surface finish that hides an inadequate sub-base. The depth of the sub-base depends on the surface it's supporting, the weight that will have to be carried and the nature of the ground. But always make sure that your builder lays at least 100mm of well-compacted hardcore topped with a layer of ballast or sand.

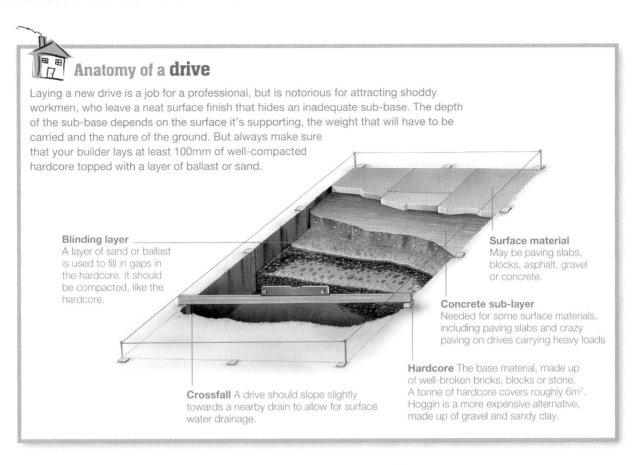

Blinding layer
A layer of sand or ballast is used to fill in gaps in the hardcore. It should be compacted, like the hardcore.

Surface material
May be paving slabs, blocks, asphalt, gravel or concrete.

Concrete sub-layer
Needed for some surface materials, including paving slabs and crazy paving on drives carrying heavy loads

Crossfall A drive should slope slightly towards a nearby drain to allow for surface water drainage.

Hardcore The base material, made up of well-broken bricks, blocks or stone. A tonne of hardcore covers roughly 6m². Hoggin is a more expensive alternative, made up of gravel and sandy clay.

---

isn't, then you'll be forever battling against the weeds and it may be worth the expense of lifting the gravel to lay a membrane down.

● Carefully pull up any weeds whenever you spot them or, if the weeds have spread over a wide area, spray once a year with weedkiller.

● Once a year, rake the gravel to redistribute it if it has become unevenly spread, and top up with a little new gravel if necessary.

Easy fixes

● **Fixing spalled concrete** If concrete wasn't cured properly or the mix contained too much water, the surface will eventually chip or flake in a process called spalling. Chips can also be caused by a heavy impact.

● You don't have to repave the entire area. Instead, break up all the damaged concrete with a small sledgehammer (you should hear a hollow sound when you hit weakened concrete). Using a wire brush, scrub the surface until all the loose material has been removed, then rinse well. Once it has dried, cover the surface with latex patching compound or a mixture of portland cement, fine sand and water. Smooth it with a trowel or float.

● Always wear safety goggles when breaking up concrete and use a chisel with a hand-protector built in.

● **Removing oil stains from the driveway** A car leaking oil can leave unsightly stains that can also damage the surface. There are plenty of commercial stain removers available, but a simple home solution can work just as well. Spread a thick layer of ordinary cat litter over the stain,

smart idea

An ecologically sound alternative to hard paving (which can increase water run-off and contribute to flash flooding) is to lay a honeycombed grid of recycled plastic over 200-300mm of compressed ballast. Each hole in the grid can be filled with gravel or sand, or with a mixture of soil and fertiliser that can be sown with grass seed to create a hard-wearing grass surface.

Hire a tamper to patch potholes

grind it in with your heel, cover with newspaper and let it stand overnight. The next day, sweep up the litter, cover the stain with a paste of washing powder and water and let it sit again overnight. In the morning, remove most of the soap paste and scrub the stain with a stiff bristle brush, adding more water and paste, if needed, as you work.

● **Patching potholes** Ashpalt can crumble at the edges or potholes can form, but you can patch the surface yourself.
● Use cold-roll asphalt and store it indoors overnight before you use it. The material is easier to work with when it's warm. Rake out any crumbled asphalt and brush the remaining solid surface with bituminous emulsion. Lay some of the patching asphalt in the hole and ram it with a fence post or a hired tamper until it's solid and firm. If you can, place a board over the patch and drive your car backwards and forwards over it a couple of times to compact it further.

● **Topping up a gravel drive** Refreshing a gravel drive that has worn thin is heavy work, but not difficult. A builders' merchant will deliver gravel in 1 tonne bags and tip it straight onto your drive. One tonne will cover around 16m². Pea gravel is more rounded than standard gravel and larger sizes (20mm rather than 10mm) are less likely to get stuck in shoe soles or tyre treads. Use a rake to spread the gravel then go over the area with a garden roller.

Fixing cracks in **concrete and asphalt**

To fix this ...	Do this ...
A small crack (less than 5mm wide) in asphalt	Dig out any weeds or grass, then clean off remaining dirt with a broom. Next, use a stiff brush and a premixed driveway cleaner (or a solution of laundry detergent in water) to scrub away residual oils or dust. Rinse well and let it dry. Patch the crack with asphalt crack-filler and smooth it with a putty knife.
Potholes and wider cracks in asphalt	Follow the preparatory steps above, leaving the area wet (but with no standing water). Use a trowel to fill the hole with cold-roll asphalt (see 'Patching potholes', above). Half-fill holes deeper than 100mm with coarse gravel and tamp it down before putting asphalt on top. If more than one layer of patching is needed, tamp down after each application, and let it dry before applying the next layer. Asphalt patches require 24 to 48 hours to set completely.
A hairline crack in concrete	Dip a rubber-gloved finger in some car body-filler, press it into the fissure and smooth it. You can also use any urethane-based sealant to fill cracks up to 2.5mm deep.
Larger concrete cracks	Use a narrow cold chisel to chip out loose edges, then clean out any remaining pieces of cement and dust with a wire brush. Use a trowel to fill in the crack with latex patching concrete, and smooth it with a wood float.

Steps

The good news is that concrete steps need little maintenance or special care. Edges or corners may chip or crumble, but not for many years, unless they're damaged by a dropped heavy object, and even this can be fixed without too much trouble. Regular cleaning is the most important task, as steps coated in grime or algae can become dangerously slippery.

Care and maintenance

● **Keep steps clean** Keep concrete steps well swept and hose them down regularly, or wet them and scrub with a stiff broom. This will get rid of muddy footprints and other abrasive material that can wear down the steps' surface and be carried into the house to cause damage there.

● **Seal and waterproof concrete steps** To keep concrete steps from getting stained, seal the surface. Dirt and grime will then wash away easily, without staining the concrete itself. Scrub the steps with detergent and water to get them clean and rinse well with a hose. When they dry, apply a masonry waterproof coating, which doesn't make the steps slippery but should make them easier to keep clean.

● **Be alert for loose slabs and uneven steps** Each spring, inspect all steps in the garden to make sure that they're still safe. Paving slabs may have come loose in the winter frosts, edges may have crumbled, plants

SAVE £100

Cost for a builder to repair a chipped concrete step in the garden.

How to repair a chipped concrete step

1 Cut back a crumbling edge using a cold chisel and club hammer. Wear work gloves and safety goggles to protect you from shards of concrete. If the surface is worn down, score it with a brick bolster and hammer to provide a good grip (key) for a new layer of concrete.

2 Fix timber edging round the step, using pegs and bricks to keep it firmly in place. If renewing a worn surface, set the edging about 15mm higher than the surface, with the side pieces allowing a forward slope of about 10mm for water to run off.

3 Brush away dust and debris, then prime the area with a mixture of PVA adhesive and water according to the container instructions – usually one part adhesive to five parts water.

4 Use a trowel to make repairs with concrete filler. To resurface a step, coat it with a solution of three parts PVA adhesive to one part water, then apply concrete made up from a bagged sand-cement mix. Level the area and cover for three days.

from surrounding borders may have spread onto the steps or the surface may have become slippery with moss or algae. These are all potential hazards, but all are easily fixed before someone is injured. If concrete steps have become uneven and water is puddling on the surface, consider resurfacing them (see page 271) or laying new slabs on top, if the surface is sound enough. Always make sure that steps are an even height within each flight – if some are higher than others you're likely to trip or fall.

Easy fixes

● **Seal narrow cracks before winter** Check concrete steps in autumn and seal any narrow cracks before winter comes, as water that gets inside and freezes will expand and make the crack worse. Brush away any loose concrete and dirt, then fill the crack with an exterior urethane or silicone-modified acrylic sealant rated for use on concrete. Smooth the sealant to blend with the surrounding surface.

● **Fit a handrail to make steps safer** If you have children or elderly relatives in your household, a handrail can help to make steps in the garden much easier and safer to use.
● To install a simple wooden handrail alongside freestanding steps, sink fence posts (cut down in length) into post spikes in the ground next to the steps or sit them in a bolt-down post base fixed to the surface of the steps. You could also bed the posts in concrete, as if you were building a fence.
● Use a string line or length of wood to join the posts before you make your final fixings and measure down to the ground along the length of the handrail to make sure that it will follow the gradient of the steps.
● Use smooth, planed wood to make a handrail that will not give users splinters. You can buy outdoor-grade handrails from wood decking suppliers, who also sell balustrade posts to go between the fixing posts. A balustrade is an important safety feature, particularly if the steps are next to a drop or steep slope.

● **Installing upside-down bolts** Railings attached to concrete steps often work loose because their bolts rust, or water gets into the bolt holes, freezes and expands, pushing out the bolts. If you have a loose railing, improve the original installation when you fix it by anchoring new bolts upside down to make the railing sturdier.
● Detach the railing from the wall by removing the screws or wall brackets, if appropriate. Then use a nail bar to lever up the floor-mounted bracket and pull the old bolts out of the concrete.
● Use an electric drill fitted with progressively larger masonry bits to widen the bolt holes until they will accept the heads of new bolts.
● Brush the insides of the bolt holes with masonry bonding agent, then slip the new bolts into the holes upside down. Mix and pour special anchoring cement around the bolts, and let it set for at least an hour.
● Once the anchoring cement is firm, apply a layer of masonry waterproof coating around the bolts. Then reposition the railing and secure it with locking nuts and washers.

smart idea

If your steps' surface becomes grease-stained, sprinkle some dry cement over the stain and let it sit for an hour to absorb the mess. Then sweep it up with a broom and dustpan. If you don't have dry cement, try plain sand or cat litter.

Patios and paths

Keeping the surface clean and safe is the most important maintenance task for patios and paths. Loose or damaged paving slabs or stones should be reset or replaced as soon as possible, slippery moss needs to be eliminated and loose path materials, such as gravel or woodchips, should be evenly spread and replenished as needed.

Care and maintenance

● **Give patios a clean sweep** Don't allow dead leaves, fallen tree blossoms, seedpods and other garden debris to pile up on your patio. In addition to being unsightly, decaying organic matter can harbour insects and leave behind dark spots on concrete and flagstones. Keep patios neat by regularly sweeping them with a stiff broom.

● **Scrub away stains** Grease from barbecue grills, stains from rusty patio furniture, bird droppings and leaf tannins can all leave their marks on your patio. Fortunately, most can be rubbed out with a bit of scouring.
● Spot-treat rust stains with a solution of one part lemon juice to four parts water, then cover the area with plastic sheeting, weigh it down and leave it to stand for ten minutes. Test this lemon solution in an out-of-the-way place first if you have coloured slabs, as the lemon juice may bleach out the colour. Scrub the stain with a stiff-bristled brush and rinse well with water.

SAVE £600

What you would pay to have a neglected 3m x 4m patio removed and new concrete paving professionally installed.

Hiring tools for a professional finish

Equipment spotlight

Professional tools make light work of the heavy jobs involved in laying a new path or patio, but it doesn't make sense to buy large equipment that you may never use again. Most hire shops will rent block-cutters and heavy-duty plate vibrators by the day or weekend – and some will deliver them, too.

● Don't leave with the equipment until someone has demonstrated how to use it safely, and always stop immediately if you feel unsure or unsafe.

● It's crucial that you also buy and use the appropriate safety equipment when using these tools. The hire shop should always explain what you need and be able to supply the equipment.

A hydraulic splitter cuts slabs

A plate vibrator compacts the base

- Remove rust stains from concrete by sprinkling some dry cement powder over them and rubbing with a small piece of flagstone. This pumice-like combination effectively scrubs off the stains.
- For other stains and to give your patio an annual spring clean, scrub well with a long-handled, stiff-bristled brush and a biodegradable patio cleaner that won't harm the surrounding plants. Rinse the area with a hose when you have finished.

Bricks or setts make good edging

- **Brick edging makes a flexible shape** Edging your patio with bricks or granite setts gives the area an attractive finish. It also means you can accommodate irregular shapes or areas without having to cut down large slabs to an awkward size or shape. Use a string line to guide you (left) and bed the bricks onto a damp mortar mix, tamping them down until they're all level.

- **Power wash your patio** A few blasts from a pressure or power washer can work wonders on a tired-looking brick, stone or concrete patio.
- To avoid damaging the patio material or injuring yourself, don't use a 'pinpoint' nozzle. Instead, use a fan nozzle to spread the jet. Also, take care to avoid positioning the jet too close to the patio as this can cause the water to etch the surface of the stone – and be careful not to damage or dislodge any mortar joints. A patio-washing attachment will help to avoid all these potential problems and could be a wise buy if one is available for your particular model of pressure washer.
- Pressure washers can be hired by the day for your annual spring clean. As with all hire equipment, if you've never used a washer before, request a demonstration and detailed safety guidelines from the hire shop.

- **Rid your stone patio of moss** If your patio is shaded by a tree, you may struggle with moss in damp, dark corners, which can make patios and steps perilously slippery.
- The easiest way to get rid of moss is to scrub it away with a stiff-bristled brush, using a solution of one part household bleach in two parts water. If you have coloured stone or concrete in your patio, test the solution on an inconspicuous corner to make sure it won't make the colour fade.
- To keep moss from returning, seal the surface with a brick sealer.

- **Evict ants from your patio's crevices** If mortar joints between your paving stones have cracked and come loose, or if the joints are just filled with brushed-in sand, your patio may get infested with lines of ants in summer. Before you reach for the ant powder, try flooding them out by pouring boiling water over the nest mounds and around the affected area.
- Another approach is to spray the mounds and surrounding area with a 50/50 solution of water and white vinegar, or commercial glass cleaner mixed with some washing-up liquid.

smart idea

Keep a few extra paving stones or bricks on hand in case you need to replace any in your patio. To ensure that your surplus stock will weather at the same rate and be the same colour as those you may want to replace, store them outdoors.

How to replace a loose or damaged slab

1 Use a spade to chop through any mortar at edge joints. Push the spade under the slab to lift it and slip a broomstick or pipe underneath to roll it out. A sunken or see-sawing wobbly slab can be re-laid, but renew a cracked or chipped slab.

2 If the slab was bedded on sand, loosen up the old sand with a trowel, add more sharp sand and lightly level the surface with a length of wood. Fill any sunken areas so that the slab will be level with the surrounding ones when it's put back into place.

3 If the slab was bedded on mortar, remove the old mortar from the hole, or the back of the slab if you're going to re-lay it, with a hammer and chisel. Mix new bedding mortar in a dryish mix of one part cement to four parts sharp sand (or use a bagged sand-cement mix) and spread it over the surface with a brick trowel to a thickness of 30-50mm. Roughen the surface with the trowel point.

4 Slab edge joints may be flush or with gaps. If there are gaps, place 10mm thick wooden spacers along

one long and one short edge before rolling the slab into position on a broomstick or pipe. It's difficult to pull back the slab if you have rolled it into the hole and butted it up against its neighbours. Make sure the gaps are even all the way round.

5 Lay a 50mm thick piece of flat wood on the slab as a cushion while you use a club hammer to tap it down flush with the surrounding slabs. Check that it's flush using a length of straightedged timber.

6 If you cannot tap the slab down flush, lift it again and skim off some of the bedding material. Or, if it sinks down too far, add more of the bedding material.

7 Wait at least two days before filling in the joints with mortar in case the slab settles and needs to be adjusted.

● Sprinkling ground black pepper or cayenne pepper on top of the mounds may also work to discourage the ants and send them elsewhere.

● **Rake and replenish your path** Loose path material – gravel, pebbles, or wood or bark chips – typically gets displaced over time to the edges, where there's less traffic. To restore its even distribution, use a lawn rake to pull the material back into place. This also serves another purpose, helping to dislodge weeds, leaves, twigs and other debris, which you can collect and discard as you work. Don't forget to replenish your path material as needed to prevent it wearing thin.

● **Make paths a weed-free zone** Any area of gravel or bark should always be laid over a continuous sheet of weed-suppressing membrane. If your path or seating area is plagued with stubborn weeds, it may be that the loose material is simply spread directly over the compacted earth.
● An annual application of weedkiller, together with regular weeding when weeds start to sprout, should keep the weeds in check, though this can be an endless task. Consider scooping up the loose surface material and laying a membrane yourself – sometimes sold as 'landscape fabric', it's widely available from garden centres and DIY stores and usually sold by the metre from a roll. Make sure that you overlap the sheets wherever you need to make joints, then replace the gravel or bark and rake it level.

Mark and cut flagstones to size

● **Seal your stones** Natural stone slabs, slates, flagstones or bricks should be coated with a water sealer to enhance their colour and provide protection against stains. Clean the stone before applying the sealer, using a power washer if necessary to lift engrained dirt. Reapply the sealer every two to five years to keep your patio in top condition.

Easy fixes

● **Cutting flagstones down to size** When you need to cut a paving stone to replace a broken one, or to fit an awkward shape when laying a new patio, you don't need a masonry saw to get it right. Simply score the desired cut a few times on one side using a stonemason's or straight chisel and a lump hammer. Then flip it over and score the other side. You may have to repeat this a few times before the pieces break off. The secret is to take your time – rush the job and you'll have a cracked stone. Make sure to wear goggles and work gloves to protect against shards of broken stone.

● **Stop sand washing away** If the sand in your stone path is slowly washing away, it might be that the joints between the flagstones are too wide. If you need to reset the stones, set them in sand as before, but instead of filling the joints with plain sand, mix a little dry portland cement in with the sand and pack it firmly between the stones. Sprinkle a little water over the joints to set the filler – use a watering-can with a fine rose – and the sand should stay firmly in place.

● **Repairing broken tiles** Period town houses often had elegant tiled paths and porches – some with simple quarry tiles, others with elaborate patterns – and you may be lucky enough to have an original outside your front door. Unfortunately, these tiles are easily broken and many paths have been replaced with a more hard-wearing surface. It's easy to replace broken tiles if you can find a matching replacement (see below). Use a chisel to prise out broken pieces, and if you need to chip away stubborn stuck pieces of tile always work from the edges in towards the middle to avoid breaking the surrounding tiles, too. Chip away mortar left in the hole before laying the new tile, making sure it's level with those around it.

● **Making a match** When one slab or tile in an otherwise sound path or patio has been badly damaged, it's usually simple to replace. But what if you don't have any spares? If you can no longer buy matching paving stones or tiles – and in any case, brand new ones will stick out when surrounded by the existing, weathered, old ones – try hunting in local salvage yards for second-hand ones.
● If buying new is your only option, you can still save yourself the cost of a whole new patio by making a feature of the odd tiles or paving stones. Look at the position of the broken slab and lift and replace a few others around the patio at the same time to make either a regular or random pattern of contrasting slabs. Depending on the position of the broken slab, you could also replace it and a few others with a square of gravel or soil planted with a low-growing perennial plant to add interest and texture.

take care!

A muriatic acid solution (brick acid) is sometimes recommended for removing stains from natural stone and brick, but use it only as a last resort. Muriatic acid is a diluted form of hydrochloric acid and is extremely dangerous. If nothing else has removed the stain, mix one part acid into at least ten parts water in a plastic bucket (never use a glass or metal container). Pour the acid carefully into the water, never the other way around, to avoid splashing it over yourself. Wear protective gloves and goggles, long sleeves and trousers, and stout shoes, and don't let the run-off drain onto the soil or plants.

Decking

Wooden decks are quick and easy to install, and make popular and attractive outdoor seating areas. But they need more regular maintenance than a stone patio to keep them in good condition and they're unlikely to last as long. You can help to prolong the life of your decking and keep it looking its best with regular cleaning, occasional refinishing and by looking out for potential structural problems and fixing them promptly.

Care and maintenance

● **Keep your deck dry** Standing water is an invitation for rot, so make sure that any nearby guttering is directed away from your deck and keep the gutters and downpipes clean to avoid overflows from blockages puddling on the decking. Your decking should drain freely, but if puddles form after rain, sweep them away with a stiff broom. Clear any blocked gaps between boards that are preventing water from draining away.

SAVE £1,000

Cost to replace a badly deteriorated 3m x 4m area of decking.

● **Keep fixings tight** As the wood in a new deck dries and shrinks, connections that were bolted or nailed together can loosen and become unsafe. Once a year, in spring, check below the decking if you can and tighten every nut and bolt. Hammer in any nails that are about to pop.
● At the same time, look for discolouration, mould and other signs of rotting wood, both below the deck and on its surface. Poke a screwdriver into boards that look suspect – if the tip penetrates the wood easily, replace that piece with a new board.

● **Let air circulate** Good air circulation underneath a deck is essential to preventing moisture build-up that can cause rot and attract pests. If you can access the space beneath your decking, clean it out once a year to prevent the build up of leaves and other debris. If you want to conceal the area below a deck, use wooden trellis panels, which hide untended ground,

Deck furnishings do's and don'ts

● Don't leave mats or outdoor rugs on deck surfaces, because they'll collect rot-inducing debris and moisture. If you want a mat or a rug on your deck, remove it regularly to clean and air the underlying surface, and don't replace it until the surface is completely dry. Pick up a rain-soaked mat or rug and dry it out thoroughly before replacing it.

● Do elevate planters on rolling plant stands or pot feet instead of placing them directly on your deck. Placing a saucer underneath a planter isn't enough, because the saucer can leave stains.
● Do move furniture often to clean underneath, especially if it has closed-weave or otherwise solid sides that reach down to the ground.

TRY TO ELEVATE YOUR POTS TO AVOID STAINS.

SWEEP YOUR DECKING REGULARLY:
WET LEAVES ARE SLIPPERY AND CAN
STAIN THE WOOD.

or stored items, while allowing air to flow freely. Make sure the trellis sits at least 25mm above the ground so that its bottom edge doesn't rot.

● **Give it a clean sweep** It's important to sweep decking regularly to get rid of leaves, twigs and other debris that can stain wood surfaces, make them slippery or trap moisture that will lead to rot. Use a heavy-duty broom to sweep your deck clean, making sure that the bristles get into the gaps between boards to clear out any trapped leaves and pine needles. If even after a good sweep with a heavy-duty broom you still see debris lodged between the boards, use a putty knife to clean out the gaps.

● **Caring for composite deck material** Not all decking is solid wood. Harder-wearing, low-maintenance, composite materials are also available – generally a combination of recycled hardwood and polymer resins. They do have their own care requirements – for example, certain cleaning products may fade the planks – but a pressure washer may not damage their surface as it can with softwood decking. There's also no need to oil or refinish your decking every few years. If you're unsure how best to care for your decking, ask your supplier or local DIY store.

take care!

A power washer may seem like the perfect tool for cleaning decking, but it can do more harm than good. Too much water pressure or the wrong spray angle can disturb wood fibres, raising the grain and leaving a fuzzy surface that doesn't wear or weather well. In most cases, a standard garden hose with an adjustable nozzle – in conjunction with a deck-cleaning solution and a stiff broom – is a much better tool for the job.

How to clean and seal your deck

Depending on how much you use it and whether you have overhanging trees, your decking will probably need washing once or twice a year. Every two to three years you'll need to reseal the boards, and you can do this job at the same time. To see if your deck needs resealing, splash a glass of water on the deck boards. If the water beads up, the surface is still water-repellent; if it soaks in, it needs resealing. Wear wellingtons, safety goggles and rubber gloves, and pick an overcast day to tackle the job. Warm, sunny weather will cause your deck-cleaning solution to dry before it has a chance to work.

1 Clear the decking of furniture and planters and trim or tie back any branches that are touching its surface. Also moisten and cover any nearby foliage that might come in contact with the cleaning solution.

2 Mix a ready-made deck-cleaning solution following the manufacturer's directions; unless your deck is badly stained, use a bleach-free formulation. Use a stiff-bristled brush to scrub all parts of the deck (railings, steps and floorboards) with the solution, starting at the top of the railings and working your way down to the floorboards. To make washing the boards easier on your back and knees, use a long-handled floor brush.

3 Allow the cleaning solution to sit on the wood surface for about 15 minutes, then rinse away all residue with a garden hose. Also rinse nearby plants that have been splashed with cleaning solution. Let the deck dry completely (usually for three to four days) before replacing furnishings and planters.

4 If you also need to reseal your deck, sweep it thoroughly once it's dry and apply a clear or staining wood sealer. A roller attached to a pole can make quick work of the boards, or use a natural-bristle brush, especially for the railings and any edges that a roller cannot reach. Alternatively use a pump-style garden sprayer. Treat the entire surface of the wood (top, sides and bottom) and pay extra attention to the ends of the boards, as they're the easiest entry points for moisture.

A WELL-CARED-FOR DECK WILL LAST FOR YEARS.

Easy fixes

● **Bleaching stains** If mildew and stains are spoiling your decking's surface, remove them with a relatively gentle but effective oxygen bleach wash. Mix 40ml of oxygen bleach in 5 litres of warm water (don't substitute chlorine bleach, which can break down the lignin that binds wood together and harm nearby plants).

● Apply the solution to stained areas with a mop or brush, let it sit for 15 to 20 minutes, then use a hose to rinse off the solution.

● Some commercial deck cleaners also contain bleach and are specially formulated to remove tough stains, mildew and unsightly tree sap.

● Whether you use a commercial or homemade bleach-based cleaner, you'll need to reapply wood sealer after washing, since bleach removes it along with the dirt and stains.

● **Fixing popped nails** Over time, as the wood shrinks, swells and shifts, nails used in the construction of your deck can pop out, creating safety hazards and possibly leaving rust stains.

● If the nail head is just barely above the surface of the wood, hammer it back in, using a nail punch to drive it just below the surface.

● If the nail has worked itself loose, pull it out as soon as you notice it. Instead of hammering in a replacement nail, use a 75mm stainless-steel decking screw. This will bite more deeply and securely into the wood. It's also rust-resistant and won't stain wood decking.

take care!

Pressure-treated wood has been impregnated with potentially toxic chemicals that protect wood from burrowing pests and decay-causing fungi. When handling pressure-treated timber, wear eye protection and a dust mask. Wash your hands well before eating and wash your work clothes in a separate load from the rest of the laundry. Finally, don't use pressure-treated wood for any structural elements that could come into contact with drinking water or food, or as framework for raised vegetable beds.

Retaining walls

A wall built on a solid, level and well-compacted base shouldn't need much care. Simple maintenance like replacing loose stones, keeping plants from weakening the structure and checking for low spots behind the wall is usually all that's needed. Replacing a retaining wall – or worse, dealing with the mess and damage from a collapsed wall – is disruptive and expensive, so get to know the signs of trouble and act fast when you spot a problem.

Care and maintenance

● **See if your wall is settling** Watch out for excessive settling or low spots behind your wall that can allow water to pool or build up. Over time, such areas will get larger and collect more water, which can eventually seep behind the wall, resulting in a weight build-up that could cause a collapse. Prevent problems by lifting the mulch or sod on top of the wall each spring and adding enough new backfill to raise the cap back to its correct level.

● **Replace loose stones** One loose stone in a wall always seems to beget another. If one or two stones become loose due to freezing and thawing, or following the impact of a car bumper, for example, they are soon likely to be joined by their neighbours and the weakness will spread fast along the wall. To avoid a major repair job, reset stones as soon as they become loose. Use mortar to keep them in place if necessary, even if the rest of the wall is constructed dry.

SAVE £1,000

Cost to reconstruct a collapsed 4m length of brick retaining wall, just five courses high – higher walls are much more complex and expensive.

Anatomy of a **brick retaining wall**

A sound foundation is critical to the strength and long life of a retaining wall. A wall like this should be no less than a full brick's width thick, with a strip foundation at least 450mm wide and 300mm thick. Below the lower ground level, two or three courses of frost-resistant bricks are important to prevent compromising the wall's strength in cold weather. Regular drain holes above the lower ground level will help to stop moisture building up and pressing against the wall, so it's vital to check these from time to time and keep them clear. In a long run of wall, movement joints should have been built in to allow the bricks to shift slightly with natural movement. You should see vertical joints at regular intervals, filled with exterior-grade mastic. The wall is back-filled behind with a base of hardcore then topsoil.

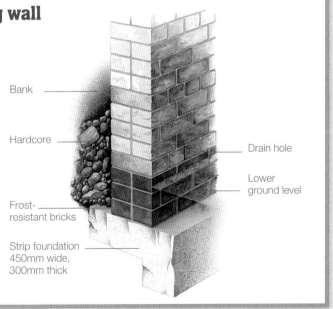

Bank

Hardcore

Frost-resistant bricks

Strip foundation 450mm wide, 300mm thick

Drain hole

Lower ground level

DON'T GIVE WEEDS A TOE-HOLE IN YOUR WALL.

● **Pull out interloping weeds and plants** Weeds, vines and seedlings can take hold in the smallest of gaps in a wall, even where there appears to be no soil at all. Although they may look harmless – pretty, even – the weight of a vine or a sapling's roots can shorten your wall's longevity. Hand-pull anything you see growing on top of or on the face of your wall, or give the wall an annual spray with weedkiller.

Retaining wall pros and cons

There are three basic types of retaining walls: natural stone, wood timber and modular concrete. Each has its own strengths and weaknesses.

Material	Pros	Cons
Natural stone 	Attractive and long-lasting; wide variety of materials to choose from; can be installed to accommodate curves and contours.	Requires more time and skill to install; more expensive (unless you have access to free stone); soil can wash through gaps.
Wood timber 	Inexpensive; quick installation; requires only carpentry tools for installation.	Short lifespan (10-25 years); limited colour and design options; requires regular maintenance to keep it looking good.
Modular concrete 	Goes up quickly once first course is in place; wide variety of colours and shapes; easy to integrate steps or multiple tiers.	Moderately expensive; heavy (some blocks can weigh up to 34kg); special tools required for cutting.

Fences

Not only does a fence provide privacy and security, it can change the look of your garden. Maintaining a fence requires diligence, though – always be on the lookout for structural problems and take care of them right away. Making simple spot repairs can add years to the life of your fence, and save you the huge expense of replacing it.

Care and maintenance

SAVE £500

Cost of replacing a wooden fence around 12m, or six panels, long.

● **Inspect the perimeter** Check fences every few months for trouble spots. Use sealant to fill any gaps between the fence posts and concrete footings to prevent water from seeping in and causing rot. Wooden fences – except for unpainted cedar fences – should be completely painted or stained every two to three years. In the meantime, scrape off flaking or peeling paint or worn stain whenever you notice it and reapply a fresh coat to prevent the wood from being exposed. Replace any rusted screws, brackets or wire ties before they break and make sure that all gate hinges are tightly secured and well oiled.

● **Keep vegetation at a safe distance** Many gardeners aim to cloak fences in more attractive flowers and foliage, but climbing plants and bushy shrubs growing near a wooden fence will increase moisture in the area and severely cut back on needed air circulation. Keep plants clear of the base of the fence by putting down a weed barrier of landscape fabric on both sides of the fence and covering it with gravel.
● Pay special attention to the condition of your fence around and behind plants, looking out for signs of rot.

● **Trim or cap fence posts** Flat surfaces on wooden fence posts allow water to sit and soak in, which encourages them to rot. Solve the problem by trimming or cutting posts to a point, slope or arched shape (right) so rain will run off them. Alternatively, use preformed metal or wood caps (far right) to protect the supports.

● **Power wash unfinished cedar** Unpainted cedar fences weather to an attractive finish, but you can still improve their appearance from time to time by cleaning with a pressure washer. Use an angled spray to clean rather than damage the fence and don't get the nozzle any closer than 40cm. Swing the jet slowly along the length of the boards and the wood's colour will brighten as the grimy surface is stripped away. Stop washing when the wood stops changing colour.

● **Staining and preservative on a fence** Most fences need treating with preservative every two to three years. The best time to do this is when the wood is dry but the sun is not too hot – late summer, after a dry spell and when no rain is forecast. Traditional creosote preservatives

A spray gun makes light work of applying preservative

are unpleasant to use and damaging to plants and the environment, but many water-based or natural oil products are now available. Apply the preservative with an old paintbrush or with a spray gun (above).

Easy fixes

● **Replacing a fence panel** Fortunately, fence panels come in standard sizes, and rotten or damaged panels are usually easy to replace. If the old panel is nailed in place you'll need a pry bar to detach it from the posts. If it's fixed with clips you should find that one end of the panel has clips that can be unscrewed.

● If you're going to nail the panel to wooden posts, drill six pilot holes in each end of the panel first, three on each side. Ask a helper to hold the panel in position, matching it to the height of its neighbours, then nail it to the posts. Drive the nails in at a slight angle so that they will not pull straight out if the fence comes under pressure,

● You should be able to reuse existing clips. Replace like with like if any are damaged, but use fresh galvanised screws.

Strengthen a damaged arris rail

● **Repairing wooden rails** Arris rails, horizontal rails used to add strength to fence panels, can sometimes become loose or split, either through natural deterioration or during high winds. If the damage is in the middle of the rail, you can strengthen it by screwing a metal arris-rail bracket over the split – use galvanised or alloy screws that won't rust. Damage near the end of the rail can be fixed with a flanged arris-rail bracket (left) that also screws into the post. If the post is concrete, use a masonry bit to drill into it and wall plugs to hold the screws.

● **Replacing a rotten post** Support the panels on each side of a rotten post with lengths of timber wedged under the top rail, then remove the fixings holding the panels to the post. Dig down beside the post to free it. Make the hole deep enough for the new post to be at the right height when sat on 150mm of well-rammed hardcore. Check that the post is vertical, then pack round it with more hardcore to support it and reattach the panels. Back-fill the hole with hardcore and soil, or with concrete post fix.

Sheds and greenhouses

Garden buildings need to be functional and sturdy and not add to the list of household repairs. Small tasks, like inspecting your shed's wood for worn spots or signs of rot, keeping your greenhouse clean and well ventilated, and tightening loose bolts on arbours and pergolas, will allow you many years of safe use and enjoyment outdoors. Remember to fit a strong lock to your shed to safeguard the tools and equipment you keep inside.

Care and maintenance

● **Tighten fixings in spring** Temperature changes over the year cause wooden structures to expand and contract. This, in turn, causes the metal fixings holding them together to loosen, letting in moisture, pests and plant growth. Each spring, check your shed and any other structures, tightening loose screws and re-hammering wobbly nails. If some nails are too loose to reset, replace them with larger, galvanised nails or screws.

● **Protect unfinished wood** Apply a coat of water-repellent wood preservative (see page 283) every few years to keep wooden sheds, arbours and greenhouses in good condition. Sheds constructed with pressure-treated 'tannalised' timber should not need re-treating.

● **Protect greenhouse plants from frost** Traditional horticultural glass looks good, but twin-walled polycarbonate sheeting has a better insulating effect, protecting plants from frost and reducing the need for artificial heating if you keep plants in your greenhouse all year round. Polycarbonate also diffuses sunlight, reducing the need to whitewash the glass to protect plants from leaf-burn.

SAVE £600

What you would pay to replace a mower, power tools and garden equipment stolen from an unlocked shed.

● **Keep greenhouses well ventilated** Good air circulation is essential to grow healthy plants, but it also prevents mould growth and other problems developing within the structure of the greenhouse. While outside temperatures are rising in the morning, keep window vents or the door open, but close them in the afternoon to conserve the heat. To avoid having to manually adjust the vents, consider installing automatic vent openers, which can be set to open and close at predetermined temperatures.

take care!

Pergolas and arbours may look lovely covered in grapevines, but birds and wasps will also be attracted to the fruit, spoiling your enjoyment of the quiet spot and leaving mess behind. To get the best from these structures, don't use them to grow crops; choose ivy or a flowering, fragrant climber like honeysuckle or jasmine instead.

A LITTLE ROUTINE MAINTENANCE CAN GO A LONG WAY IN KEEPING OUTDOOR BUILDINGS IN GREAT SHAPE FOR YEARS.

• **Give your greenhouse a summer clean** Use the summer months, when plants are moved outdoors, to clean and repair your greenhouse. Wash windows and shelves with detergent and disinfectant (both are necessary for battling insects and diseases, but avoid contact with plants). Use an algaecide to remove slime from flooring and benches. Also, inspect the windows for damage. Temporarily repair cracks with glazing tape, but replace broken panes as soon as possible. Check irrigation hoses for leaks, and repair or replace rusted shelving, frame parts or taps.

Scrub greenhouses well in summer

Easy fixes

• **Refelting a shed roof** The traditional bituminised felt used for most shed roofs should last for 10-15 years, but it will eventually become brittle and can leak or tear. You can lay new felt over old, but you'll do a neater job by stripping away the old first and removing any nails left behind. This also makes it easy to check the roof itself for damage or rot.
• Cut the new felt to length. The strips should run parallel to the ridge and overlap by 25mm at each end. Start at the eaves, using 13mm galvanised nails to fix the felt in place, then finish with an overlapping sheet laid over the ridge. Use adhesive where two sheets overlap.
• For a more attractive and long-lasting finish, use felt shingles. These come in strips and are nailed on in a pattern so that the galvanised nails are covered by the next course of shingles – just like a real slate roof.

A new roof renovates an old shed

How to **choose a new shed**

There are a wide range of sheds and outdoor stores available. To get the best value for money think about how you'll use it, the style you prefer, permanence, size and budget. Always buy bigger, not smaller, if you're undecided, and you'll be less likely to need to upgrade later on.

• **USAGE** Look at how many tools you have and wish to store and all the other things you may want to put in the shed, such as bicycles and garden toys. If you plan to store valuable items, such as power tools, choose a strongly constructed shed, perhaps even a metal store with an integrated base, and secure the door with a good padlock. Consider doing without a window, as this is another potential entry point for a burglar: thefts from garden sheds are common.

• **STYLE** Try to choose a shed that's sympathetic to its surroundings, both in style and size. A single pitch 'lean-to' shed may tuck away down the side of the house or against a fence, while a larger garden could accommodate a much bigger and grander structure.

• **PERMANENCE** Wood and metal sheds and other small outbuildings can often be taken apart if you move, whereas more substantial buildings become permanent structures and additions to the house.

• **SIZE** Wooden sheds in kit form start at about 1.8m x 1.2m, rising to 3m x 1.8m. You'll need an appropriate base: either a concrete slab or timber bearers on paving stones.

• **MATERIALS** Wood is the traditional option, usually made with panels of feather-edged or shiplap boards. Tongued and grooved boards are more expensive, but also better quality. Untreated timber will need regular maintenance, but tanalised timber is longer lasting.
• Metal stores are lightweight so must be fixed down to a secure base, usually concrete, paving slabs or posts sunk into concrete. Other styles have their own galvanised base. Metal sheds require little in the way of maintenance and, because they simply bolt together, make a good choice if you wish to move in the future.
• The windows in most timber kit sheds are made from perspex, and they can often be removed easily from the outside. To make the shed more secure, consider upgrading to toughened glass.

Ponds

A pond is an attractive and wildlife-friendly addition to a garden. Get it right and nature will take over most of the maintenance for you. Make sure you position it in an appropriate place and make it safe if you have children in the household or who visit your garden.

Care and maintenance

● **Options for new ponds** The easiest way to construct a pond is to buy a preformed rigid plastic liner. Dig a hole to fit the shape and line it with sand, then drop the pond in place. Alternatively, use a rubber pond liner and create any shape you like. Include ledges and different depths and a gentle slope on at least one side for wildlife to get in and out. Fit a sheet of underlay to protect the liner from damage from stones and another sheet over the liner, covered with pea shingle, for extra protection.

● **Keep out falling leaves** Dappled light falling onto the water's surface makes for a charming scene, but when the leaves fall in autumn they can quickly clog your pond. Stretch a fine nylon net over the entire pond and secure it with bricks or tent pegs around the edge. Keep the net taut to prevent birds becoming entangled and clear it of leaves regularly.
● A nylon net isn't strong enough to stop children falling into the pond, but if you make a strong wooden frame covered with a tough grade of chicken wire, this will double up as a safety net and leaf catcher.

SAVE £100

Cost to replace 3.5m x 4m butyl pond liner damaged by careless maintenance.

Garden pond maintenance

Watch out for signs of these common garden pond problems and follow the simple repair tips to keep your pond healthy and watertight. Always remember that a pump used to drain a pond or to power a fountain must be plugged in to a safe outdoor electrical socket.

● **PUNCTURED LINERS** The hardest part of fixing a hole in a pond liner is finding its location. To narrow down your search, let the water level drop – the water will stop draining at the level of the leak. Areas where ponds flow over waterfalls or into other ponds are common problem spots. Carefully move plants and rocks and examine the liner. Once you find the leak, scrub the area with a scouring pad to remove dirt, then dry it thoroughly. Using a repair kit (available from most garden centres), apply the adhesive and patching material, then let it dry and cure based on directions.

● **DROOPING LINERS AND WICKING WATER** Flexible liners can settle and water will creep over the edge. Look for wet spots around the edge of the pond, then prop up the sagging liner by raising the edge up with soil. Water can also use plants or exposed areas of soil to climb up and out of a pond, known as 'wicking'. The solution is to move the plants away from the edge of the pond or create a break in the 'bridge' to stop the wicking.

● **PLUMBING LEAKS** Check the soil around pumps, valves and hoses for wet areas. If the leak is in a pipe or hose, carefully unearth the pipe, then, with the pump running, track down the exact location of the leak. Sometimes the solution is as simple as retightening a hose clamp. If a hose or pipe is leaking, the most effective repair is often to splice in a new section.

How to spring-clean a pond

Around every five years, a garden pond will probably need a thorough clean-out.
Do this in early spring, before fish and other creatures start breeding.

3 Scoop out the mud from the bottom using a net or sieve – don't worry about removing every last bit. Pile the mud on a plastic sheet next to the pond and leave it there for a couple of days so that any creatures can crawl back into the water.

1 Remove all pond plants and place them in buckets part-filled with pond water. Prepare three large bowls of clean water. Scoop out fish and other wildlife, and keep fish, spawn and snails in separate bowls (fish need wide containers for plenty of oxygen). Put some plants in with the fish for shelter and food.

2 Use buckets to bale out the pond, or siphon off the water with a hose, collecting the water in buckets, bins, paddling pools and other large containers.

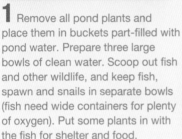

4 Scrub inside the pond with a stiff brush and clean water – don't use detergents. Bale out and discard the resulting dirty water. Refill the pond, using a combination of rainwater and the water salvaged from draining the pond, balancing them so that the water looks clean. Top up with tap water, if needed, then replace the plants.

5 Allow temperatures to stabilise for a day or so before replacing fish, spawn and snails.

Store pumps for winter

Your pond will become dormant for winter, so now is the time to lift and clean a submersible pump. Lift it out of the water, with the brick on which it is mounted (right). Carefully remove the filter (far right) then clean the pump thoroughly in fresh water. Drain the pump and allow it to dry before putting it away for winter. Drain an external pump and wrap it in bubble wrap to insulate it.

6 HOME PROTECTION

Dealing with emergencies and disasters is all about staying calm, knowing what to expect and being prepared. This section will help you to guard against some of the worst disasters, such as fire and flood, with tips about minimising damage, safeguarding yourself and your family, and advice on clearing up in the aftermath.

There's also advice on dealing with invasive pests or insects, problems with mould and rot, and the perils of bad weather. Read on to learn how to avoid these setbacks and how to tackle them when they do arise.

You'll also find out how best to secure your home against intruders, whether you're popping to the shops or leaving the house empty while you go on holiday.

Fortunately, there are many precautions you can take to guard against all these potential threats and keep yourself, your family and your home safe. Read through these pages carefully, do what you need to do and then relax, knowing that you're prepared for anything.

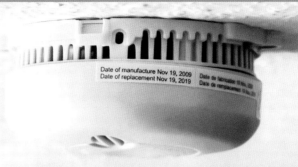

Date of manufacture Nov 19, 2009
Date of replacement Nov 19, 2019
Date de fabrication 19 Nov. 2009
Date de remplacement 19 Nov. 2019

Fire and
carbon monoxide safety

A fire in your home is devastating, both emotionally and materially. Fires can destroy your property and threaten the lives of your family. The good news is that there are easy steps you can take to protect your family and your home from a fire and from dangerous fumes released by household appliances. Follow these tips to be prepared, stay safe and make sure that everyone in the house knows what to do in an emergency.

Be prepared

● **Maintain your smoke detectors** Battery-operated smoke detectors are effective and easy to install but won't do you any good if they're not operating properly. Follow this simple but vital routine:

● Once a month, check each detector by pressing the test button until the alarm sounds. If the unit has no test button, light a candle, blow it out and hold the smoking wick near the detector. If the alarm doesn't sound in 30 seconds, replace the battery. Keep spare batteries in the house so that you can put in a new battery as soon as it's needed.

● Twice a year, open the case and gently vacuum inside using the cleaner's soft-brush attachment. If the case doesn't open, vacuum through the holes.

● Change the battery once a year. Do it on your birthday and you'll be unlikely ever to forget.

● After ten years, install a new detector.

● A mains-powered smoke alarm removes the risk of failure through dead batteries, but it must be fitted by a qualified electrician and wired into the electricity supply. Back-up batteries are included in case of a power cut. The alarm should still be checked every month to make sure it works.

SAVE £1,000
Cost of relining a flue that's damaged by a chimney fire.

• **Rehearse a family escape plan** Don't wait for a fire to break out to start thinking about an escape strategy. Draw a rough plan of your house, showing all its doors, windows, hallways, porches and low roofs. Devise two escape routes for each room, mark them on the map and make sure that your whole family understands them. Without frightening everyone, it's worth holding occasional fire drills at night so that it becomes routine and everyone can follow the shortest routes to the outside automatically. Just as in an office or school, establish an outdoor meeting place where you can count heads and know that everyone is safe.

• **Fewer false alarms in the kitchen** Smoke alarms in or near kitchens can be set off by cooking fumes or burnt toast. After too many noisy interruptions, it's tempting to disable the alarm. Instead, move it to a less sensitive position or consider fitting a heat sensor alarm in its place. These sound when the temperature rises to a level that indicates a fire, rather than reacting to the smoke in the air.

The do's and don'ts of fire prevention

Do ...

• Install and maintain smoke detectors and keep appropriate fire extinguishers on hand in garages, workshops and kitchens.

• Keep passageways, doors and stairways clear and easy to navigate.

• Keep curtains, bedding and upholstered furniture away from heaters, fireplaces and stoves.

• Unplug televisions, computers and other electrical appliances when you won't be using them for a while.

• Sleep with your doors closed. If there's a fire, this will help to contain it while you wake up and escape.

• Check extension cords for defects and replace any that are damaged.

• Keep tea towels, kitchen roll and other flammable items away from stoves and hobs.

• Replace doors leading to an integral garage with steel doors, or at least solid wood ones, which have a greater fire resistance.

• Regularly clean your tumble dryer's filter – a common cause of fires.

• Keep a torch near your bed in case a fire causes a power failure.

• Position your barbecue at least 60cm from anything that could burn. If it's a gas barbecue, make sure it's totally rust-free; a rusted area could develop into a gas leak that creates a fire.

Don't ...

• Smoke in bed, in an armchair or on a sofa in front of the television when you're tired or have been drinking.

• Overload electrical circuits. Multiple devices plugged into a socket can cause a fire.

• Leave unattended candles burning.

• Allow children to play with matches, lighters or candles.

• Keep anything combustible within 1m of your boiler.

• Try to restart a dwindling fire by squirting it with lighter fluid. Add kindling instead.

• Keep piles of newspapers, oily cloths or flammable chemicals indoors. If they become too warm, they may catch fire through spontaneous combustion.

• Keep tins of paint in an understairs cupboard. They may catch fire and set fire to your main escape route.

TEST EACH SMOKE DETECTOR
ONCE A MONTH.

In case of fire

● **Contain small fires quickly** If a small fire breaks out, get everyone out of the house and dial 999 for the fire brigade. Then, if the fire is still small, try to put it out with a fire extinguisher, but remember that any fire can escalate fast, producing deadly smoke and fumes. If you're in any doubt, don't try to tackle the blaze.

● When using an extinguisher, position yourself between the fire and an escape route. Work with a sweeping motion, aiming the nozzle at the bottom of the flames. If the fire gets out of control, leave the house quickly, closing all doors behind you to help to contain the fire.

● Make sure you use the correct fire extinguisher. If you spray a water jet onto an electrical fire without first turning off the electricity at the consumer unit, you can make the situation much worse. Use a dry-powder (blue label) extinguisher for fires in electrical equipment, and water (red), foam (cream) or dry powder (blue) on freely burning materials, such as wood, textiles and paper.

● Keep a fire blanket in the kitchen for smothering cooking fires caused by overheating oil. Alternatively, throw a damp tea towel over the flames.

● **A safe escape** At the first signs of smoke or fire, get everyone out of the house as quickly as possible. Don't stop to collect valuables or keepsakes. Don't even stop to call the fire brigade: call from outside on a mobile phone or from a neighbour's house. When escaping from a burning house, follow these tips to keep yourself and your family safe:

● Don't panic. Keep a cool head and concentrate on getting to safety.

● If you're trapped in a room, stay near the floor. If you can't get out through the window, open it to let in fresh air and let smoke out.

● If you can get out and you know where the fire is, use a route that moves away from it.

● Remember the escape map you drew and take the safest exit route.

● Close all doors behind you as you pass through the house to the outside.

● Feel any door in your path with your hand. If it's hot, don't open it. If it's cool, open it slowly and stay behind it. If you feel heat or pressure coming through the door, slam it shut.

● If a hall or stairway is filled with smoke, try to find another way out.

smart idea

Cleaning up after a fire is very different from regular house cleaning. If you've had a major fire, hire a fire restoration contractor to do the work for you. You should be able to find one in the telephone book.

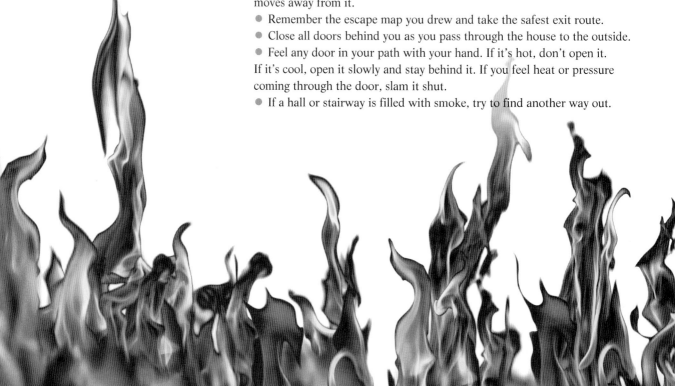

Smoke detectors

The best defence against fire is early detection. It's critical that you install smoke detectors on all levels of your house, including the basement if you have one, and outside each sleeping area. Put one inside any bedroom that houses a large electrical appliance, such as a television or computer. Install alarms at a safe distance from steamy showers and cookers that could trigger the sensor unnecessarily.

● There are two basic types of alarms. An ionisation unit emits a small amount of radiation that's detected by a sensor and sounds an alarm when smoke blocks the radiation from reaching the sensor. This type is best for detecting fast-burning fires from paper, wood and fat. A photoelectric (optical) unit, triggered when smoke breaks a beam of light, is better at sensing smoky fires, such as smoldering mattresses, and is less likely to go off accidentally. Combined models are also available. Always make sure your unit carries the British Standard Kitemark and meets British Standard BS 5446-1.

Mains-powered, linked smoke alarms

Most smoke detectors are battery-powered (right), but some alarms are wired into your home's electricity supply, so there's no danger of the battery running out. They even have back-up batteries, which take over in the event of a power cut. A mains-powered smoke alarm must be fitted by a qualified electrician.

● Fitting several alarms all linked together could dramatically increase your escape time, particularly in large houses or if someone in the house is hard of hearing. With this kind of system all the alarms will sound as soon as one of them detects signs of a fire, so you'll be woken upstairs as soon as a fire triggers the downstairs unit. With stand-alone smoke alarms, the upstairs alarms wouldn't be triggered until the smoke or flames themselves had filled the house and reached the landing or the bedroom.

● If you must pass through a smoke-filled area, crawl along the floor, where the air is clearer.
● In a smoke-filled area, take only short breaths through your nose. Cover your nose with a damp handkerchief, if possible.
● Once outside, don't go back into the house.

● **Stop, drop and roll** If clothing catches fire, act quickly. If it's your own clothing, cross your arms over your chest, drop to the ground, and roll over and over slowly. If a wool blanket, coat, rug or heavy curtain is within reach, wrap yourself in it and roll on the floor.
● If someone else's clothing catches fire, get them on the floor quickly, even tripping them up. Smother the fire with a wool blanket, coat, rug or curtain. Spray the person with a fire extinguisher if one is handy, but be careful to keep the spray away from the person's face.
● Once the fire is out, don't be tempted to pull burned clothing away from the skin as you might cause serious injury. Call for an ambulance straight away.

5 ways to minimise the risk of carbon monoxide poisoning

1 Have your heating system, boiler, any gas fires or heaters, chimneys and vents checked and serviced annually by qualified, CORGI-registered gas engineers and a professional chimney sweep.

2 If a pilot light on your boiler goes out, relight it immediately. Before activating the ignition spark, open a nearby window and wait for a while to make sure the air is free of gas that may have escaped while the pilot light was out. Domestic gas has a strong smell to prevent leaks going undetected. A pilot light that repeatedly goes out can be a sign of another fault, so get your boiler checked by a professional.

3 Never operate fuel-burning appliances inside your home, garage or any enclosed space unless they are safely vented to the outside.

4 Never leave a car running in an attached garage, even with the main garage door open. Carbon monoxide may seep into the house.

5 On every floor of your home and near sleeping areas, install a carbon monoxide detector that meets the requirements of the current British Standard BS 7860 and carries the British Standard Kitemark. Make sure it's not blocked by furniture or draperies.

A CO detector is cheap and easy to fit

Preventing carbon monoxide poisoning

● **Know the signs of carbon monoxide (CO) poisoning** Inhaling carbon monoxide causes headaches, dizziness, nausea and drowsiness. Get anyone suffering these symptoms into the open air quickly and call for an ambulance. Once the person is safe, quickly open all doors and windows in the contaminated room, turn off any combustion appliances and leave the house. Call the fire brigade and Transco Gas Emergency line and report what has happened. Before turning your fuel-burning appliances back on, make sure a qualified technician checks them.

● Apart from symptoms of illness in a victim, there are other signs of a carbon monoxide leak to look out for. The boiler pilot light continually blowing out, a gas flame burning orange or yellow rather than blue, soot or a musty smell around a gas appliance or a scorched area on the appliance, and an increase in condensation on windows can all signify a fault in a gas appliance that could be giving off carbon monoxide.

● **Install a CO detector** The best models have test buttons and digital displays (left) that show the room's level of carbon monoxide. All sound an alarm when levels are too high. The concentration of carbon monoxide is measured in parts per million (ppm). Exposure to levels of 1 to 70ppm is harmless to most people, but those with heart problems might experience an increase in chest pain. Levels above 70ppm may cause headache, fatigue or nausea. Levels above 150ppm can cause disorientation, unconsciousness and even death.

● **Test your detector once a month** Hold the test button for 10 to 15 seconds; if the alarm doesn't sound, replace the battery. If that doesn't work, the unit is malfunctioning: replace it.

Home security

Keeping your house safe from burglars is mostly a matter of making it look like it's more trouble than it's worth for thieves to break in. The easiest way to keep your home from looking like an easy target is to keep your doors and windows securely locked. But there are other ways you can fool intruders, too.

Preventive measures

● **Secure all doors and windows** It won't do much good to lock your doors and windows unless they are solid and perfectly secured. The following measures can all help to increase security:

● Replace hollow-core outside doors with steel doors or solid wood.

● Don't rely on easily broken door chains. Fit deadbolts instead (see page 300).

● Install a wide-angle (180 degree) peephole in your front door. Simply drill a hole to put it in. If the bell rings and you don't see anyone through the peephole, don't open the door.

● Add key-operated locks to all windows, even on a first or second floor. Keep the keys close to hand so that you can still escape in an emergency, but not where they can be reached through an open or broken window.

● Trim overgrown shrubbery bordering your home. This allows you a clear view through your windows, and prevents burglars from lying in wait behind the bushes.

● Install deadbolts on outside doors – and use them.

● If you have an integral garage, secure the interconnecting door as well as you would your front door. If a burglar can get into your garage by lifting an up-and-over door, it's possible to work out of sight and undetected to break into the house.

● If you have cellar or basement doors that lead to the outside, secure them from the inside with sliding crossbars.

SAVE 12.5%

Potential annual saving on a home contents insurance policy if you install a burglar alarm with 24 hour monitoring.

More home safety do's and don'ts

Do ...	Don't ...
● Build a fence with gates around your property (but don't obscure windows).	● Leave packaging from new computers, televisions or appliances outside the house. They let burglars know you have expensive new equipment inside.
● Store valuables in a fireproof, waterproof safe.	
● Establish a neighbourhood watch scheme, and advertise it in the area.	● Leave ladders or tools unlocked and in plain sight: they can be used to break into your home. Lock ladders securely to brackets fixed to the house wall if you cannot store them in a locked shed.
● Install motion-activated security lights to help to prevent intruders from working undetected.	
	● Forget to cancel milk and paper deliveries whenever you go away.

How to fit a deadbolt to a door

A rack bolt, or deadbolt, adds security to a door, making it harder to break down. It can be operated from inside with a key or by fitting thumb-turn knobs.

1 Mark a central point on the edge of the door where you want to fit the bolt. Use a try square and pencil to continue the mark onto the inner face of the door.

2 Drill a hole into the edge of the door to the diameter and depth of the body of the bolt.

3 Wind out the bolt and push it into the hole. Mark round the faceplate, withdraw the bolt with pliers and cut a shallow recess for the faceplate with a chisel.

4 Hold the bolt flush with the face of the door and mark the spot for the key. Drill a hole (following the manufacturer's instructions to gauge the correct size) through the inside face of the door only.

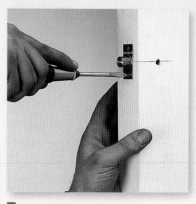

5 Push the bolt back into the door and screw the faceplate to the edge of the door. Check that the bolt operates correctly. If necessary, enlarge the keyhole.

6 Screw the keyhole plate to the inside of the door.

7 Close the door and wind out the bolt to mark the door jamb. There's usually a pimple on the end of the bolt to mark the wood.

8 Open the door and drill a hole to the required depth at the mark in the jamb. Check that the bolt will go smoothly into this hole.

9 Hold the cover plate over the hole, draw around it, cut out a shallow recess and screw the cover plate in place. Check the operation of the bolt and make any necessary adjustments.

A motion-sensitive light is a deterrent

● **Put your lamps on a schedule** Programming your lamps to turn on and off while you're away can help to make potential intruders believe that you're home. There are several ways to do this. One way is to screw light-sensing sockets into standard lamp sockets that will turn the lights on automatically at dusk. You can also use a plug-in timer to turn lamps on and off at certain hours. Finally, you can replace a standard light switch with a switch timer that you set by turning a dial. Some models memorise and repeat your daily lighting pattern; others can be set to go on and off at random times to give the appearance of normal activity.

● **Light up your home's exterior** Install lights at each side of your entrance door and leave them on all night, or fit them with dusk-to-dawn light-sensitive bulbs – if one burns out, you'll still have an illuminated entrance. It's also a good idea to ask an electrician to install floodlights with motion-sensing (PIR) switches – if anyone approaches your home,

PROGRAMMING LAMPS TO TURN ON AND OFF WHILE YOU'RE AWAY MAY MAKE INTRUDERS BELIEVE THAT YOU'RE HOME.

STOP MILK AND NEWSPAPER DELIVERIES. PILED-UP NEWSPAPERS AND ROWS OF MILK BOTTLES ARE A SURE SIGN YOU'RE AWAY.

the lights will detect their movements and turn on, alerting you to the interloper's presence and possibly discouraging them from going any further. You can adjust the direction of the sensors, the size of the detection field and the sensitivity of the system to avoid the light being triggered unnecessarily by passing traffic, cats or even swaying branches. Most models have an override switch.

● **Take precautions before you go on holiday** When you're away for longer than just a day, it can soon become obvious to potential burglars that your house is empty. Follow this advice to keep your home safe – it's as much part of preparing for your holiday as packing the cases.

● Stop milk and newspaper deliveries and arrange a temporary 'stop mail' service with the Post Office. Piled-up newspapers and post, and rows of mik bottles, are a clear sign that no-one is home. Better still, ask a relative or neighbour to go in every day to check the house and pick up any post.

● Ask a neighbour to mow your lawn and water your plants so that the garden doesn't look neglected towards the end of your holiday.

● Leave a car parked in your driveway, or invite a neighbour to park their own car in your driveway periodically.

● Install timers on lamps around the house so that they turn on and off automatically, giving the impression that you're home.

● Leave curtains and blinds open, as you would if you were at home during the day. You could also ask someone to close and open curtains for you or install time-operated automatic closers.

● Tune a radio to a talk station at a volume loud enough to be barely heard outside, but not understood. Put the radio on a timer programmed to turn it on and off and it can give the impression that people are talking inside the house.

● Leave a key with a friend, along with an itinerary and instructions on how you can be reached. Leave the phone numbers of your plumber and electrician with the neighbour in case of an emergency.

● Turn on all security alarms and timers as you leave.

● **Lock up last thing at night** Just being in the house isn't enough to guarantee that your possessions are safe. Many burglaries happen when the homeowners are in another room, in the garden or asleep in bed. Never leave the front door open – it's too easy for someone to slip in unnoticed and steal valuables or help themselves to a key for use later. Lock the doors if you're home alone and taking a shower or bath, or are in the back garden, and always lock up last thing at night. Be alert to the risk of distraction burglaries, where a caller to the front door occupies your attention while an accomplice slips in through the back.

● Don't risk locking yourself in so securely that you cannot escape in the event of a fire. Mortise locks are perfect for when you're out, but can cost you time if you need to fumble to find and use a key when you're in a panic and in the dark. A better solution is to fit a deadbolt (see page 300) that you can operate with a permanently fixed thumb-turn, or to use simple throw-bolts from the inside at night.

GIVE A FRIEND A KEY WHILE YOU'RE AWAY.

Which alarm system is right for you?

Don't rely on your barking dog to alert you to burglars. If you want maximum security, have a burglar alarm system installed. There are two basic types of burglar alarms: perimeter systems and motion detectors.

Perimeter systems

A perimeter system sounds an alarm if someone opens a door or window. Magnetic sensors are installed on closed windows and doors, and adjacent switches are recessed into the frame. When the door or window is closed, the magnet and switch are close enough together to form an electric circuit. If the window or door is opened when the system is armed, the circuit is broken and the alarm sounds. Glass-break alarms that stick to any glass window or door and sound when the glass receives an abrupt shock are another option.

Motion detectors

If something moves inside a room with a motion detector, cutting across its invisible beam, it sets off an alarm. This kind of detector should be installed across doorways and other passageways around a metre above the floor. If it's too low, it may be activated by household pets, but if it's too high then intruders can easily move beneath the beam. It's also a good idea to position sensors in the corners of each room near the ceiling to survey the main areas of foot traffic. Sensor pads can also be used, fitted beneath carpets in doorways or at the top of the stairs to trigger the alarm when they're stepped on.

● All alarm systems consist of sensors that are connected to a control box, a remote-control key switch to turn the system on and off, and an alarm that rings a bell or siren or dials the police (or security company) or your own mobile phone. The control panel should be near the door you use most often, but out of reach from the outside if a window is broken.

● The most efficient burglar alarms are hard-wired systems that combine both perimeter alarms and motion detectors. There are also wireless systems that use radio frequency signals to monitor the components, many of which simply plug into standard electrical sockets or are battery-powered.

● A full burglar alarm system is best installed by a professional, although it's simple to fit individual motion detectors that scan single rooms and sound an alarm if anyone enters.

Pest infestations

We may enjoy some wildlife in our gardens, but few of us welcome it in our home. The best way to keep insects, mice and other pests at bay is to understand the ways in which they try to get in. Keep unwanted guests at bay with vigilance, preventive maintenance and a rapid response to problems that arise. If you don't act fast you could find yourself with a hefty bill from the pest-control company.

Preventive measures

● **Inspect your home yearly** Take an annual walk around your house, inside and out, looking for telltale signs of insect infestation, such as rotting wood, mud tubes leading from the soil to door sills and other wooden areas, or ants congregating close to the house. If you spot insects, deal with the problem fast to stand the best chance of eradicating them.

● **What to do about woodworm** The telltale holes – like holes in a dartboard – that signal the presence of woodworm can be guaranteed to send any homeowner into a panic, imagining collapsing beams and ruined floorboards. But in fact, woodworm is rarely a problem in modern homes and not all woodworm is cause for alarm. If your home is kept dry, through normal modern heating and ventilation, most woodworm will be unable to survive.

● You need only worry about evidence of woodworm in houses without central heating as the beetle larvae that cause the problems only thrive in these conditions.

SAVE £120

Cost for a professional pest-control team to eliminate a mouse infestation and proof your home against further invasions.

A MOUSE CAN SQUEEZE THROUGH A GAP AS NARROW AS A PENCIL.

● Most wood-boring beetles lay their eggs in freshly fallen sapwood in the wild, as this makes the most nutritious habitat for their young. The same applies within houses, where most woodworm damage occurs in new timbers, in new builds or extensions. Once the house is lived in and dries out, the woodworm will move elsewhere.

● **Ants in your pantry** It's easy to see that ants and flies are attracted to all things sweet, so a simple but important step in keeping them out of your home is to avoid tempting them in with food left on kitchen surfaces or food preparation areas left with scraps on them.

● Spring-clean your food cupboards once a year, emptying them, wiping them with an all-purpose household cleaner and throwing away any old food before you restock the shelves.

● Stop ants at the doorstep by using an insecticide 'pen', sold in supermarkets and DIY stores, to draw a line through the point at which they are entering your home. They will not cross the line.

STOP ANTS AT THE DOOR.

● **Keep rodents at a distance** The best way to control mice and rats is to block any possible entry points into your home. A mouse can squeeze through a gap as small as the width of a pencil, so check all round your walls and window frames, cupboards, doors and air bricks every year for signs of deterioration that could leave gaps big enough for rodents. Check holes in walls where drainage pipes run out, too. Seal any gaps with exterior-grade mastic, steel wool, fine metal mesh or anything else that will effectively block the gap.

● Signs that you have mice in the house include scratching or scurrying noises; small, dark droppings left along walls or in cupboards; teeth marks on wood, plastic, cables or other hard materials that have been gnawed; and a distinctive ammonia-like smell, particularly noticeable in enclosed spaces. You may even find a nest of shredded paper or fabric.

● Act quickly if you think you have mice, before they multiply into a big problem. Wooden mousetraps or humane live traps are widely available.

● **Don't let your pet bring trouble into the house** If your dog or cat catches fleas, you can find your home infested within a matter of weeks. While the fleas don't carry disease, they do bite and are no-one's idea of a welcome houseguest. Make sure that your pets wear flea collars or have regular treatment to keep them free of fleas, and be sure to vacuum regularly, particularly around your pet's favourite spot, using the strongest suction you can. Try to encourage your pet to stay in rooms without carpet.

● **Dealing with a wasps' nest** If you spot wasps repeatedlly going in and out of a particular spot in your eaves, house wall or garden shed, you may have located a nest built in your loft, within the cavity of the wall or in the eaves of a shed or garage. Wait for a cool day or late evening then treat the nest with a proprietary aerosol spray or foam. Wear protective clothing and take care to aim the spray through the entrance hole.

● Keep pointing in good condition to prevent wasps and bees getting into your wall cavities through cracks in the brickwork.

Mould and dry rot

It's just not possible to eliminate mould and fungi completely from your house. A more realistic goal is to control their growth, and the best way to do that is to keep moisture at bay. Even dry rot – despite its name – is moisture-related. Good ventilation and moisture control are the keys to preventing serious problems that could even cause structural damage.

SAVE £5,000

The average cost to eliminate an area of dry rot and repair damaged timbers in a floor, where the rot is caused by a simple blocked air brick.

smart idea

If you keep potted plants on a wooden floor or deck, avoid moisture problems by setting the planters on pot feet (available at garden centres and DIY stores), which allow air to circulate underneath.

Preventive measures

● **Patrol your property** Inspect your house regularly for signs of mould and rot and the moisture problems that cause them.

● At least twice a year, check your roof for leaks. Look for loose roof tiles and cracks in pointing at the eaves (see page 131).

● Inspect your basement (if you have one), crawl spaces (if you can access them), loft, porch, house perimeter and any other areas, such as gullies on the roof, where water can collect or seep in.

● Check roof eaves and door and window frames for the signs of dry rot: soft, crumbly wood and a powdery surface.

● Keep gutters clean and free of fallen leaves, which trap moisture and can cause the gutters to overflow. Leaking gutters or pipes that are soaking nearby timber joists and rafters could lead to wood rot.

● Examine the sealant around windows, doors and pipes that run through external walls, and renew it as needed. Make sure weather stripping around doors and windows is doing its job of keeping moisture out.

● If you have a wooden deck, inspect the ground-to-post contact points.

● Inside the house, check bathroom and kitchen plumbing for leaks. Look for signs of mould growth around showers and baths and on tiles. Dry rot is commonly found below leaking baths and shower trays, so be alert for any signs of leaks and fix them promptly.

● Make certain that vent pipes from cooker or bathroom extractor fans, and the tumble dryer vent pipe, if it has one, aren't cracked or split and are venting efficiently to the outside, not directing warm, moist air into your loft or wall cavity, where it could encourage mould and rot.

● Condensation that forms on single-glazed windows will soak wooden frames and lead to rot. Open windows slightly to minimise condensation and wipe them down to remove the moisture.

● **Keep bathroom air circulating** Good ventilation is essential to discouraging the growth of mould and mildew in bathrooms. After showers and baths, run the extractor fan for about 20 minutes, or long enough to dry out the room. If your bathroom doesn't have a fan, open the window – but consider having a fan installed, as this is a much more effective solution. Fans are now a requirement in any new bathrooms.

● Automatic extractor fans make it impossible to forget this crucial ventilation habit. Fans can be wired in to the light switch so that they

Damp can seep through rotten window frames or a leaking roof

Ventilate wardrobes to avoid mould

come on as soon as the light is switched on and continue to run for a preset time after it's switched off. More sophisticated models incorporate a humidistat, which turns the fan on when humidity in the room reaches a predetermined level.

● To increase air flow to bathroom cupboards, consider replacing solid doors with louvered ones.

● **Bleach it** To remove surface mould from tile corners in showers and baths, use a solution of one part bleach to ten parts water in a plastic spray bottle. Make sure the room is well-ventilated – open windows and keep the bathroom door open – before spraying directly on the mould spots. Wait for 15 minutes, then wipe with a damp sponge.

● **Blast it** To remove deep-seated mould and keep it from coming back, use a solution of 1 teaspoon of water softener, 1 tablespoon of ammonia and 1 tablespoon of vinegar in 200ml of warm water. Wipe the walls with this mixture then rinse with fresh water and buff the tiles dry.

Single glazing is prone to condensation

● **Freshen up** To get rid of musty smells, you need to remove the moisture problem itself: ventilate the room and scrub affected walls with a bleach-and-water solution (see above) and a nylon-bristled brush. If necessary, paint walls and ceilings with a paint that contains fungicide.

● **Keep loft vents clear** Warm, moist air will rise through the house and collect in the upper reaches of your loft, where it can lead to damage in your structural roof timbers. Make sure that soffit vents and any roof vents in the loft are kept clear (see page 155).

● **Direct water away from your house** Make sure the ground slopes away from the walls of your house. Channel water from downpipes away from the foundations into the main drainage system or a well-maintained soakaway (see page 141). Trim overhanging branches and plants at the foot of the walls: these both provide opportunities for moisture to collect, and roots near the foundations can interfere with your drainage systems.

take care!

Cleaning up a heavy mould infestation is often a job best left to a mould-removal specialist. If you do tackle surface mould or mildew yourself, avoid contact with the mould and caustic cleaning products by wearing rubber gloves, goggles and a face mask. To minimse the risk of the problem recurring, throw away any items that were affected by the mould as they may harbour spores.

Bad weather

High winds, snow and floods can wreak havoc on your home and property, but a well-maintained house and garden should be able to withstand all but the worst of the British weather. Follow these simple tips to prepare yourself and your home so that you can shelter inside in safety and let the storm rage around you. Don't forget about sheds and outbuildings and do what you can to avoid your house being damaged by trees or fences from your own garden.

SAVE £100

Cost to repair a window smashed by a falling tree branch snapped off by high winds.

💡 **smart idea**

Check the small print of your home insurance. Make sure you know exactly what you're covered for and which potential problems fall outside the scope of your policy. If you live in a known flood-risk area, for example, you'll need a special flood-risk policy.

Pre-winter checks

● **Check your roof** Roofs are vulnerable to high winds, which will lift any loose tiles. Driving rain will then find and enlarge the tiniest openings, resulting in leaks that can damage the rooms below. Before winter, check the roof (see page 131) and repair problems right away.

● Building Regulations require every roof tile to be 'mechanically fixed', or nailed, around the eaves and verges (open edges) as well as every fourth or fifth course, or row. The regulations only apply to new roofs, but if you do need to replace tiles, it's worth asking your roofer to nail them down.

● If your garden is exposed, check the roof fixings on sheds and outbuildings, too. Corrugated plastic sheeting often used on lean-to stores or shelters is particularly prone to wind damage and must be well fixed.

● **Keep your trees trimmed** During a windstorm, trees and branches can fall onto your house and cause severe damage. If you have a large tree close to the house, prune away some inside branches to open up the crown of the tree. The less dense the branches, the more wind can pass through them, reducing the risk of branches breaking. You should also check your trees for signs of weakness: remove any trees that are drying out, leaning more than 15 degrees or have heavily damaged roots.

If bad weather is forecast

● **Trim troublesome trees** If a storm partially uproots a tree, splinters a large branch or causes a major split at a fork (where two major branches meet) the tree or heavy branches may weaken in time and fall onto your roof or pose a threat to passers-by. Ask a professional tree surgeon to remove or trim large branches or trees. For small trees or small, low branches, you may be able to do the job yourself (see page 263).

● **Repair broken fences** Loose or damaged fence panels that wobble a bit on normal days can be ripped apart and even become dangerous missiles in high winds. If you've been putting off making a repair, prioritise it when high winds are expected. You can brace a loose panel temporarily by driving long stakes into the ground at an angle on either side and wedging them under the top rail or a lower horizontal rail of the panel, but it's better to make a more permanent fix.

● Reinforce a loose fence post by sinking a concrete spur next to it and bolting the two together – these short concrete posts are usually supplied by DIY stores with holes pre-drilled, but you'll need to drill corresponding holes through the existing timber post. Make sure that the post is level before ramming hardcore around the base of the post and bedding it in with concrete.

● Repair rotten or split horizontal rails and replace entire panels that are damaged beyond repair. For more tips on fence repairs, see page 284.

● **Anchor down sheds and greenhouses** Even a well-stocked shed can be upended in high winds, as the wind blows through the gap underneath it. And greenhouses, which do not usually have an integral base, are easily tipped over. Fix a heavy-duty hook to each corner of the building (right) and keep four strong guy ropes and pegs inside. When a storm is forecast, peg the shed down.

Tether your shed if winds are forecast

General precautions

● **Get flood insurance** If you want to avoid catastrophic costs due to floods, the number one rule is to have proper insurance. Most house insurance policies don't cover losses due to floods, so if your house is in an area prone to flooding, buy separate flood insurance.

● Flooding is becoming more common, not necessarily because of climate change but because more homes are being built on flood plains and more people are paving areas of their garden for parking, which puts added pressure on drains and can contribute to flash floods.

● You can check whether your home is in a flood-risk area by visiting the Environment Agency's website. This check is a standard part of the searches your solicitor performs when you're buying a house.

● You can help to prevent small floods within your own grounds by keeping drains and surface-water gullies clean and clear at all times. Don't allow leaves and other debris to build up, as this will prevent water from draining away during a heavy storm.

● **Take an inventory** Make a detailed list of your home's contents, and take photos of everything. If a flood causes damage and you want to make an insurance claim, this will help to prove what exactly was inside.

● **Keep an emergency kit at the ready** If you live in a remote rural area, store some emergency essentials all together, including torches and candles, a first-aid kit, a small supply of energy bars and tinned food (don't forget a can opener) and blankets.

take care!

If there's danger of a flood in your area, tune in to a local radio or television station to keep track of what's happening and the level of the risk. If you're advised to evacuate, do so – but first turn off the gas, electricity and water supplies. Lock up the house and leave quickly.

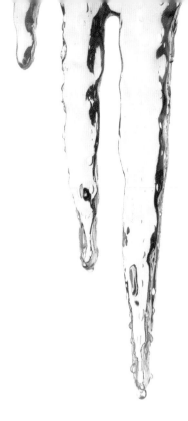

● **Don't go anywhere during a flood** If you're at home when a flood begins, stay there. Don't try to wade through the water to drier ground unless the emergency services are there to guide you, and, above all, don't drive through flooded streets. Even moving water less than knee-deep can sweep people off their feet – 30cm can wash away a vehicle. About half of flood-related deaths occur when people are trapped in cars that stall while being driven through flooded areas. If your car stalls, abandon it immediately. Instead of leaving home, stay put and do the following:
● Pile sandbags at doors to try to keep back the water.
● Lift any furniture you can off the floor to minimise damage, but don't waste time doing this if the water is already coming in – it's more important to keep yourself rather than your belongings safe.
● If the waters start creeping in and you cannot leave the house, move upstairs. Take warm clothing and your emergency care kit with you wherever you go.
● Fill sinks and baths with water. You may need it later if the water supply becomes contaminated.
● If the floor is flooded or any wiring gets wet, turn off the electricity at the main consumer unit (see page 174).

● **Keep your water pipes from freezing** Frozen pipes are probably the most common cold-weather problem that homeowners face. Water expands as it freezes, and eventually pipes, whether they're PVC plastic or copper, burst. The most susceptible pipes are the ones that run through unheated areas of the home, such as to outside taps or through the loft, above the loft insulation. Burst pipes result in major plumbing bills and the water that gushes out can ruin floors, furniture and other belongings. To prevent these headaches, remember the following:
● Before winter, turn off and drain the water supply to outside taps or fit lagging to the pipes and an insulating jacket to the tap.
● Insulate pipes that run through unheated spaces, including those that carry hot water. These pipes can still freeze when the water heater isn't operating. See pages 222-223 for tips on insulating pipes.
● If you plan to be away from home for an extended period during cold weather, leave the heating on, at a low setting.

● **Tips for a warm and cosy winter** Follow these simple suggestions throughout the winter to keep out the cold:
● Clean gutters and downpipes (see pages 139-141) in late autumn – after the last leaves have fallen – to prevent blockages that can cause gutters to overspill and prevent rain from draining freely away.
● Check areas that let in cold air, such as lofts, garages and spaces under kitchen and bathroom cabinets. Seal any openings or add insulation.
● Trim any tree branches that may damage the house or the outside wiring in a storm.
● Check weatherstripping on doors and windows to make sure that they are watertight and draughtproof (see pages 157-159).
● Turn radiators in unused rooms on at low, to prevent the rooms from

becoming vulnerable to cold and damp. Close the doors to conserve the heat in the rest of the house, but air the rooms from time to time.

Easy fixes

● **Thawing frozen pipes** If you turn on a tap and only a trickle of water comes out, a section of pipe is probably frozen. Find the frozen spot by swabbing along the pipe with a moist rag – frost will form when you reach the ice. Thaw the pipe along its length before it bursts, starting at the end nearest a tap. Leaving the tap open, apply heat with a hair dryer, portable space heater, electric heating pad or hot-water bottle, or wrap the pipe in rags or towels and pour boiling water over it, catching the water in a pan beneath the pipe. Never use a propane torch (blowtorch), as it may heat the water in the pipe to boiling point and make the pipe explode.

APPLY HEAT WITH A HAIR DRYER TO THAW FROZEN PIPES.

● **Patching leaking pipes** If a frozen pipe develops a leak, you can fix it temporarily while waiting for a plumber. First, shut off the water supply and dry the pipe. Fix a small leak by wrapping plastic or duct tape tightly around the damaged section. For a larger repair, slit a section of rubber hose and slip it over the pipe, then hold it in place with tightly twisted wires or two or more hose clamps.

● **Drying out after a flood** Whether your flood was caused by a river bursting its banks or a pipe bursting in the house, the quickest way to dry the affected area is with a combination of dehumidifiers and desk fans. After a serious flood, always get your electrics checked before switching anything on.
● The main flood damage is usually to carpets and plasterboard walls. If your home has been flooded and is in a flood-risk area, consider installing solid, tiled floors and brick or blockwork walls when you make your repairs.

What should I use **to insulate my pipes?**

A variety of insulating materials are available at hardware and DIY stores. You can buy lengths of preshaped foam pipe insulation, cut them to length with a knife and secure them around pipes with clamps or tape. You can also wrap pipes with aluminum insulating tape or felt bandage – with each wrap, overlap the tape by 1cm and secure the ends with duct tape (see pages 222-223).

Pipes that run through stud partitioned walls or within the loft can be bedded in loose-fill loft insulation or mineral wool blanket insulation. You could even wrap the pipes with thick layers of newspaper, held in place with tape. Make sure you wrap joints, bends and valves as thoroughly as straight runs of pipe, just leaving valve handles exposed for use.

Index

PICTURE CREDITS
T = top; C = centre; B = bottom; A = above; L = left; R = right

Images supplied by The Reader's Digest Association, Inc., with the exception of the following:

Front Cover Getty Images/David Fisher/Stockbyte; 2 iStockphoto.com/Andrew Rich; 4 Getty Images/Jeffrey Coolidge; 6 iStockphoto.com/Milos Luzanin; 8 T iStockphoto.com/ Sergey Tumanov, C Getty Images/Tooga, B iStockphoto.com/Jakub Krechowicz; 9 T&C iStockphoto.com/Knape, B iStockphoto.com/Marcela Barsse; 10 iStockphoto.com/Sergey Tumanov; 13 iStockphoto.com/Inspireme; 14 iStockphoto.com/Kutay Tanir; 15 (broom) iStockphoto.com/Floortje; 16 L iStockphoto.com/Scubabartek; 17 iStockphoto.com/Acilo; 19 TL iStockphoto.com/Mirith, R iStockphoto.com/Thomas Perkins, B iStockphoto.com/ Sergei Ivlev; 20 T iStockphoto.com/David Morgan; BL ShutterStock, Inc./Pandapaw, BR ShutterStock, Inc./Alexirius; 21 Alamy Images/Fancy; 22 R ShutterStock, Inc./Simon Krzic; 23 CL iStockphoto.com/Scrambled, C iStockphoto.com/Thumb, R iStockphoto.com/ Frank Boston; 24 TL iStockphoto.com/Irina Tischenko, TR iStockphoto.com/DNY59, CL iStockphoto.com/Floortje; 25 TL ShutterStock, Inc./Joe Belanger, TR iStockphoto.com, BL iStockphoto.com/Roman Milert; 26 TL iStockphoto.com/DeadDuck, CL iStockphoto.com/ Anatoly Romashchenko; 27 R iStockphoto.com/Graphicola; 28 B iStockphoto.com/Patrick Heagrey; 29 T Getty Images/Photo Alto/ Laurence, B iStockphoto.com/Donald Erickson; 31 Getty Images/Stockbyte; 32 C iStockphoto.com/Doug Cannell, R iStockphoto.com/Prill Medien Design & Fotografie, L iStockphoto.com/Carlos Gawronski; 33 iStockphoto.com/ Frank Boston; 35 iStockphoto.com/Andrew Howe; 36 iStockphoto.com/Alex Slobodkin; 37 iStockphoto.com/Gaby Jalbert; 38 Getty Images/Tooga; 48 iStockphoto.com/ StockSnapper; 50 TL iStockphoto.com/Doug Berry; 52 iStockphoto.com/Björn Kindler; 53 iStockphoto.com/Tulcarion; 56-57 B ShutterStock, Inc./Matthew Jacques; 59 T iStockphoto.com/Makkayak; 63 Getty Images/ Photodisc; 64 T iStockphoto.com/Nick Schlax; 67 ShutterStock, Inc./Ingrald Kaldhussater; 70 iStockphoto.com/Joerg Schwanke; 74 Getty Images/Studio Blond; 76 iStockphoto.com/Christina Richards; 77 iStockphoto. com/Aga & Miko Materne; 78 T ShutterStock, Inc./Curt Ziegler, B ShutterStock, Inc./STILL FX; 79 iStockphoto.com/Kata Ribanszky; 81 Top to Bottom: iStockphoto.com/Trevor Hunt, iStockphoto.com/drflet, iStockphoto.com/Linda & Colin McKie, ShutterStock, Inc./Vanessa Nel; 82 Alamy Images/Fancy; 83 iStockphoto.com/Design56; 84 T ShutterStock, Inc.; 86 iStockphoto.com/Jakub Krechowicz; 89 iStockphoto.com/DNY59; 91 T iStockphoto.com/ Lisa F. Young; 93 iStockphoto.com/10320385; 96 iStockphoto.com/Marcus Lindström; 101 iStockphoto.com/Eyewave; 102 Getty Images/Antenna; 104 R iStockphoto.com/ Enviromanic, CA & B iStockphoto.com/Soubrette, CB iStockphoto.com/Adam Dodd; 105 iStockphoto.com/Jelena Popic; 111 T iStockphoto.com/Edward Shaw; 119 BR iStockphoto. com/Rickard Blommengren; 120 ShutterStock, Inc./Home Studio; 121 iStockphoto.com/Dave White; 122 iStockphoto.com/Jack Kelly; 123 iStockphoto.com/Duard van der Westhuizen; 125 B iStockphoto.com; 127 iStockphoto.com/Christine Glade; 136 iStockphoto.com/ Alexander Dunkel; 138 iStockphoto.com/Mitch Aunger; 142 iStockphoto.com/Richard Watson; 143 T iStockphoto.com/Merlin Farewell, B iStockphoto.com/Artur Synenko; 145 iStockphoto.com/Bruno Uhernik; 148 T iStockphoto.com/Betsy Dupuis; 150 iStockphoto.com/Don Nichols; 153 iStockphoto.com/Chris Elwell; 159 T ShutterStock, Inc./Marc Dietrich; 160 iStockphoto.com/ Dead Duck; 165 Getty Images/Image Source; 166 iStockphoto.com/Knape; 170 iStockphoto.com/Morgan Lane Studios; 171 L www.energysavingtrust.org.uk, 171 B & 172 iStockphoto.com/Carlos Caetano; 177 C iStockphoto.com/Pixhook, B British Standards Institution; 179 iStockphoto.com/ Stocksnapper; 180 iStockphoto.com/Andrew Parfenov; 182 T iStockphoto.com/Jonathan Maddock; 186 Getty Images/Momentimages; 190 iStockphoto.com/Craftvision; 191 iStockphoto.com/Dejan Nikolic; 193 T iStockphoto.com/Red Helga, B iStockphoto. com/Mark Richardson; 194 T iStockphoto.com/Brian Brew, BL iStockphoto.com/Maxwell Attenborough, BR iStockphoto.com/Nick Schlax; 197 iStockphoto.com/Sweetym; 199 iStockphoto.com/Laurent Renault; 200 iStockphoto.com/Stocknshares; 201 iStockphoto. com/Bruce Lonngren; 206 iStockphoto.com/Izabela Habur; 207 iStockphoto.com/Jamie Grill; 209 T iStockphoto.com/Tomm L; 211 iStockphoto.com/Jan Rysavy; 212 iStockphoto. com/Redmal; 213 iStockphoto.com/Dave Bolton; 215 Red Cover/Sophie Munro; 217 T iStockphoto.com/Tarek El Sombati, TR iStockphoto.com/Martti Salmela; 220 B iStockphoto.com/Derek Dammann; 221 iStockphoto.com/Mark Gabrenya; 222 iStockphoto.com/Andy D; 228 B iStockphoto.com/Rollover; 230 T iStockphoto.com/ John Janssen; 233 iStockphoto.com/Paul Kazmercyk; 238 L www.gassaferegister.co.uk, R www.oftec.org; 239 ShutterStock, Inc./Feng Yu, 241 iStockphoto.com/Dane Steffes; 242 iStockphoto.com/Tomm L; 243 iStockphoto.com/Luseen; 245 iStockphoto.com/Vladimir Liverts; 246 L iStockphoto.com/Rocks under Water; 247 ShutterStock, Inc./Frank Reporter; 249 iStockphoto.com/Gabriel Moisa; 253 L ShutterStock, Inc./Juriah Mosin, R iStockphoto. com/Dori O'Connell; 254 iStockphoto.com/Knape; 257 Getty Images/Alison Miksch; 259 iStockphoto.com/Pamela Moore; 261 iStockphoto.com/Pawel Gaul; 263 B iStockphoto. com/Juan Estey; 264 iStockphoto.com/Don Bayley; 265 BR iStockphoto.com/Charles Brutlag; 266 T iStockphoto.com/Ryan Ruffatti, B iStockphoto.com/Robert Kyllo; 267 iStockphoto.com/Eric Delmar; 277 iStockphoto.com/Dem10; 278 iStockphoto.com/ Rita Jacobs; 279 iStockphoto.com/Thomas Eckstadt; 280 iStockphoto.com/Susanna Fieramosca Naranjo; 282 T iStockphoto.com/Don Nichols, CA & B iStockphoto.com/Yenwen Lu, CB iStockphoto.com/drflet; 288 iStockphoto.com/Tamara Murray; 290 iStockphoto.com/ Marcela Barsse; 293 iStockphoto.com/Inga Nielsen; 295 Getty Images/Digital Vision; 296 iStockphoto.com/imagedepotpro; 297 iStockphoto.com/James Wright; 298 iStockphoto. com/Domto; 299 iStockphoto.com/Onur Döngel; 300 B iStockphoto.com/Anita CM; 301 iStockphoto.com/Gloria-Leigh Logan; 302 iStockphoto.com/Stephen Boks; 303 iStockphoto.com/Uyen Le; 304 iStockphoto.com/Eric Isselée; 305 iStockphoto.com/ Arlindo71; 308 iStockphoto.com/Anton Zhukov; 310 iStockphoto.com/Wolfgang Amri; 311 iStockphoto.com/Robert Gebbie; Back Cover centre Getty Images/Photodisc.

PROJECT TEAM
Project Editors John Andrews and Alison Candlin
Art Editor Simon Webb
Designer Jane McKenna
Consultant Jeff Howell
Photographer Gary Ombler
Illustrator Pat Murray/Graham-Cameron Illustration
Proofreader Matthew Griffiths
Indexer Marie Lorimer

FOR VIVAT DIRECT
Editorial Director Julian Browne
Art Director Anne-Marie Bulat
Managing Editor Nina Hathway
Picture Resource Manager Sarah Stewart-Richardson
Pre-press Technical Manager Dean Russell
Product Production Manager Claudette Bramble
Senior Production Controller Jan Bucil

Colour origination by FMG
Printed and bound in China

Save £10,000 with a Nail
Published in 2011 in the United Kingdom by Vivat Direct Limited
(t/a Reader's Digest), 157 Edgware Road, London W2 2HR.
Save £10,000 with a Nail is owned and under licence from
The Reader's Digest Association, Inc. All rights reserved.

Copyright © 2011 The Reader's Digest Association, Inc.
Copyright © 2011 The Reader's Digest Association Far East Limited
Philippines Copyright © 2011 Reader's Digest Association Far East Limited
Copyright © 2011 Reader's Digest (Australia) Pty Limited
Copyright © 2011 Reader's Digest India Pvt Limited
Copyright © 2011 Reader's Digest Asia Pvt Limited

Adapted from *Save $20,000 with a Nail* published by The Reader's Digest
Association, Inc., in 2008.

Reader's Digest is a trademark owned and under licence from The Reader's
Digest Association, Inc. and is registered with the United States Patent and
Trademark Office and in other countries throughout the world.
All rights reserved.

All rights reserved. No part of this book may be reproduced, stored in a retrieval
system, or transmitted in any form or by any means, electronic, electrostatic,
magnetic tape, mechanical, photocopying, recording or otherwise, without
permission in writing from the publishers.

We are committed both to the quality of our products and the service we provide
to our customers. We value your comments, so please do contact us on **0871
3511000** or via our website at **www.readersdigest.co.uk**

If you have any comments or suggestions about the content of our books,
email us at **gbeditorial@readersdigest.co.uk**

ISBN: 978 0 276 44594 1
Concept code: US 5097/L
Book code: 400-356 UP0000-1